SOCIOLOGY

BY JOSEPH H. FICHTER

SOCIOLOGY

SOCIOLOGY

SOCIOLOGY

THE UNIVERSITY OF CHICAGO PRESS

Library of Congress Catalog Card Number: 57-6272

THE UNIVERSITY OF CHICAGO PRESS, CHICAGO & LONDON
The University of Toronto Press, Toronto 5, Canada

Foreword

This introduction to sociology has been designed as a "beginners' book." It is, however, a sociological work and not a preliminary to the study of sociology. There has been no attempt here to produce a simple and easy, "do-it-yourself" type of explanation. This approach recognizes the complexity of the sociocultural system and the fact that the serious student, even with the help of textbooks, lectures, and instructors, is expected to "work at" the process of gaining knowledge. Technical terminology is defined and used throughout, and the difficulty of the subject matter of sociology is not camouflaged by "talking down" to the student.

A decade's experience in teaching this introductory course has emphasized the importance of systematizing the relevant and of pruning out the irrelevant. Introductory sociology should not be cluttered up with materials from other related disciplines like history, economics, geography, biology, and psychology. This book avoids also the various value slants that in a hidden or open way are lodged in most introductory sociology textbooks. Above all, it does not moralize from any particular ethical point of view.

To systematize the relevant sociological material means simply to bring together, define, clarify, classify, and co-ordinate those principles of sociology upon which there is common consensus among the most empirical of all social scientists, the American sociologists. The first part starts with the minimum unit of the society, the social person, and evolves to the largest collectivity, the total society. The second part starts with the basic component of culture, the behavior pattern, and evolves to the total culture. The third part analyzes the manner in which society and culture and their components are inescapably intertwined in the whole sociocultural system. The key concepts of sociology are shown in the diagram on the following page.

Footnotes have been completely omitted from this text, not only because beginning students never read them, but also because it seems pedantic to refer to sources of common elementary knowledge. Much of what is now part of the storehouse of sociological knowledge was at one time the original discovery, insight, or formulation of an individual. But

v

it seems quite unnecessary still and always to refer to Sumner's folkways, Cooley's primary group, Ross's social control, Stonequist's marginal man. These and many other concepts are now an integral part of social science.

A bibliography and "outside readings" have become part of the equipment of the introductory college course in sociology. The former

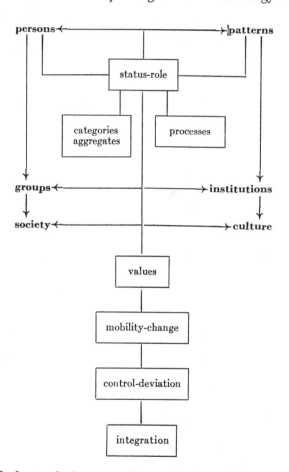

is provided after each chapter and is confined to a brief list of the best-known and most available books. These works are included more as a stimulant to further knowledge than as a confirmation of what is contained in the present text. The bibliography will probably be more useful to the teacher than to the student. As an aid to study and review, there is also a list of discussion questions at the end of each chapter which acts as a kind of outline of the chapter.

The extra volume of "outside readings" which frequently accompanies the introductory text is replaced here by a series of "original readings" in each chapter. These discuss various American phenomena pertinent to, and illustrative of, the principles and generalizations contained in the chapter. This concentration on American materials helps to bring the scientific data alive, calls attention to the sociocultural system in which the student himself lives, and avoids the exotic behavioral trivia which social scientists have turned up among primitives and other non-American societies.

The debt that this book owes to the great American sociologists, both living and dead, is obvious on every page. My acknowledgment is due also to Loyola University of the South, where this material has been taught to many students. It was "tried out" in mimeographed form for two years before going into print. This testing period has helped, especially through the suggestions of Lawrence Bourgeois and Charles Palazzolo, to clarify the material further and to assure an internal consistency in the whole work. I should like to thank also Anne Block and Myra Monahan for typing many revisions of the original draft.

JOSEPH H. FICHTER

Contents

Rational—Ideal and Real Patterns—Patterns as Norms of Behavior—Explicit and Implicit Norms—Behavior Patterns Are
Structured

1. Some Political Patterns. 2. Patterns of Lawlessness. 3. Some
External Religious Patterns. 4. Recreational Patterns. 5. Patterns of Food Preparation

The Group Mind—Patterns and Consensus—The Range of Conceptual Patterns—Social Principles and Ideology—Variations in
Social Thinking—Classifications of Conceptual Patterns—Judgments and Prejudices—Attitudes and Stereotypes—Public Opinion and Propaganda—Wishes and Advertising—Ambivalence—
Ethnocentrism

1. Patriotism and Ethnocentrism. 2. Fads in Conceptual Patterns. 3. Opinion Polls and the American Public. 4. Propaganda
in America. 5. Prejudices and Discriminations

Role and Social Personality—Role and Status—Roles and Relations—Content of Roles—Expected and Actual Roles—Social
Sanctions on Roles—The Formation of Social Roles—Roles and
the Individual—Classification of Roles—Key Role—The General
Role

1. The City Politician. 2. The Traveling Salesman. 3. The Professional Athlete. 4. The Elementary-School Teacher. 5. The
Scientist

Relations and Roles—The Content of Processes—Universality of
Social Processes—Classification of Processes—Co-operation—Accommodation—Assimilation—Conflict—Contravention—Competition—Complexity of Social Processes—Conceptual Matrix of Social Processes

1. The Value of Competition. 2. American Teamwork. 3. The
Americanization Process. 4. Examples of Contravention. 5. Minimizing Conflict in America

What Is Sociology?

Sociology is the scientific study of patterned, shared human behavior. The social behavior of human beings has been an interesting subject of study all through the recorded history of man. The ways in which people act toward one another, that is, their *social relations,* have been scrutinized, discussed, and described by historians and politicians, by poets and storytellers, by theologians and philosophers. The story of "what happened," whether told by expert historians or by the reporters in today's newspapers, is the story of people in social life. To analyze this story of social events from a scientific point of view is the task of the sociologist.

What a sociologist studies is not a newly discovered thing. It is not an invention or a new combination of previously existing things, like the products of laboratories in the physical sciences. Finding existing patterns in social life is the sociologist's business. He cannot imitate a chemist by putting things together in a test tube. He does not invent things in the way that Samuel Morse invented the telegraph. It is true, however, that social changes occur, new forms of group life appear, new techniques evolve for social action—and these are more and more the subject of the scientific study of society.

The basic subject matter of sociology has been "in existence" as long as human beings have lived together on earth. In certain aspects it has differed in time and place, sometimes changing rapidly and sometimes slowly, but the essentials of social life have always been the same. This fact of essential similarity makes possible the scientific study of social behavior. Certain regularities and uniformities are always present. These can be observed, described, analyzed, and interpreted, and it is only after men have learned to do this that we can properly speak of a science of sociology.

The term "sociology" was used first about a hundred years ago by Auguste Comte, a Frenchman. The scholars of that day who called themselves sociologists were what we today would call social historians and social philosophers. Some of them quarreled over whether heredity

or environment made man what he was, as if it had to be all one factor or all the other. Some of them talked of a social "soul" in terms
more religious and philosophic than scientific. During the past fifty
years, especially in the United States, sociology has acquired a body
of practical research information, has brought its theories down to
earth, and has gained a central place in the college curriculum.

A definition of sociology must distinguish it from the other social
sciences. Economics places its focus upon the material things that human beings require to live on earth, how they are produced, exchanged,
distributed, and consumed. Political science places its focus upon
power and authority, the ways in which these are employed and distributed to make an orderly public life possible. Sociology focuses upon
the fact of human "togetherness"; it studies the patterned regularities
of social behavior as they exist everywhere in society. As a body of
knowledge, it centers around the fact of human relations; and anything
that contributes to, or flows from, this human association is sociological.

The Content of Sociology

No definition can provide anything more than an identification of
the thing defined. When we say that sociology is the scientific study of
society, or of human relations, or of social behavior, we have merely
given an indication of its contents. This whole book is a discussion and
explanation of the definition of sociology, that is, it treats the contents
of the science. As an introductory book, it must necessarily be a survey
of basic and essential knowledge in this area of study. We shall not
have time to describe the more specialized and highly technical and
detailed studies made by individual sociologists.

When we say that sociology is a "scientific study," we do not mean
merely that it is an intellectual exercise or that it is only a peculiar
approach to certain human phenomena. It is both of these, but it is
mainly a body of knowledge about society. The word "science" immediately implies that there is something (content) which is studied and
that there is a way (method) of studying it. This book summarizes the
basic content of sociology, and the way in which it presents the material of study indicates the method which sociologists employ.

The content of sociology frequently is called "social phenomena,"
but that is too vague. It is better to say that we are studying human
relations, for our daily experience of human relations—with family,
friends, enemies, and strangers—is the basic stuff of the science. Not

only do we make some kind of response toward all the people whom we meet, but we make approximately the same kind of response over and over. Our social behavior is standardized and patterned.

The phrase "patterns of social behavior" expresses a prime idea in sociology. The unique, abnormal, private activities of people interest us only secondarily, because we pay attention to social relationships as they happen in repeated order. Someone who swims the English Channel does not interest the sociologist so much as do the thousands who ride the London subway to Piccadilly Circus day after day, year after year. In essence, the sociologist studies social persons performing social patterns.

The Conceptual Framework

Social behavior occurs concretely, that is, personally among flesh-and-blood people in a definite time and place. In order to understand this behavior, however, we must form concepts that identify a similarity in the acts of behavior wherever they take place. We train ourselves to call a relationship between a man and a woman in Afghanistan and a man and woman in Sweden "marriage," though their customs differ. We make of our broadest concepts a framework on which we distribute the content of sociology. The concepts enable the sociologist to think of "species" of behavior rather than just specific acts. The naturalist talks of the species "lion" when he wants to include both a lion in a zoo in Chicago and a lion in the hills of Africa. The sociologist talks of the concept "society" when he wants to include both a human organization in Australia and one in Italy.

Social behavior occurs in the concrete, but in order to analyze and understand it we must learn to conceptualize it. This means that we must learn to abstract essential generalizations from the concrete occurrences. We are then able to distribute and arrange these generalizations or concepts, the content of the science, upon a framework. This provides for us two parallel sets of key concepts. The first set is made up of patterns, roles, institutions, and culture. The corresponding set is made up of persons, relations, groups, and society.

For example, from our observation of people in society we recognize certain *patterns* of social behavior clustering around the social function they are meant to perform. This set of patterns is conceptualized as the *social role* that the individual enacts. Thus your role as a student has been standardized and patterned quite differently from the role of your professor. Each acts in expected ways and toward the aims for which the actions are intended. But the conceptualization goes further. When you bring together all the patterned roles which center upon a certain social function, you have a *social institution*. Finally, all of the institutions, combined as a totality and existing among a given people, are conceptualized as the *culture*.

We must remember that we are studying not only social patterns, but also *social persons*. The student and the professor associate and interact in *human relations,* and this is observed wherever reciprocal social roles exist. These human relations occur in social *groups* in which people co-operate toward the fulfilment of social needs. Since these social needs are quite varied, we must conceptualize and classify a great variety of groups. The major groups in the society employ corresponding major social institutions. Thus, the persons who are in educational groupings follow the patterns and enact the roles consonant with the institution of education. When all of the groups are conceptualized as a connected and ongoing totality, we have the abstraction called *society*. This rough description shows that the particular society employs a culture peculiar to it.

Are We Studying Real Things?

When we speak of the conceptual framework of any science, we speak, of course, of generalized abstractions existing in our minds. But if our concepts are not realistic, and if they do not correspond with the concrete social and cultural system in which human beings live, they cannot lend themselves to scientific study. The subject matter of sociology actually exists in the real order, but it is not the function of the sociologist, as social scientist, to evaluate the reality of social phenomena. He accepts them as given data and leaves it to the philosophers to make final declarations concerning their existence and essence.

This question of social reality is of great importance for the beginning student of sociology. He is likely to be confused by certain contributions to sociological literature that go far beyond the field of sociology. These appear in pseudometaphysical and speculative discussions that deny the existence of objective norms of behavior and particularly of social values.

This problem of social reality is pertinent in the numerous and imaginative "analogies" which have been employed to explain and describe social life. One reads, for example, that society and culture constitute an "organism" or a "superorganism" which has its regular stages of birth, growth, and decay. Mechanistic explanations have been put forth to deal with "stresses" and "forces" as though people in their human relations were so many parts of a gigantic engine called society. Psychological explanations start with the premise that some sort of group mind or collective consciousness is the central fact of social life.

An analogy is a comparison of two objects that are partly similar and partly dissimilar. Biological, mechanical, and psychological explanations of society and culture are in themselves erroneous. If similarities are pointed out merely as illustrative clarifications, they are relatively harmless, but the terminology of social science has developed to the point where these analogies are in general quite useless. The objective fact is that social reality cannot be reduced to the terms of biology, physics, or psychology. But this does not mean that social phenomena exist in a vacuum or that they are completely divorced from other aspects of reality.

Distinction from Other Disciplines

Sociology has come of age as a science not only through the research and theory that have uncovered and arranged the facts of social life. In this process of development to scientific status, sociology has also gradually purified itself of its "analogous" interpretations. Without switching his scientific role, the sociologist has learned these basic facts about the analogy of being from the philosopher. Similarly, he learns from other disciplines and builds up certain prerequisites of knowledge that prevent him from misinterpreting the genuine subject matter of sociology. These may also be termed "extra" requisites because they are outside the field of sociology and preliminary to it.

The distinction of sociology from other academic disciplines can be better appreciated through a series of illustrations. For example, the student of society must learn the facts of heredity from the biologist. There is no doubt that physiological heredity has an influence upon some aspects of cultural behavior. Similarly, it is a fact that the physical environment in the form of climate, terrain, and various other aspects of geography exert an influence upon behavior patterns. The social scientist turns to the geographer for the necessary factual information of this science. Again, the presence of human psychological aptitudes has an effect upon social behavior. The field of individual psychology is quite distinct from that of sociology, but it provides many important and fundamental teachings for the social scientist.

This is also true in the area of ethics and morality, in which the experts have developed important principles and concepts.

Every educated person should have some minimum knowledge in each of these various academic disciplines. No one can always and exclusively be a "pure" sociologist, and an adequate specialization in any particular field of knowledge requires a broad general education. The scientific role, limited to one area of knowledge, is only one of the many roles that the social scientist as a human being enacts within society. Sociology is a clearly definable science, an area in which a student may obtain specialized knowledge, but this specialization must not be pursued at the expense of more generalized education.

The various disciplines provide important knowledge that the sociologist must accept in the form of assumptions. The factual information supplied by philosophy, biology, geography, psychology, and ethics is assumed by the sociologist to have been tested and proven in these fields. These facts are assumptions, not to the experts in those fields, but to the sociologist. The encyclopedic, all-embracing concept of sociology has long since been abandoned. The social scientist does not take time out to investigate and prove that man has the power of self-direction, that objective moral values exist, or that the physiological structure of people differs in various ways. The student of society should know these things, but he should not expect to learn them from the sociologist.

Is Anything Constant?

The beginning student of sociology is often perplexed by the bewildering array of information he learns concerning the variety of behavioral patterns in different societies. He hears and reads so much about variations in social customs that he wonders whether there are any constants at all. As we proceed further into the study of sociology, we shall perceive that certain constant elements must be present in every society and culture. As a matter of fact, the so-called principles of sociology, constituting the contents of this book, are the constant, universal elements. A glance at the chapter headings will indicate what these are.

The student of society must learn to distinguish between the constant similarities and the changing differences. Every culture must contain the basic major institutions, and every society must have the corresponding basic major groupings in which people function together toward social goals. One may say that it is the nature of social life that these constants be present. These fundamental institutions and groups—familial, educational, recreational, economic, religious, and political—are found wherever people live in organized social life. The components of institutions and groups, as described in this book, are also necessarily present everywhere.

The student of society ought not to look so hard for essential similarities of behavior that he is fooled by accidental similarities. Elections in Poland and elections in England, for instance, are roughly the same in outward appearance, but their social meaning is entirely different. The student also must not be tricked by accidental differences. The fact that an American greets people on the street informally while a Japanese bows to the people he meets does not mean that Americans lack courtesy. The fact that in one society alcoholic drinks are outlawed and in another society wine is served at every meal does not make one set of people better than the other.

The wide variation of the sociological constants in different places and among different people simply indicates that society and culture are extraordinarily flexible and changeable. In one society children receive all their formal education from their fathers or uncles. In another society children are sent in groups to a person who is a specialist in education. The daily routine of an Arab watering his date trees in the Sahara seems far different from the activities of an Eskimo hunting seals in Alaska. The important point here is that the educational and the economic institutions are common to all cultures. The same fundamental social needs exist in every society, but the manner of satisfying them differs widely.

Is Anything Worthwhile?

This problem of constants and variables is closely connected to that of the relativity of values. If there is so much change throughout the world and if people satisfy their needs in so many different ways, is there anything of enduring value in social life? The student is a moral person and, in a sense, a citizen of the world. He is responsible and accountable for his own behavior and logically concerned about good and evil in society. This concern is obviously a matter of conscience, of ethics and morality. It cannot be satisfied although it is often aroused by the scientific study of sociology.

From a scientific point of view, sociology is not aligned with any particular moral system. Social science in itself cannot be democratic or totalitarian; it cannot be Christian or Mohammedan. The sociologist, as scientist, tries sincerely to avoid moral judgments about the cultures and societies that he studies and analyzes. He observes that value systems differ from one society to another and even from one group to another within the same society. If he says that one system is as "good" as another or that some are "worse" than others, he is making a value judgment which emerges from his moral role rather than from his scientific role.

Social values are those items which the members of a society consider highly important and worthwhile, and according to which they tend to standardize their behavior. Probably no student of society can be completely impartial in his attitude toward social values. It would be like playing a child's game to suggest, for example, that the scientific sociologist recognizes no moral difference between a gang of criminals and a committee of church vestrymen. Probably no sociologist can entirely purify his lectures and writings from the values that he personally holds. He implies by the very adjectives he uses that he sees a moral difference between an "oppressive" system of child labor and a "free" system of management-labor relations.

This means of course that even the secular scientist, which every sociologist must be, cannot divorce himself completely from the culture in which he is himself involved. His own personal values in some way reflect the social values of the culture in which he has been socialized. It is important that the beginning student of sociology recognize this fact in his own attempt to be impartial and objective. We shall see more of this when we discuss ethnocentrism, which is the tendency to judge other groups by the norms and values currently held in our own group. It is the very nature of personal and social life that people must hold values and act according to them, and this fact often impedes the student of society from understanding and analyzing different kinds of value systems.

Social values are the norms, or measure, by which members of a society standardize their behavior. Among conservative French families, for example, the only "correct" way for young people to marry is according to their parents' wishes. In the United States, on the other hand, many young people feel that the only "correct" way to marry is according to mutual romantic love. The sociologist himself, exposed to the values of his society long before he becomes a scientist, is not so impartial as he would like to be. Even his most scientific behavior implies two value judgments: (a) scientific investigation is a worthwhile activity; (b) man in the group is a proper object of such investigation.

A sociologist who grew up in a society that detests cannibalism and protects children tends to reflect these attitudes when he writes of a society that practices cannibalism and infanticide.

The question of what is *ultimately* worthwhile goes far beyond the limits of sociology. The question of the existence of a body of objective and irreducible value principles is not part of the study of sociology. In actual social life, however, there is everywhere a relativity of social values; what one society values highly, another may spurn as worthless or even harmful. This the social scientist readily recognizes. He studies the *social fact* of existing values; he analyzes and interprets them. This is in itself an absorbing area of study: to understand how these values originate and develop, what function they perform, what effect they have on society, how widely people conform to them. To go beyond this and to attempt a judgment concerning their ultimate and immutable validity requires the assistance of the expert in ethics.

Sociology a Difficult Subject of Study

People accustomed to the mechanical conveniences of our modern generation tend to ignore the tremendous problem-solving that made these conveniences possible. It is exceedingly simple to turn on a television or radio set, an air-conditioning or deep-freeze unit, to dial a number on the telephone, or to walk up the steps into an airplane. The very simplicity of these actions gets the same results whether or not we are aware of the enormous system of co-ordinated technical knowledge and productive facilities which have made the action so simple for us.

Similarly, most people are unaware of the factors and elements which make an ongoing sociocultural system possible. The student, like every social person, has been doing these things all his life; he has been following patterns of behavior, holding social values, and living in groups without giving much thought to these facts. It is sometimes surprising for him to learn that sociology is one of the most difficult areas of study into which the human mind can enter. This difficulty arises from three main facts: (*a*) the complexity of the subject matter of sociology; (*b*) the operation of multiple causality in society and culture; (*c*) the variability and impermanence of solutions to social problems.

a) The complexity of sociology. The beginning student usually does not recognize that society and culture are highly complex, even in the so-called simple or primitive forms of group life. Patterns of behavior are inherited from previous generations, and the individual gradually gets accustomed to them without either analyzing them or comparing them with the accepted cultural patterns of other societies. It is only when he begins to study the variations and combinations of social thought and action possible to human beings that he comes to realize their variability and complexity.

Sociological analysis is difficult because there are so many elements of the social situation that have to be recognized *simultaneously*. For example, one cannot understand even the oft-expressed concept of "social institution" unless he realizes that an institution is an intricate network of different but co-ordinated and related patterns of thought and behavior, which in turn are directed toward social ends and governed by social values. The institutions of a culture also intermesh, and it is difficult to understand one institution like the educational or the familial without also having some knowledge of the economic, political, and other major institutions.

Another pertinent example is the intermeshing of social roles of different persons in the same social situation. One does not enact the role of daughter in a vacuum. The ways of acting and thinking of a daughter in a family are related to the roles of other members of the family. There is a reciprocity of rights and duties, of expected patterns of behavior, between parent and child, between sister and brother. Although the roles of each necessarily differ from those of others, all the roles must necessarily be correlated. The individual social person is also a complex of multiple social roles. Each role differs somewhat according to the social group and situation in which it is enacted, but the person still remains an integrated human individual.

b) Multiple social causality. The same problem of multiformity and complexity is present to the social scientist concerned with ends and means, that is, with the reasons why things are done and the ways of doing them. It is obvious to any careful student of society that social facts do not "just happen." The theory that society and culture evolved by regular, progressive stages has long since been abandoned by sociologists. Nevertheless, various deterministic theories are still prevalent, especially among people who have not studied social science. This most often takes the form of a theory of single causality, that is, attributing either the total sociocultural system or any part of it to one, all-embracing cause.

In normal conversation we often hear a simple, sovereign cause used as an explanation of social phenomena. For example, one hears that the social problem of American race relations is caused by the immorality of Negroes. Or that climate makes the southern states politically conservative. Or that the introduction of machinery caused secularization of our culture. Or that international Jewry is responsible for economic depressions. Or that the cost of living is being forced up by organized labor unions. The list of these simple, single "explanations" is almost inexhaustible.

The student ought to keep a record for one week of all the "single explanations" he hears. By comparing his list with the lists of his classmates, he will see that a few tired ideas are used over and over by many people to explain almost everything in life. He will be amazed at the lengths to which people will go to save themselves the trouble of thinking.

The single-causality approach is probably the most widespread and most consistently recurring error in the social thinking of people. There seem to be two main reasons for this error. First, the single "explanation" is the easiest answer to the complex question of human relations. The lazy thinker expresses what to him seems obvious. Second, people often lack scientific knowledge about society and culture. This ignorance is sometimes accompanied by the arrogance of prejudiced attitudes. The study of social science is an important means for clearing up both ignorance and arrogance.

Almost any question of human relations, from the simplest item of child care to the most serious decision of a corporation president, has behind it a whole series of interrelated factors. People do not act merely "on instinct"; they do not make "on the spot" decisions without a great deal of preliminary social and cultural experience. Even the theory that "great men" cause historical change has been tempered by the realization that leaders are themselves the product of their culture and can operate only within the limitations of the sociocultural environment.

c) Impermanence of social solutions. Besides the complexity and multiple causality of social phenomena, there is also the difficulty of change in society and culture. Change is an ever present social fact wherever human beings live together, and it is further complicated by the variability of both the rate and direction of change. Even traditional and conservative societies that appear to be almost static are constantly subject to adaptation and variation. In this sense, social change is in itself one of the sociological constants, and it is treated in some detail later in this book.

The changing character of society gives the sociologist difficulty. The geologist is finished with part of his work when he discovers what the earth's crust was like at one stage and how that led to the next stage. The sociologist, however, may find that some of his facts about a particular society become obsolete after a few years. In 1940, for example, he could not predict in detail what television's effect would be on our society now.

The fact of change does not belie the presence of structure and order in society, but it does make more difficult the whole study of social problems. Many causes are at work bringing about this change, the most important of which appears to be man's own power of selection and decision. A "free society" is likely to be a more dynamic society because the individual social person has greater latitude in his patterns of social behavior. The ancient philosophical problem of unity and diversity in the world is here present in the modern scientific garb of the co-ordination of social function and structure.

Sociology is not social reform, but the essential principles of sociology are a prerequisite in any proposed solution of social problems. It is desirable, of course, that "solutions" be found for the problems of society and that certain universal principles of social life be established. But in concrete social situations of real life we always find certain individuals and groups who deviate, who will not "stay put" in the nicely arranged categories, and who will not consistently behave according to the principles uncovered by social science. Just as there are no single causes of social phenomena, so also are there no permanent solutions; and this is why the artificial blueprints of social Utopias are of only minor sociological significance.

Social Engineering and Sociological Research

The student may take the attitude that he studies sociology only for its own sake, only because he wants to know more about society and culture. Beyond this he may seek knowledge of social life because this knowledge enriches his mind, gives him a more thorough understanding of other people, and provides a satisfying objectivity of judgment concerning others. There is no question of the fact that a tremendous storehouse of this kind of knowledge has been built up in recent decades from the scientific research of sociologists. The modern student can depend upon the validity of sociological information and is no longer forced to choose among a series of mere speculations.

The student is also a moral person and citizen, an actor in the various social roles which his society demands of him. In this sense, mere knowledge does not satisfy him. As an intelligent and concerned person he probably seeks the application of sociological knowledge to the social situations in which he finds himself. This is a transition that neither a textbook nor a professor, but only the student himself, can make. A person can be an expert in sociology and still behave as a social deviant, just as a man with deep theological knowledge may be a great sinner or a learned economist may spend his own money foolishly.

In general it may be said that study and research are almost always ultimately directed toward "doing the thing better." The emphasis in an introductory course in sociology must be on factual knowledge resulting from long research by social scientists. This is the scientific aspect of any study: to obtain exact and universally true information that one can study in a systematic way and about which one can have a high degree of certitude. The human and personal aspect of any study is to render it useful and fertile. Sociological study lends itself to helping the individual and his society achieve results in terms of better social relations.

The planned improvement of society is practically impossible without the scientific knowledge provided by sociology. The term "social reform" has gone somewhat out of fashion because of its apparently moralistic overtones. One speaks now of its synonym, "social engineering," which in turn may be objectionable because of its overtones of mechanism and manipulation. Whichever term one employs, the fact remains that administration and planning are essential elements in organized social life.

Social engineering therefore involves the intelligent application of sociological knowledge. Much of the social planning of the past has been done on the basis of shrewd guesswork and hit-and-miss experience. Every family, school, and church, every club, business, and municipality, works out plans for the future, seeks to solve its problems, administers its personnel, recognizes and pursues its social goal. This is nothing more or less than social engineering, and it is eminently more intelligent and productive to perform these functions on the basis of the exact and valid knowledge provided by sociology than on the basis of haphazard, trial-and-error experimentation.

Why Study Sociology?

We assume that most readers of this book are college and university students. What we have said previously about social research and engineering helps to answer the question why sociology is an important area of study for them. Relatively few students become professional sociologists; but all students are participants in society, and they become more and more involved in various social roles after they finish their formal academic training. The more prominent and influential a person expects to be after his college years, the more useful and important will sociological knowledge be for him.

Since everybody must at all times live in society, associate with people, and enact social roles, it is obvious that sociological knowledge is a basic help in every career and vocation. Positions in journalism, teaching, salesmanship, business administration, law, preaching, politics, and others where an essential occupational activity is "dealing with people," require more than ordinary knowledge of human relations in society. Even participation in the family, the neighborhood, and the community is more intelligent and successful when based upon scientific sociological knowledge.

It is not the function of the sociologist to argue whether knowledge or virtue is more important in the development of the "good society." Every responsible person is presumably interested in a "better world," but in the last analysis social improvement is not achieved by merely willing it, or by having good intentions, or even by constantly practicing social virtue. There is a great difference between passive virtue and active virtue, between unthinkingly accepting change and intelligently promoting change.

Highly ethical people are certainly a desirable asset in any society, but if they are ignorant of the technical analysis of roles and institutions, processes and functions, they will probably contribute little to intelligent social advancement. Reliable knowledge about social phenomena is an essential and basic prerequisite for a better society, and this is what a textbook in sociology is intended to provide.

DISCUSSION QUESTIONS

1. Explain the statement that sociology is a relatively new social science studying an old subject.
2. Distinguish the focus of sociology from that of other social sciences.
3. How does the "content" of sociology differ from the "conceptual framework" of sociology?
4. Why is the term "behavior pattern" a key concept in sociology?
5. What is meant by the statement that the subject matter of sociology is "real"?
6. What is the scientific utility of physical, mechanical, and psychological analogies?

7. How and why does the sociologist use "assumptions" from other disciplines?
8. Explain the difference between variables and constants in the field of sociology.
9. Explain the statement that the science of sociology cannot be aligned with any particular moral system.
10. Why is it difficult for the sociologist to keep his own personal values out of his social science?
11. What accounts for the complexity of the study of sociology?
12. Why is the single-causality approach an easy error to make in sociological analysis?
13. What is meant by the relative impermanence of social solutions?
14. How is social engineering related to sociological research?
15. In what personal and social ways is sociology a significant area of study?

SUGGESTED READINGS

CUBER, JOHN F. *Sociology: A Synopsis of Principles.* 3d ed.; New York: Appleton-Century-Crofts, Inc., 1955, chaps. i, ii.

DAVIS, KINGSLEY. *Human Society.* New York: Macmillan Co., 1949, chap. i.

LaPIERE, RICHARD T. *Sociology.* New York: McGraw-Hill, 1946, chap. i.

LUNDBERG, G. A., *et al. Sociology.* New York: Harper & Bros., 1954, chaps. i–iii.

SIMPSON, GEORGE. *Man in Society.* Garden City: Doubleday & Co., Inc., 1954.

TIMASHEFF, N. S., and FACEY, P. W. *Sociology: An Introduction to Sociological Analysis.* Milwaukee: Bruce Publishing Co., 1949, chaps. i, ii.

WILLIAMS, ROBIN M. *American Society: A Sociological Interpretation.* New York: Alfred A. Knopf, 1952, chap. iii.

The conceptual approach to this introductory study of sociology is that social persons are the unit of society and that behavior patterns are the unit of culture. In this first section we proceed from the smallest unit, the person, through the various ways in which he is associated with others, to the total society.

We analyze first the social person and the process of socialization (chap. i), then the social status of the person and the manner in which he obtains this position in society (chap. ii), then the various ways in which people are placed in social categories (chap. iii), in social aggregates (chap. iv), and in groups and associations (chap. v). The final chapter of this first section deals with society as a whole (chap. vi).

PART I

Person
and
Society

CHAPTER ONE

The Social Person

The irreducible physical unit of social categories, aggregates, groups, and societies is man, the human being, the individual, the person. All of these terms are synonymous, and they are used interchangeably throughout this book. The sociologist is not concerned with subhuman levels of life, with the gregarious instincts or the herd-life of brute animals. The notion that social behavior is nothing more than an instinctive and predetermined response to environmental stimuli has long since been abandoned by serious social scientists.

Definition of Person

The human being is distinguished from the subhuman being by his ability to think in abstract terms and to make decisions and choices. The person is a self-directing animal. He can do "paper work"; he can plan and arrange for the future. He can reflect on his own actions and reactions. He is accountable for his own behavior, and he can develop a sense of responsibility toward others.

Society and culture are scientifically meaningless without reference to these abilities and competencies of the human being. Experience and observation show, of course, that people are not equally social, intelligent, and volitional. Not everybody uses his mind and his other abilities to the best advantage. Some, like imbeciles and idiots, are never able to develop these human qualities. Some become social outcasts, criminals, or other kinds of social deviants. Nevertheless, the potentiality for normal, standardized social behavior is in all of these people, and for this reason they too are persons.

The human being is a unit; he is one person, and any attempt to identify him as a continuous part of his physical or cultural environment, of a group mind or a world soul, must result in sociological frustration and in scientific nonsense. On the other hand, this "oneness" of the human person does not mean that he can be studied from only one point of view. The human person has many "aspects," or facets. He is a single but composite and complex being.

As a *physiological* unit, the person is studied by biologists, anatomists, biochemists, pathologists, and others. As a *moral* unit, who can do right and wrong, he is studied by ethicians, moralists, theologians, lawyers, and others. As a *psychological* unit with conscious desires and subconscious drives, he is studied by psychiatrists, psychoanalysts, psychologists, and others. This does not refer to different kinds of persons, nor does it mean that the same person can be divided up into separate segments. The human being studied under all of these different aspects is the same person studied by the sociologist, but under a still different aspect.

The Social Person

All human beings, as distinguished from non-human animals, are social persons. The terms "rational" and "social" are not synonymous, but one quality does not exist without the other. The very fact that we say an individual is a rational person necessarily means that he is a social person. These are characteristics only of people. When we say that irrational animals learn or that they are social, we are speaking only analogously.

When a sociologist says people are social, he does not mean that they are charming, urbane, or accomplished and refined. He does not refer exclusively to the social events or social leaders described in the "society pages" of the newspapers. The limitation of the words "social" and "society" to the recreational and congenial activities of people or to the gracious and hospitable virtues is a restriction upon their full meaning.

A person is social in the sense that he has both an inclination and a need for human association. Robinson Crusoe, Peter the Hermit, or any modern solitary recluse must be considered a social person even though direct relations with other people do not occur. The term "social" is derived from the Latin word *socius,* which means companion or associate. Social science, therefore, studies people only under this one aspect. The student of society is interested in the way in which persons are related to other persons. The fact that the person is a sociological unit, that he can be, and is, studied only under this aspect, must be kept in mind as a central point of reference throughout the reading of this book.

Nature and Nurture

It is obvious that there is a vast difference between a person at the age of thirty days and a person at the age of thirty years. Quite aside from the physical, moral, and intellectual change, the older person is sociologically different. He knows his way around in groups and societies; he knows how to behave in relations with other persons. To what do we attribute the development of these abilities?

Most sociologists speak of original *nature* as the "raw material" with which a person is equipped both actually and potentially at birth. Frequent speculation about the contribution of this original nature to the development of the mature social person, because it is for the most part merely speculation, does not provide adequate scientific knowledge. The scientific difficulty lies in the fact that one cannot adequately measure the "natural person" completely unaffected by social factors.

The term *nurture* in its most general meaning refers to all of the external influences affecting the individual person. More specifically for the sociologist, it refers to the social and cultural factors that help the individual to develop his "original" and natural social potentialities. We study the individual already present in society, whether as a relatively helpless infant or as a relatively self-sufficient adult.

It appears to have been futile to debate whether nature or nurture is more important in the socialization of the individual. The baby is certainly born with abilities to respond to external influences, but what these abilities are in their "raw state" concerns physiologists and psychologists more than it concerns sociologists. The latter are content to accept "given data" and study them, and the given data here are the readiness and the abilities of persons to react to external influences. The most reliable scientific conclusion appears to be that *both* nature and nurture contribute to the socialization of the individual person.

Creature and Creator

The important point to remember is that the person responds and reacts. In other words, the human individual is not an inert but pliable object which the society molds to its purposes. He is not merely a puppet of his culture, performing exactly and always in the way the culture demands. As an agent, with the ability to discern and decide, the human being can alter his own behavior and can influence the society in which he lives. If human beings did not have this ability to create and to produce changes in their human relations, there would be no culture in the strict sense of the word, and there would be no society of acting and interacting persons.

It is true also that persons are in many ways the product, the creature, of their culture and society. Most individuals appear to be much more influenced by their social and cultural environment than they are influences upon it. We are not only socialized; we are socialized in particular ways. This fact has been dramatized by large numbers of farm laborers who migrate to industrial cities. They find the ways of the city people and the industrial workers quite strange, and they often have tragic difficulties in attempting to adjust their own behavior to the new cultural setting.

The reason for this difficulty is that the person from an isolated rural area is a cultural creation different from the person who has been conditioned by the big industrial and commercial city. This has been recognized in the universal caricatures of the farm boy and the city boy. Even greater differences in the human cultural products are observed when we compare an Oriental with a Westerner. A Chinese is more similar to his fellow Chinese than he is to an American. The similarity between a Chinese and an American may be in their "original nature," the fact that both are persons, with intellectual and volitional and emotional potentialities at birth. Their behavioral differences, however, develop in each mainly because of the culture and society in which they have grown up.

Socialization

Socialization is a process of mutual influence between a person and his fellow men, a process that results in an acceptance of, and adaptation to, the patterns of social behavior. It does not mean that the person ceases to be an individual. Just as we cannot say that a person "becomes human" when he learns to use his intellect, so we cannot say that a person "becomes social" when he learns how to get along with other people. The human being is a social person from the beginning of his life, but he undergoes continuous adaptations and changes as long as he lives.

Socialization can be described from two points of view: objectively, from that of the society acting upon the individual, and subjectively, from that of the individual responding to the society. *Objectively*, socialization is that process by which the society transmits its culture from one generation to the next and adapts the individual to the accepted and approved ways of organized social life. Thus, the function of socialization is to develop the skills and disciplines which are needed by the individual, to instil the aspirations and values and the "design for living" which the particular society possesses, and especially to teach the social roles which individuals must enact in society.

The process of socialization is continuously at work "outside" the individual. It affects not only children and immigrants when they first come into the society but all people within the society all of their lives. It acts upon people; it provides for them the patterns of behavior which are essential to maintenance of the society and the culture.

Subjectively, socialization is a process which goes on in the individual while he is adapting to the people around him. The person "takes on" the habits of the society in which he lives. From infancy on, he becomes gradually "society-broken." As an immigrant, the person becomes sociologically "naturalized" to his adopted society. It must be stressed that this is a lifelong process, that much of it is a kind of subconscious conformity, and that it is always particularized in time, place, culture, and society. It is important to note that a person does not become socialized in a haphazard, generalized fashion, as a sort of citizen of the world or as a member of human society. The process makes him into a recognizable American, Mexican, Frenchman, or whatever.

The Social Frame of Reference

The accumulated experiences of the individual in his society form the background from which he undergoes new experiences. The sociologists say that the culture becomes "internalized," that the individual "imbibes" it, and that in this way "from the inside" it continues to influence his conduct. Thus the culture is not merely something external to the individual. His whole social background tremendously and constantly influences the patterns of thought and behavior which the person follows at any given moment.

The ways of life he has learned, the ideas he holds, the values he treasures, all in some way come originally from outside of him. These are the results, the products, the materials of the socialization process. The person tends to meet new experiences and to interpret current happenings in the light of these past experiences. In a sense he tends to think and act according to the degree of conformity that he has achieved.

The social frame of reference has as its content the social experiences of the individual. These are the vantage points from which he looks out on the world; they are the points of reference and of comparison against which he forms opinions and judgments and according to which he behaves, often without any conscious reflection. This is the storehouse in which a person readily finds how he is expected to behave in the usual and frequently repeated situations of social life. It is also the storehouse on which he draws for similarities out of the past when he is confronted with a novel social situation.

Not all social experiences are equal in importance and intensity. The social frame of reference can be analyzed on three levels. Social experience is (*a*) common to all human beings, (*b*) unique to each person, and (*c*) specific to a particular culture and society. The basic concepts of sociology deal with elements which are found everywhere: patterns of behavior, human relations, status and role, institutions, and so forth. Each person, however, experiences these things through his own personality in a way that no other person can share and in a social setting that is different from all others.

These three aspects of social experience can be demonstrated with numerous examples. Friendship and the primary group are found wherever human beings live in society; but each person experiences friendship in a unique (that is, never exactly duplicated) manner, in this time and place, with these particular persons. The manner in which friendship is demonstrated and symbolized differs from one society to another. In one society, adult males who are friends greet each other with a kiss on the cheek, in another society with an embrace, and in still another by shaking hands.

Social Learning

The process of socialization can ultimately be reduced to the fact that the individual learns by contact with society. The process refers not to individual knowledge, which also comes from contact with others, but to shared knowledge which has social significance. From this point of view, the manner in which he learns does not differ from that of simple learning. The difference between simple learning and social learning is not in who learns, or in how he learns, but in what he learns.

Social scientists have taken over from the learning experts and educators certain terms and concepts that apply to the learning process. There is the *drive*—biological impulse, subconscious wish, or conscious desire—to acquire certain satisfactions. This is a characteristic of the human individual and describes the fact that people want to learn. The *cue* is the characteristic of the idea, object, or situation to which the person is drawn. The interaction between the learner and the thing learned is called the *response;* it is what occurs when the particular drive in the individual is co-ordinated with the particular cue in the object. The *reward* refers to any object or event which strengthens or makes easier the response of the individual in striving to learn.

This abstract terminology may give the impression that each facet of the learning process is a single, separate item. The fact is that concretely each is a complex aspect of the whole process. For example, a boy wants to learn the game of football so that he can become a star on the high-school team. This is a drive for learning, the desire to achieve local glory and popularity, but it is overlaid with other wishes —to get recreation, to release physical energy, to prove that he is "tough." The cue to which his attention is drawn is in the techniques of the game, the system of rules for the team on and off the field, the various kinds of trick plays. The response is his actual practice and performance, achieving perfection in the patterns of play and in co-ordination with other players. The reward, too, may be multiple—the actual winning of games, the appreciation of the coach, the applause of the spectators.

From the point of view of social science, there are certain conditions and qualifications surrounding the process of social learning. All of these have to do with the manner of learning in relation to other persons. We are not concerned about original thinking and discoveries, the composition and invention of ideas, trial-and-error research in the privacy of one's study or laboratory. The process of learning in social situations is a process that occurs with and among people and therefore always involves social relations.

The subprocesses of social learning are numerous; the principal ones are the following:

a) Imitation is the human action by which one tends to duplicate more or less exactly the behavior of others. It is commonly recognized not only in the way children "ape" their parents but also in the way adolescents and even mature adults take on the characteristics of people whom they appreciate and admire.

b) Suggestion is a process outside the learner. It is found in the works and actions of those who are attempting to change the behavior of the learner. A person may "take a suggestion" not only from the conscious and deliberate persuasion of another but also without the other person knowing it.

c) Competition is a stimulative process in which two or more individuals vie with one another in achieving knowledge. It is peculiarly important in social learning of children because it is often involved in the desire of the child to obtain the approval of others. Competitive learning is a clear indication that people tend to learn and to conform to the approved ways of behaving in society and to shun the ways that are disapproved.

It must be obvious from these brief remarks concerning the sub-processes of imitation, suggestion, and competition that the essential prerequisites of social learning are contact and communication. The few authentic studies of individuals socially isolated, of children who were kept apart from society, show that association with others is an essential condition of social learning. Within certain limits, the number and kind of contacts and relations a person has during his lifetime are also a measure of the extent to which he becomes socialized.

Hindrances to Normal Socialization

Normal socialization is a process producing at least the minimum learning that any person requires to get along in his particular society. The term "normal" must necessarily be left indefinite because the society does not demand exactly the same degree and kind of response from all of its members. More is expected from some than from others. Some are able and willing to respond more readily and quickly than others. No person can fully exploit all the potentialities of his society and culture for himself.

No matter how ambitious or brilliant a person may be, he is constantly limited by time and circumstances from realizing more than a fraction of his own cultural and social potentialities. The development of a highly specialized society has increased the number of possible roles and functions generally available, but it has decreased the number specifically available to the individual. Selection must necessarily be made among numerous roles, and concentration of effort is required once the choice has been made. It is seldom that a person completely fulfils his normally expected roles, familial, occupational, religious, and others. It is even less seldom that he realizes his potentiality in more than one occupation. The expert physicist, for example, cannot also have a career in music or in political science.

Hindrances to the full development of the social capacity of the individual come from many directions. The individual person may be simple-minded or lazy, sick or crippled, or handicapped in other physical ways. The social structure and its assignment of power and prestige may repress individual opportunities for learning, as when a small ruling class subjugates the large masses of people. The culture itself, with its beliefs and attitudes and values, may impede learning by emphasizing the traditional and the static. The physical and geographical environment of a society may make such demands upon the people that their energies are expended in mere survival.

Agencies of Socialization

In general, it may be said that the total society is the agency for socialization and that each person with whom one comes into contact is in some fashion an agent of socialization. Between the large society and the individual person there are numerous small groupings, and they are the principal agencies for the socialization of the person. The obvious beginning of the process for the newborn child is his immediate family group, but this is soon extended to many other groups.

Preschool influences act upon the child from many directions. The little circles and relationships in which he participates with parents, relatives, friends, nurses, and others are all important in showing him how to be a "good little child." Even in these early years media like television, radio, and comic books begin to provide patterns of behavior. The neighborhood, the school, and in some instances the church are important agencies of socialization for young people.

Other media of socialization have varying effects at different stages of a person's life. Since social learning is a continuous process at every age level, the person is constantly being checked in some drives and encouraged in others. Frustrations and satisfactions, strains and readjustments, all constitute experiences which are ways of learning. The mother who explains the differences in the way her various children have gone through their growing stages indirectly says that she herself has learned a great deal from these experiences.

All forms of adult groups and associations, in business and professions, in recreation and politics and religion, continually influence the change and development of the social person. The modern media of communication like movies, television, radio, and mass-circulation magazines are more influential in forming social behavior than most people realize. Parents and teachers who are concerned about the impact of these agencies upon small children do not often realize that they themselves are following examples and suggestions and picking up opinions and attitudes through the same process. They are being subconsciously socialized.

Individualization

We have seen that every individual internalizes and personalizes his social experience. This is what we mean by the individualization of culture. Patterns of behavior in order to be scientifically observable and measurable must be expressed by concrete persons in actual social situations. In spite of the imagination of fiction writers, we do not really know what a spaceman is, how he behaves and acts with others. This is because no one has ever internalized the patterns pertinent to such an individual. Similarly, only a person who has been a mother can ever actually fulfil all of the role expectations of motherhood.

The social personality is never a perfect reflection of the culture and society in which it has been developed. It is physically impossible for two people, even twins, to have exactly the same experiences with the same people at the same time and in the same situation and to respond in exactly the same way. No pair or cluster of individuals can ever be completely identical, and no individual is ever completely predictable in his social behavior. Individualization, however, is not the opposite of socialization. It is merely the process which personalizes one's experiences. This is simply another way of saying that each has a unique and variant personality and that even social experiences and social relations are productive of differences between individuals within groups.

Thus it is true to say that every person is both unique and social. Nobody lives in a vacuum, and the person is individualized by the adjustments he makes to the influences exerted upon him and by the personal interpretation of what he has learned. The sociologist studies that which is social, common, and shared in many people rather than that which is unique, peculiar, or personal to the individual. The agencies of socialization have a *similar* effect upon a *large* number of people, and it is these similarities shared by pluralities of people that make possible the study of social science.

The Social Personality

We have said that a person is characterized by the ability to think and to make decisions and that the human individual can be studied for different purposes from different points of view. The concept of the social personality, as a complex of various social roles, is an extremely useful device of the sociologist. The individual is a social person from birth, but his social personality develops constantly through the socialization process. In general terms, the social personality includes all the ways in which the individual acts in relation to and with other persons. In specific terms, all these ways may be analyzed under the headings of the various social roles which he has developed and according to which he acts.

We shall later analyze social roles more closely and in greater detail. It suffices here to note that the person follows a patterned way of behavior in each of the major groups in which he participates. He is the father in his family, the vestryman in his church, the superintendent in his factory, a member of a parent-teacher club, of the country club, and of the local Republican party. These are more than just facets or aspects of his person. Each one of them requires that he enact a role corresponding to the objectives of the group and to his participation in the group. When we put all these roles together, study their origin, function and interrelations, or structure, we are studying the social personality of the individual.

AMERICAN SOCIALIZATION AND THE SOCIAL PERSON

1. The "Spoiling" of Children

Americans of the older generation and foreign visitors to our country are "horrified" at the way in which we bring up our children. Older people often complain that children are being brought up without manners. Europeans feel that our children are seen too often and heard too much, that parents are doting and overindulgent, and that in some sense children rule the American home. As evidence of the trend in this type of socialization they point to truancy and deviltry in secondary schools, to juvenile delinquency in our large cities, to the prevalence of crime and rackets among our adult citizens.

It is to be assumed that the socialization of children in any society tends to be integrated with the patterns of thought, the goals, beliefs, values, and ideals of that society. This integration is never perfect, but it helps to "make sense" of what may appear to be erratic and undisciplined behavior. A consideration of the following items may help to explain the type of socialization of children found in America.

a) In the United States there has been traditionally a high evaluation of the individual personality. This is not likely to be confined only to adults or to be appreciated and applied suddenly at some transitional point in a person's life. Even the very young child is accorded this respect.

b) There is also an emphasis on the future. Unlike most older populations of Europe and Asia, the American people have little regard for traditions as a guide to conduct. Children are the "wave of the future." In them lie the aspirations of many parents who have themselves not achieved success.

c) The lack of social apprenticeship prevents the girl child from assimilating adult female patterns and the boy child, adult male patterns. Learning by doing, by imitation of and companionship with the parents is more consonant with stable, agricultural family life. On the American scene there are numerous "substitute" parents performing family functions with the children.

d) The relative isolation of the immediate conjugal group prevents the child from developing diffused emotional ties to a large group of adult relatives. He gets his security and love from parents only and not from relatives in the larger kinship group, like grandparents, aunts, uncles, and cousins.

e) The inconsistency of standards of conduct tends to bewilder the child. This is especially noticeable around the ages of seven to ten when the child begins to question why he must tell the truth, go to Sunday school, and avoid certain "bad words" when his parents' conduct does not conform to their preaching.

f) The child has an extraordinary dependence upon the mother who symbolizes love and security for him, while the father tends to be a sort of stranger. The bringing up of children is seldom a function shared by both parents in the American society.

g) The scientific and rational tendency of the American culture is seen in the American parents' dependence on expert and pseudo-expert advice on child-rearing. The natural and almost automatic rearing of children has been replaced by a desire to do the intelligent and the scientific thing.

Research in this field of socialization is only gradually accumulating among American social scientists, and our analyses are still imperfect. The above trends, however, are fairly well marked in the American society. They are not meant to be a full explanation of the problem of spoiling children, nor are they universally applicable. There are many local, regional, and class differences in the bringing up of children.

The number of immigrants has sharply decreased in the past two decades, but in so far as some families in the United States behave according to the ideals of foreign cultures, there are noticeable differences in socialization. This makes a problem for children of such families, especially when they discover that the home life of their school companions is quite different from their own.

To some extent the rural pattern of socialization differs from that of the urban family. The possibilities of a larger kinship group, of closer co-operation between husband and wife and between children and parents, the conservatism and traditionalism of the rural family—all these mean that the socialization of children in the villages and on the farms is not so hindered by lack of social apprenticeship. Rural patterns of behavior are, however, changing rapidly as the urban culture invades the rural areas through the mass media of communication.

2. Standardization and Individualism

It is a commonly held notion that the American is or will soon become the standardized product of the machine age. This concept is built upon an analogy running something like the following: The American productive system has been able to provide, at relatively low prices, a vast flood of commodities. This has been possible because of a standardized process and product. From this fact a peculiar logical leap has been made to the notion that because Americans produce and consume standardized commodities, the Americans themselves have become standardized.

We are interested here, of course, in the question whether the social person in America is a standard product, whether there is even a remote similarity between the production of American goods and services and the American production of social persons. From the point of view of process it would appear that only some extreme form of socialism and regimentation in the rearing of children from infancy could bring this about. This is so far from American reality that it is hardly even an academic question.

From the point of view of the product, that is, of the American person, the following observations indicate that he is not a standardized and uniform person. Even the standardization of things has not progressed to the extent that casual observation may lead one to believe. The standardization of American people does not begin to approach that of people in most of the major nations of the world.

a) The enormous variety of our biological and physical stocks immediately belies standardization of physical features. There is probably no nation in the world where one encounters more differences in bodily features and types. Our people exhibit the total range of known skin color, facial characteristics, and hair types.

b) The offspring of intermarriage among the various racial and ethnic stocks is providing, at least temporarily, an even greater diversification of physical types. As this process continues over the generations, it must eventually produce a more or less standardized physical type of American. At the present time, however, we are many generations removed from this homogeneous product.

c) The number of different religious bodies in America is larger than that of any other country in the world. Although Christianity is the basis of many of our religions, the varied interpretations of it have resulted in more than 250 distinct and formal religious bodies.

d) The types of architecture differ enormously. This is noticeable, not only in factories, schools, churches, and office buildings, but especially in residential construction. The identifiable styles of homes, like Colonial, Georgian, Southern, Spanish, ranch-type, and others, are many; but the ingenious combination of styles often makes identification and enumeration almost impossible.

e) The trend to the single-family dwelling reflects individualization, not only in the material surroundings of life, but also in a further isolation of the families themselves. Even in the cities it is questionable that multiple-apartment houses and public housing projects provide a community setting for the development of behavior conformism. The continuing migration of families to the suburbs tends to counterbalance the so-called mass-living in cities.

f) The rich variety of available clothing styles for both men and women belies even the external appearance of standardization. Men's clothing, traditionally much more conservative in color and cut than that of women, has developed a multiplicity of styles and combinations. Almost any American department store offers a greater choice than any European store in size and style of women's shoes, hats, and dresses.

g) From the sociological point of view, the standardization of patterns of behavior is more important than all the foregoing. No doubt a recognizable "American type" of social person is gradually emerging, but American differences in this regard are often more striking than the similarities. Some of these differences are those between rural and urban people and between lower and upper classes, but the most dramatic of them are recognizable on a regional basis. Distinctive cultural variations still exist in the Deep South, New England, the Middle West, the Southwest, and California.

Strangely and unexpectedly, the assembly line and the mass-production system have had results almost opposite from what some theorists predicted. Deadly uniform standardization has given way to differentiation and individualization. In other words, the American economic system, and this includes both the technological and the social organization of the system, has made possible a richer variety than has ever existed in the world before.

Because of refrigeration, transportation, and food preservation, the American is no longer tied to the seasons and cycles of nature. He can vary his diet in ways unknown to his ancestors and to most of his international contemporaries. Because of inventions and gadgets, he can live comfortably in the desert in the cold of winter or the heat of summer. He can travel faster and by more ways than the people of other countries. Admittedly, these are external items; they do not touch immediately the character or the soul of the American. But these material things are the product of the kind of person the American is—pragmatic, imaginative, energetic, and rationalistic.

3. Is the American an Individualist or a Conformist?

Like most questions concerning culture and society, this one cannot be answered in absolute terms. Some critics of American society confuse standardization of things with conformity of social persons and behavior. Americans, on the other hand, boast of freedom, private rights, individual enterprise, and equal opportunities as though these were full and absolute characteristics of our society.

The sociological truth appears to lie somewhere between these two extremes. The rugged individualist could hardly survive in any society, because everyone needs his fellow men; and the complete conformist would probably become a neurotic, because everyone needs a minimum of independence. Restraints are placed upon the individualist in America, and, at least in limited ways, the self-expression of the social person is encouraged.

a) The socialization of the American is strongly flavored with economic and materialistic influences. The shrewd businessman in the tradition of the Yankee trader is given high social approval. The salesman who is a go-getter, who outsells his competitors month after month, is encouraged to put his individual personality into his work. He is often held up as a model of American conduct, as a hero who should be imitated.

b) The mystic and pious individualist tends to be considered odd by his fellow Americans. He is not prevented by any law from practicing his beliefs, nor is he forced in any external way to conform to accepted standards of conduct. But holiness sects are often held up to ridicule, and in this way social pressure is brought to bear upon them. There have been extreme forms of religious prejudice and discrimination, including physical attacks on the property and persons of religious minorities.

c) The pursuit of private interest is therefore both encouraged and discouraged. The complete and unrestrained individualist is an impossibility in any society, but the notion still remains in our folklore that if each person persistently pursues what is best for himself, the best interests of the total society will somehow be achieved. In practice, however, this notion largely disappears. When we take into account the duties as well as the rights of the individual, we often place loyalty to church, family, or other groups above loyalty to the individual.

d) Convenience often brings conformity among Americans in their social life. Social pressure serves as a means of bringing about conformity in the sense that models and examples of behavior and of organization are set up. Often it is convenience rather than compulsion that moves Americans in their group life, in the setting up of luncheon clubs and friendship cliques, in the use of household gadgets and mechanical equipment. This is, of course, an example of the rational approach that characterizes the American.

e) Conviction and conformity sometimes conflict among Americans. Non-conformity may even reach the point of violence in the handling of Communist spies, in the treatment of racial minorities, like the Japanese during the last war and the Negroes in some areas of the country. This means, of course, that not all Americans hold exactly the same detailed body of convictions, and they are therefore individualists rather than conformers in those areas where their strongest convictions lie.

f) Specialization, particularly in occupational roles, has given the impression that the American is highly individualistic. The rise of the expert has made a difference in American society because it has given opportunity to the development of peculiar and personal talents. There tends to be conformity within the same occupational area, however, especially in scientific pursuits, because there exists a relatively open exchange of knowledge.

From this list there emerges a fairly balanced picture of the American person. In his ideals and attitudes he stresses individualism, and in his overt patterns of behavior he finds that a relatively high degree of conformity is essential. There is a conscious effort in America to prevent social conformity from engulfing the individual, but only to a degree.

It must be obvious that although the socialization process is lifelong and continuous, it slows down considerably as one grows older. The person in his early twenties, who has little stake in property and home, in a job, and in community status, conforms much less to patterned

American expectations than the person in his early forties. This is not merely a matter of psychological awareness, aptness, and readiness to change. It is also a question of the social situation in which he finds himself, the commitments he has made, the social relations that influence him to conformity.

4. The Adaptive American Personality

The analysis of the American character, that is, of the kind of representative personality found in the United States, has been attempted by both social scientists and popular commentators. Some of these are serious and scholarly attempts, and some are highly impressionistic and biased caricatures. The social personality of Americans cannot be a matter of statistics, of the sheer numbers who conform to the definition, whatever it may be. Usually, when it is of any value at all, it centers upon a status type of American, like the upper-middle class, urban, white person.

Whatever else this typical American person is, the scientific consensus appears to focus on his adaptiveness. This is a logical deduction from the enormous dynamism of American society and culture, as well as a generalization based upon direct and empirical observation. Opportunities are so numerous, inventions are so frequent, aspirations are so optimistic, that the American is almost forced to adapt himself to the constantly changing situation. This readiness to shift, implied in the term "adaptiveness," is the central tendency of the American ideal-type personality.

a) The influence of the past, in fact, the presence of a long and hallowed history, is often said to be the reason why a society and its social units become stable. It is absurd to suggest that the United States has no traditions or that our people are not influenced by them. The fact is that one of our most important cultural heritages is precisely the tradition of change and the willingness to change. This has been imbedded as a high value, and it is reflected in the adaptive personality.

b) The influence of the future is not a contrary or opposite influence to that of the past. The American emphasis on progress is a constituent element of the body of social values that stretches back into American history. Neither progress nor the desire for progress appears to be slowing down in our society. In this sense, the American possesses a "future-directed" personality, and adaptation to future situations, whether foreseen or not, is an essential ingredient of the American character.

c) Dependence on self is a strongly urged virtue inculcated into American youth. This does not mean a rigid isolation as a lone wolf or as the captain of one's own soul and destiny. It is simply the confidence of the American that he can make the grade, that he must find within himself the resources to respond to every stimulus, or at least to the stimuli that he considers worthwhile.

d) Dependence on others is an expression of self-confidence of the American rather than a relationship of helplessness and subordination to others. The American feels that he should be accepted by anybody anywhere, that he can depend upon others to appreciate him, or at least to tolerate him. The typical American expects a great deal of understanding from other persons, without the need to philosophize and to explain his motivation.

e) The need of approval is probably more openly expressed and more widely extended in the American than in other people. The American personality is expansive in this regard; it wants the appreciation of as many people as possible in addition to family and intimate friends. The American wants to be known as a "good guy," but he does not want to be "taken for a sucker."

f) The mobility of people in American society contributes to the development of the adaptive personality. This means not only social mobility but also the physical and residential movement of individuals and families. It is estimated that the urban family moves its residence approximately three times a decade. In the occupational sphere the shifting of jobs is a social phenomenon unique in its frequency and extent. The sheer amount of travel for pleasure and business has made the United States a nation on wheels.

An analysis of this kind does not pretend to delve into the inner motives of Americans in their constant process of adaptation. It may be said, however, that the attitudes and values held by persons tend to conform with the outward expressions of behavior. The American personality has to adapt itself to these social and cultural factors. It must meet the social situation in which it exists.

Any discussion of the adaptive personality must imply the important question whether the social person is the means or the end. If the social person is the center of the society, the important irreducible physical unit of the group, would one not expect that the institutions and values should be adapted to him rather than vice versa? This is probably an oversimplified question that cannot be fully answered in this form because of the complex relationship between the individual and the society.

Basic social needs are the same everywhere, but the ways of satisfying them differ. People tend to develop the kind of culture that suits them, and the culture tends to develop the kind of people who can best utilize it. A dynamic culture will be employed by dynamic people. Adaptive persons will have an adaptive society. In short, adaptability is a central characteristic both of the American personality and of the American society and culture.

5. The Neurotic American Personality

It is commonly remarked by critics of the American scene that the fast pace of modern life is making of us a nation of neurotics. The thesis is that speed itself somehow generates neuroses, that the inability to keep up the pace leaves people frustrated and nervous, that the ever increasing tempo makes demands which should not be expected of normal human beings. As evidence for this they point to the growing number of neurotic and psychotic cases, the fact that mental patients occupy more hospital beds than physical patients, that psychoanalysts are more and more in demand.

There appears to be a logical fallacy, however, in the relationship between "speed of living" and the development of the neurotic personality. The neurotic person is usually one who is confused in his behavior. The sociological question of importance is not whether the modern tempo has quickened or whether change is inherent in the American culture and society. The question is whether the inner conflict of the personality reflects, is caused by, or causes an external social and cultural conflict.

Neurotic persons are considered abnormal because they do not react to other people, to their social and cultural environment, in expected and approved ways. For a long time it has been the fashion to seek inside the individual for the explanation of abnormal behavior, to delve into his psyche, to search his dreams and fantasies, to measure his instincts, to unravel his traumas and fixations.

If the explanation of the neurotic personality lies wholly within the afflicted individual, this is not an area of study for the social scientist. If his condition is, however, a reaction to, and a reflection of, the culture in which he lives, the problem is of prime importance to the sociologist. Certainly one of the criteria we commonly use in judging people is whether their patterns of behavior are congruous with those we call accepted and normal patterns. The criterion is not what any particular individual would judge to be socially normal but what the society itself generally agrees upon. Thus, what is perfectly normal in the American culture may be considered abnormal in the Turkish society, and vice versa.

The mental conflict at the basis of some neuroses among Americans appears to come from outside of the person himself. It appears also that only the relatively intelligent persons who recognize cultural inconsistencies and the relatively scrupulous persons who try to resolve them are the ones most likely to be affected. Some of these inconsistencies are as follows:

a) The contradictory aspirations to success and humility tend to drive persons in two opposite directions. This does not mean that a successful person cannot be humble. But the meek do not inherit the earth, at least not the American earth. To be successful you are expected to be aggressive and self-assertive, and the constant attempt to follow this line of conduct almost certainly prevents humility.

b) Emphasis on the motives of both profit and service makes it difficult to compromise between them. This is simply another aspect of the attempted balance between self-seeking and self-interest, on the one hand, and brotherly love and universal charity, on the other. In the economic sphere the American often considers service a salable item and actually provides excellent service in order to make more profit on the commodity he is selling.

c) Both honesty and shrewdness are extolled as social virtues in the American culture. The semiprofessionalism of college athletics is a glaring example of this. The suggestion that a student should follow the honor system is made on the very campus where there is a shrewd circumscribing of the amateur code. Within certain limits, the person who "gets away with" dubious practices achieves a kind of prestige even while he convinces himself that honesty is the best policy.

d) Conflicting standards of sexual morality are unquestionably a source of puzzlement to young people. They are told to be decent and proper in their relations with the opposite sex, but they are barraged almost from infancy with sensual pictures, advertisements, stories, movies, and songs.

e) Both physical ruggedness and bodily comfort are held up as ideal American goals. The largest appeal in the advertisements of most products is the appeal to easier and more comfortable living. But, at the same time, bodily exercise, strength, good health, and sturdiness are highly valued.

A much longer list of these contradictory aspirations can be made or found in almost any introductory textbook in sociology. Why does such a system of values not result in a still greater increase in the neuroses of the American people? The main answer seems to lie in the fact that a person can be socialized to accept as normal both ends of the contradiction. If the child is accustomed from his early years to the compromise patterns in his elders, he tends to accept them without question. This is a prime example of the culture molding the individual. The culture overcomes logic. Since everybody is thinking and acting in these ways, the individual is inhibited from questioning the obviously approved system of behavior, contradictory as it may be.

The personality whose neurosis can be traced to the culture is exceptional as well as abnormal. He has sufficient insight to be troubled by inconsistencies, and in this he is an exception to most people in the society. He is abnormal from the point of view of the society because he does not conform to its standards.

A final warning must be emphasized, however, and that is that the recognition of cultural inconsistencies and contradictions does not necessarily make a person neurotic. Most careful students of American society realize the presence of these trends, and it cannot be assumed that they are abnormal personalities. On the other hand, most persons are constantly subject to cultural influences without being fully aware of them.

DISCUSSION QUESTIONS

1. What is meant by a person? A social person?
2. What are the various aspects under which a person can be studied?
3. How does the sociologist resolve the "controversy" over nature and nurture?
4. In what sense is the individual a creature, and in what sense a creator, of his culture?
5. Define the objective and subjective processes of socialization.
6. What is meant by the "internalization" of culture?
7. On what levels can the social frame of reference be analyzed?
8. What are the identifiable mechanisms of both the learning and the socialization processes?
9. List and explain the limitations to the full development of the social capacity of the individual person.
10. Why are some agencies of socialization more effective than others?
11. In what sense can one say that every person is both unique and social?

12. Give the sociological definition of the social personality.
13. What patterns are emphasized in the socialization of the American child?
14. List some of the evidence that the American is not a "standardized product."
15. Give some explanations for the fact that Americans in general are not "rugged individualists."
16. What is the difference between the adaptive and the neurotic personality?
17. What are some contributing factors explaining the adaptiveness of the American personality?
18. What are the cultural inconsistencies that appear to be partial explanations of the American neurotic personality?

SUGGESTED READINGS

Cuber, John F. *Sociology: A Synopsis of Principles.* 3d ed.; New York: Appleton-Century-Crofts, 1955, chap. xii.

Gillin, John P. *The Ways of Men.* New York: Appleton-Century-Crofts, 1948, chap. xxvii.

Hertzler, J. O. *Society in Action.* New York: Dryden Press, 1954, chaps. iv, v.

Rose, Arnold. *Society.* New York: Alfred A. Knopf, 1956, chap. vi.

Woodworth, R. S. *Heredity and Environment.* New York: Social Science Research Council, 1941.

Young, Kimball. *Sociology: A Study of Society and Culture.* New York: American Book Co., 1942, chap. xv.

CHAPTER TWO

Social Status

Every social person has his "place" in the groups and the society to which he belongs. Society is not a haphazard, accidental conglomeration of human beings; it is an orderly arrangement; and the social structure can be conceptualized as a kind of scaffolding on which each separate part can be recognized. Although person and status always go together, it is possible to think of them abstractly as separate concepts. Social status is the place the person occupies in the social structure, as judged and evaluated by the society.

Everybody "has" social status, and the term does not refer merely to high prestige and rank. Nor does it refer to the subjective opinion the individual holds of himself. A person's social evaluation of himself may be quite erroneous when tested by objective criteria. Social status, therefore, is the position, or rank, which the person's contemporaries objectively accord to him within his society.

The Origin of Status

The scientific concept of status is not fixed by mere volatile public favor or disfavor, which may make a person very popular one year and reject him the next. Furthermore, in the maintenance or change of one's social status the person is not an inert subject of the society's whims. How, then, does a person come to have one particular social status rather than another? A study of the origin of status answers this question. Social scientists recognize in the main two ways by which status can be obtained.

a) Ascription of status refers to the fact that the society applies certain criteria of evaluation to the individual without any action on his part. The clearest example of this is the criterion of ancestry, since a person has no choice whatever about being born into an Italian or Irish family, a royal or peasant stock, the Negro or the white race. Although it is true that ultimately all status is ascribed to the individual by his society, we refer here only to those characteristics that are, at least originally, out of the control of the individual.

b) Achievement of status refers to the socially evaluated results of effort on the part of the individual. This achievement works in two directions. A brilliant physicist not only enhances his own social prestige by his performance but also reflects honor and prestige on his whole scientific profession. If royalty as an ancestral criterion decreases in social prestige in a particular country, it may be possible that an efficient and successful king will through his own achievement raise the social value of the royal status. Thus a person is not merely a passive recipient automatically placed in a social status. His own behavior raises or lowers his status.

Sociologists sometimes speak also of "assumption" of status in reference to the individual's voluntary choices at entrance into a new status. A person may choose law as an occupation instead of carpentry; he may choose to marry or to remain single, to marry into a "better family," to assume parenthood within marriage, to accept a political appointment, to enter the ministry, or to become a foreign missionary. These are all examples of the voluntary assumption of status which attaches to the acceptance of new social roles. But it must be remembered that each of these roles requires preparation, and in this sense it has an aspect of achievement rather than of mere assumption.

It must be noted also that there is an interplay and overlapping of the ways in which status originates for the individual. People are neither completely and passively at the mercy of society's judgment, nor are they completely and actively the creators of their own social status. In the ultimate analysis, social status refers not to what you do, or what you are, or what you think you are, but to what people in the society think you are.

A person may work very hard all his life in an ascribed lowly position and never achieve much difference in social status. On the other hand, he may step into an occupational opportunity that automatically carries high status. It is possible, too, especially in the less competitive societies, that a person be relatively indifferent to social success, do hardly anything to achieve it, and still enjoy fairly high social status.

Determinants of Status

When we talk about determinants, or factors, of high or low status, we do not mean that these items of themselves give status. Status is a mental construct, a degree of esteem or disesteem which people in a society display toward individual persons. Ancestry and wealth, for example, are not inherently status-giving items. The kind of ancestry and the amount of wealth help us to determine objectively the status of the person, but this is possible only because these items are given social significance by the way in which people in the society evaluate them.

There is considerable variation throughout the world from society to society in the significance of the status symbols, or determinants. But since status is socially defined, that is, determined by factors outside the individual, there exist certain universal criteria of social approval and disapproval, esteem and disesteem. In most general terms, these are contained in the social values, that is, the things that people consider important and worthwhile. In specific terms, these criteria can be broken down into a series of determinants, or factors, universally present, in combination and in varying degrees of emphasis, wherever people lead a group life.

In attempting to judge the social status of any individual, as well as any family or any social category, the following criteria must be used. They can be more or less objectively measured. No single one of these criteria is sufficient for the evaluation of status; they must be taken in combination.

a) Ancestry gives one a privileged or inferior position because the fact of being wellborn or lowborn has a certain value even in a professedly democratic society. The esteem or disesteem of a particular person's ancestry rests on several factors: legitimacy or illegitimacy, reputation of the family, and its length of residence in the area. One's racial background is often given prominent consideration, as the difference in Negro, Indian, Asiatic, or Caucasian; and one's ethnic or national background, as English, Mexican, Italian, or French, is also usually of considerable importance.

b) Wealth, in one form or another, is likewise a universal criterion of social status. It is a convenient, objective measurement because possessions are tangible items. They can be counted and graded. They allow the possessor to display the degree to which he can afford to live in style, comfort, and general well-being. The source of one's wealth is also socially significant, since newly acquired or ill-gotten wealth does not give so much prestige as inherited wealth or that obtained in a socially approved fashion.

c) The functional utility which a person serves is also an important criterion of social status. A person is ranked according to what he "does" in a society, and this again depends upon what the people think is worth doing. In a society where the economic institution is paramount, a person will be scored heavily on the basis of his gainful occupation. On this criterion alone, we may say that the president of a bank is socially valued higher than the janitor of a bank. It is also true that certain functional categories (like medicine or engineering) may be ranked higher than others (like school teaching or police work).

d) The amount and kind of education are determinants of social status in every society. In some societies there are sharp distinctions between the illiterate and the literate. In societies where education is compulsory, the gradations are numerous and more subtle but nonetheless real. A person with higher education also has higher social status. The college degree is a symbol of status, and this has even more value if it is earned at colleges and universities with high social prestige.

e) The kind and degree of religion one professes are also determinants of social status. The general values of society always include some attitude toward the supernatural. In most societies this is an attitude of approval; in a few societies formal attempts have sometimes been made to lower the esteem of religion as a criterion of social status. In a society where only one large religious body exists, one's relation to, and position in, that religion has great significance for social status. In a society where numerous churches and denominations exist, these religious bodies themselves tend to be rated on a hierarchy of status.

f) Biological characteristics are important criteria by which a society places any particular individual in a higher or lower social status. Sex appears to be a universal criterion in the sense that most societies accord the male a higher status than the female. Femininity is generally subordinated to masculinity as a social value. The differences of degree are vast from society to society, for in one place and time there may be a tendency toward equality of the sexes, and in another the lines of inequality are rigidly preserved. Age is also a universal physical criterion of social status, at least in the sense that adulthood is valued more highly than infancy. The application of this criterion also differs widely. In some societies aged persons are valued, respected, and almost venerated, while in other societies there is a notable accent on youth. Closely allied to both age and sex is the concept of *physical beauty* as appraised by the people. The standards of beauty are variable, as to height and weight, bodily contours, facial profile, skin color, and hair type, but standards do exist universally.

The Transfer of Status

Although the person and his status are always intimately connected, we have been analyzing them in the abstract as separable items. The description of the social person tells us *what he is,* while the description of the social status tells us *what he possesses* of value in the opinion of the society in which he lives. What we are saying is that the social status is transferred to the social person himself. That which the society approves or disapproves indicates also in this transfer those whom the society esteems or disesteems.

Transfer of status may be demonstrated by several familiar examples. It is usually the head of the family, the husband and father, who represents to the outside world the social status of the family members. Generally speaking, therefore, we may say that the wife and children reflect and share his social status, so that in a sense his social status is transferred to them. Another example of status transfer is that of a person holding an important office in a society. A president or a premier, a cardinal or a bishop, may have great personal popularity based upon his intelligence, charm, and competence. These are subjective abilities by which he achieves increased prestige, but, in addition, he is held in high esteem because of the office he occupies, and one may say that this status transfers to the person himself.

Social Power and Status

It is sometimes said that social power, that is, the influence that a person is able to exert over others in society, is a criterion of the status which he possesses. Although one may use social power as a quick and ready rule of thumb to measure social status, this influence is a consequent rather than a determinant of social status. It is obvious that people with high social status have much more influence in a community than people with low social status. Even the person who may be said to have "achieved power" has done so mainly because he first achieved the social position from which to exercise influence.

It appears that this is the main reason why some people seek to improve their social status, not merely to enjoy a feeling of superiority or of self-satisfaction, but because the possession of high status makes it possible for them to get concrete results in their dealings with others. This is especially noticeable in a dynamic society where opportunities for upward social mobility exist. The person who is a "nobody" socially may have great ambitions, but he is hindered in many ways in the achievement of his ambitions.

We need not at this point go into the characteristics of leadership and personal influence in modern society. The personal ability to persuade others is given much attention by psychologists, but the student of society is interested in the social origins and effects of this leadership. It must be pointed out that although social power accompanies and accrues to status, the latter is not the only source of influence and power. We have already seen that an individual may achieve higher status through personal effort, and it is also through effort and ability that he may achieve social power. The "king-maker," the "man behind the throne," the manager for a political figure, and similar persons frequently wield an extraordinary amount of power and influence.

Types of Status

The quantitative concepts of higher or lower, more or less, better or worse, inhere in the very notion of social status. Therefore, it requires no special insight to recognize a classification of persons on this basis. In fact, the whole concept of class and of stratification refers to one's status in relation to the status of others. It is useful, however, to recognize *institutionalized status*, that is, the relative position of the person in the major institutionalized groupings of the society.

The major and basic social groups are the familial, educational, recreational, economic, political, and religious. As we shall see further, these groupings are structured in the arrangement of the positions of persons within them. This makes it possible for us to speak about a person's *group status*—family status, economic status, religious status, and so forth. Within the family, for example, the individual may have the status of grandfather or of infant daughter; within the school system that of college professor or second-grade pupil; within the church that of bishop or sacristan.

It is possible, but quite unusual, that a person will enjoy high status in all these major groups in which he participates. The fact is that there is in every society an ordering of the groupings themselves by rank in the sense that one type of basic group will have more social importance than another. This question centers on the relation of the major institutions to one another. In a society where the economic institution is predominant, the economic grouping and the status of the individual in the economy will also be of great importance.

Key Status

Each person has as many statuses as there are groups in which he participates, but he has also one principal status. The determination of this key status for any particular individual depends not only upon the status that he has assumed and achieved but also, and mainly, upon the values current in the society. In a society where economic values and institutions carry high prestige, a person's gainful occupation will usually indicate his key status. This would obviously differ in a society where the family, or the church, or the state, is the dominant grouping.

The key status is an important sociological concept in the analysis of the total social personality. The key status is the largest "window" which the person opens to the world about him, and it is through this window that the society sees and interprets his other statuses. It is at this point that what a person does, that is, his social role, is closely associated with his key status.

It is sometimes said that social status is what people think you are and social role is what people think you do. Evaluation, measurement, and judgment by others thus enter into the concept of both role and status. There is a clear distinction between these two concepts, but in the concrete social situation they go hand in hand. A person does, or is expected to do, certain things in accord with his status; that is why we say that the achievements of the individual affect his status. Certain roles carry higher status than others, and a person's key status attaches to the role his society considers the most significant.

In general terms, we may say that the social roles carrying the highest prestige in the society are relatively scarce. They usually require certain skills and abilities not shared by large numbers of people. There are few corporation presidents in comparison to the rank and file of employed persons, and the skills required in the role of corporation president are considerably greater than those required in the lower industrial positions. There is only one heavyweight boxing championship title. To hold this title and to enjoy the status that accompanies it, the pugilist has to fulfil the requirements of the role. Thus the key social role refers to the functions that accompany the key status, while the key status refers, at least in part, to the evaluation that people place upon the function.

Station in Life

The complex analysis of the social person, as he is seen and judged by others, demonstrates that each individual has many statuses but that only one of these is adjudged his key status. The person is a social totality, and he has a "total social status" which is called his station in life. This is a combination of all of his social statuses; it is the generalized position that emerges when all of the criteria of status are combined to form a single evaluation of the person. Station in life is heavily influenced by, but is not identical with, key status. It does not refer merely to a person's position in his family, in industry, in political, educational, recreational, or religious groupings.

The sociological reality of one's station in life is readily recognized in the fact that class status is a universal social phenomenon. It is the individual's known "class position." Most people in any society have a rough concept of the meaning of upper, lower, and middle classes, and they recognize that one's station in life is his position in one class or another. As a matter of knowledge at this point of our study, social class may be defined as a category of people whose station in life is roughly similar; they are on a similar status level; they are socially accessible to one another more readily than they are to people on other social levels.

It is sometimes said that social class itself is a criterion or determinant of social status and of station in life; but this statement appears to be tautological. The two terms reflect each other and are at best two ways of looking at the same phenomenon. From the point of view of the person himself, his station in life places him automatically in one or another of the social classes. From the point of view of the class category, the evaluation of the class depends upon the station in life of those persons who constitute it.

Status and Stratification

Since social status is the rank of one person in relation to others, and since social class is the rank of one category of people in relation to others, it is logical that the same criteria are employed to identify both. In other words, ancestry, wealth, function, education, religion, and biological characteristics reflect social values around which people are clustered into classes. People who have low status, as measured by all of these criteria, are people who "belong" to the lower class. Social class, like social status, is a generalized position emerging from extrinsic evaluation. It is a mental construct that results from social consensus, and it does not refer to inherent or developed moral qualities in the individual.

Social stratification refers to the horizontal "layers" or strata into which the people of a society are arranged. A social stratum is conceptualized in relation to other strata in order to include large numbers of people placed similarly. Since every person is unique, it is possible that the infinitesimal shadings of differences would allow a continuum from one end of the social hierarchy to the other. This attempt, however, would probably be as useless as it is difficult to realize. General similarities are recognized in any society so that people conveniently fall into stratified categories. It has long been customary to speak of lower, middle, and upper classes, but in a highly stratified society there are recognizable differences within each of these broad categories.

From the point of view of status, every group is stratified, and from the point of view of class, every society is stratified. Thus stratification of some degree and kind is universally present in social life. Even a recreational club has leaders and active and passive members. The positions of subordination and superordination are obvious in schools, churches, factories, and wherever else people have systematic social relations. Thus the aspiration for complete democracy or for perfect equality among people is without scientific validity. Similarly, the promotion of an ideal of a classless society is both unrealistic and impossible.

It is nevertheless true that the effort to introduce equality of opportunity and democratic human relations has resulted in a rearrangement of the class structure. Numerous societies have traditionally maintained a system in which a relatively small, wealthy, and powerful upper class controlled the large mass of people in the lower class. The so-called "revolt of the masses" appears to be stirring currently in many of these societies. In the democratic, Western societies, the spread of political, economic, educational, and other opportunities to the largest number of people has resulted in the growth of a relatively stable middle class and of a more complex and multiple system of stratfication.

Social stratification is a highly complex arrangement, which to be understood requires a careful analysis of the multiple criteria of status. The concept is rendered practically meaningless by adherence to a simple distinction between the rich and the poor, the capitalist and the worker, the haves and the have-nots. This kind of distinction is prevalent in a society where economic activities are socially valued. It must be emphasized, however, that neither wealth nor a person's position in the economy determines his social class. In almost any large concentration of population, there are people of "good family" who are relatively poor, and there are people of great means who strive unsuccessfully to "break into" the upper class.

Social Inequality and Mobility

Social status would have no meaning if there were no inequalities among the persons in the society and no scarcities in the items that people value as the criteria of prestige; since equality in the distribution of these items is impossible, complete social equality is impossible. Thus, a status-less and stratum-less society is unthinkable. This statement is true from both the subjective and the objective point of view. Subjectively, individual persons have different degrees of competence, intelligence, and energy, and this is important in so far as it helps them to achieve or to assume status. Objectively and extrinsically, the criteria of social status cannot be shared equally.

A person's possession of these valued items may increase or decrease in most instances. He may decrease his wealth and increase his education; he may adhere more closely to, or fall away from, approved patterns of religious behavior. There is little he can do about ancestry, sex, or age, but people have been known to invent genealogies, to accentuate their physical beauty, and to make themselves appear younger or older than their years. Emphasis on one social criterion may change in relation to another so that there will be "shifts" in those items that people consider important. For example, the athlete or actress may have higher status in one time and place than in another. But these shifts of values and of emphasis on values are usually slow and unspectacular.

Status and class are universal social phenomena relatively enduring and unchanging in a society. Social mobility refers to the shifting of a person from one status to another and from one class to another. Traversing the "social distance" between any two statuses is the manifestation of vertical social mobility. This means going up or down, being more esteemed or less esteemed in the opinion of the society, and if the distance covered is large enough, it means going up or down from one class to another.

The amount and rate of social mobility vary greatly from society to society. An "open-class" society is one in which the opportunities for social mobility are relatively numerous. This is especially characteristic of a dynamic, progressive society in which competition has a high value, closed aristocracies of birth are belittled, and individual prowess is applauded.

PECULIARITIES OF STATUS RELATIONSHIPS IN AMERICA

1. The Changing Status of Women

Since the turn of the century the American reading public has been constantly made aware of women's rights, of the influence of women in public life, of the striving for sex equality, of the subtle dangers of "Momism." There are many evidences that the social status of the contemporary American female is quite different from that of women in most other modern countries. The periodicals, television and radio shows, newspaper columns, books, and lectures that have dealt with the "woman question" indicate that female influence is increasing and that women's status is being raised.

Female status cannot be measured except in relation to the status of males. This does not mean that a change in female status necessarily results in the masculinization of women. It does not mean in any gross sense that women are becoming less feminine in either physical appearance or in biological function. In fact, the trend indicates the opposite: that the secondary sex characteristics are being more accentuated than ever before.

The changing status of the American female can be deduced from the following observations:

a) In our society's recreational groupings, women have demanded and obtained a greater freedom of activity. Most fields of athletic competition, including even professional wrestling, have been opened to them. They patronize gambling places, taverns, and night clubs. In some few larger cities, exclusively male grills, clubs, and bars have been established to stem the "invasion" of women patrons. But other areas of recreation make deliberate efforts to attract female interest and women customers with special devices like "Ladies' Day" at the ball park and cut-rate tickets for women's clubs.

b) The change in the political status of women is evident in the fact that women may vote. In addition women have become active party workers in the political precincts and in county and state politics, and have appeared at the national conventions of the major parties. They have reached the rank of cabinet membership, of ambassadorships and consular posts in foreign countries, and of congressional office. Politicians listen respectfully to the League of Women Voters and to various civic groups that press for political change. Large numbers of women are employed in government agencies.

c) Probably the most far-reaching change of all is that in the economic status of women. The stereotype of the helpless female who knows nothing about finances, is careless with money, and is completely dependent upon males for material support has vanished from reality although it still exists in fiction. Women have come to possess wealth, a very important criterion of social status. It is estimated that more than half of the corporation stock in the United States is registered in the names of women and that about 90 per cent of the purchase of consumers' goods is made on the decision of women. Unlike the ownership of stock, the making of retail purchases indicates the control of wealth. The deference paid to women customers hinges around this fact, and this deference is tantamount to a rise in status.

d) The rise in women's status is seen in the fact that females are often a symbol of male social mobility. It is not historically unusual that the successful male demonstrates his status by adorning and exhibiting his womenfolk, but this has reached unprecedented proportions in the American society. The male wants his wife to "have the best," and the result is a curious mixture of social pressure, upward mobility, symbols of status, desire for comfort, and response to advertising. Clothing, household appliances, automobiles, and female participation in luncheon and garden clubs are not only demonstrations of the female rise in status but also reflections of the station in life of the head of the family.

e) The functional utility of women to the society has also been an indicator of the rise of social status. Women are often the "culture bearers" in the sense that they preserve the values of a society. This function in the family and community is of great significance. Functional utility is widened also in the area of gainful employment. The tremendous increase in service occupations in our industrial economy has been largely handled by women. The great majority of telephone operators, secretaries, stenographers, file clerks, retail-sales people, schoolteachers, and social workers are women. With the exception of heavy industrial labor, women have accepted and performed adequately most of the gainful occupations previously reserved for males. Women are not only gainfully employed; they are contributing useful functions highly valued by the society. This utility is a criterion of their increased status.

f) The level of female education is rising and this too has contributed importantly to higher social status for women. More women are being formally educated in America than ever before; they are spending more years in higher education; the kind of education they are receiving is not specifically feminine; they are matriculating at and graduating from the traditionally best colleges and universities of the country.

It must be noted that all these changes have contributed to a higher evaluation of women in our American society. This does not mean that earlier American females were treated with dishonor and disesteem. In fact, the scarcity of women and the moral climate of the colonies helped to keep women on a peculiar pedestal. To a large extent this was chiefly ascription of status. The fundamental difference at the present time in the rise of female status rests in the fact that women have been granted the opportunities to achieve status.

2. The Ambiguous Status of Youth

The American sociey is remarkable in the modern world because of its youth problems. The extent and intensity of delinquency among our urban adolescents, the intractability and restlessness of our young people, the worry and scolding on the part of social authorities—all these indicate a peculiar social problem. Probably no major society in the history of the world has had to grapple with a youth problem of such magnitude and complexity.

We have seen that a person's age is one of the criteria of his social status in any society. We are speaking here of the status of young people as a general population category as well as of youth as a criterion of status. Youthfulness, the desire to stay young and to look young, has an extraordinarily high value in the American culture. The cult of youth as a criterion of social status has become almost a fetish. The social presure to "keep young and fit" is exerted even upon the aged in the style of clothes and cosmetics for both sexes. Slenderizing is not merely for health's sake; and sport's enthusiasm and interest are expected of older people. The "old grads" seem to be more devoted to the football heroes than are the college students themselves. Youth as a social status appears to be valued and appreciated by everyone except the teenager.

Some of the factors which make this ambiguity of status possible in our society are the following:

a) Youth in America is largely functionless, except in a preparatory fashion. We have said that the utility of the function performed is an important criterion of social status. American youth has no specific function except to "grow up." It is in a waiting period, rather than a transitional period, between dependent childhood and independent adulthood. In most societies the great majority of boys and girls are gainfully employed at the age of fourteen or fifteen. They are "doing something" that is considered important and is taken seriously by their contemporaries and by themselves.

b) From another point of view this is an extended adolescence. There is no sharp and formal distinction, no rites of passage, between the status of child and the status of adult. The male or female who is physically and intellectually an adult and is able to assume the responsibilities of adulthood is often socially still a boy or girl. This situation is fraught with strains and frustrations. The refusal of adults to take adolescents seriously results often in the refusal of adolescents to take adults seriously.

c) The prolonged education of youth often leads to restlessness and ambivalence although it ultimately gives the individual greater social prestige as an adult person. Because Americans value formal education so highly and provide educational opportunities for all, the young people here stay in school much longer than do the youth of other countries. The American belief that anyone with talent should be given the opportunity for college education is sometimes given the added meaning that anyone who can afford to pay for higher education should have it. Young people are expected and urged to continue their schooling even when they have no interest and less competence for further learning. It is little wonder that some high-school and college students find an outlet for their interests and energies in an excessive pursuit of recreation and in secret sororities and fraternities.

d) Youth is more easily adapted to change than is adulthood. The process of socialization, especially the willingness to accept new and progressive ideas, is quicker and more extensive in youth, resulting often in a clash of values with older people. Because he is confused about his own status, the youth seeks greater varieties of self-expression. The dynamic aspect of American society and culture is nowhere so dramatically demonstrated as in our adolescents with their characteristic volatile fads and fashions and their slogans and catchwords.

e) American youth often has the duties of a child and the privileges of an adult. Dating, which has no direct connection with marriage preparation and which starts at fourteen or fifteen involves the operation of automobiles and many adult forms of recreation, such as patterns of drinking, including the frequenting of taverns and night clubs. The girl is encouraged by her parents to be "popular with boys" but also to keep herself chaste and decent. Even here the standards of popularity and decency are ambiguous and sometimes in conflict because the terms are understood differently by parents and children.

These circumstances indicate the lack of a clear-cut, universally acceptable youth status in the United States. There are differences from region to region, and from class to class, but this does not constitute the basic ambiguity concerning the status. The ambiguity exists both in the minds of youth and in the minds of adults. Neither can say clearly and in detail how the general criteria of status apply to youth and how the expectations of behavior are patterned. The fact is that youth is in "flux" in a way peculiar to the society itself rather than to the physical characteristics of youth.

This discussion should not lead to any alarmist conclusion about the future of American society. It is probable that our dynamic, open, progressive, adaptive society requires this kind of youth status. The fact that the majority of young men could meet satisfactory standards of military discipline and efficiency and that they "settle down" later to become competent employees, dependable citizens, and responsible fathers and husbands; the fact that the majority of young females assume their adult roles in a satisfactory manner—all of this indicates that the ambiguity of the youth status does not spell doom for the American society and culture.

3. The Changing Status of American Negroes

The sociological "laboratory" of race relations in the United States provides an opportunity for the student of society to test the generalizations of social science. Here we are concerned only with the status of the American Negro, and particularly with application of the criteria of social status. This "laboratory" has become more and more open to the gaze of foreign observers and has become the scene of intensified activity by Americans themselves.

What we have before us is the dramatic upward shift of a whole social category from slave status, that is, from a position below and outside the American citizenry. The continuous rise of the social status of Negroes is not a proof of the change in criteria by which status is judged. These criteria are universal in every society, but the emphasis on one or another of the criteria changes. A process of interaction has taken place. The evaluation of the Negro by whites has changed because of the achievement of status by Negroes, and this achievement has been made possible largely by white ascription of status to Negroes. In other words, the complete explanation does not lie either in the statement that "the Negro has pulled himself up by his own boot-straps," or in the statement that "whites have changed their attitudes toward Negroes."

All Negroes do not possess the same social status, either in their own judgment or in that of whites. The range of social status from highest to lowest is probably not so great as that found among whites because the upper-class Negroes have not attained the station in life reached by some whites. The following are indicative of the changing Negro status:

a) Change in occupation has effectively changed Negro status. The rural Southern Negro has migrated to commercial and industrial centers in large numbers. Negroes have received higher wages even in menial jobs and in domestic service. They are eligible for more kinds of employment and have more economic opportunities. They have gained important positions in music and the arts, and especially in sports. At a time when the service occupations are becoming more and more important in our society, the Negro is no longer considered merely a servant in the American economy. The concept of a permanent servant class is incongruous with American values.

b) The legal status of the Negro has changed in the sense that theoretical and abstract rights have in many instances been translated into concrete terms. Negroes have won practically every federal court case in which they have charged a transgression of their educational, political, and other rights. The rights to vote and hold office, to use public facilities like schools, libraries, parks, theaters, and means of transportation, to accumulate and dispose of property, and many others have been spelled out and have been more and more enforced.

c) The consciousness of democratic and egalitarian values in the general American society has greatly influenced the change in Negro status. This consciousness is partly a consequence of the way in which social goals were emphasized in the war effort and partly a reaction to the world situation in which the free nations are at odds with the totalitarian nations. The practical acceptance of social values and ideals has worked constantly in favor of the Negro.

d) The level of education of the American Negro has been continuously on the rise. The percentage of American Negroes attending colleges and universities is higher than the percentage of all citizens obtaining similar education in any of the other major countries in the world. American Negro education is meaningful, however, only in relation to the general level of education in the United States. The high value placed on education in our country necessarily raises the status of persons having that education.

e) The bodily characteristics of the Negro are peculiarly important to his social status. His skin color and facial features are highly distinctive and often set him apart because they do not coincide with the traditional Anglo-Saxon standards of physical beauty. Among Negroes there is a tremendous range in these characteristics, and there is no doubt that even the shade of skin coloring affects the relative social status of the individual. Toleration and approval of all shades of color by the American society would lessen the effect of this criterion of status. Meanwhile, there is little that the Negro himself can do about it.

f) The racial ancestry of many American light-skin Negroes can often be identified only because there is community knowledge of it. Even though the great majority of American Negroes are "part white," the sociological definition places anyone in the category of Negro who has some known Negro ancestry. The anonymity of the urban society is allowing many of these persons to pass as whites, but while "passing" raises the status of the individual, it does not change the status of the race as a whole. Here again the change of status will depend upon a revision of the criterion of ancestry.

g) The development of middle-class behavior patterns among many Negroes is having a subtle but marked effect on the change of social status. As the Negro family rises in social status it adopts a relatively rigorous standard of conduct in the raising of children, in forms of recreation, and in moral and religious practices. At the same time the family standards of many upper-middle class whites appear to be relaxing. These changes are simply an indication that a family with established social status can "afford" to relax the mores while a family which is striving for higher status tends to conform to the mores.

From the institutional point of view there are many other factors which contribute to raising the status of the American Negro. He is shifting in large numbers from the emotional religious sects to more conservative and even liturgical forms of religion. He is participating in higher status forms of recreation like golf and tennis and is accepted in professional and collegiate competitive sports. The barriers to achievement of status have gradually broken down in the major economic, political, and educational groups of our society. All of these add up to a new and higher social status for the American Negro.

4. Religion as a Criterion of Status

Religion is one of the major institutions which are found in every society. The extent to which religion may be used as an important indicator of social status depends very much on the values the society puts on religious participation and practices. The United States is said to be a secular society with a this-worldly culture, and if this is true, one may assume that measurable secular items are more effective criteria for social status than intangible supernatural ones.

It is probably true that social status has always in every society been measured more on secular than on sacred factors. Even in theocratic societies, poverty, humility, and charity—the measuring rods of holiness—probably did not help appreciably to elevate a person to high social status. Family status, wealth, and education have apparently always been more significant values to the great masses of people. Religious status might add to or detract from general social status, but religion itself has not been one of the most emphasized criteria.

In the United States organized religion is considered respectable. Church affiliation is an asset for persons like politicians and businessmen who have to meet and please the public. There is probably no high public official who would admit to having no religion. Governors of states, and even higher officials, have been known to get themselves baptized and to join a church. It is estimated that about 40 per cent of our population are not members of churches, but seldom does an American admit in an interview or on a questionnaire that he is an atheist.

a) The kind of religion to which one belongs both reflects the social status of the individual and contributes to his status. The emotional, noisy, "shouting" religions may satisfy a need for some individuals, but they are followed mainly by people of low social status. The dozen major religious bodies of the United States vary in their influence depending largely on their region and on the local composition of the church.

b) The conservative and traditional churches which pursue their functions unobtrusively and do not put great demands upon their members are typical of the high-status religions. They represent a kind of haven for the energetic and harassed American. They provide reassurance and comfort and satisfy the important American quest for security. It is as though everything else must change, but these upper-class religions must remain stable.

c) The tolerant church is also highly appreciated by those who are attempting to maintain or to achieve high social status. The fiercely evangelical and openly proselytizing church is a disturbing element; it makes a great ado over relatively "unimportant things" like theological doctrines. The broadmindedness of doctrine, which allows various private interpretations, represents an attitude that many Americans consider worth striving for.

d) Americans expect their churches to have a social welfare approach, but mainly in the sense of providing recreational facilities and congenial atmosphere for the membership. Churches with upper-class membership sometimes provide professional marital counseling and even psychiatric help. They usually support certain "good works" for the unforuntate in other parts of the city. The individual can demonstrate his social status by contributing generously to these "causes."

e) The opportunity for lay participation in the actual administration of the congregation, especially among the Protestant churches, also provides an avenue for upward social mobility. A person may gain social recognition through these activities when he finds himself blocked and frustrated in the secular channels of mobility. Many of the functions thus performed are in essence secular but they are given an extra value in that they are being done "for the church."

In the last analysis it may be said that religion in America conserves social status for the individual. This is probably more true in the smaller towns and in the growing suburbs than it is in the anonymous metropolitan areas. Religion is the slowest-changing major institution in the American culture. The religious groups, especially those with the highest aura of social prestige and respectability, tend to conform to, rather than to change, the secular milieu in which they exist. Thus they help the individual himself to conform to his social status.

5. Achievement versus Ascription of Status

America is called the land of unlimited opportunities, not only by foreigners who are anxious to immigrate, but also by many Americans themselves. It is part of our folklore that anyone can go as high as his competence will allow. The youngster is urged to compete seriously because there is "always room at the top." Any newborn infant has the chance some day to become President of the United States, provided it is not a female or a Negro, does not belong to the Jewish or Catholic religion, does not have an Italian, Polish, or Russian name, and is not of Asiatic ancestry.

The realistic fact is that achievement of social status is quite carefully circumscribed by many limiting conditions, even in the United States. In the ultimate analysis, as we have seen, all social status is ascribed, because it depends upon the way in which the society judges the individual, his family, and his class. While there is room for achievement of status, there are also definite hindrances. Some of the more obvious hindrances to achievement of social status are the following:

a) A ceiling exists for industrial workers because the specialization of function requires highly trained and educated personnel. It is no longer realistic to think of entering a factory as a mechanic's helper and working up to the presidency. Specialists are being channeled in from the colleges at those levels to which and through which the ordinary skilled worker cannot penetrate. This is a structural limitation on ascending social mobility which will probably become even more rigid.

b) The quota system is sometimes used in areas which could be normal avenues for upward mobility. Jews and Negroes, and sometimes others, are limited or excluded from certain preparatory schools, colleges, and universities and from some country clubs and resort hotels. In these instances the achievement of social status is thwarted before it can begin. These practices will tend to decrease to the degree that the American people become more liberal and tolerant.

c) Restrictive covenants in residential areas can no longer be validly defended in the American courts, but there are innumerable gentlemen's agreements not to sell choice properties to "undesirable elements" of the population. A good address is more than a mere symbol of social status or a place for comfortable and convenient living. It also involves the opportunity for social relations with those persons, and with that class, which is known to live in the neighborhood.

d) Limitations on marriage opportunities, while not so rigid in the American society as in other societies, are nevertheless real. It is not only people of the upper class who warn their children to be careful about their dates; most American parents are concerned that their children "marry well." The American "in-law problem" is not merely a problem of psychological maladjustment between relative strangers; it is more often the attitude that the son- or daughter-in-law is not "good enough," that is, is not of sufficiently high social status.

e) Regional disparities often hinder the bright boy or girl from making the most of opportunities. This is partly a matter of rural isolation and partly a matter of the relative poverty of some regions of the country. To achieve higher social status a person has to be in a location where facilities for self-improvement exist. This lack is most noticeable in areas where schools are inadequately staffed and the number of school days are kept at a minimum.

f) Identification with "foreign ideologies" appears to be a relatively recent limitation on achievement of social status. For example, the mere fact of having been associated in the past with persons who belonged to Communist organizations brings one under suspicion. This "guilt by association" is sufficient to interfere with a career that may have had potentials of high social status. This may be an indication of increasing conformity to national values and ideals. In effect it is analogous to social ostracism and to religious excommunication.

These hindrances to the achievement of social status are to some extent variable. In some respects they appear to be increasing and in other respects decreasing in intensity. At any rate, they are an indication that the dream of equal opportunity for all is a quite restricted dream. The nature of social stratification, and of the criteria upon which status is judged, ultimately implies inequalities. The American society, like every other society, contains these inequalities, but they are not so numerous or so restrictive here as in many of the less dynamic societies of the world.

DISCUSSION QUESTIONS

1. Explain what is meant by social status.
2. What is the difference between ascription and achievement of status?
3. List the universal determinants of social status.
4. If these determinants of status are universally present, why does their application differ from one culture to another?
5. Give examples to demonstrate the "transfer of status."
6. Explain this statement: "Social power is a criterion of status."
7. What is meant by "institutionalized status"?
8. Distinguish between key status and station in life.
9. Why is the key status an important sociological concept in the analysis of the total social personality?
10. In what sense is station in life synonymous with class position?
11. Define social stratification. How does it differ from, and how is it related to, social status?
12. Why is a society without status and strata impossible?
13. What is meant by social mobility and social distance?
14. List the evidences for the changing status of the American female.
15. In what sense can we say that youthfulness is itself an American social value?

16. Why is it sometimes said that the status of American youth is "ambiguous"?
17. By what criteria can we demonstrate the rising status of the American Negro?
18. What aspects of American churches tend to contribute higher social status to their members?
19. List the main conditions which limit the achievement of status in the American society.

SUGGESTED READINGS

BENNETT, JOHN W., and TUMIN, MELVIN M. *Social Life, Structure and Function.* New York: Alfred A. Knopf, 1948, chap. vi.

DAWSON, C. A., and GETTYS, W. E. *An Introduction to Sociology.* New York: Ronald Press Co., 1948, chap. xvii.

EBERSOLE, L. *American Society.* New York: McGraw-Hill Book Co., 1955, chap. xii.

HILLER, E. T. *Social Relations and Structures.* New York: Harper & Bros., 1947, chap xxii.

QUEEN, STUART A., *et al. The American Social System.* Boston: Houghton Mifflin Co., 1956, chap. vi.

WILLIAMS, ROBIN M. *American Society: A Sociological Interpretation.* New York: Alfred A. Knopf, 1952, chap v.

CHAPTER THREE

Social Categories

We have seen that a person's social status depends largely upon what people in the society think of him. But this evaluation of the individual, this degree of esteem or disesteem, depends in turn upon the degree to which a person possesses the various criteria of social status that the society values highly. Thus, social status is not purely mental or imaginary; it has its basis in the objective and real presence of items of social value.

Similarly, a social category is not merely mental or imaginary. A social category is a plurality of people who are "thought of" as a social unit because they are actually similar in one or more ways. This is demonstrated in the example of social class, which is made up of people who have similar social status. Because of its family background, degree of wealth, education, and other qualifications, the upper class in any society is mentally constructed as a social unit, even though the people in this class may not form an organized and recognizable social group.

Definition of Category

Similarity, or the sharing of common characteristics, is the essential note in the definition of the social category, and it is also the important difference between a social category and a social group. The persons in the category need have no contact with one another, no reciprocal communication or human relations, nor even proximity. The labor force, children of preschool age, marriageable females, suburbanites, and many other social categories, fit the definition of a plurality of people who are recognized and studied as a social unit because they share one or more common characteristics.

The forming of categories is one of the most common mental processes in which human beings indulge. Categories are basic to every science because they make possible the intelligent understanding of the qualities and behavior of things which are similar. A simple exercise in this process is the attempt to subdivide and classify all material objects. Two broad categories are immediately perceived: that of living things and that of non-living things. Living things can be subdivided into animals and those which are merely vegetable; the animal beings into brute and human animals. Human beings can be subdivided into all kinds of categories: the young and the old, the males and the females, the married and the single, and many others.

In one sense the social category exists "only in the mind," but if it is a scientifically valid category, it has a basis of real existence in external and objective human beings. This objective basis is a similarity, a common characteristic, which actually exists in the people who are thought of as a social unit. Thus, the category itself is a logical or mental plurality, but the people, and their similarities, have their existence outside the mind. When we talk about the rich or the blind or the illiterate or the intelligentsia, we have a pretty good idea of what kind of person is included and what kind is excluded from these different categories.

Kinds of Social Categories

The social scientist does not bother to classify people according to every possible characteristic that they may have in common. The list of shared items among people is almost inexhaustible, but most of these items are of little sociological significance. The chiropodist, and perhaps the manufacturer of corrective shoes, would be interested to know how many people in a county or state have flat feet. Health programs were advanced tremendously when it was discovered that there are only four types of blood and that all human beings belong in one or another of these four categories. But this kind of information and this type of categorization would have at best only secondary significance for the social scientist.

This is another way of saying that while all categories are statistical, that is, the people who have the common characteristic can be numbered, not all categories are social. And not all social categories are of equal significance in the study of society. In any particular instance the importance of the social category studied depends largely upon the purpose that the social scientist has in studying it. If he is analyzing the patterns of political behavior, he may arrange his data into categories of voters and non-voters, radicals and conservatives, male and female voters, old and young voters. In a more general way, however, the important social categories are those that are measured against the main criteria of social status. As we have seen, these represent the values of the society, and the arrangement of people according to these criteria provides one of the most important insights into social persons.

The Source of Data for Categories

The only way through which accurate and exclusive categories can be known is the tedious process of counting people. Important as this is, it is merely the preliminary step to the analysis of social phenomena, because statistics, no matter how well refined, say nothing of themselves. The largest source of data on which categories can be arranged is the national census. Some countries maintain a "live" census that is constantly kept up to date and contains a wide variety of information about the population. Other countries take a census only every ten years and collect only limited amounts of information.

A sample of the items tabulated in statistical categories is the following: age, sex, marital status, race, number of births, place of birth, place of residence, occupation, home ownership, number of rooms, kind of heating and plumbing, ownership of automobile, radio, television, refrigerator, and many other items. The refinement of the data allows the combination of several characteristics in specific localities.

When this information is catalogued and studied one obtains a general picture of the "population characteristics" of the society. A comparison of the statistics from one census year to another provides a picture of trends and changes. This census data constitutes the raw material with which the demographers, or population experts, work and from which they make their analyses and deductions. It is extremely important information, and every student of sociology must know at least the general outline of the population characteristics of the society in which he lives.

The Utility of Categories

There are two extreme attitudes to be avoided in the matter of statistical categories. The first is the notion that they are "just statistics," that they are just a matter of "counting noses" and therefore of no importance. The other extreme is the belief that the study of sociology is nothing but the study of statistical categories. Statistics provide necessary and basic information for the student of social science, and without these data he tends to speak in vague generalizations.

In many instances the statistical category constitutes the "universe" being studied. This term means simply the total number of persons who are involved in the study. If we say that "a thousand babies were born in this town last year," we cannot say whether or not this is a significant number unless we know how many people live in the town. It would represent a much higher birth rate if the town's population were five thousand people than if it were twenty thousand. The total selected population is the universe studied. The plotting of population trends requires the accurate numbering not only of the total population of a given area but also of the age, sex, and marital categories. In this way, the larger categories must be divided into meaningful sub-categories.

The knowledge of social categories has practical utility in many ways. If we know how many children were born six years ago and how many fourteen years ago, we have a fairly accurate knowledge of how many pupils will be entering elementary school and how many will be entering high school this year. This can be even more specifically refined by school administrators if they study the mortality rates from infancy to fourteen years of age. This is precisely the kind of information upon which insurance companies depend in fixing the rates on their policies. They arrange people in various categories according to age, sex, race, occupation, and others. They study the morbidity and mortality rates among miners or construction workers as compared to those among salesmen and teachers, and are thus able to fix differential premiums.

It is obvious that a knowledge of social categories is important to politicians, public officials, manufacturers, religious leaders, educational administrators—in fact, to anyone who must plan in relation to large numbers of people. It must also be obvious that statistical categories in themselves tell us nothing. The analysis, interpretation, and comparison of categories must be made before any significant conclusions can be reached. The fact that statistics can be manipulated to "prove a point" is not an argument against the study and use of categories. The popular fallacy that statistics and lies are somehow synonymous simply means that people sometimes lie with words and at other times with numbers.

Categories and Groups

One of the most common errors in everyday language is the confusion of categories with groups. People speak of a minority group, a religious group, or a youth group when for the most part they mean a category of people who fit these descriptions. It must be emphatically pointed out that the compilation and analysis of statistical categories is not the study of social relations and structures, although the analysis of groups is. The number of married people as compared to divorced people by itself gives no real information concerning the operation of the American family. The various categories indicating the amount of education that people have had give no inkling concerning the patterns of behavior current within educational institutions. The number of skilled workers as compared to unskilled workers does not tell us anything about the problems of human relations in industry.

This is simply another way of saying that social categories are not social groups. The category is made up of persons who share one or more characteristics in common but who are not in contact or communication. The category, therefore, represents a point of view, a mental approach or construct, and the persons studied are "together" only in the mind of the individual who studies them. It is obvious, of course, that some of these people may be "together" in the technical sense of concrete group life. All teen-age girls in a city constitute a social category, but some of these teen-age girls associate in various kinds of actual groups.

The distinction between all and some, between category and group, is neither deep nor difficult. The common characteristics that are the basis of the category may also be the basis for attraction into actual associations and human relations. "Consciousness of kind" means that persons recognize and appreciate and tend to associate with other persons who are similar to them. Old men form a clique of cronies, young boys form gangs; people of the same religion or race, or education, are sometimes attracted to one another on the basis of that which they share in common. It must be noted, however, that similarities are only one of many reasons, and not the principal reason, why people form groups. College girls are a category, but a sorority is a group based on something more than similar age, sex, and college attendance. Married men are a category, but a family is a primary social group.

Categories and Stereotypes

Both categories and stereotypes are mental constructs; the difference between them is that one is true and the other false. The stereotype is based upon common characteristics that are imagined to exist but that actually do not exist in the people to whom they are applied. This does not mean that the category says only "good things" about people while the stereotype says only "bad things" about them. When someone says that "American Negroes are illiterate people," he is expressing a stereotype; when he says that "Many rural Negroes do not finish elementary school," he is making a true statement about an actual category of people.

While stereotypes are preconceptions, or prejudgments, we must be careful to note that some preconceptions may happen to be true to reality. A person may prejudge an individual, a group, or even a total category before he has investigated the actual concrete facts in the case, and he may happen to be correct in his preconception. This method of accidentally "hitting upon the truth" without actually knowing the objective facts is hazardous and unscientific. It is in a sense also illogical because judgment logically follows objective knowledge of the facts.

Stereotypes are false preconceptions while categories are true conceptions. The first is a judgment without a basis in fact, while the latter is a judgment based upon the facts. An expressed stereotype, therefore, is always a false statement, indicating a bias for or against the persons about whom it is made. A stereotype may be complimentary or uncomplimentary. Generalizations like the following: "French women are intellectuals" or "American women are vivacious" or "Mexican women are beautiful" are stereotypes as much as the following: "Asiatics are treacherous people" or "Caucasians are exploiters" or "Indians are lazy." These stereotypes, both flattering and unflattering, are open to so many exceptions that they are sociologically meaningless.

The habit of using stereotypes is so widespread that it is worthy of special note for the student of society. As we have seen, stereotyping is quite different from categorizing. The recognition of a social category is the result of careful observation and judgment. The use of stereotypes is often an attempted short cut but actually a blockade to objective thinking. It is much easier to lump people under one heading than it is to analyze the facts and make a precise and careful statement. This prejudgment by which we give general opinions before knowing the facts is the basis of prejudice. The tendency to stereotype runs in two directions: generalization and specification.

a) Generalization is that mental process whereby we apply the fact we know about one person, or a few, to all persons who belong in the same category. If your generous uncle has large ears, you may conclude that generosity is common to all persons with large ears. If a bald-headed man has stolen something from you, you may conclude that all bald-headed men are thieves. This slovenly mental process is usually accompanied by emotional attitudes. It is the careless extension of sympathy or antipathy to a large number of people merely on the basis of experience with one or a few persons.

b) Specification is the converse process whereby we apply to an individual the stereotype which we hold of the whole category to which he belongs. This appears to be a much more common process than that of generalization, and it is usually learned in the process of socialization. The culture of any society contains many traditional stereotypes, both positive and negative, which are handed down from generation to generation. People may have certain preconceived notions about Jews or Catholics and then apply these notions to each Jew or Catholic. Stereotypes abound about Negroes and Asiatics, and these are easily specified to the individual person. There are "nice" stereotypes about Anglo-Saxons, the intelligentsia, the Mayflower descendants; and there are "nasty" stereotypes about Mexicans, the proletariat, hillbillies, and crackers.

Categories and the Criteria of Status

The categories worth studying are those that involve social values. The most logical classification of social categories therefore is according to the criteria of social status. These criteria are extremely numerous in any given society and no listing will encompass them all. The fact is, however, that people do form categories on the basis of social status, and that all of the principal social categories can be included under these headings:

a) Wealth categories are those in which the possession or absence of wealth is used not only to evaluate the individual social person but also to place similar persons together. The simple Marxist division of people into capitalists and proletarians is ultimately based on this criterion. The way in which people talk about the rich and the poor as contrasting categories indicates that wealth is the basis of the distinction. In fact, any society in which materialistic values are held high tends to categorize upper and lower classes merely on the basis of wealth.

b) Ancestry categories are those that lump people together according to family, racial, and ethnic background. Most of the minority categories in modern society are of this kind. Immigrant people are thought of as a social unit principally because they are known to be of foreign parentage. The census data give the distinctions between native-born and foreign-born, and also distinguish between Negroes and whites, Indians and Orientals. Immigrant and racial minorities can be assimilated into the society when their ancestral background is more or less obliterated. This is one of the reasons why some people with "foreign-sounding" names change their names to others more in accord with the values of the social majority.

c) Functional categories are those that are based principally on the way people are gainfully employed. Terms indicating broad categories like the working class, white-collar workers, the service trades, or management are in very common usage. Specific occupational categories run into the thousands and are recognized in the "help wanted" sections of the newspapers: welders, bricklayers, typists, secretaries, waitresses, and others. But the functional categories are not limited to the gainful occupations alone; they include housewives, church vestrymen, Sunday-school teachers, amateur precinct workers, and so forth.

d) Educational categories do not refer only to people who are professionally engaged in the educational system as teachers, administrators, and professors. Education, as a basis of categories, primarily distinguishes the literate from the illiterate, the intelligent from the unintelligent. The achievement and intelligence scores given to pupils at all levels result in handy social categories. Terms like men of learning, liberal scholars, and scientists, with all their subdivisions, are examples of educational categories in wide use.

e) Religious categories tend to be built upon the manifestation of the religious values that people hold. The terms "sacred" and "secular" have come into wide use among sociologists and refer more often to categories of people than to actual churches and denominations. The terms Catholics, Protestants, and Jews refer not so much to the organized religious groups so designated but to the disconnected plurality of persons who are identified by these general religious names. The religious category is also a handy way of labeling minorities in any society.

f) Categories based on the criteria of biological characteristics are also extremely numerous. A quick classification is made when one says that persons are blond or brunette, tall or short, stout or slender, young or old. The age categories are roughly infancy, childhood, adolescence, adulthood, middle age, and aged, and these are further refined by census data into one-year and five-year categories. The sex categories are a common tool of the social scientist. The large category based on racial similarity, which we have placed under the criteria of ancestry, may be refined and subdivided under the criterion of bodily features, and this is particularly true where skin color is a high social value. The terms "beautiful" and "handsome" indicate ready-made and frequently used social categories.

Categories and Stratification

We have seen that it is possible to form categories in one's mind on the basis of any real item that is common to a number of people. We have seen that the items of similarity are selected for many different reasons and for many purposes of study, and that not all common characteristics lend themselves to the formation of sociologically relevant categories. The fact is that the student of social science must be selective in the study of social categories, and this selectivity centers upon the values that the people in any given society hold.

All similarities among people are not equally valued by the society. This means that just as there is a hierarchy of social values and a stratification of social statuses, so also categories are ranked in a certain order. Depending upon the characteristic around which the category is formed, the category is "placed" higher or lower in relation to other categories. The number of people who have blond hair is not nearly so important to a society as the number of people who have finished college. The number of people who have curly blond hair is not so important as the number who graduate with honors.

Stratification in a sociological sense refers to the "layers" of social categories as they are ranked from highest to lowest in the esteem of the people in the society. This concept is most frequently exemplified in the discussion of social classes; the rough difference among upper, middle, and lower classes is recognized by everyone. The notion of stratification is seen also in the discussion of the various kinds of minorities in a society. Any particular social minority is identified as a category because the people within it have a lesser share in the socially valuable items, whether they are migrant farm workers or part of a racial minority. This "lesser share" immediately places these people in a lower social stratum than the people who are not in the minority.

The Principal Combinations of Criteria

The student of society cannot be satisfied to learn only those social categories that are based upon one criterion of status. This is, of course, the simplest kind of knowledge, but mere casual observation will indicate that each person shares numerous characteristics with other persons. The human being in society is not merely rich or poor, educated or non-educated, pious or impious; he is also of definite family background, does many things in society, and represents a certain biological type. This means two things: first, that any individual can be placed in as many social categories as there are criteria he shares with others, and, second, that any combination of characteristics in him can be matched by similar combinations in other people.

It is this sharing of a combination of similar characteristics that accounts for the most important social categories in every society. It is on this basis of combined similar characteristics that a meaningful and scientific analysis of social categories can be made. It is also in this area that the unsophisticated observer makes most of his mistakes in stereotyping people, that is, in assuming that one set of characteristics must necessarily accompany another set.

The most important social categories, formed on the basis of combined similarities, appear to be the following:

a) Social minorities are categories of people who share a combination of similar disadvantages. They are therefore esteemed "below" that level at which the normal, the average, the acceptable, is fixed. We are talking here not of a numerical minority, since in this sense almost any social category is a minority. Powerful minorities have governed and controlled societies through force and military might, and, numerically, the upper class is a minority everywhere. To be a social minority, the category must be *underprivileged*. It may represent one-third, or two-thirds, or even more of a nation, or it may be a relatively small segment of the population. Its members are not necessarily persecuted in every instance, nor are they always and deliberately prevented from attaining the privileges enjoyed by the rest of society. In a static society the status of minorities changes very slowly; in a dynamic society the tendency is to absorb and ultimately to assimilate minorities into the general population.

The three principal categories of this kind are the foreign-born, the racial, and the religious minorities. *Religious minorities* exist in every major society of the present world. We view them here not as people who form social groups because they profess the same religious beliefs but from the point of view of others who think of them as a social category. The extent to which the religious minority, like the Jehovah's Witnesses, differs in its beliefs and worship from the accepted norms of the majority also measures the extent to which it has low social status. The criterion here, however, is not merely religious affiliation;

and it almost always includes aspects of foreign origin and of economic and educational levels.

Foreigners form a major social category often divided into many subcategories according to country of origin. They, too, are social minorities. The principal criterion on which they are considered is their ancestry, their ethnic origin, especially if it represents peasant stock. But other criteria combine with the fact of foreign ancestry: the educational, with reference to language and literacy; the economic and religious; and even the biological characteristics if these differ markedly from the accepted norms of the majority. The Irish immigrant in Liverpool, the Polish miner in Germany, the East Indian in South Africa, are examples of foreign minorities.

Racial minorities form those social categories that are principally characterized by the criteria of ancestry and biological difference from the majority. This type of minority includes the largest number of the criteria of social status we have discussed. Their degree of wealth and education both affect and are affected by their racial background. The utility of their function in society, especially of their occupational activities, is also an important overlapping criterion of their social status.

b) Social classes are the most obvious examples in any society of the combination of criteria of social status. In fact, the social class cannot be objectively studied except as a social category that depends upon the value judgments existing in the minds of people. Whether one speaks roughly of two or three social classes, or of the numerous strata existing in the more complex societies, it is essential in discussing class to include and to combine *all* the criteria of social status. A class is a plurality of people who are thought of as a social unit because they are actually similar in several respects and who are "rated" at a certain level of stratification.

Social classes are mental constructs, but a person's class status has a much greater concrete effect upon him than do the more general statistical categories in which he may be included. The reason for this is twofold: first, because his class is a category based on multiple similarities that often put him in actual social relations with other people, and, second, because the value of these similarities is determined by other people's opinion of them, and, therefore, by the esteem or disesteem in which the person himself is held. We say that a person is affected by his class status mainly because of what other persons think of him and how they act toward him. They consider him "better or worse" because of his class status, and, at the same time, he belongs in a higher or lower social class because he has or does not have what people in general consider the better or worse social characteristics.

It is a problem of research methodology to discover, first, the actual social values the society holds, and, second, which people in any given area possess the combination of characteristics thus evaluated. Involvement in, and study of, a particular society reveals frequent reference to the characteristics the people hold in high regard. Hearing the people themselves talk about one another helps one to "place" them in their objective social class. For example, in one locality the "better people" may be categorized by the fact that they are of Creole ancestry, send their children to Catholic preparatory academies and private eastern universities, and belong to certain exclusively Gentile clubs that have Greek or Roman names. In other areas the specific details of these general characteristics will differ, but they will still act as a clue to discovering membership in the upper class.

Social scientists also frequently employ certain quantitative measurements in order to fix the class status of a person or family. The student of society can always learn that a certain section of the city, or one suburb rather than another, is considered the better residential area, that one type of dwelling reflects higher social prestige than others, that certain types of occupation and kinds of financial income have greater social approval than others. Such items can be counted and measured and balanced. The data are comparable and objective and can be interpreted to indicate the number and size of the various social classes.

c) Publics are a more subtle type of social category that has increased in importance in urban and commercial societies. The public, like the class and the minority, is also a mental construct in which persons are thought of as a social unit because they possess certain common characteristics. But this is merely secondary. Unlike minorities and classes, publics are sociologically significant because the attention of those who categorize them is focused upon them.

In the technical, scientific sense, a public does not refer to the total general population, nor does it refer to an organized social group, although both of these meanings are sometimes erroneously applied to the term. A public differs from an aggregate because the latter is marked by physical proximity and the former is not. For example, the radio comedian is addressing himself to his public, a category, while the stage comedian is addressing himself to his audience, an aggregate.

This distinction may appear to be highly minute, but it shows clearly the difference between two kinds of social units.

When a preacher, lecturer, writer, manufacturer, or politician is asked, "Which public are you appealing to?" the question implies the focus of attention upon one social category rather than another. Thus there are many publics. Even the "consuming public" to which the advertiser appeals has many subcategories, sometimes vaguely referred to as "discriminating people," "men of distinction," or "those who want the best," and sometimes more specifically, as the teen-agers, the housewives, the suburbanites.

The appeal to the workers, or to the proletariat, is not simply a reference to a class category. These people combine certain shared characteristics on the basis of which they are considered a public. The readers of mystery fiction or of detective stories, the fans of wrestling, baseball, or football, the intelligentsia, the "arty" people, in fact, any plurality of people to whom appeals are directed, must be considered a public. Each of these categories can be studied separately and each will demonstrate the presence of similarities of educational and economic levels, of functional utility and also often of sex and age characteristics.

PECULIARITIES OF AMERICAN SOCIAL CATEGORIES

1. Class Consciousness of Americans

The oversimplified interpretation of the democratic way of life in America has resulted in such statements as: "Everybody is as good as everybody else," or "We don't have social classes like European countries," or "We cherish our traditions of freedom and equality." These are sometimes the remarks of the naïve and sometimes of the opportunistic, and they reflect often a state of wishful and unrealistic thinking. Every society has differences of social status among individuals and some sort of stratification of social categories. We have here apparently a peculiar combination of an actual stratified society and a general unwillingness of most Americans to admit the presence of stratification.

Social consciousness here refers to an awareness of differences of social status and strata and does not mean an awareness of social problems, an attitude of civic duty, or of patriotism. Following are some of the reasons why social consciousness is minimized in the American society:

a) Americans tend to disparage or to avoid titles. They are noted for familiarity in social intercourse and for breaking down formal barriers even with strangers. The term "Mister" fits every adult male, but even here subordinates and employees use terms like "Boss," or "Chief" to avoid the stiffness of the title. Social peers use first names among themselves, and persons in superior positions also address others by their first names. This type of familiar social address is unthinkable in most other major societies.

b) The diffusion of an egalitarian ideology is a most important means of preventing class consciousness. The child is taught in his early school years about independence, opportunities, and self-reliance. He learns a great deal about his own rights; and this emphasis upon rights is widespread in the adult society. Slogans of equality are the stuff of which political speeches are made, and the various movements for equal rights which have dotted our history have been important determinants of attitudes.

c) The criteria of social status are most often recognized as personal differences rather than as social and class distinctions. The American tends to admire and respect the individual who has made his way, who has achieved success and made a name for himself. He focuses upon the person as an individual rather than as representative of a social stratum related to other social strata.

d) The availability of material symbols of status tends to compensate for lack of actual high status. The fact that automobiles, television sets, refrigerators, and other items can be bought on the instalment plan, that reasonable imitations of "exclusive" clothing styles can be purchased, and that there are few traditional types of apparel which identify a person's class—these are all weighty factors in minimizing the recognition of class differentials.

e) The relative lack of exclusion or segregation in public and commercial facilities tends to decrease the actual separation of classes. Except in areas where racial discrimination is practiced, the American, if he has the price, may sit in the best seat at the opera, the horse races, or the championship prize fight. He has access to libraries, museums, schools, and colleges, to transportation and communication facilities. When there are "exclusive affairs" or when facilities are denied to him, he usually understands that this is done on the basis of the private right of those who are excluding him, not because of his own lower social status.

f) By and large, the American is treated and expects to be treated as an equal in political, legal, and military procedures. Jury duty, the voting franchise, military service, the right to bring suit and to stand a fair trial, the right to police protection and fireman service—all these are intended to apply impartially to all Americans. The fact that they are not always so applied must be noted by the student of society. But the fact that these practices are widespread and that their presence is emphasized tends to give the American the feeling that he is living in a classless society.

These few evidences concerning the de-emphasis of class consciousness among Americans are also evidences of the importance of categories as a mental construct. Even though the class structure exists as a concrete reality, and even though class status has immediate, personal, and objective consequences for individuals, there is still a tendency to belittle, or even ignore, its reality. What people try to believe constitutes in itself a social fact of great significance. Because of the all-pervading ideology of democracy and all that it implies, people attempt to lessen the implications and consequences of the actual stratification of categories.

2. The Shifting Negro Category

There is a vast difference between the manner in which American Negroes live in our society and the way in which most white people categorize them. Every person with even the least degree of known African ancestry is automatically placed in the Negro category. The "color line" is arbitrary and unique to the American racial situation. An American is considered either Negro or white even though only a few, if any, "pure" Negroes or "pure" whites, actually exist in our country.

This method of classification is sociological rather than biological or physical. In most of the European colonies, especially those controlled by the British, people of mixed ancestry were recognized as a category between those of European stock and of native stock. In some of the South American countries there is a tendency to categorize as white even those relatively dark-skinned persons who are known to have some degree of Caucasian ancestry. Unlike these South American and colonial societies, the American tendency is to bunch all persons of mixed ancestry into the category of Negro.

The interesting sociological fact is that American Negroes share many more characteristics in common with American whites than with non-American Negroes. Most of the important criteria of social status are fairly well distributed among them. Negroes are in no sense foreigners; they can trace their American ancestry back further than most whites can. They share the same language, the same religions, and the same major social values with the whites. But the extraordinary emphasis placed on the recognizable difference of ancestry and of physical features seems to suffice to place all American Negroes in a single social category.

In spite of these generalizations, the concept of the Negro as a separate social category is rapidly changing, and the following are some of the indications of this change:

a) The American Negroes are not socially organized as a whole population, and many of the exclusively Negro groupings are going out of existence. As a total category, the Negroes exhibit most of the differences and levels of social status and strata which are seen among the whites. The necessity of forming their own religious, recreational, educational, and professional associations was forced upon them by the policy of white exclusion. They are now gradually abandoning these; in fact, their strongest groups are those which are now fighting against the need for racial groups.

b) Migration out of areas of high Negro population is proceeding very rapidly. The percentage of Negro people is steadily decreasing in states like Mississippi, Alabama, and South Carolina where they previously constituted almost half of the population. Meanwhile, their proportion is rising in northern and midwestern states, and even in the Far West. Like the immigrant categories, the Negroes tended to be treated as a separate category as long as they remained concentrated. When these concentrations break up, the separateness decreases in the minds of others.

c) The shift in occupational status has meant a change from the traditional rural, agrarian, and menial levels of employment to opportunities on the urban, commercial, industrial, and professional levels. Since functional utility is an important criterion of social status in any society, this shift appears to be an upward one. Continued high employment, general prosperity, attitudes of both labor unions and management, and the restriction of foreign immigration have all been instrumental in this rise in Negro occupational status.

d) The physical characteristics of the American Negro appear to be changing gradually toward the norms which are esteemed among white people. It is estimated that almost 90 per cent of the American Negroes have some degree of non-Negro ancestry. Whether "racial mixture" will continue over succeeding generations to lighten the

Negroes is a question of social and cultural trends. Negroes still are distinguished as a separate social category, however, primarily by visible physical characteristics.

e) The general climate of opinion is widely favorable to the integration of Negroes as fully accepted Americans. Executive orders of the last three Presidents have been very important in the integration of Negroes into the armed services and into all branches of government service. Decisions of the federal courts have removed barriers in schools, busses and trains, playgrounds, libraries, and other public facilities. The findings of social scientists and their teaching in our colleges and high schools have provided knowledge on race relations and helped to improve attitudes.

f) The world situation in which America stands as the foremost proponent of democracy, freedom, and human dignity has inspired a reassessment of the ways in which these ideals are followed within the nation. The so-called "Negro problem" has been used as a propaganda weapon, often shaped in crude and distorted fashion, among the colored peoples of the world. The effectiveness of this weapon in attacking American moral and political leadership in the world has been recognized. The result has been an attempt to guarantee the rights of Negroes within the nation.

The change in status of the Negro category, brought about by these and many other factors, has sometimes been called the greatest "success story" in history. Most Negroes were brought to this country as slaves; they were "outside" the general framework of American society at that time. They have risen from this position, so that many individual Negroes now have high social status, and the whole Negro population is gradually rising in status even though it remains a separate social category.

It is an interesting fact that at the very time when the Negroes' status has improved, the term "caste" has come into wide usage as a reference to the Negro category. As long as the color line remained rigid and the notions of Caucasian superiority and Negro inferiority were widespread, we could speak logically of the upper white caste and the lower colored caste. The shifting of the Negro category in American society means a movement upward and out of this strict caste classification. This movement away from former Negro-linked disabilities appears to imply the eventual disappearance of the caste barriers.

3. The Tendency To Label People

Anyone who knows the American colloquial language realizes that it contains a vast number of labels which are applied to persons in minority categories. Nicknames are used for age, sex, class, regional and religious categories, but in a pejorative sense they are used most frequently for racial and immigrant minorities. To some extent this indicates a consciousness of the social status of "other" people even by the individual who does not like to be considered class conscious.

Labels for immigrant categories are particularly widespread since all Americans who are not Indians have a "foreign name." The American population contains descendants of practically every known nationality on earth. This helps to account for the diversity, if not the number, of nationality nicknames and labels which are employed here. The custom persists even though immigration restrictions and rapid Americanization have decreased the factual differences among these people. The last census showed that less than 6 per cent of our population, mainly people beyond middle age, are foreign-born, and the great majority of these are naturalized citizens. American-born persons of foreign-born parentage constitute another 11 per cent of the population.

The important point here is that many Americans do not restrict the use of labels merely to the foreign-born, or even to the children of foreign parentage. The label persists over generations. To call a person an Irish-American, or an Italian-American, is to place him in a valid social category; to call him a "dumb Mick" or a "dirty Wop" is to stereotype him. The latter use is a disparaging stereotype because it implies a whole series of other negative common characteristics, most of which are not present in the individuals so named.

While the immigrant minority and its descendants are a readily labeled category, other groups in American society are also stereotyped. The southeasterner tends to label all other Americans as "Yankees" in a derogatory sense. The farm boy coming to the city is labeled everything from "rube" to "yokel" and is subject to further refinements of stereotyping depending upon the section of the country from which he comes. People in religious minorities also come in for their share of name-calling.

The following list of the occasional characteristics of the subjects of stereotyping is a partial explanation of the American tendency to label people:

a) The various immigrant groups have different social status, with the British, Irish, and Germans among the "older" immigrants and the people of southern and eastern Europe among the "newer" immigrants. Feelings of superiority of the former give rise to a tendency to place distinctive labels on latecomers, and the reaction of the latter is a retaliation with similar labels.

b) Conscious efforts at self-identification are exhibited by some immigrant minorities, especially those who were strongly persecuted at home or who had developed a lasting nationalism. These people, such as the Irish, Italians, and Poles, perpetuate their songs, stories, and folklore. They are for the most part proud of their lineage even though they tend to castigate immigrants from other places as un-American. In some instances, their efforts to preserve foreign forms of religious practices among their offspring have also helped to identify an immigrant category.

c) The tendency to population concentrations, especially in the larger cities, has made some minorities easily identifiable as a separate social category. Most of the large American cities still have sections in which one or another of the immigrant minorities lives. In the Southwest there are Mexican quarters, in the Northeast are French-Canadian sections, and in several cities there are Chinatowns. As the immigrants become more assimilated the significance of these "ghettos" is diminishing.

d) The preservation of behavior patterns has made it easy to label immigrant minorities. Immigrants to some extent keep their family behavior—husband and wife, child and parent relationships—and to a greater extent their habits of food consumption. Certain types of "dishes" are typical of certain nationalities, although they are more often served in restaurants than within the family.

e) Immigrants may be identified by traces of speech accents even to the second and third generation. While urbanization and compulsory education, together with the general ignorance of foreign languages in this country, lessen the speech differences, the mimicking of foreign accents is still the stock in trade of some comedians and other entertainers, and the particular accent used immediately labels the nationality category which is being represented.

f) The physical appearance of a person tends to type him in the minds of observers. Since there is a tremendous diversity of physical types in the United States, this is a factor of identification mainly when it is accentuated by the manner of speech, style of clothing, or behavior patterns of the individual. It is diminishing through the biological mixing of the various immigrant "stocks" in our population.

The possibility of labeling these characteristics is gradually diminishing. The relatively constant factor which remains through them all, and the one upon which the label and stereotype most frequently hinge, is the family name of the individual. In some instances even this characteristic has been removed by the legal change of name to a more "Americanized" spelling, or perhaps to one of the British names, which are in themselves a label for one of the oldest immigrant minorities.

4. Categories Reached by Advertisers

A highly commercial and profit-conscious culture like that of the United States must inevitably recognize the categories of the people with whom commercial transactions are made. The analysis of the innumerable subcategories of the consuming public has developed a highly scientific approach to advertising and selling of commodities and services. The statements "The customer is always right," "We aim to please," and "Service is our motto," imply that the seller knows who the customer is, what it takes to please him, and how service to him is to be performed.

The techniques which the advertisers use to reach these different categories are in themselves a study of social psychology. American advertising is not the haphazard, "scatter-shot" process which it may at first glance appear to be. It is scientifically refined and it is aimed at certain categories. This is not because the manufacturer is unwilling to sell to everybody, but because the concentration on certain segments of the population is a more economical and more efficient way of selling products. Following are some of the principal bases upon which the consuming public is subdivided into social categories by advertisers:

a) The appeal is often aimed to the age category of persons most likely to respond. It is no accident that the cowboy and spaceship television programs are scheduled for late afternoon when children can view them and that they sell various kinds of breakfast foods, candies, chocolate milk, and other edibles. The department stores have sections for junior misses, or teen-agers, and even for those of college age.

b) Many advertising programs are directed to one or the other sex. Sports events of various kinds are used as broadcasting opportunities to sell razor blades and beer to the masculine audience. The manufacturers of feminine cosmetics develop the type of program which they feel will appeal to the female buying public. The importance of the female public as potential consumers can be recognized in the host of women's magazines containing advertising specifically aimed at them.

c) Advertising on the basis of the functions of the category appealed to highlights especially the position of the housewife as a potential buyer. The so-called "soap operas" almost always advertise household goods and are broadcast at the times of day which are most convenient for the housewife. Every major occupation, profession, or business in the United States provides outlets for manufacturers in technical journals and trade papers. They are deliberately and specifically aimed at various functional categories in the population.

d) Advertisers appeal to people who are assumed to have a desire for social prestige. Ostensibly this advertising is aimed only at the higher status categories, but it is known to have an effect, perhaps the strongest effect, on those who are striving for higher social status. More expensive commodities like jewelry, high-priced automobiles, fur coats, and other luxury items are advertised in those periodicals known as prestige journals. All the other commercial media of mass communication are also used for this purpose. "Keeping up with the Joneses" is sometimes considered a humorous phrase, but nothing demonstrates so dramatically the presence of status categories and the extent of status competition among the American people.

e) Ownership is the basis for another advertisers' category. There is a direct appeal to homeowners, automobile owners, insurance-policy holders, and others who may be urged to purchase connected goods and services. Larger items which are registered or licensed make it possible for the salesman to go directly to the owner. He may neglect all other possible social categories and concentrate only on those from whom results may be expected.

There is, of course, a certain amount of overlapping of characteristics in most of the categories to which advertisers appeal; there are also many subcategories which may be recognized under the various criteria, and combinations of criteria, mentioned above. The housewife who is interested in a line of cosmetics or of kitchen utensils may also like to know what kind of beer to serve her husband's guests or what type of apparel is attractive to her teen-age daughter. It is an index of the genius of the American businessman and of the American economic system that these devices for categorizing prospective customers have been so widely recognized and so efficiently employed in this country.

5. Unequal Treatment of Social Categories

We have seen that the very definition of social status and strata implies an unequal possession of socially valued items among the persons in different social status categories. This is true in every society, including the American, where the cultural creed professes the basic dignity and equality of all human beings. Inequalities of social status, however, do not always imply inequitable or hostile relations between the persons of different status. In fact, there are innumerable examples of reciprocal relations of kindness, generosity, friendship, and love between persons of higher positions and persons of subordinate status. This is seen in certain social situations across class lines, and even across racial, ethnic, and religious barriers. It is seen in the play activities of very young children who have not developed an awareness of status and also in the relations of some adults who recognize the personal qualities of intelligence, character, and virtue in a particular lower- or higher-class individual.

In spite of these exceptions there are several glaring instances of unequal treatment accorded to certain social categories in America. Not included in the following list are criminals who have "forfeited" the right to equal respect.

a) The social status of women has been steadily rising, but it is still true that most women employees performing work equal to that of men do not receive equal pay. Females as a social category are sometimes discriminated against by religious groups, labor unions, political parties, schools, and colleges. They are favored in some respects over males, however; for example, there are laws protecting them from nightwork, regulations providing rest facilities and sick leaves, and customs preventing them from doing heavy industrial and mining work.

b) Illegitimate children and dependent orphans form a category of socially disadvantaged persons. Through no fault of their own they are in a position of social inferiority. American society's increasing awareness of these children, together with the more intelligent approach of social workers, philanthropists, and other social reformers, has mitigated the condition of these children. They are receiving temporary, immediate, and material aid, if not an effective raising of their status.

c) The category of child labor in certain rural areas and urban slums is also the object of inequitable treatment by the American society, in spite of child-labor laws which were designed to prevent the exploitation of children by unscrupulous employers and to provide time and opportunity for normal schooling.

d) Upper-class people in every community are the objects of favorable discrimination by the several agencies of public service. The police treat with more deference the adult traffic violator or the potential juvenile delinquent from an upper-class family. The streets are cleaner, the pavement is more quickly repaired, the fire department responds more readily, and the garbage is more neatly collected in those sections of the city which are the better residential areas.

e) The most obvious objects of discriminatory treatment have been the racial minorities, especially the American Negro. We have seen that the social status of the Negro is changing for the better, but there still exist numerous state laws which discriminate against him. Laws preventing intermarriage or the use of certain hotels, restaurants, playgrounds, places of public amusement, railroads, streetcars, and schools are still in force. These are bolstered by local and regional customs that are prejudicial to this social category.

There are other and smaller social categories, including certain religious minorities, dependent people of no income, physically and mentally handicapped, and even some political categories, that receive unequal treatment from the majority of the American society. Those we have mentioned provide sufficient evidence that there are many levels of unequal treatment, and that social distinctions have certain concrete effects even in our democratic society.

DISCUSSION QUESTIONS

1. Why are categories basic to every science?
2. In what sense do categories "exist only in the mind"?
3. What is the difference between statistical and social categories?
4. Give some examples of the practical utility of the knowledge of social categories.
5. Distinguish between categories and groups. Give examples of each.
6. Are preconceived stereotypes always erroneous? Explain.
7. Define and give examples of generalization and specification in the categorizing process.

8. What is the connection between the classification of categories and the criteria of social status?
9. What is meant by the "ranked" order of categories?
10. In what sense can we say that all minorities are underprivileged?
11. Show the difference among the principal minority categories.
12. Why do social classes affect the individual more than do the other types of social categories?
13. Explain: "Publics are sociologically significant because they are a focus of attention for those who categorize them."
14. List the reasons why class consciousness is minimized in America.
15. What is meant by the sociological classification of Negroes?
16. Why is the concept of the American Negro as a separate social category rapidly changing?
17. Give the main characteristics according to which some minority categories in America are stereotyped.
18. List the principal bases upon which advertisers categorize potential customers.
19. Identify the largest categories of people who are most frequently accorded unequal treatment.

SUGGESTED READINGS

BENNETT, JOHN W., and TUMIN, MELVIN M. *Social Life, Structure and Function.* New York: Alfred A. Knopf, 1948, chaps. xxiv, xxv.

EUBANK, E. E. *The Concepts of Sociology.* Boston: D. C. Heath & Co., 1932.

HILLER, E. T. *Social Relations and Structures.* New York: Harper & Bros., 1947, chap. xxxviii.

O'BRIEN, ROBERT W. (ed.). *Readings in General Sociology.* Boston: Houghton Mifflin Co., 1951, chap. vi.

WILLIAMS, ROBIN. *American Society: A Sociological Interpretation.* New York: Alfred A. Knopf, 1952, chap. v.

CHAPTER FOUR

Social Aggregates

Sociology, by its very definition, studies people who are related to one another, and every social unit must contain persons who are somehow together. We have seen that the people in a social category are together, not in physical, external reality, but in the judgment of the observer who notes that they possess one or more common characteristics. The social aggregate, however, takes us a step further. It does not depend for its unity upon the mental construct of the observer. The social aggregate is an assemblage or plurality of people who are in physical proximity, but without reciprocal communication.

A social group, in the technical sense, involves various degrees of interaction and communication and social relations. From this point of view the aggregate must be conceptualized somewhere between the category and the group. In the former the people are not even physically present to one another; in the latter the people have enduring social relations. A football team is a group; the crowd watching the game is an aggregate; the totality of football fans in the country constitutes a category.

Characteristics of Aggregates

The people who make up a social aggregate are "together" in a peculiar way. One may say that they are "amassed" in the sense that they are only loosely assembled. Some of the more common examples of the social aggregate are the so-called population units, the slums and the various districts, quarters, and sections of the city; the uptown, downtown, and midtown areas, the various urban zones, the political wards, school districts, and police precincts. These are not the only kinds of aggregates, but they fit the characteristics of the aggregate.

A more complete definition and description of the social aggregate must include the following elements: (*a*) The persons who make up the aggregate are relatively *anonymous* in that they are almost strangers to one another. (*b*) The social aggregate is *not organized;* it does not have a structure with a hierarchy of positions and functions.

(*c*) There is only *limited social contact* even though the physical proximity may be very great. (*d*) There is at best only a *slight modification of behavior* on the part of those who are in the aggregate. (*e*) Most social aggregates are *territorial* and their social significance is limited by certain physical boundaries. (*f*) Most aggregates are also *temporary* in the sense that people shift in and out of them and from one aggregate to another.

The term "aggregation" is frequently used as a synonym for the term "aggregate," but this use is scientifically valid in only one meaning of the word. Aggregation used transitively refers to the process by which people are brought into a collectivity. From this point of view, people are "aggregated" when they migrate from the country to the city, when they come into the theater for a play, when they move into a new neighborhood. Aggregation is not synonymous with, nor sociologically so important as, the processes of socialization and assimilation. Aggregation used substantively refers to the actual collectivity of people and has the same meaning as social aggregate.

It must be noted that aggregation represents only one focus in the study of people. The typical urban apartment house in which the occupants of the various apartments have at most a nodding acquaintance with one another is a modern example of a social aggregate. But this does not deny that the individual family which occupies each apartment is a group. The building contains an aggregate of groups. The individual person may be both the unit of an aggregate and the unit of a group at one and the same time.

Classification of Aggregates

The classification of social aggregates can be done in many ways depending upon the basis chosen for analyzing them. Any one of the characteristics already mentioned may be used as a basis for measuring a range of aggregates. For example, anonymity of persons may be complete, as when a number of strangers casually stop to look at workers excavating for a new building, or it may be only relatively present, as when a number of office workers step into an elevator and vaguely recognize one another because they have been working in the same building for years.

The other characteristics also represent a continuum in which they are present to a greater or lesser degree. The people in attendance at football games may be momentarily and vaguely "organized" in responding to the cheerleaders; there may be some passing remarks among total strangers which indicate social contact; and other minor movements and responses indicate some modification of behavior. Casualness, rather than intent and planning, is an important indicator of the social aggregate, and it is seen in both the territorial characteristic, as when urban neighbors hardly ever see one another, and the temporary characteristic, as when passengers on a ship or train meet on one occasion and are never again assembled. There is a range also in size, from a few persons to a relatively large number.

The problem of classifying social aggregates is intensified when one attempts to deal with population units. The total human race is "assembled" on the face of the earth, but it is difficult to conceptualize this world population except as a social category. The human race is sometimes called the total "human society" but the lack of constant and reciprocal relations among the earth's dwellers makes this an almost meaningless extension of the technical definition of society. It is true that the recognition of "one world" has become significant in our times, but the association of people across intercontinental and international lines is for the most part merely through representatives.

The population within a nation, state, or city is more likely to be termed an aggregate, but even here because of the large numbers there is frequently a confusion of terms. While these social units constitute statistical and social categories in so far as they share common characteristics without contact, they can be seen as roughly organized social units, brought together at least under political and civic administration, and to some extent also sharing common values.

When a person speaks of the masses, the proletariat, the workers, the underprivileged, he is speaking of social categories. When politicians direct their appeal to "the people," they are referring to an identifiable social category which is not in fact assembled except in the mind of the speaker. This is an example of the political public, which we have defined as a social category. But when the politician appeals to the voters in a particular city ward and perhaps even comes into the ward to address a mass meeting, his audience is an aggregate rather than a category. Thus the distinction between aggregate and category is made on the basis of size and physical proximity or assemblage.

Principal Kinds of Aggregates

The dynamic aspects of human relations makes difficult the scientific classification of social aggregates. There is a certain amount of confusion and overlapping in the application of sociological terminology because there is confusion and overlapping in the concrete social system. People simply do not "stay put" so that you can say they are in each instance either in a group or an aggregate, nor are their forms of aggregation always so easily identifiable as may at first appear. In spite of these difficulties it is necessary to use terms as accurately as the changing social phenomena studied will allow.

If the nature of social units creates terminological difficulties, these are multiplied by the common, non-technical usage of words. There is much inexact use of terms like "crowd," "mob," "audience," and "mass." People talk of mob psychology when they mean mass psychology. The typical mob is sometimes called an "angry crowd," and audiences are sometimes called "crowds." Terms like "radio audience," "television audience," "racing followers," and the like, really refer to publics, that is, social categories, and not to social aggregates.

The following classification of social aggregates into crowds, mobs, audiences, demonstrations, and residential and functional aggregates is an attempt to cut through some of these terminological difficulties. We discuss here only those clearly identifiable social aggregates which are sociologically significant. They show the two most important characteristics of social aggregates: the people in them are physically and proximately assembled, and they have among themselves a minimum of social relations and communication.

a) The crowd is an ordered, relatively non-interacting aggregate of persons. From the point of view of the totality it is aimless and is not performing any common function; it is simply occupying physical space. This does not mean, however, that the individuals who compose it are purposeless or bewildered. Each individual can probably "explain his presence." The crowd is peaceable and non-excitable; it is amorphous and exhibits only a kind of "external" unity.

There are nevertheless recognizably different kinds of crowds, and the student of society can usually make distinctions among them merely through observation. The individuals in the afternoon shopping crowd that is casually and idly watching a construction job can be distinguished from the crowd waiting to cross the street when the traffic light changes, and from the people who are milling into a football stadium.

b) The mob is a social aggregate said to "get out of hand" because it lacks both internal and external control. It is disorderly rather than unorderly. It tends to act as a social unit on a short-lived, large-scale basis. The persons making up this aggregate are usually charged with intense emotions. This term is almost always used in a pejorative sense, indicating that the mob is destructive, antisocial, and belligerent. It is usually a protest phenomenon.

Riots and lynchings are mob activities most frequently incited by "ringleaders." Interaction among the separate individuals in the mob is at a minimum, but there is almost always some sort of relationship between the leaders and the followers of the mob. This is an essential difference between the crowd and the mob. It is possible also to distinguish among the different types of mobs from a knowledge of the kind of protest which each is making. Mobs are aroused by racist feelings, by economic exploitation, by political upheaval, by religious fanaticism. Mobs have been known to form on the basis of outraged artistic sensibilities and in reaction to the decisions of referees and umpires in athletic contests.

c) The audience is a social aggregate of persons who deliberately assemble to watch and listen to a performance of some kind. We use the term here only in its strict reference to a physical collectivity within a limited spatial area. The people in an audience differ from the mob in that they are listeners and spectators rather than active performers in any joint action. They differ from the crowd in that they endure longer and their attention is more closely focused. Audiences are expected to react to a common stimulus, and they are sometimes judged on the degree and kind of reaction they give to this stimulus: appreciative or dull; boisterous or quiet; approving or disapproving.

Audiences may be classified more meaningfully on the basis of that which attracts them than on the basis of their response to the attraction. Audiences gather for all kinds of performances: for athletic contests of various kinds, for lectures on innumerable topics, for theater and movie productions, for debates, and for beauty contests. Even the persons assembled in a church congregation, to the extent that they do not participate as a group in the religious services, are an audience.

d) Public demonstrations form a social aggregate of persons who are deliberately assembled for the purpose of promoting some idea, belief, movement, or person. The people who make up the demonstration are not merely spectators or listeners; they actually participate in some kind of collective behavior in the presence of others. The demonstration is usually organized only in the sense that some previous planning has occurred, and the participants are only loosely assembled in relation to one another.

Demonstrations are a social phenomenon peculiar to urban life. They are a social aggregate differing from the crowd, mob, or audience. The most common examples of the demonstration are mass meetings, political rallies, religious processions, and the various kinds of parades. A demonstration may be a one-time occurrence like the celebration at the end of a war, the march of the unemployed, or a procession of silent prayer in protest of religious persecution. Other demonstrations, like parades and processions, have become celebrated annual occurrences in certain large cities. The St. Patrick's Day parade in New York, the Mummers' parade in Philadelphia, the Mardi Gras parades in New Orleans, are examples.

e) Residential aggregates can be recognized in all large cities. The relative anonymity and the frequent residential mobility which characterize the large city tend to develop the social aggregate in any given urban section. To the extent that people live near one another but remain relative strangers, have practically no contact or interaction, and are unorganized, they remain a social aggregate. This is more likely to occur in the so-called transient areas with rooming houses, hotels, and large apartment houses, than in the stable and "old, settled neighborhoods."

These observations concerning the urban residential area apply only to the totality of people in the area seen as a whole. Within the area there are smaller, organized groupings. Families and friendship cliques are found everywhere.

The concept of the residential social aggregate is clarified when it is contrasted to that of the neighborhood. The latter term implies association, contact, communication, and friendly exchanges among *all* the people within a given residential area. The fact that many residential areas tend to be aggregates only is demonstrated by the constant effort of civic and religious leaders, of politicians and businessmen, to create or awaken a "community consciousness" by which people will identify themselves with their residential area. This sort of effort is not required in a genuine neighborhood.

f) Functional aggregates are constituted by people to whom territorial boundaries are more or less arbitrarily assigned. For example, police precincts, school zones, and political wards are arranged conveniently for certain functional purposes, but they can in no technical sense be termed groups or communities. Similarly, the total aggregate of people who function in a shopping district, a financial center, or a theatrical district tends to lack the characteristics of a group. Because of a discernible function performed in these areas, it is logical to distinguish them as aggregates from residential areas.

Aggregates and Groups

It is quite simple to distinguish between the social aggregate and the social group when each clearly possesses the characteristics by which we identify them. In concrete everyday social life, however, there is a zone of transition between the two which makes it difficult to classify some particular social units. This is merely another aspect of the dynamism and complexity of the phenomena studied in social science. Groups dissolve into aggregates, and aggregates develop into groups.

The descriptions and definitions of the various types of aggregates given above may suggest that all the persons within them are completely separated from one another. The fact is, however, that in almost any large aggregate of people there are contained some groups and paired relations. Not all the people in a movie audience are total strangers to one another, nor does each one come to the theater separately and unaccompanied. Parents and children may be together as a unit in the church congregation, in the crowded streetcar, or on the boardwalk at the seashore. Only when we look at the aggregate as a totality do we recognize its technical sociological meaning.

There are many instances, however, in which a social aggregate, or a segment of it, develops into a group. A collectivity of persons, casually assembled at a revival meeting, may decide to establish a new religious sect. Chance acquaintances who meet on a train or a ship, in a bar or a restaurant, may form a lifelong friendship. A mass rally instituted by a civic leader may develop into a taxpayers' association. A small number of students, assembled at first as a relatively passive audience in a lecture course, may eventually establish a social group.

Conversely, one sees the disintegration of groups into mere aggregates. When an organization lacks leadership, loses sight of its purpose, or fulfils it, or when the membership loses its mutual interests, the group tends to slip into an amorphous aggregate, and perhaps eventually to disappear as a recognizable social unit. Social scientists note these tendencies away from groups and toward aggregations particularly in the large urban places, and so the study of social aggregates has been more and more sharply focused on the changing life of the modern city.

The Person and the Aggregate

The impression is sometimes given that the aggregate is similar to a herd of passive social animals that are not exercising their abilities as rational beings. It must be obvious from what we have said so far that this is not the case. The social aggregate, as a midway point between the mental construct of a social category and the actual solidarity of a social group, empirically "contains" people. The individual person has a relation to the aggregates in which he is a unit, and this relation is seen in several ways:

a) The person is necessarily present in a social aggregate. We have seen that physical proximity is necessary before an aggregate is created; it is also true that no one, especially no city dweller, can avoid social aggregates. He is in them and part of them at all times. His mere physical existence at some permanent address in some section of the city places him in a residential aggregate. Whenever he moves about the city he is certain to be in crowds and audiences of one kind or another. Therefore, he does not have much choice even if he decides to remain isolated at home.

b) Since social aggregates are unstructured, the individual person has virtually no social status within an aggregate. Social status depends upon the recognition and judgment of others, and the individual's status is always a position in relation to other positions. If he has status within, for example, a mob, it is only in the sense that there is a vague understanding of the difference between leaders and followers in the mob. The aggregate in which the person is a unit, however, may influence his status in a group which is outside the aggregate. In so far as the person chooses to be in different audiences, to be a fight fan rather than an opera-goer, or a ready participant in mobs, his social status may be affected.

c) There is a small degree of patterned behavior to which the person conforms as a part of a social aggregate. When women are present, men remove their hats in hotel elevators but keep them on in the elevators of commercial buildings. Women in a shopping crowd may jostle one another in a manner unthinkable in a church audience. The patterns of behavior at an athletic contest are much more "relaxed" than they are at a symphony concert, and they differ even from one type of sport to another. It must be noted that the modification in the behavior of the individual results from the type of social aggregate in which he finds himself and not from interaction with the other particular individuals who happen to be in the aggregate.

d) It may be said that the person exhibits collective behavior in aggregates rather than social behavior. This distinction means that his action is, in the presence of others, simultaneous and often similar to that of others, rather than for, or against, or with, others. Social behavior implies communication, contact, and interaction, and this is precisely the type of behavior that occurs in groups but not in aggregates. Collective behavior does, however, have a social effect. The presence of an attentive crowd may inspire workmen to steadier, more consistent, and more productive work; the roar of the crowd and the applause of the audience are often purposeful and effective.

e) The individual person tends to submerge his identity in the social aggregate. This is not necessarily a decision on the part of the person himself, but rather a resultant or concomitant of the nature of social aggregates. Anonymity and lack of personal knowledge of the other persons may be noted especially at demonstrations such as rallies and parades, where the voice of the individual is hardly heard or where he does not care to express it.

f) It is a well-known fact that personal responsibility decreases in social aggregates. To be a "part of the crowd" or to "follow the mob" means that the individual is largely surrendering his own accountability for the collective action. Much of what is done by the person in these instances is spontaneous and unreflecting. The "spirit of the crowd" is often contagious in the temporary gatherings of people, while in the residential aggregation personal lack of responsibility increases because of the very transitoriness and anonymity of one's residence.

The Aggregate Masses

A society in which social aggregates of various kinds are numerous and influential is sometimes called a "mass society." Scientifically this is a contradictory term, however, because masses are unorganized and discrete aggregates, while societies are systematic and organized arrangements of groups and people. The terms "mass population" or "aggregate masses" appear to be preferable for this social phenomenon, but we are using these words here to indicate social aggregates, not mere statistical and social categories.

Who are the masses? They are not simply the working class, or the lower class, or the so-called proletariat, in any given population. These words refer to social categories fixed in the minds of people and evaluated by the various criteria of social position. In a strict technical sense, the masses are the totality of all social aggregates which typify the modern urban society. We have noted that the various kinds of aggregates—crowd, mob, audience, demonstration, residential and functional aggregates—are typical of densely populated urban places. When we view all these aggregates together, we see the masses, not the systematic and organized society.

The aggregate masses are more than merely a point of view or a mental construct. They exist concretely in any given society as the aggregation of all the social aggregates. They can be viewed as a totality because they have certain features in common. We have described the differences by which we could classify the various principal kinds of social aggregates. We now indicate the following characteristics shared in common by the aggregate masses.

a) The masses are a heterogeneous composition of persons. There is great diversity in all those criteria which account for social status. The people differ widely in wealth, ancestry, occupation, education, and in religious and physical characteristics. It is practically impossible to identify an aggregate according to these shared characteristics; it is totally impossible to attempt such an identification of the total masses.

b) The masses exhibit great variation of mores. There are, of course, certain outside limits of conduct imposed by the society in which these aggregates exist. No set of mores is commonly shared by all the persons who make up any single aggregate at any one time. This wide range of behavior patterns is accompanied also by variability of mores, in the sense that patterns of behavior change rapidly in the masses. This means that social aggregates are not dependable or predictable.

c) The masses as such are not highly institutionalized. This is another way of saying that traditions and customs that develop in groups and associations tend to be dissipated rather than strengthened in the aggregate masses. Whatever institutionalization has taken place within the urban masses has been neither common to all aggregates nor uniform among all. The rules of conduct and the ways of acting change so rapidly that they do not have the chance to develop a uniform social pressure on individuals.

d) The personality of people in the masses tends to be individualistic. This is a function of urban anonymity and lack of contact, as well as of the constant necessity for adaptation and adjustment, in the various aggregates. A highly individualistic personality is not a paradox in the midst of aggregates which tend to behave on a uniform level. The person simply does not become an integrated part of the aggregate in thought and convictions even when his external behavior is similar to that of others.

e) The masses are unstructured. This is an obvious consequence of the fact that the various aggregates which combine to make up the mass society are themselves unorganized. The masses cannot act concertedly as a total collectivity, they have no central purpose, no direction from inner leaders. Although there are elementary forms of leadership occasionally apparent in the separate social aggregates, one cannot speak of mass leadership unless the masses are somehow organized into associations.

SOCIAL AGGREGATES IN THE AMERICAN SOCIETY

1. The Urban Spatial Neighborhood

American cities contain many rural-born people who have migrated for various reasons. Even after they have lived in the city for twenty years they claim that "you don't get to know anyone," or that "your neighbors won't even talk to you." They still miss the kind of personal relations they enjoyed back in the village and on the farm. They are articulating the lonelines and the anonymity of the city. In scientific terms, they are talking about the difference between living mainly in social aggregates and living mainly in social groups.

In this discussion we must keep clearly in mind the distinction between the social neighborhood and the merely spatial neighborhood. The American urban trend is away from the former and toward the latter. The social neighborhood is a numerically small community in which people have close contact, share similar values and beliefs, and co-operate for recognized common goals. The spatial neighborhood is a small physical area in which people live in close physical proximity but in which there is relatively little group contact among them.

The typical city dweller in America has neighbors only if the term signifies people who "live nearby." This is the apparent incongruity of city life: a maximum of spatial neighbors and a minimum of social neighbors. It would be a mistake, of course, to speak in absolute terms of the complete isolation and atomization of persons in the city. The next-door neighbors, whether the door is down the hall or down the street, are only relative strangers.

Urban American spatial neighborhoods exhibit certain common features by which they can be identified and which can be analyzed in detail. Some of these distinctive features are as follows:

a) Spatial neighborhoods are nameless. Certain relatively large urban areas, like Yorkville, the South Side, the French Quarter, are neither social nor spatial neighborhoods. They are usually functional areas—enterprises from a commercial point of view, or directional guideposts from a territorial point of view. Even a city section, identified as a political ward, a police precinct, a school zone, a church parish, is in essence merely a cluster of nameless small spatial neighborhoods.

b) There is a rough economic similarity within these neighborhoods since similar rentals tend to attract persons and families of similar income. One does not find an impoverished family living next to a wealthy family. People speak of low-income areas and high-income areas, but there are subtle differences in the wide range from the high to the low.

c) Such neighborhoods are small in area and may be confined even to one multiple apartment house in some places, or to one or two streets in a section of single-family dwellings. This small area, however, may contain as many as three hundred people.

d) Human contacts are casual in the immediate neighborhood. The greeting or the nod is a characteristic and normal contact, and borrowing a dustpan, a cup of sugar, or a loaf of bread exemplifies the casual contact. It may extend even to the invitation to "drop in for a drink" on New Year's Day. Actual visiting between families is the sign of a friendship group and not of a social aggregate.

e) Contact between neighbors tends to be through women and children rather than through adult men. This is to be expected since women and children spend more time in the neighborhood, meet neighbors at the grocery or drugstore, and pass them on the street. Here, again, reference is not to the child's playmates or school friends with whom he forms a primary group rather than a social aggregate.

f) Knowledge about neighbors is characteristic of this type of social aggregate. The people do not know one another well, but they tend to have opinions of, and attitudes toward, the neighbors. Many of these appear to be stereotypes based on some observable external evidence. They distinguish the "noisy ones" from the "quiet ones," the "flashy people" from the conservatives, the friendly from the aloof.

It can be seen that modern spatial neighborhoods are very different from the "old" neighborhoods that were characterized often by community life of people with similar ethnic, religious, and immigrant background. They are also quite different from the communities which are now developing in the newer suburbs where a conscious attempt is being made to develop and maintain social relations. It is sometimes said that the large American metropolis has reached its maximum growth in population, but it is probable that the conditions giving rise to the urban neighborhood, as described here, will continue to exist.

2. Economic Factor in the American Masses

Chains of causation in the discussion of sociological phenomena tend to be scientifically questionable. It is, however, a common assertion that economic change has been the principal cause for the widespread emergence of American social aggregates. The reasoning is something like this: The application of technological inventions to the mass production of goods required not only large concentrations of capital goods at the source of power but also large numbers of people at the place where the work was done. Large industries meant large cities, and it is in large cities that the characteristic social aggregates of our time have been assembled.

Thus the aggregate masses are said to compose the industrial, commercial, and urban society. Social scientists commonly observe that the economic institution is the predominant institution of our culture and that the economic groupings are the most influential in our society. Industrialism, commercialism, urbanism, and mass aggregation of people are said to be linked in a causal chain. While this is an oversimplified statement, it provides the basic and bare conceptualization of the processes that have made the emergence of social aggregates an outstanding feature of American life.

In somewhat more detail the following phenomena indicate the way in which the social organization and direction of American economic life have almost necessarily accompanied, if not caused, the social aggregates of the "mass society."

a) The breakdown of traditional skills has meant the disintegration of the bonds that once held skilled craftsmen together. Many skills that were the trade secrets of a craft, that required many years of training and were shared by the experts in the field, were simply wiped out. Machines could do the work faster, and often better, than the hands of the craftsman. There was no longer need for these ancient and hard-won skills.

b) The fellowship of skilled workmen disappeared when the skill they shared was no longer needed. This meant that a group of workmen, organized around a craft to further their own interests and that of the craft, no longer had a central function. The group as such tended to disintegrate and its members became units in social aggregates.

c) The social status of the skilled worker, based upon age, experience, functional competence, and reputation, has been drastically lowered. His position as a producer could be challenged by any trained young worker who could quickly learn to tend a machine and who, because of his strength, dexterity, and youth, could probably outproduce the older worker.

d) The physical isolation of factory workers has increased the social distance between individuals. The principal relationship has become that between the man and his machine rather than between one man and another. In other words, co-operation, the social process that unites people in groups, is neither as possible nor as necessary as it was.

e) The personality of the individual became less important than his production efficiency. This is true also of clerks, stenographers, and other white-collar workers in the large business enterprise. The point of sociological relevance is that personality is an essential element in the formation and maintenance of groups but is negligible in social aggregates.

f) The specialized division of labor has tended to separate workers still more from one another. This means that workers have even less to talk about, less in common from a functional point of view, since they hardly know how their item of production fits in with those produced by others. It is interesting to note the parallel contrast between the highly co-ordinated and efficiently operating machinery which delivers a complete and integrated product at the end of the assembly line, and the series of disconnected, highly individualistic persons who have tended the assembly line.

This brief review of the social phenomena which accompany the economic conditions of American production must not be interpreted as a glum and hopeless picture of the group relations of industrial workers. The economy has undoubtedly contributed directly to realignment of workers in social aggregates and at least indirectly to the increase of the urban aggregate masses. These facts and their consequences have been carefully analyzed through the research of social scientists.

Both organized labor and large-scale management have co-operated with social scientists in an intelligent interpretation of these social facts and in an attempt to offset the desocializing effects of the modern

American technological system. Programs of education have informed the worker of the meaning of his contribution to the total product. The importance of co-operation and teamwork has been emphasized through the deliberate creation of primary groups in the work situation. Deliberate attempts are made to relieve the monotony of repetitive operations, to raise the social appreciation of work, and to elevate the esteem of the worker for himself. These are all efforts to restore some of the sociological advantages of group life into a system of social aggregates.

3. Lack of American Mass Movements

Theoretically, one might suppose that a society characterized by large numbers of different social aggregates would also have a history of mass movements, but the United States is notable for its lack of them. Aggregates are people in the mass, and, when the American aggregate organizes, it usually becomes some kind of association. It does not form with other aggregates into a "people's movement." The conditions for mass movements appear to be present in our society, but all attempts to create such movements have been short-lived.

Historically, of course, the United States has experienced all kinds of movements, but they have been social movements of a relatively specialized nature. They have not included the masses as a whole, the heterogeneous aggregations of people in our country. There has not even been a class movement in the sense in which the Marxists define the working masses. The only attempt to organize the heterogeneous masses of the American society was that of the Knights of Labor, who invited to membership all who worked for a living, including business and professional men. This attempt was unsuccessful.

The women's movement for political suffrage was one of the specialized movements; it disappeared when women were given the vote. Farmers' protest organizations had some of the aspects of a social movement and have been effective through lobbies. The labor movement still remains a fairly specialized operation and has not crystallized into a solidaristic mass movement. The most recent and effective movement is that of Negroes for equal rights. It is historically and sociologically significant that these specialized movements tend to succeed one another rather than to occur simultaneously.

Following are some of the factors that, taken in combination, help to explain the fact that mass movements do not appear among the American masses:

a) The institutional adaptiveness of our culture to the reasonable demands of the people tends to satisfy the needs for which mass movements are organized. The major political parties are generally willing to study and to react to the needs of the people. The readiness of all three branches of the federal government to reinterpret the laws in the light of modern social developments has forestalled the formation of mass movements.

b) The success of the democratic process has provided pragmatic confidence that "something can be done." Although Americans are notoriously apathetic voters in comparison with the people of some other countries, the "threat" of the polls has often influenced the elected officials. Reliance on their representatives, who must make an accounting to them in the next election campaign, accompanies the political inertia of the great masses of people.

c) Specialized movements succeed largely through lobbies and pressure groups, which concentrate on piecemeal advantages and particular issues. These are specialized interests, rather than the general interest or the common good that a mass movement would be presumed to promote. This means of promotion is an indication of the rational and scientific approach characteristic of the American people.

d) The mass solidarity which accompanies mass movements has not crystallized in the American society mainly because of the successive waves of immigration. The population has been subdivided by differences in language, religion, and ethnic, racial, and national background. This cultural pluralism, unique in the history of the world, has hindered cohesion of thought and action. While some of these differences are gradually disappearing, they have been historically effective as a preventive to mass movements.

e) There has always been an immigrant lower class of people who were more eager to establish themselves as Americans than to reform American society. These people have never at one time been numerous enough, nor well enough acquainted with the American society, nor in sufficiently effective communication with other Americans, to form the basis of a mass movement. The southern rural Negroes who move into the large urban centers are now replacing them with somewhat the same effect.

f) The upward social mobility of individuals has meant that much of the organizing talent that could have formed and led mass movements rose above the ranks of people who would most benefit by such movements. Each generation has "sent upstairs" the potential leaders of mass movements. This opportunity for advancement in social status has been one of the greatest advantages for the individual, and the development of individualism is an antidote to the development of mass action.

g) The material success of America, which provides a constantly rising standard of living for more and more people, has cut the ground out from many of the "causes" around which social movements build. This standard of living is not the same as government-provided "bread and circuses." In the American society the people have obtained material objects through their own work in their own economic roles.

These conditions explaining the absence of a mass movement in the United States are not necessarily enduring or permanent. Since social aggregates continue to multiply, it will be interesting to observe the future trends. As long as the relatively exclusive immigration laws remain in effect, the population is certain to become more homogeneous as people of differing ethnic, racial, and national backgrounds continue to intermarry. Whether this cultural and biological mingling will be great enough and important enough to offset the other obstacles to mass movements cannot be predicted with any degree of accuracy.

4. American Parades as Social Aggregates

Every society has its own way of staging public demonstrations. Folk festivals and religious processions, often carefully planned in advance, bring the people out into the streets. The American street parade has developed a pattern that appears to be uniquely American and is peculiar to the large urban populations.

The street parade is not a casual accident any more than an athletic or theater performance is unplanned. The participants in parades form a social aggregate that is transitory and anonymous; it behaves like a crowd on the march; once it begins, it is organized only in the sense that it has a physical direction in which to march. The typical parade is an occasion when the crowd on the sidewalk watches the crowd on the street. There are numerous kinds of parades, but they are all essentially the public celebration of some significant event.

a) The hero parade appears to be the most spontaneous and the largest of all American parades. The hero who is being honored may be anyone, a Channel swimmer, a golf champion, a returning general, a group of military veterans, a baseball or football team. These are for the most part "victory" parades, celebrating some feat or achievement which meets with popular acclaim and approval. This type of demonstration has become more mechanized in recent years, consisting of a kind of caravan of automobiles. The throwing of ticker tape and other wastepaper from the windows is an added feature in the big cities, especially in the business districts.

b) The patriotic parade is probably the most frequent type of parade since it occurs even in the small cities and towns in America. The best known of these are the parades on Independence Day, Memorial Day, and Veterans Day. Other national and state holidays are also celebrated by a parade. These are marches on foot with musical bands spaced along the line of march. Most often these bands are pressed into service from the elementary and high schools of the city.

c) Organization parades are those that often form a part of the agenda of the annual convention of associations like the American Legion, the Veterans of Foreign Wars, the Shriners, and others. Since participation in these parades is usually permitted only to the membership of the organization, they seem to go beyond the classification of social aggregates. Nevertheless, the annual convention of national organizations gathers together people who are virtual strangers to one another, and the relationship that exists among these persons on such occasions tends to be that of the crowd rather than that of the group. The so-called "carnival" or Mardi Gras parades also come under this category since they are planned and executed by organizations.

d) The commercial parade is becoming increasingly frequent in American cities. This may be anything from a circus parade, which is designed to sell tickets to the show, to an outright commercial demonstration designed to emphasize products like cotton, oranges, coal, and other commodities. Most of the commercial parades are advertising media and the participants may be temporary employees who gather simply for this occasion. In this regard they fulfil the characteristics of the social aggregate.

e) The political parade appears to be going out of fashion in the United States. There are still a few political machines and organizations which utilize this type of advertising and propaganda, but other media like radio, television, and the mass rally seem to have supplanted the parade in importance. In some large eastern cities the St. Patrick's Day parade, ostensibly a religious demonstration, has political and ethnic overtones as well.

f) Workers' parades are also relatively infrequent in our society. The date officially set for this demonstration is the national Labor Day holiday in September, and organized labor attempts to make a show of numbers and strength in its street parades. This day is also part of a long week end, however, and most union members appear more willing to pass it in recreation than in marching through the streets. The representatives of socialist labor organizations have attempted to import the European pattern of May Day into the United States, and their street parades on this annual occasion have sometimes turned into another type of social aggregate, the unruly mob.

In the United States parades are usually considered a form of recreational activity. For the most part neither the participants nor the spectators take them seriously. They are meant to mark joyous occasions more often than sad ones. The public funeral procession is uncommon, and even the occasional public religious procession is often called a parade or a rally. Recreational and leisure-time activities are increasing in all forms except in parades, for commercial entertainment enterprises have developed many other means of relaxation.

5. Slums as Social Aggregates

The United States has been slow to awaken to the fact that urban slums are a public and social responsibility. There are probably two main reasons for this slow realization: the first is the strong emphasis on private enterprise as the bringer of all goods and the curer of all evils; and the second is the tendency to think of slums in terms of material property, as houses and streets, rather than as persons and families. Since the economic depression of the 1930's, there has been a growing awareness of the slums as a social problem, and our society has begun to invest in public low-cost housing and in urban redevelopment.

Slums exist in all large American cities and are usually measured by the indexes of substandard housing: the need for major repairs, lack of sanitation facilities, and overcrowding. This last item is the key to the social scientist's study of slums. The cities are crowded places, and no part of them is more crowded than the slums. While there are social groups and organized social relations everywhere in these blighted areas, the slums, when viewed as a totality, are a series of social aggregates.

The following items clearly demonstrate that the urban slums can be defined as social aggregates, but they must not lead to the conclusion that complete social atomization exists, or is even possible, in the slums.

a) An extraordinarily high proportion of unattached individuals live in the slums. We usually think of the family, that is, of husband and wife, or of parents and children, as the social unit in residential areas. The slums have a high proportion of unrelated boarders living with these units. This number of legitimate single persons is increased by the numbers of "homeless" men living in rooming houses or sleeping in flophouses. There are also the outlaws of society who flock to the slums: criminals, prostitutes, and others.

b) Transiency is more characteristic of the slum than of any other type of residential area. While there are many long-term dwellers in the slum who cannot find their way out to better living conditions, there is a great deal of movement from one house to another, and from one slum to another. While economic prosperity makes it possible for some to leave the slums, their numbers are more than equaled by rural migrants drawn to the city by prospects of a job.

c) Upward social mobility is slower in the slum than elsewhere, and the reverse, downward mobility, is more often the case. The unattached person entering the slum tends to go from "bad to worse," that is, gradually to lose status even in this low-status area. There are certainly differences of status among slum dwellers, although the range of status is not great because the valued items which serve as criteria of status are in short supply.

d) From the point of view of the total society, the slum dwellers constitute the lowest class category. In fact, they are often forced to remain there because they are the "undesirables," those who have the lowest ranking in the criteria of social status. This does not refer merely to lack of wealth and education, nor to low occupational functions. The immigrant, racial, and ethnic ancestry of these people is an important factor of their class status.

e) The limited choice in social relations is also characteristic of the slum as a social aggregate. People are living in enforced physical proximity with others whether they wish it or not. The individual may desire to avoid some people and to be friendly with others. Neither voluntary avoidance nor voluntary acceptance is left completely to his decision in the crowded conditions of the slum. This is an example of the coexistence of horizontal social distance with physical proximity.

f) Relatively ineffective formal groupings characterize the slum areas of our large cities. Schools exist in the slums, but parent-teacher associations are difficult to maintain. Missions and churches exist there, but formal church clubs of the middle-class pattern hardly exist. Political groups have been interested in getting out the votes, but the slum dwellers find it difficult to participate in organized political action.

g) The people of the slums are even less socially articulate than the general mass of American citizens. The prospect of improving their condition appears to lie less in their own protests and actions than in outside forces. Even though they constitute the classical rootless proletariat, they have never been socially cohesive enough to organize their protests effectively. Nevertheless, one of the potent factors for arousing the public conscience about the slums has been the fear that "subversive elements" might infiltrate to gain control of the slums. Crowds and mobs have frequently formed, and incidents have occasionally occurred in the form of riots and near-riots, but these are not sustained and articulate movements.

h) The presence of racketeers and of juvenile gangs indicates a more permanent type of social organization in the slums. It must be noted that this type of grouping is not found only in the slums, but the conditions for its formation are more favorable there than elsewhere. These conditions are a combination of most of the items we have already listed above.

The description of the American urban slum given here is focused upon the definition of the social aggregate. It cannot be emphasized too often that this is not the only way in which the sociologist can study these people. They can be viewed from the different definitions of social categories, or they can be studied in more detail from the point of view of groups and organizations. The perspective of the social aggregate has already been explained in the text, and it is possible to study meaningfully not only slums but any residential area from this perspective.

DISCUSSION QUESTIONS

1. Distinguish briefly categories, aggregates, and groups.
2. What elements must be included in a complete description of social aggregates?
3. What are some of the difficulties in classifying aggregates?
4. Name, define, and give examples of the principal kinds of aggregates.
5. Do large aggregates ever contain small groups? Explain.
6. Distinguish between residential area as an aggregate and neighborhood as a group.
7. Explain with examples how an aggregate may become a group and how a group may become an aggregate.

8. List the various ways in which a person is related to the aggregate of which he is a constituent unit.
9. In what sense is the term "mass society" an apparent contradiction?
10. List and define the characteristics of the aggregate masses.
11. Distinguish between the spatial and the social neighborhood.
12. What are the distinctive features of the American urban spatial neighborhood?
13. Discuss: "Economic change has been the principal cause of American social aggregates."
14. What is the difference between a mass movement and a specialized social movement?
15. What factors explain the lack of mass movements in America?
16. In what sense is a parade a social aggregate?
17. Distinguish among the various types of American parades.
18. Why has America been late in recognizing slums as a social responsibility?
19. List and explain the sociological characteristics of slum dwellers.

SUGGESTED READINGS

BENNETT, JOHN W., and TUMIN, MELVIN M. *Social Life, Structure and Function.* New York: Alfred A. Knopf, Inc., 1948, chaps. xxx, xxxi.

GREEN, ARNOLD. *Sociology: An Analysis of Life in Modern Society.* New York: McGraw-Hill Book Co., Inc., 1952, chap. xii.

LaPIERE, RICHARD T. *Collective Behavior.* New York: McGraw-Hill Book Co., Inc., 1938, chap. xviii.

MERRILL, F. E., and ELDREDGE, H. W. *Culture and Society: An Introduction to Society.* Englewood Cliffs, N.J.: Prentice-Hall, Inc., 1955, chaps. xv–xviii.

PARK, ROBERT E. (ed.). *An Outline of the Principles of Sociology.* New York: Barnes & Noble, Inc., 1939, chaps. xxi–xxii.

CHAPTER FIVE

Groups and Associations

As we have seen, the social person is a unit in different kinds of collectivities, and the previous discussion of categories and aggregates helps us to understand the definition of the social group. Because the group actually exists outside the minds of men, it cannot be called a social category. Because of the kinds of relations which persons have within it, the group is not merely a social aggregate. The persons in a group associate with one another and have patterned interaction among themselves. Thus, the briefest definition of the group is "human beings in reciprocal relations."

Any study of the origin and formation of groups can refer only to the specific group which has a beginning in time, continues for a while, and then goes out of existence. It cannot refer to group life as such. Group life and social relations are coextensive with the existence of persons. Like categories and aggregates, they are universally present wherever people live. Where there are persons, there are groups; and where there are no persons, there are no groups.

Characteristics of the Group

The sociological meaning of the term "group" is much more detailed and technical than we have indicated. A more complete definition of the group must include the following:

a) The social unit called a group must be identifiable as such, both by its members and by outside observers. This does not mean that every member must be known personally to every other member or to non-members. Secret societies, lodges, and fraternities have a recognizable existence, although their membership may be exclusive and hidden. The groups in any large city are so numerous that no individual could have personal knowledge of all of them; but they are knowable, that is, it is possible to find out about them.

b) The group has a social structure in the sense that each part, or person, has a position related to other positions. Thus, social stratification, or the ranking of social status, is present even in the smallest informal groupings. There is always at least a trace of subordination or superordination even in the most equalitarian groups.

c) There are individual roles in the group. In fact, this is what group participation signifies and it is the aspect under which participation is studied. When the members cease to enact their roles, the group ceases to exist. A group in which there is no personal action of a patterned sort is sociologically unthinkable.

d) Reciprocal relations are essential to the group. In other words, there must be contact and communication among the members of the group. This must be a mutual or reciprocal process, even if it is limited to only two persons in the group at any one time.

e) Every group has norms of behavior that influence the way in which the roles are enacted. These need not be written rules or regulations; but they are usually certain patterns of behavior which are understood and followed by the members. Thus, there is necessarily a modification of the behavior of the individual when and because he is in the group.

f) The members of the group have certain common interests and values. In some instances these may be only vaguely defined, but that they are present is seen in the fact that a conflict in values will almost invariably split the group.

g) Group activity, if not the very existence of the group itself, must be directed toward some social goal or goals. This answers the specific question why, for what purpose, does the group exist.

h) A group must have relative permanency, that is, a measurable duration over a period of time. This is one of the important distinguishing marks between a transient social aggregate and a social group.

Taking all these characteristics together, we can now give the following complete definition of the social group. A group is an identifiable, structured, continuing collectivity of social persons who enact reciprocal roles according to social norms, interests, and values in the pursuit of common goals. It may be noted in passing that a total society, like the American or French or Mexican societies, is a combination of all of the groups existing within it. Groups within a society are distinguished from one another mainly by their central functions, while major societies are distinguished from one another mainly by their cultures.

Recruitment to the Group

If a group is to continue in existence it must have ways of recruiting new members. Persons come originally into the conjugal family group by birth or adoption and into the extended kinship group by marriage. All other groups admit new members through one or a series of qualifying elements. This may be a merely informal understanding that a person is welcome to join a friendship circle. In other groups he may be elected or appointed or invited to membership. He may have to pass certain tests or examinations, conform to rituals and ceremonies of the group, and in some instances pay an initiation fee.

The question of recruitment to the group is not the same as the study of the formation or origin of groups. It is obvious that people live in groups because they are social beings. In most instances they simply discover themselves taking part in the activities or groups without reflecting on the manner in which they happen to be in these particular groups rather than others. Thus, on the part of the individual there is often an almost non-rational and subconscious entrance into the group. A boy may associate with his neighbors in a play group, or he may become a member of an organized Boy Scout troop.

Classification of Groups

Social groups are so complex and so varied that their classification must necessarily be multiple. We have said above that the major groups in a society can be identified and classified by their central social function, but this is simply one of numerous approaches. The ways in which groups can be differentiated and arranged are as numerous as the points of view from which they can be studied. Many of these approaches are useful only for the purposes of a specific study.

Some of the "easier" classifications may of themselves be of little sociological value. Ranging all groups on a continuum of size, for example, from the smallest to the largest, is not particularly significant, unless the numbers of people are related to some other sociological characteristic. Ranging all groups on a basis of permanency, from the oldest and most enduring to the newest and most quickly changing, may be an interesting exercise in historical perspective, but, to be scientifically important, permanency and impermanency must also be linked with other features of the group.

Every social group must have the characteristics already defined, and it is posible to classify all groups on a continuum according to each of these characteristics. Some of these are more important than others. One may classify all groups according to *structure,* placing them on a continuum from the most rigidly to the most loosely structured; or according to *social roles,* from those that make the most demands to those that make the fewest demands on the members; or according to *reciprocal relations,* from those in which communication is the most to those in which it is the least frequent and intimate. One may classify groups according to the *standards of behavior* expected of the members; according to the kinds of *social values* they share; and according to the kinds of *social goals* toward which they direct their behavior.

Common Bases for Groups

One of the most widely used systems of group classification, and perhaps the simplest to grasp for an introductory understanding, is that of the four common bases for group association. This is a common-sense rather than a scientific approach, but it has the advantage of providing a quick, broad, and universal outline of group life. This most general classification embraces the largest number of groups in the fewest categories. The four bases upon which all people associate in group life are: (*a*) common ancestry, (*b*) territory shared in common, (*c*) similar bodily characteristics, and (*d*) common interests.

a) Common ancestry is traditionally the strongest tie that binds human beings in their social relations, although its importance has been greatly lessened in the modern, complex, and large-scale societies. The groups based upon common ancestry are sometimes called "blood" groups, those in which members are related by birth, marriage, or adoption. Both the immediate conjugal family, consisting of parents and children, and the consanguine family, including cousins, aunts, uncles, and so forth, are of this type. The extended kinship group includes all who are in any identifiable way related to each other. In primitive societies this extended group is often called the clan or tribe.

b) Territorial proximity is also a very broad basis for social groups. Since all groups are necessarily existent in time and space, it is obvious that they must somehow be limited to a physical territory. The sociological neighborhood that is not merely a social aggregate, and the true community, are modern examples of territorial groups. In so far as the persons within a political division, like a village, a suburb, or a township, constitute a collectivity in reciprocal relations, they may also be studied under this category. Many different kinds of groups, such as athletic teams, parent-teachers' groups, and civic clubs, are identified with the name of the place in which they exist.

c) The classification of groups based on bodily characteristics is widely used in modern society, and the listing of groups under this heading would be interminable. In the isolated, primitive societies, the similarity of biological characteristics is closely allied to the facts of common ancestry and common territory. In the compex modern society common racial features are still a basis of imposed social grouping, but other characteristics lend themselves to a great deal of voluntary association. For example, youth clubs, various female organizations, men's lodges, fraternities, and clubs show that age and sex are frequently used as a basis of groups. Physical strength and aptitude are common bases for groups of football players, wrestlers, and other athletes.

d) The sharing of common interests is the basis for a great variety of modern social groupings. In fact, the "interest group" is sociologically more significant than most of the other groups discussed above because common interest implies the willingness to function together in the pursuit of a common goal. The multiplication of scientific, business, and professional associations is merely one indication of the tremendous number and variety of this kind of group.

It must be emphasized that these four bases for social groups do not represent four exclusive classifications. They are abstractions from concrete reality, a way of looking at the same persons from different points of view and according to the varying relations they have with their fellow men. There is, in fact, an overlapping of persons, a multiple membership of the individual, in the various types of groups discussed. It would be difficult to find a normal adult who is not in some way a member of all four types of groups.

The Major Groups

The most satisfactory and sociologically significant classification of groups is that which centers on the major universal social functions that human beings in group life must perform if society is to continue in existence. Human beings everywhere and at all times must cooperate in some way to satisfy the social needs implied in familial, educational, economic, political, religious, and recreational activities. These essential needs and functions are sometimes called the social and cultural prerequisites in the sense that without them no society could continue to exist. It is obvious, therefore, that they are universal, and empirical studies have shown that they are also variable.

The universality of these major social groups has been established without question by social scientists. But although these groups are found in every society, without exception, this does not mean that each is given equal emphasis within any particular society. They are all essential to the continuance of the society, but in one place the economic groups may be the most important, while in another place emphasis is upon the political, or the religious, groups. Nor does this universality mean that every social person is simultaneously enacting a social role in all of them in any given society.

Most adults in every society join with others in the fulfilment of familial and recreational needs. The father of a family may also be a member of a poker-playing group. All children submit to the socialization process and are, at least for a time, participants in informal and formal educational groups. The businessman plays a role in his parish church and his political party, and the economic, religious, and political groups engage the attention of varying numbers of people. The significant fact is that some people in every society must at all times be performing the central functions of these major social groupings.

The diversity and variability of these major groups have also been scientifically established. The fact that these social needs, functions, and groups are present in every society does not mean that they are present in the same way. Different forms are emphasized in different societies, and greater variations are permitted in some societies than in others. Polygamy is practiced in some places; the economic groups in an industrial society differ from those in an agricultural society. The variety of recreational and religious groups is tremendous throughout the world. The way societies structure their groups for educational and political purposes varies greatly. Somehow or other every society manages to reproduce itself, educate its new members, provide material sustenance and means of relaxation, maintain public order, and satisfy the religious needs of people.

The advantage of classifying groups in this way is that every group which has a clearly defined single social goal can be included under one of these headings. The fact is, of course, that many groups have multiple functions, but even here they can be arranged for purposes of study under the principal activity in which they engage. The following is a brief résumé of the groups which come under each of the six major headings:

a) The family group is made up of those persons engaged in satisfying the basic needs of family life: the arrangements for sex relations, the birth and care of children, and mutual affection of the members. In some societies the concept of family extends vertically and horizontally to include all who are in any way related by marriage, birth, or adoption. It is sometimes also synonymous with the word "household" and includes domestic servants, retainers, serfs, and even slaves.

b) The educational groupings are those in which the essential social function of transmitting the culture to succeeding generations is performed in informal and formal ways. In simple societies this is often done within the family itself, but in more complex societies there is a great variety of schools, institutes, academies, and scientific and learned associations. No matter where and how it is done, the fact is that this function is recognized as a social activity performed by people together.

c) The economic groups are those in which the members produce and distribute the material goods and services necessary for the physical maintenance of life on earth. Here again there is a great difference between the society in which the family members co-operate to sustain themselves and a society in which the division of labor has become highly specialized. All kinds of business and professional associations are primarily economic although they may have other subfunctions, like scientific research, the training of employees, or the maintenance of lobbies for political purposes.

d) The political groups are all those which perform the function of administering and governing, of maintaining the public order, of making, interpreting, and enforcing the laws. The political parties, the whole court system, the penitentiaries and jails, the military units of all kinds, must be included under this heading. The central function of the political groups can always be recognized even though certain governmental functions may become quite diffused and diverse. Large modern governments must concern themselves with almost everything from soil conservation and atomic research to hospital administration and radio communication.

e) The religious groups are constituted by those persons who share in a patterned and social way the relationship between God and man. The piety and private worship of the individual is affected by the kind of religious bodies present in the society, but the social scientist focuses upon the groups of people who share similar religious values and enact common religious behavior patterns. Most of these groups perform also other subfunctions, running parochial schools and sectarian colleges, operating social-work agencies, and even providing playgrounds and other recreational facilities.

f) The recreational group is made up of persons who are satisfying in a social way the need for relaxation. Recreation does not mean simply play and athletics and physical exercise. There is a great variety of activities which are considered recreational, and they include serious aesthetic organizations as well as hobby clubs. The term "commercial" recreation indicates that the economic factor may play an important part in the formation and maintenance of recreational groups, and there can be no doubt that the entertainment "industry" in modern large societies is big business.

Groups and Associations

It has become customary in sociological literature to make a distinction between primary and secondary groups. Both of these are genuine social groups in the strictest technical definition of the term, but the tendency has been to identify the secondary groups as associations. This distinction is not merely an instrumental and conceptual device that enables us better to understand the composition of society. It is a distinction between two general types of groups that actually exist in large numbers.

When we discuss the various kinds of societies in the next chapter, we shall see that some societies are characterized by a predominance of primary groups while others emphasize secondary groups, or associations. The type of society which places an emphasis upon primary groups carries a long list of labels, each depending upon the taste and point of view of the social scientist who is describing them. A society of primary groups is called communal, established, *gemeinschaftlich*, mechanical, closed, solidaristic, familistic, folk, and traditional. An Irish fishing village, a wood-carving town in Bavaria, a community of Louisiana trappers, and rural French-Canada exemplify these primary-group characteristics.

Unlike the distinctions among the major social groups which focus upon a single essential social function, the distinction between the primary and secondary groupings is based upon a combination of characteristics. If we consider the terms which contrast with those given above for the primary type of society, we have a rough description of the secondary type of society. A society which emphasizes secondary groups is called associational, adaptive, *gesellschaftlich*, organic, open, anomic, contractual, complex, industrial, and dynamic. As we learn more and more about groups and societies, it becomes increasingly clear that modern urban America is developing all these characteristics.

Two important facts must be pointed out here. The first is that both the primary and the secondary groups fit the strict definition of the social group given above. This is true even though the secondary group is more frequently identified simply as an association. The second is that the identification of these types of groups is mainly a matter of the partial presence of certain characteristics. They are "types" in the sense that they represent the two poles of a range of groups. If all groups in a society were placed on a continuum, some would appear to be in a transitional stage, sharing some of the characteristics of both the primary and the secondary groups.

The difference between the primary and secondary groups is mainly, but not exclusively, in the kind of reciprocal relations and communication that exists among the members of the group. When these social relations are intimate, personal, face to face, and frequent, they are characteristic of the primary group. The social relations in the secondary group, or association, are obviously on a different level. They are relatively impersonal, more formal, and less frequent, and are characteristic of larger and loosely organized groups.

Primary Groups

The primary group is a relatively "tight" collectivity of people who have frequent face-to-face relations, a feeling of solidarity, and a close adherence to common social values.

The face-to-face group is primary in the sense of being fundamental to the individual person. His earliest and most formative experiences are with the primary family group. Here he has his most effective and long-lasting lessons in socialization. Much of his social personality results from this contact and communication. The intimate groups with which he associates all during his life are primary also in the sense of being closest to him. They are made up of the people he loves and trusts and admires. They are the ones with whom he has his most worthwhile social experiences. They make life worth living. These groups are primary, too, in the sense that the individual's "true" personality is revealed in them. He may be constrained more to enact the rigid expectations of his social roles in the secondary associations, but in the primary groupings he is more "himself."

The social person's primary group is called the "in-group" only in the strictest sense of the term. In it he has a feeling of belonging, a consciousness of cohesiveness, which tends to place all other people in out-groups. This distinction between in-group and out-group is not synonymous with that between the primary group and the secondary association. The various out-groups may be either primary or secondary depending upon their composition and characteristics. They simply refer to the groupings with which any individual person is not on a basis of close personal relations. The in-group is the one to which the individual really belongs, that is, to which he adheres and upon which he depends. In the last analysis, the in-group contains his friends and confidants; the out-groups are made up of mere acquaintances and strangers.

Secondary Groups

The secondary group, or association, is a looser collectivity than the primary group. Individual persons enter into these secondary relationships voluntarily and purposively and often, in an unspoken way, "contractually." These relationships are regulated by law and justice, by formal customs and agreements. They are more careful and calculated; a person has to "watch himself," has to be "on his best behavior." When a man asserts among his business associates that "my word is my bond," he is attempting to inject into a secondary group the highly regarded mutual trust and understanding characteristic of the primary group.

It must be noted that the social person, with the possible exception of the youngest children, belongs simultaneously to both primary groups and secondary associations. The immediate family is his primary group, but the large, extended kinship to which he belongs is a secondary group. The people with whom the adult associates most in his church are his primary group, the other members of the parish or congregation form his secondary group. In his economic relations he associates more closely with some than with others; the former are primary, the latter secondary.

It is a mistake to assume that only the familial and recreational groups can be primary groups. This assumption occurs because sociological literature frequently gives only the close family and the play group as examples of primary groups. Nevertheless, the fact remains that, as in most sociological classifications, the dividing line between primary and secondary groups is not in every specific case clear and distinct. Some primary groups may be in the process of becoming looser secondary associations; some secondary groups may be in the process of "closing ranks," limiting membership, and developing primary social relations. The Communist cell, as a close-knit action group, is an example of the deliberate formation of a primary group within the structure of the larger secondary association.

Associations and Aggregates

The secondary group or association stands midway between the primary group and the social aggregate. The same person is found in all three of them; in the primary group he is close to others, in the secondary group he is organized with others, and in the social aggregate he has only casual and fleeting contacts with others. The difference between a spatial neighborhood and a social neighborhood is largely a difference between a social aggregate and a secondary group. In the first the persons hardly know one another; in the second they tend to live a community life.

The student of society must be careful to distinguish not only between the primary and the secondary groups, but also between the secondary group and the social aggregates. We have seen that these aggregates, such as crowds, mobs, and audiences, are marked by transitoriness, fluidity, lack of organization and of continuing reciprocal relations. This is not true of secondary groups, which are relatively large associations of people, like a university, a city parish, a factory, a country club, a local political party. Human relations in these groups are less personal and intimate than they are in primary groups, but the people are formally organized and are identified as members of the association.

It is commonly asserted, and with fairly objective and sufficient evidence, that any urban industrialized nation tends to become a society of associations and aggregates. This generalization must be accepted and interpreted with caution. If it means that the people are spending more time in secondary groups and in aggregates than ever before, the statement can be well substantiated. But two points must be emphasized in reference to this generalization. The first is that both primary and secondary groups exist, and the person belongs to both of them simultaneously by virtue of his membership in any of the major social groups. The second is that primary groups do and must exist in any ongoing society. The degree to which the primary groups are strong and numerous is an index of integration and solidarity in the total society. If its primary groups are weak and insufficient, the society itself tends to "disintegrate."

CHARACTERISTICS OF AMERICAN GROUP LIFE

1. The Decline of Primary Groups

It is apparent to even the casual observer that social aggregates and secondary associations are increasing in American urban society. Since people are limited in their time, energy, and abilities, this increase in other forms of human relations almost necessarily implies a decrease in primary relations. It is not necessary, however, merely to deduce this fact. One can observe all about him, and in his own experience, the measure to which his time, energy, and abilities are employed in secondary rather than in primary groups.

Primary groups are as essential to the continuity of the American society as to that of any other society. There is a minimum level, which we have not reached and probably cannot know empirically, at which the decline of primary groups seriously threatens the existence of a society. Thus when we talk about the decline of primary groups in our society, we are discussing a sociologically serious *trend,* but we are not implying the *absence* of primary groups—a sociological impossibility. On the other hand, it is true that urban Americans are adaptive and resilient, and they have accustomed themselves in many ways to the social change which emphasizes secondary associations.

Some of the indexes and factors in the decline of primary groups in the American society are as follows:

a) Americans are geographically the most mobile people (except for nomadic tribes) in the world. This population mobility has reached the point where an estimated 20 per cent of the people change their residence within any given year. Primary groups develop through stable, continuous relations with the same persons. When a family moves, the members of the family continue their primary relations among themselves but tend to break off relations in the non-family groups.

b) The discontinuity of generations is also a factor in the decline of primary groupings. This refers to the fact that in the American society the newly married couple is expected to leave the parental family and to "shift" for itself. While this throws the members of the young family closer together and theoretically ought to strengthen their primary relationships, it tends also to take away the support of the many primary groups formerly surrounding them in the parental home and neighborhood.

c) The extremely high incidence of divorce in the American society is one of the indexes of the decline of primary relations. Whether or not it is also a cause of this decline is not clear. No human relation is more intimate and personal than that of marriage, and the breakdown of the marital relation is synonymous with that of the primary relation between the people involved. It must be noted here that most divorced people remarry and that their second marriages are relatively stable and permanent arrangements.

d) While we have classified primary groups under the major social groupings specified according to function, it is also true that there is a dispersal of social functions in many primary groups. The primary school group that shares in religious and recreational as well as educational functions is likely to be more cohesive than one which concentrates only on learning. The primary familial group that shares in economic, recreational, educational, and religious activities is likely to be more cohesive than one that allows these functions to be performed away from the home.

e) The urbanization of church life is also a characteristic of the American society. Theoretically the high values of religion, with its emphasis on love and fellowship, should strengthen the primary relations. As the city churches become larger, however, they tend to become a secondary group. It is estimated that while 40 per cent of Americans are not expressly affiliated with churches, many of those who are formal church members participate only casually and sporadically in religious services and groups. This does not mean that the percentage of church membership is declining but that the intimate primary religious groups are declining in numbers and significance.

f) The decline of the social neighborhood in the urban areas means the decline of those friendly personal relations that characterize primary groups. This appears to be part of the price we pay for population density and the general anonymity of the urban way of life.

g) The growth of specialized commercial services has helped to break down the primary group. The person pays to have something done for him, rather than do it himself in the company of others. He does this frequently for sports and entertainment, but also for the various services in restaurants, hairdressers, launderettes, supermarkets, and other places. The efficiency and promptness of these services are very attractive to the individual city dweller.

In the midst of these facts concerning the decline of primary groups, there is a paradox which requires interpretation. This is the multiplication of the individual's primary relations. A person associates with different persons in each different primary group. For example, the urban male may associate with one group of males in the shop or office, another group in the tavern, still another on the bowling team, in the church congregation, the political club, and, of course, his own family. This kind of multiple social relationship is a corollary of the decrease of the multiple functions in the family itself. Usually, there is a certain amount of crossing-over and sharing of members in the different primary groups, but, to the extent that the individual participates in completely separate groups, he tends to weaken his primary relationships.

2. American Pressure Groups

The pressure group is an organized collectivity of persons seeking to promote their own special interest in the total society. Every self-conscious group tends to do this in some respect, to seek higher status, to be well regarded by others. But the special-interest group is identified by its use of social pressure, its attempts to gain power and advantages in relation to other groups. There is often a "conflict of interests" between two or more groups and this is what gives the pressure group its peculiar characteristic in the American society.

The pressure group is usually a secondary association built upon a broad base of membership and represented at its top by expert, efficient, and hard-driving smaller groups of individuals. These people's function is to put over the interests of their membership, and, in so far as they are active in the political arena and influence government and legislatures, they are called lobbies. The government is sometimes thought of as a mediator among the pressure groups, but it is more often the agency from which favorable action is requested.

It is not accidental that a pluralistic, democratic society like the United States should have a large number of pressure organizations of great variety, including the following:

a) The business groups probably exert more pressure, spend more money, and have a greater effect on American society than any other type of pressure group. This is to be expected in an economic-dominated society. The National Association of Manufacturers and the United States Chamber of Commerce are the best known and the most powerful of these, but there are also innumerable trade associations and specialized groups from all the industries and businesses in the country.

b) The functional pressure groups also exert a tremendous influence, sometimes against the business groups and sometimes in co-operation with them. The best known are the American Medical Association, the American Bar Association, and the various organized labor unions. Concerned with furthering their particular interests, they publish newspapers and sponsor radio programs through which they attempt to bring their cases before the people.

c) In some respects the farm groups are even more successful in building up power in the American society. Because of their rural background, and the nostalgic sympathy of most Americans for the rustic life, the farmers are often not thought of as an organized pressure group. Many of these groups are not representative of the family farmer but of the corporate farmers who specialize in the industry-like production of citrus, dairy, and other foods. The cattlemen and wheat growers have especially powerful lobbies.

d) The military veterans' pressure groups advertise a strong moral claim on the special attention of the nation. The patriotism and loyalty characteristic of our present society have made it inadvisable for other pressure groups to oppose the demands of the American Legion, the Veterans of Foreign Wars, and other similar organizations. Political leaders have been especially sensitive to these demands.

e) The pressure groups representing various minorities are also characteristic of the American society. These operate mainly in promotion of the rights of racial and ethnic minorities that are constantly fighting for recognition. The Negro groups, and to some extent the Jewish defense groups, have become more prominent than the older hyphenated-American groups representing minorities of various nationality backgrounds. This is the main area in which there are also strong anti-minority pressure groups, designed especially for anti-Negro and anti-Semitic activities.

f) The term "pressure group" is not often used in reference to American religious bodies, but each of the twelve major churches uses organized means to gain influence in both national and regional activities. This is a matter not merely of propaganda and proselytizing for new members, but also of influencing legislation and guarding against presumably threatening activities.

It is clear that pressure groups do not by themselves exhaust all the agencies and channels that represent special interests in the United States. There are individuals who are socially powerful because of their high status, and there are also broad "impersonal" interests that permeate a climate of opinion, such as the vague "states' rights" movement, or the promotion of federal subsidies for education, or the opposition to international bankers, and others.

The number and variety of these groups of "special pleaders" constitute a network of contravening, if not conflicting, forces. They indicate the complexity of the American society and invalidate simple interpretations of its conflicts like "capital versus labor," or "the businessman versus the farmer." These dichotomies express at best only a small segment of the mosaic of American group life, often bypass the great amount of co-operation among groups, and de-emphasize the twofold relationship of the pressure group to the political system and to the general population.

3. American Women's Clubs

Adult American women have more leisure time, more money to spend, more freedom of movement, and a greater variety of interests than the women of any other major modern society. Since they are social persons living in an urban society which multiplies its social aggregates and associations, it is to be expected that females will organize themselves in numerous kinds of groups. Association of persons along sex and age lines is not something recent or novel; female groupings have existed in all societies.

In an earlier period, women's clubs were organized for church activities, and, since religious bodies have traditionally separated the males from the females, the old from the young, the married from the single, this was an almost automatic and enforced type of association. At a later period, as women demanded more freedom and equal rights, they also banded together voluntarily to seek and defend these rights.

The classification of large secondary female organizations indicates that women have grouped themselves around almost as many and varied interests as men have. These are not merely "ladies' auxiliaries" to associations primarily masculine in membership; they are also separate groups in professional, business, military, academic, political, and religious activities. The various sisterhoods, missionary-aid societies, and temperance leagues are like the older religious interests. Women are notoriously poor members of labor unions, but they have been relatively successful in groups dedicated to civic and political reform.

We are concerned here, however, with the informal primary groups of women as an American social phenomenon. Typical of these are women's clubs dedicated to self-improvement and congeniality which meet in an aura of vague "do-goodism." Most of the women members are over forty years of age; their children are at least in the late adolescent stage; they are not gainfully employed; and they have a great deal of "time on their hands." More often than not, these are the women with whom foreign visitors come into contact and from whom they take back to their countries an erroneous generalization, a stereotype, of American womanhood.

What makes for this phenomenon? What are the elements which

account for the emergence and continuing increase of this type of primary group?

a) These women's clubs fulfil a need for their members. The married woman in this age category has performed her social function in bearing and rearing children. She is not needed for the economic support of her home; she has not been trained toward activities of a solitary or meditative nature; her housework requires a minimum of time and interest; she feels a need for social relations outside the home.

b) Because these clubs are relatively exclusive, membership in them is a reflection of one's social status. They differ in status from one to another, but the women who belong to any particular club are of relatively the same social stratum. This social accessibility for the most part indicates that their husbands are also in the same social class. Membership for the woman helps to maintain the status of the family.

c) This type of women's club always puts an emphasis on congeniality. Whether it is a luncheon club, a garden club, a bridge club, or any other kind, the members must be able to "get along" well together. Friendliness is more important as a personal quality than charm and poise. The members are genuinely fond of one another and meet on a basis of face-to-face relations.

d) Hardly any of these groups are primarily maintained for an ameliorative purpose, but almost all of them have some charitable project as one of their activities. They may donate to an orphanage, promote help for handicapped children, sponsor an opera guild, or encourage any of the numerous activities for civic betterment of the community.

e) The central purpose, however, is almost invariably recreational. Even though the ladies feel that they must be "doing something for somebody," their acknowledged goal is relaxation and enjoyment, to have in a temperate and moderate way a "good time." This may be paradoxical since it is the very surplus of leisure time and the relief from pressing social duties that makes possible the proliferation of these women's groups.

f) Although the social relations within these groups are primary and informal, the group almost always has a formal structure. There is a chairman, secretary, and treasurer, dues are collected, new members are formally invited. Often, of course, the business meeting, or that portion of a meeting devoted to business, is at best a perfunctory affair.

It must be pointed out that this description is not applicable to all the various types of female organizations that flourish in our society. It refers only to that type of women's club which is so often unfairly caricatured. One cannot dismiss them as innocuous groupings of people who are wasting their time. They have a definite place in our kind of urban society, and it is difficult to see what kind of group and activity could replace them.

4. Urban Youth Gangs as Primary Groups

Another social phenomenon current in the American urban society is the gang. Social scientists sometimes speak of the "gang age" because the members of these groups are teen-agers. The gang usually grows out of a spontaneous play group within a closely limited urban area. These groups are for the most part boys' gangs, although there are a few instances of similar girls' groups, and of girls' auxiliaries to the boys' gangs. The term "street gang" has come to have a negative connotation, as though all behavior of the participants were suspect and delinquent.

The fact is, however, that there are many more "good" gangs than there are "bad" gangs. The function of the gang is essentially recreational in nature. It is a friendship clique, a primary group of young people who like to associate with one another and who are for the most part given to harmless pranks. The "tough" gang with which the police are concerned is usually found in the crowded slums and adjacent areas where social and economic conditions are largely disorganized.

Youthful recreational groups are present in all societies in one degree or another. But the "tough" American street gang is unique in its large numbers and in the peculiar importance attached to it by its members and by the society in general. Following are some of the factors which contribute to its formation. It must be noted that no "single cause" is adequate, nor can any "single solution" be offered for the social difficulties which arise from these gangs.

a) Population density and substandard housing are characteristic of the urban areas where gangs develop. This means, of course, the constant overcrowding of homes. If there were only a few overcrowded dwellings in a city block, this would not be a large factor, but, when each apartment of each building is overflowing with people, it is natural that these people spend much of their time on the streets.

b) Family disorganization accompanies urban overcrowding. The economic conditions, the presence of boarders, the lack of privacy, the feeling of young people that their parents, especially the father, are failures—all of these tend to weaken the emotional security a youth needs. The family fails to meet the minimum standard of living which the American society expects and values. The socialization process, through which the youngster is expected to develop into a responsible citizen, does not work to good advantage in this situation.

c) One of the reasons for the restlessness of American adolescents in general is their relatively functionless status, and in a crowded city young people are likely to seek status in disapproved ways. In other societies, where the great majority of teen-agers become gainfully employed and are already started on their economic careers, juvenile delinquency is minimized.

d) It is a recognized fact that American youth seeks status through peer approval more than through parental approval. This means that the "natural authority" of the older generation is weakened, and the young person tends to follow the patterns of behavior of his contemporaries. The youth seeks an outlet in the gang and prefers the approval of the gang to that of his parents and family.

e) The confusion of behavior standards is highlighted in the juvenile gang. The schools and churches with which the youth has some contact represent to him a standard of behavior that seems unrealistic because it is so far out of line with what he sees in his everyday experiences. The propositions for the "better life" offered in the whole system of American advertising are also, to his mind, completely out of his reach. Many of the behavior patterns he sees around him every day are very different from those said to be in existence in the "outside world."

f) Meanwhile, the tremendous flood of movies, radio serials, comic books, pictures, and pulp magazines that portray crime and violence represents to the gang member a style of behavior that seems more suitable to his own life situation. The models of delinquent behavior, ostensibly censured by the society at large, are offered to him in detailed patterns of action performed in surroundings and by characters he recognizes. The youth certainly has access to the more "positive" representations in these media of communication and entertainment, but these often seem to him lifeless and unreal.

g) The lack of approved recreational facilities in the crowded urban areas is also a conditioning factor in the formation of gangs. Supervised recreation cannot be the single solution in a situation where all these other conditions exist. The fact is that the combination of boredom and tension is an important psychological factor in the formation of gangs and in the type of behavior which they pursue. Adequate playgrounds and meeting places, organized sports and dances, would help to relieve the tension and boredom.

It must be noted that the youth gang is simply a socially abnormal instance of the universally present primary group. There are leaders and followers in these gangs, a code of behavior which the members consider important, frequent and informal social relations, a feeling of belonging, an attitude which stresses the welfare of the group. These are in many ways intensified characteristics of the primary group.

5. Associations of American Labor

In some ways the United States is a highly organized society. We have seen the various bases upon which people tend to associate with one another, not only the major social groups found in every society, but also the various subgroupings peculiar to each society. Americans often form groups and join existing groups on the basis of similar economic function. People who are gainfully employed organize to protect their interest and to promote their particular function. This is as true for doctors, lawyers, nurses, and teachers as it is for manufacturers, distributors, white-collar workers, and industrial workers.

The American labor unions, as social groups, have some of the characteristics found in all organizations of gainfully employed people. But the term "labor union" appears to have been limited by social usage mainly to those who are organized manual workers. Teachers and social workers, bankers and doctors, for example, do not like to call their professional associations labor unions, even though one of the primary functions of these groups is the economic protection of their members.

Unlike the labor organizations of most other major societies, the American labor unions have limited themselves mainly to immediate economic gains. They have acted as pressure groups, have exerted political influence, have issued statements on most of the contemporary social and world problems. They have not, however, formed a political party and have no serious ideology other than that of the American capitalist system. They have no interest in "taking over" either economic or political management in the society or in establishing a proletarian and "classless" society.

Following are some of the features of American labor unions, which include in their membership a little more than one-fourth of all gainfully employed persons in our society:

a) The labor unions are secondary associations in which the social relations of members are largely standardized and impersonal. In any union local there are unquestionably primary groups made up of the most active and interested members, and in any national union the top officials in frequent contact with one another also form a primary group. But the very nature of large-scale industry in America has required a parallel large-scale organization of labor in which primary groups do not flourish.

b) Worker solidarity, the dedicated co-operation of members, is largely a myth in these unions. The aspirations of workers, like those of most other Americans, are directed toward higher social status and better material standards of living. The "middle-class mentality" of American workers has been the despair of Communist and socialist labor leaders. The worker has a certain loyalty to his union and is often willing to endure the suffering of strikes, but this loyalty appears to be built on gratitude for benefits received and on the hope of more to come, rather than on a personal attachment to, and solidarity with, his fellow workers.

c) The growth of bureaucracy within the large labor unions parallels that which exists in government and industry, and even in educational and religious structures in America. Policies are determined at higher levels and subordinate officials are expected to execute them. Bureaus of special functionaries have emerged so that the top officials are surrounded by labor lawyers and strategists, labor accountants and economists, public relations experts, and other specialists.

d) The democratic process has imposed peculiar difficulties on the maintenance of labor unions. The voter apathy characteristic of the American people is seen also in unions. Factory-wide and industry-wide voting on particular issues has been facilitated by the co-operation of management and government. But the conduct of local meetings and the election of officers are hindered by the mass apathy of workers. Labor leaders depend upon popular elections for their continuance in office. Unlike a salaried manager, they cannot dictate to their membership; they are constantly forced to "prove their worth" and must periodically test their position, like the politician, by "going to the people."

The labor unions, as a whole, are often thought of as a solid phalanx moving the country irresistibly closer to the socialist or welfare state. This opinion is generally held by people who do not realize that organized labor is a product of the American society and has developed alongside of other characteristic social structures. Opposition to unions is sometimes made by persons who pretend to be defending "free enterprise" and "rugged individualism" without realizing that these have long since disappeared from the American economic scene. The fact is that labor unions follow pretty closely the pattern of secondary associations as they have developed in the United States.

DISCUSSION QUESTIONS

1. What is the difference between the "origin of groups" and the "origin of group life"?
2. Explain the technical definition of the social group.
3. Give the various qualifying elements through which a person becomes a "group member."
4. Explain how all groups can be classified according to the characteristics of the definition of group.
5. Explain and give examples of the four common bases for group classification.
6. How can the major groupings be both universal and variable?
7. Show how the single essential social function of each is the principal means of distinguishing among the major groupings.
8. What is the main difference between primary and secondary groups?
9. How is the term "in-group" related to primary and secondary groups?
10. How does the secondary group differ from aggregates and categories?
11. Can a total society exist without primary groups? Explain.
12. What are the main factors contributing to the decline of American primary groups?
13. Explain the social structure of pressure groups.
14. Explain with examples the principal kinds of American pressure groups.
15. What accounts for the multiplication of women's clubs?
16. List the characteristics of the informal primary groups of American females.
17. What is the essential function of the youth gang? Explain.
18. What factors contribute to the formation of urban male youth gangs?
19. How do "professional" groups resemble labor unions?
20. List and explain the main features of American labor unions.

SUGGESTED READINGS

ANGELL, ROBERT C. *The Integration of American Society*. New York: McGraw-Hill Book Co., 1941, chap. iii.

COOLEY, CHARLES H. *Social Organization*. New York: Charles Scribner's Sons, 1915, chaps. iii–v.

DAVIS, KINGSLEY. *Human Society*. New York: Macmillan Co., 1949, chap. xi.

GILLIN, J. L., and GILLIN, J. P. *Cultural Sociology: A Revised Edition of an Introduction to Sociology.* New York: Macmillan Co., 1948, chaps. xi, xii.

LUNDBERG, G. A. *Foundations of Sociology.* New York: Macmillan Co., 1939, chap. ix.

MACIVER, ROBERT M., and PAGE, C. H. *Society: An Introductory Analysis.* New York: Rinehart & Co., Inc., 1949, chaps. xvi, xvii.

CHAPTER SIX

Society

In the previous chapters we have noted the many ways in which human beings are united with one another and the many points of view from which the same social person can be scientifically studied. People are thought of as united in various kinds of social categories. They are loosely associated in numerous social aggregates. People engage in various types of reciprocal relations in a number of different kinds of groups. The broadest technical meaning of the term "society" must include all these types of social units as subunits within society.

The older sociologists, who were social philosophers more than they were social scientists, studied and discussed society "in general." They made broad generalizations concerning human conduct and social forms drawn from mankind "as a whole." The modern sociologist is much more precise and modest in the limits of his science. He seeks to make the group the focus of his study and to build up general knowledge out of concrete situations and experiences.

This shift of emphasis in the study of society means that social science has gained in exactitude and that sociological generalizations now have a greater scientific validity. The real significance of this change of focus is that even society "as a whole" is now more clearly understood and more thoroughly studied than ever before. Proceeding from the particular to the general has always been essential to the scientific approach, and in this case it has succeeded in removing some of the vagueness from the broad sociological generalizations of an earlier day.

Society and Societies

Before analyzing the technical definition of society, it is useful for us to exclude confusing and misleading interpretations and usages of the term. For all practical purposes it is scientifically meaningless to define society as the total population of the world, as human society, mankind, or the human race. All human beings, of course, share certain characteristics which identify them as social persons, but this fact merely unites them in the broadest of social categories. It does not bring them together in any observable or measurable way.

There exist certain universal similarities in the different societies all over the world. The demonstrable existence of these universals (status, role, patterns, structures, relations, functions, and others) makes it possible to develop social science in the strict sense of the term. These generalized phenomena are present in widely separated and distinct societies. In each society they constitute a network, or social system, which is identified as an ongoing concern. The whole human race is not so constituted, and to speak of mankind as a world society is to attempt a meaningless extension of the technical term "society."

On the other hand, it is common usage in the English language to apply the word "society" to various secondary associations. One need not be a purist to appreciate the confusion this engenders, and one finds it in the most unexpected places. The American Sociological Society, like the Society for the Prevention of Cruelty to Animals, is in technical terminology an "association," a secondary grouping of persons pursuing definite social goals. The National Association for the Advancement of Colored People, like the National Association of Manufacturers, is more technically, and therefore more correctly, named.

It must be pointed out that there are numerous synonyms for the term "association" or "secondary group." Not only do the various "societies" fit this term, but many federations and unions and leagues are also secondary groupings. The Women's Christian Temperance Union, the League of Women Voters, the American Federation of Labor, and many other similar social organizations are secondary groups or associations, and not societies.

Definition of Society

Ultimately the irreducible physical unit of the society, as of the social aggregate and the social group, is the social person. From the point of view of the persons who constitute it, a society is the largest number of human beings who interact to satisfy their social needs and who share a common culture. This rough definition differentiates the society from the group since the latter embraces only a segment of a society and because the common culture of a society is much broader than that of a single person or group.

Pursuing this line of reasoning a little further, one may say generally that the group is made up of persons and the society is made up of groups. The study of any particular society focuses upon the groups rather than upon the persons. Since all persons in some way participate in all the major groups, it is obvious that all the basic groupings are interconnected. The personnel of any major group is roughly the same as that of any other major group. In enacting their social roles the people participate in all the primary and secondary associations that make up these major groupings. Thus a society may be defined as a network of interconnected major groups viewed as a unit and sharing a common culture.

Characteristics of Society

A more complete definition of society includes the following elements:

a) The people within the society constitute a demographic unit, that is, they can be seen as a total population. This does not mean that they are merely a large social category, although it is true that one of the valuable approaches to the understanding of any society is a study of its varieties of social categories.

b) The society exists within a common geographical area. In the highly organized modern world, this usually means that certain physical limits fix the boundaries of a nation in which a complete society exists. It is possible, however, that separate societies exist within a nation, so that the word "nation" is not synonymous with "society."

c) The society is made up of functionally differentiated major groups. There are, as we have seen, the six major groups of persons found in every society through which the basic social needs of the people are satisfied. It is obvious that a society cannot be made up of only schools, or only families, or only churches.

d) The society is composed of culturally similar groups of people. Usually they speak a common language, but the cultural similarity lies much deeper in general consensus on major and ultimate values.

e) The society must be recognizable as an over-all functioning unit. The total organized population is a dynamic going concern. There is a certain amount of co-operation, and the society can be said to act as a whole, even though, as mentioned above, there are internal functional differentiations.

f) The society must, finally, be recognizable as a separate social unit. This characteristic is probably implied in the other elements mentioned above, but it must be emphasized that each society is separate from all other societies. This separation is not necessarily and always a physical and territorial one.

The complexity of a society makes a simple definition meaningless, or at best confusing. If we combine the observations we have just made, we can, however, put the following definition into one sentence: A society is an organized collectivity of people, living together in a common territory, co-operating in groups to satisfy their basic social needs, subscribing to a common culture, and functioning as a distinct social unit.

Essential Functions of Society

When a society functions in a normal and adequate manner, things are done more efficiently and satisfactorily than they can be done by individuals alone. We know from our own experience that a person would be handicapped, slowed down, and frustrated if he were expected to do everything alone, without the aid of others. It is clear, therefore, that society exists for people. It has a number of general functions which operate throughout all of the more specifically defined functions such as those of the major groups. These *general* functions are as follows:

a) Society brings people together in time and place so that it is possible for them to have human relations with one another. This temporal and spatial condition is a prerequisite for the operation of society.

b) It provides a systematic and adequate means of communication among them, so that through language and other common symbols they are able to understand one another.

c) It saves time and energy for individuals by developing and preserving common patterns of behavior which the members of the society share and enact.

d) It provides a system of stratification of statuses and classes so that each individual has a relatively stable and recognizable position in the social structure.

The more *specific* functions of society revolve around the group response to the primary and basic social needs of people. Through the universal system of the major groups the society performs the following essential functions for the persons within it:

a) Society has an orderly and efficient way of renewing its own membership. Through courtship, marriage, family, and kinship groups it provides a systematic and approved way of bringing new human beings into its membership.

b) Society provides for the socialization, development, and indoctrination of its members through its patterned and organized system of formal and informal education.

c) In its various economic groups the society produces and distributes the material and physical goods and services needed to sustain the life of individuals.

d) The basic human need for external security and order is satisfied by society through its political administration and various civic groups.

e) The religious and spiritual needs of people are provided for in a social way by society through its various church groups.

f) Every society also contains social groups and systematic arrangements through which it provides relaxation and recreation for its members.

When we speak of a society's functions, we obviously do not mean to make any crude personification of society. From the point of view of the individual person, it is other persons acting out their roles and performing their multiple functions who are doing the things that society "does." The society is, after all, composed of people through whom it "helps" an individual to be born, raised, and educated. Without society he would not get adequate material support, political protection, or religious and recreational opportunities.

Structure and Function of Society

It has been customary for sociologists to distinguish between the static and dynamic aspects of society. For analytic purposes it is important to make this distinction, but for an adequate understanding of society we must realize that actually these two aspects are always together. Even when we study the so-called "static" aspect in social structures, we must realize that the structure is always "in movement" with regard to time, direction, and the persons within it. On the other hand, while functions are by definition dynamic, they are also necessarily structured, arranged, or ordered, and in that sense static.

The *structure* of a society refers to the arrangement of its parts or units. If we look at the total society as a composite of the major groups, we note that there is an orderly relationship and interdependence of these major parts. Thus we see that the whole structure, that is, the largest structure, is made up of these various interrelated, interdependent, and mutually responsive groupings. This view emphasizes order, arrangement, and organization; it tends to be static and fixed. In its complete analysis it discerns the status of the person within the various subgroups, the position of these subgroups in relation to the major groups, and the co-ordination of all of the major groups in the society.

If structure answers the question "How is society arranged?" *function* answers the question "What does society do?" This refers to the dynamic aspect of society—the social operations, processes, and activities. We have reviewed briefly the multiple general and specific functions of the society. The social groups that compose the society do many things, and they represent the society continuously changing, shifting, and developing, going on in time and space, and performing actions through, with, and for social persons.

The universally demonstrable fact that the total society is differentiated into the various major groups indicates that differentiation is essential. The specialization which develops within each of the major groups is further evidence of this fact. Trends toward "overspecialization" in both structure and function are often consciously counterbalanced by the people of a society when they attempt to co-ordinate and to integrate their social activities. Co-ordination is essential in the all-inclusive total society so that the various functions are fulfilled co-operatively and not at cross-purposes.

Classification of Societies

There are many ways of classifying societies, and each is probably valid according to the point of view from which society is discussed. Some of these require no great depth of analytical understanding; for example, if one places the known societies on a continuum of size, from the largest to the smallest, he is not learning a great deal about the society itself. It appears more meaningful to classify societies according to their rate of growth or decline: a rapidly increasing population has a quite different kind of society from one in which the population is rapidly decreasing.

On the more abstract level of important differences in societies, most social scientists agree that the principal distinguishing characteristic is the culture each society possesses. Societies are distinguished from one another more by their differing cultures than by their differing structures and functions. We shall discuss culture in some detail in subsequent chapters of this book. Society and culture are closely allied, and it is only by the process of abstraction that we can talk about them separately. A simple example of the cultural differences that distinguish two types of society is the comparison of the *preliterate* and the *literate* societies.

Classification by Literacy

Two "levels" of culture are indicated here. The preliterate society is often called the primitive society. All the major groups fulfilling the essential social functions are present, albeit in relatively simple and overlapping forms. The primitive or preliterate people communicate effectively through oral language; their great social handicap is that they do not have the use of a written language. They have no written records, and therefore the development of a formal educational system and the compilation of scientific information are very difficult.

The student of society must be careful not to base his understanding or explanation on any single factor, but it is obvious that literacy is an important factor in the classification of societies. Literacy is a major difference between the primitive and the civilized society. The literate society enjoys a tremendous advantage in its use of concrete symbols to preserve its ideas and its history. Even among literate societies, the varying degrees of development are often measured by the proportion of the population that can read and write.

Classification by Dominant Group

A more subtle and significant classification of societies is that which marks the dominance of one major group and institution over the others in the society. Even casual knowledge of the major world societies indicates that each is now, or has been in the past, one of the four following types:

(*a*) The *economic*-dominated society is one in which the businessman and the manufacturer have high social status; commercial and material values have great influence on the behavior of people; and more time and energy are spent in economic groups than in others. (*b*) The *family*-dominated society is one in which there are close kinship ties and great honor for the aged and deceased ancestors and where social status comes more from ancestry than from any other criterion. (*c*) The *religion*-dominated society is one in which the central focus is on the supernatural, on the relationship between God or gods and man, and in which the other major groups are accordingly subordinated to the religious. (*d*) The *political*-dominated society is that which is customarily called "totalitarian," in which power is monophasic and the state enters directly in the regulation of all other groups and institutions.

It must be obvious that in this classification we are speaking of the dominance and precedence of one major group and institution over the others. There can be no question of a society which is exclusively economic, or religious, or familial, or political. All of these, together with the educational and recreational groups, must somehow be present in every society. In some societies great emphasis is placed upon the leisure-time groups and activities, and high value is placed on education, but it is improbable that any total society has ever been dominated by either of these major groups.

Communal and Associational Societies

A still different classification of societies, also of great sociological relevance, is that distinguishing the *simple, communal* type, and the *complex, associational* type. From what we have said in the previous chapter, it is clear that the first is dominated by primary groups and the latter by secondary associations. This is not the same as the distinction between the preliterate and the literate societies, although it is true that the preliterate society tends also to be simple and communal, while the complex, associational type would not become highly developed unless it had the advantage of literacy.

The following elements characterize the simple, communal type of society, and from this list can be deduced the opposite characteristics which distinguish the complex, associational type of society.

a) The simple, communal society has little specialization and division of labor. In this sense it is preindustrial, subsisting mainly from some general occupation like farming, trapping, fishing, or cattle-raising. Most of the people gainfully employed engage in the same occupation, and many of the subsidiary maintenance functions are performed within the family circle.

b) Kinship ties are strong in this type of society; in fact, it is sometimes called a familistic society because of the importance placed upon the family as the center of most social activity. Often enough, it is a patriarchal society, and with this emphasis it is usual for older people to be given close attention and respect.

c) Although there is leadership and authority, and differential status based on age, sex, and function, the communal society has relatively little social stratification. There are criteria of social status, but there is little difference in the possession of those items upon which status depends.

d) Because there is minimum social mobility in the simple society, it is often called a closed society. Status tends to be fixed and relatively permanent according to family; the stranger finds it difficult to be accepted and is often looked upon with suspicion.

e) There is relatively strong social solidarity among the members of the simple society, especially in relation to other societies. Since their social functions are not highly specialized, the people are able to co-operate more easily in their performance.

f) The simple society tends to adhere to traditional values and to patterns of behavior inherited from the past. Thus social change is at a minimum, and innovations are difficult. Socialization of individuals is therefore less complicated, and problems of adjustment to the cultural environment are at a minimum.

g) The people in this type of society tend to be governed by informal custom more than by formal law. This does not mean that custom is more lax than law. The local political administration is unsophisticated and operates on a "sense" of what is right and wrong rather than on a carefully spelled-out reasoning process.

h) All of these characteristics indicate that the simple, communal society is relatively numerically small; it has little contact with the outside world and a great deal of permanency. It is likely that the characteristics we have described could hardly develop in a society only recently established, open to the cross-currents of strange and novel ideas, and growing rapidly in numbers.

It cannot be stressed too often that the distinction between the communal and the associational types of society is a matter of degree. For example, it is not a matter of presence, or absence, of stratification, mobility, and solidarity. These characteristics, and the others mentioned above, must be present in every society, but the manner, extent, and degree of their presence make it possible to recognize the difference between the two types of society.

The complex, associational society can be easily described by a list of characteristics in contrast to those given above. It tends to be mechanized and industrialized with a wide variety of occupational functions. People are mobile, both vertically and horizontally, because there are great variations in social status and their family ties are not enduring. Solidarity is less automatic and effective than in the simple society. An elasticity in values is accompanied by greater rigidity in the system of maintaining public order.

Community and Society

The term "community" is another of those sociological words which has come to have a variety of meanings. It is sometimes used interchangeably with words like "society," "city," "neighborhood," and even in expressions like the "Catholic community" or the "Negro community," to designate loose social categories in the larger cities. A word which is surrounded with multiple and careless meanings obviously requires careful technical definition: A community is a territorial group of people in reciprocal relations, using common means in the pursuit of common goals.

A community is only an organized segment of the total society, not a society in itself. When it is urban, it is only a part of the city, not the city itself. We have seen the difference between an urban spatial neighborhood, which is merely a social aggregate, and an urban social neighborhood, in which there exist systematic social relations. The latter is a community; and every large city contains many such social neighborhoods or communities.

A community is essentially "bound to the ground" in the sense that the people live permanently in a given area, have a consciousness of belonging to both the group and the place, and function together in the chief concerns of life. The community is always considered in relation to a physical environment. The community is essentially a cluster, or network, of smaller groups, but in its totality it can itself be identified in many ways as a large social group. The members of the community are conscious of the needs of people in and out of their immediate group, and they tend to co-operate closely.

Etymologically, a "neighbor" means a nearby inhabitant in a given place. The simple communal society is one in which most people live near to each other. Thus neighborliness is a characteristic of the communities in the rural, folk, and peasant society. It is not a common characteristic of the so-called urban, metropolitan, and national societies, which are complex and associational. To some extent, however, the term "community" still applies to "old" city neighborhoods in which the people still have similar ethnic, economic, and educational backgrounds and have lived together for a long time. The modern suburbs, which are "newer" neighborhoods, make a deliberate attempt to foster the community spirit among the people, and in some instances these, too, may be technically termed communities.

The community, however, is not exclusively an urban or suburban phenomenon. In fact, the community tends to be a stronger and more effective social system when it exists in small villages removed from urban complexities and specialization. The simple, communal type of society, which we have described above, is one in which the community flourishes. Here the people are more likely to co-operate in all of the major functions of social life, especially in economic pursuits.

This matter of basic economic co-operation is peculiarly absent from the urban social neighborhood and from the suburban community. In these latter places, the residents pursue their gainful occupations, for the most part, outside the community. The head of the family goes downtown, or to the city, to his job and there performs an economic role which is hardly related to the immediate interests of the neighborhood or community in which he lives. In spite of this difference, these places can still be identified as communities. In all other aspects of social life the people center their social relations and behavior in their own physical community. Homes, schools, churches, and recreational and civic facilities are located within a specific territory in which the community exists.

PECULIARITIES OF AMERICAN SOCIETY

1. Religion and Society

American social scientists have not undertaken thorough studies of religious groups in the way they have studied the remaining five major groups. Neglect of careful research in this area of study is probably due to two main reasons: first, the bewildering variety of religious groups and institutions as well as the large percentage of non-affiliated Americans and, second, the dominance of the economic institutions and groups, which gives the impression that religion is a negligible factor in social behavior and structures.

Religion and society are said to have a unique relationship in the United States. The frequent talk and writings about American "separation of church and state" seem peculiar to people in England, Sweden, and Spain, where there are state-established churches, and to people in Belgium, Holland, and Germany, where there are formal, contractual agreements between the state and the religious bodies. The American notion of separation between the religious and the political systems appears to be poorly understood even by many Americans.

The fact is that the religious groups are an integral part of the total American society and that the religious and political persons, functions, roles, and groups meet at many points. In order to put this relation between religion and society in clearer perspective, we may consider the following:

a) Although various statistics show that the organized religious bodies in America claim only about 60 per cent of the population as members, practically all Americans "affiliate themselves" to some form of religion. Only a very small percentage acknowledge themselves to be atheistic or irreligious or without any religion. This is not to say, of course, that most Americans are pious or that they frequently attend religious services.

b) Religion is held in high repute in official and public life; days of prayer are proclaimed; chaplains are appointed for military services. Politicians favor religious leaders and tend to curry favor from the main religious bodies. They try to avoid religious controversy; religion has not been an issue in a presidential campaign since the anti-Catholicism of 1928.

c) Religious affiliation is seldom an obstacle to economic success. There are, of course, personal preferences and prejudices at work in economic competition, but the general attitude in American business and professional life seems to be that "if a man does his job, it does not matter what his religion is." This is partly because of the deliberate emphasis on religious toleration and partly the consequence of a culture in which the economic institutions dominate all the others.

d) In spite of the multiple fragmentation of organized religion in the United States, there are certain religious beliefs common to the culture. Monotheism includes here the belief in a God who punishes and rewards human beings for their conduct here on earth; and there is some sort of general credence in salvation and the future life. There are also sacred notions, not necessarily supernatural, concerning the dignity and inviolability of the individual as well as his responsibility to God and to society.

e) In spite of this general acceptance of a basic core of religious beliefs, there are many doctrinal differences among the major religious groupings. This is actually more noticeable than the widely advertised separation of church and state. The difference between fundamentalists and liberals is in the interpretation of theology itself, while the difference between the progressives and the traditionalists is in the application of religion to life. These points of view reflect the varying approaches that are present everywhere in dynamic American society.

f) The general American values of pragmatism, optimism, and progressivism are also influential in most of the major religious groupings.

Individual churches are often handled like an enterprise which has to show by its books that it is succeeding. The concrete and the practical are shown in the emphasis on social service and morality over any deep concern with doctrinal and theological discussions, arguments, or sermons. The perfectibility of man is stressed much more than the sinfulness of man.

g) An important point is that in our pluralistic society people of differing religious affiliations meet and co-operate in all the major groups except religion. In other words, there is no exclusive identification of one religious body with one political party or with one economic system. The necessity for people of all religious bodies to participate in all the non-religious groups and to accept the mores in each of these brings about a social integration which cross-cuts any social solidarity based on religious values and beliefs alone.

Every college student can probably from his own knowledge and experience point out exceptions to each of the statements made above. Unquestionably, there are Americans who have a tendency to religious bigotry, refuse to associate with people of other religions, and condemn all who are not members of the religious in-group. There are sects which emphasize the sinfulness of man, decry materialistic culture values, and try to dissociate themselves from the "secular" society. These must be considered exceptions; they do not reflect the general trend toward a closer integration of religion into the American society and culture.

There are many other aspects of American social relations and groups which show that there is no unrealistic divorce between religion and society in America. It is true that our society is not dominated by religious groups, that the central sacred values tend to be only indirectly supernatural, and that a kind of secular expediency exists even in the religious bodies, but all this says is that religion in America is different from religion in other major societies. It means that the religious groups have been Americanized; it does not mean that they have been excluded from, or segregated within, the American society.

2. Regionalism and the American Society

It is a commonplace in any large country to identify a series of "sectional societies" within the framework of the larger national society. This is true also in the older European countries where regional idiosyncrasies have been imbedded in the local traditions and where there may be a continued adherence to local styles of clothing, forms of recreation, kinds of religious rituals, and even particular dialects. In the United States, too, we talk about types of Americans—the Texan, Midwesterner, New Englander, Southerner, Westerner, and others—as though these types of persons represented different cultures and belonged to different societies.

The specific characteristics that represent regional differences in other countries, like dress, religion, and language, are not reliable sociological indexes for an understanding of regional differences in the United States. Social scientists here have emphasized the ecological differences, that is, the relation of the people to the physical environment, and have based their comparisons mainly upon those material items which can be objectively quantified. This is not to say that each region so described can in a technical sense be termed a separate society.

The following points are important in considering the rapidly changing picture of American regionalism:

a) There is still a tendency to identify a region by the principal economic functions in the area. We speak about the Industrial North and the Cotton South, the Cattle States, the Corn Belt, the Wheat States. This indicates not only the kind of gainful occupation that the people pursue but also the main economic interest they have in relation to other parts of the country. It does not mean that the people in any particular area are exclusively engaged in these functions.

b) The spread of urbanism, in the sense of urban behavior patterns, is a tremendous factor in minimizing regional differences. This is, of course, a function of the communication and transportation systems, which reach out into all parts of the country. National networks of radio and television, movies, and magazines have tended to break down parochial and regional ideas; national networks of airlines, trains, and busses and the individual use of automobiles have brought each region physically closer to the others.

c) Mechanization has been a particularly significant factor in decreasing the economic differences between the cities and the rural regions. It has brought a change in the financial status of farmers and the eight-hour day to many farm laborers; it has facilitated the migration of surplus farm labor to industrial areas. In general, rationalization and specialization of labor have accompanied the mechanization of agricultural processes.

d) The kinds of minority categories which exist in different parts of the country have been a means of identifying regions. Human relations and social structures have been influenced by the presence of Negroes in the Southeast, French-Canadians in New England, Orientals on the West Coast, Germans and Scandinavians in the Midwest, Mexicans in the Southwest, and the Irish, Italians, and Jews in the metropolitan areas. The continuation of "mixed marriages" and the subsequent biological mingling of the people, as well as the migration of minority persons to other regions and their gradual rise in social status, are breaking down this regional identification.

e) The composition of the population from the point of view of age, sex, and marital status is strikingly different in the various regions of America. The Southeast still has a young population and one in which the rate of natural increase is great, as compared to other regions. The eastern industrial and commercial areas have an excess of marriageable females, while the big western farming areas have a surplus of young unmarried workers; and regions like southern California and Florida tend to attract older and retired persons.

f) It is probably still valid to distinguish regions on the basis of whether they are primarily communal or associational, although this distinction is gradually disappearing. Regions in which the population is predominantly urban tend to emphasize social relations in the secondary groupings, while those which are predominantly rural emphasize the primary groupings. But the associational character of American society is reaching out into all parts of the country, and this is becoming less a regional and more a national characteristic.

There are other indexes for the identification of regions, but they appear to be less valid. Traditionalism and conservatism are said to mark the agricultural and the southeastern regions, but there are many indications that these attitudes are no longer peculiar to one region alone. The political emphasis on "states' rights" in the Southeast has led to the erroneous assumption that states in other parts of the country do not insist upon their rights with equal practical vigor. In general it may be said that regionalism is not so significant or tradition-bound in the United States as in other major countries and that it is here moving fairly rapidly in the direction of a total and integrated American society.

3. "Society" in America

One of the most confusing and common misusages of technical sociological terminology is that which identifies "society" with the upper-class category and "social functions" with the type of meetings, parties, dances, teas, and weddings which are described on the "society page" of the daily newspapers. This is an unfortunate conflict between technical meanings and popular usages, and it is important for the student of social science to understand the difference between the two.

Upper-class "society" in the United States is a peculiar phenomenon which is not exactly duplicated in any of the major modern societies of our times. The emphasis placed upon it and the interest shown in it by many Americans are an indication of the actual existence of social stratification in our country. This emphasis and interest may appear odd in a society which also stresses egalitarianism, the democratic processes, and the movements of various groups and categories for equal rights.

Some of the distinctive features in the functioning of "society" in America are the following:

a) In the richest nation in the world there are very few persons who can be termed "the idle rich." There appears to be cultural disapproval of "doing nothing," and the adult American male would be embarrassed to have the reputation of being merely a "playboy." Even if his chief preoccupation is actually self-indulgence, he usually insists upon having a downtown office or a nominal position on a business board of some kind. Wealthy men of ability identify themselves with the foreign service, with government agencies, with philanthropic and civic organizations.

b) The use of titles of nobility, which persists even in European countries that have become democratic, is remarkable for its absence in the United States. These titles indicate distinguished ancestry, and, while Americans are conscious of ancestry as a criterion of social status, they do not recognize it with titles. There are not enough "descendants" of the "Mayflower" or of the American Revolution to make these distinctions socially realistic. Earned titles, like General, Governor, Professor, Doctor, and others, are of course in common usage, but they stress personal achievement rather than class identification, and they are not hereditary.

c) The criteria for acceptance into "society" are variable; they are not equally stressed in all parts of the American society. The criterion that is most often mentioned as an American ideal is that of personal, occupational achievement, which is undoubtedly also one of the main channels of upward mobility. The actual possession of inherited wealth, however, is considered in some social strata as more important than personal achievement. The care which upper-class parents take in scrutinizing the "proper marriage choice" of their children indicates that "pure lineage" is often more important than even wealth or achievement.

d) "Society" people are often identified by the modes of conspicuous consumption they can afford; through these they become known as "prominent society leaders." But upon analysis these activities—sponsoring or attending debuts, garden parties, opening nights, and so forth—are seen to be conservative and repetitive and fairly rigidly patterned. Daring innovations are not in good taste. This conservatism is reflected especially in the political and economic areas, in which these people are most often anxious to maintain the status quo.

e) While the actual social position of "society" people is attached mainly to the male head of the family, the maintenance externally of that position appears to be the concern of the adult females. Within certain limits it is the women who are the "social arbiters," the bearers and exhibitors of the family status, the guides of their menfolk in the intricacies of "society." It is an oft-repeated joke in American society, and not only in the upper class, that the woman has to coerce her husband to attend the opera, art exhibits, and other "cultural" programs.

f) Consultation of the social register, in which the names of "society" leaders are recorded, still persists in some places; but the gossip columnists and the editors of "society pages" are gradually replacing the social register as an index of the people "who count." These newspaper employees often have a thorough knowledge of the degree to which individuals actually possess the various characteristics that serve as criteria of social status.

It must be noted that the descriptions mentioned above are relative to time and place. The criteria of upper-class status and the manifestation of this status are given variable emphasis. The upper social strata of Charleston and New Orleans are recognizably different from those of Kansas City and San Francisco, and the "society people" in these areas differ again from those in Chicago and New York. It is probably true to say that density of population makes a difference in the immediate influence and actual leadership of these upper-class people. In the smallest towns they are not able to exhibit the characteristics of "society." In the middle-sized cities they probably enjoy much greater social power than in the large metropolitan areas.

4. American Society and International Relations

It was not until the first World War that the United States became a first-rate international power; and as a consequence of the second World War our country has achieved an even more influential role among the nations of the earth. In the long history of humanity this emergence of the American nation seems sudden and dramatic, and it has certain unique characteristics. The change has necessarily had an internal effect upon Americans, and it has helped to form and to re-adjust attitudes of other people toward us.

Americans are as favorably inclined as the people of other major societies toward the preservation of international justice, peace, and welfare. America, called the youngest of the nations, is in fact the oldest of the large, continuing democracies. However, the position of leadership is an unfamiliar one; thinking and dealing in international relations are still strange to most American citizens.

There is no technical sense in which we can speak of a world society. The United Nations is a secondary grouping, or association, of repre-sentatives of the major societies. American relations across national boundaries have existed for a long time, however; they are not only political but also economic, religious, educational, and recreational. Various kinds of international organizations of scientists, businessmen, professional men, students, and others have also tended to bring the people of America closer to those of other societies.

The following considerations are meant to throw into perspective the position of the American society in relation to other nations:

a) Americans have accepted only reluctantly the responsibility attached to the position of world leadership. The local pressure to "bring our boys back," not to "meddle in foreign affairs," not to "waste the taxpayers' money," is an indication of the intensely nationalistic attitudes of some Americans. This spirit of isolationism is not so strong or widespread as it once was, but it is still noticeable.

b) Threats from, or the fear of, external aggression contribute to social solidarity within a society. Americans have successfully met such threats and have had some of these fears in the so-called "cold war" with the Communist countries. Although the hunt for internal spies and traitors has aroused a certain amount of mutual suspicion and some cleavages, the general result of external threats has been to draw the American people into closer social cohesion.

c) Another important factor has been developing in the gradual internal integration of the United States society. This has been the integration of the social minorities, especially of the American Negroes. The acclaimed position of the American nation as the protagonist of democracy and of the dignity and rights of individuals has made us sharply conscious of social injustices toward these minorities. While it is true that increasing industrialization and urbanization were in themselves breaking down the discriminatory barriers, our position as the democratic model for the world has accelerated this change.

d) In a sense, world supremacy has been thrust upon us. Unlike most of the major societies which in the past have gained world ascendancy, the United States did not reach its present status of world leadership through direct conquest of other nations. It is true that we have used military force in our history, but our country has not been an "aggressor nation" in any large-scale way. For most of its history the American society has been concerned about consolidating its internal structure, developing its resources, and populating its frontiers, so that it has tended to "mind its own business" in relation to foreign societies.

e) The American society has had no need of colonies either for economic exploitation or for population expansion; the American people generally have abhorred the notion of imperialism. The fact that Hawaiians and Alaskans enjoy most of the rights of American citizenship and that their territories are being seriously considered for statehood, and also the fact of Cuban and Philippine independence, are indications of the general reluctance of Americans to develop any practical and formal system of colonialism. This attitude in international relations reaches back to the status of the early American colonies, the revolutionary war of independence, and the Monroe Doctrine in protection of Central and South American republics.

f) A most important official attitude in international relations is the American program in aid of "backward peoples." This program is based on the conviction that prosperous and contented people do not foment unrest or submit themselves to "subversive" influences. It is based also on the economic hypothesis that prosperous international trade cannot exist between poor nations and rich nations when the latter merely exploit the former. In simplest form it may be said that Americans believe that what technological progress has done for America it can do for any nation.

There is a certain amount of ethnocentrism in some of the international attitudes of Americans. Pride in the fact that people of differing nationality backgrounds have been able to get along more or less peacefully leads some naïve Americans to ask, "Why can't those Europeans stop fighting each other?" The United States is the largest democratic society the world has ever seen. While nations with smaller populations, like Switzerland and Canada, have been equally, if not more, successful democracies, many Americans tend to identify democracy with our country. They are boastful of our success, and they see no reason why we should not help others to imitate us.

5. Complexity of American Society

The complexity of an object refers to both its structure and its functions. A child's toy airplane may be pressed out of a single piece of metal and it may not fly; an actual airliner is an intricate mechanism of many parts, and it has multiple functions. A simple, agrarian society is said to have relatively few "parts" in its social structure and to have relatively generalized functions shared by most of its people. A complex industrial society, on the other hand, has multiple stratification of statuses, classes, and forms. Its functions are numerous and specialized, and each person tends to focus his time and energy on his own key role in the society.

The beginning student in social science often has difficulty in understanding this point in reference to American society. He sees that many actions are simplified in modern urban life. He goes to the supermarket and exchanges his money for a loaf of bread, a can of corn, and a carton of sliced bacon. He reflects that this is much simpler than the many actions his grandparents had to perform in growing the wheat, corn, and hogs and in processing them before they were edible. Many other examples show how simple life is today: travel by air, communication by telephone, easily available means of recreation, and a clear-cut educational system.

This simplification of the individual actions of people would be impossible, however, without the complexity of modern society. An intricate system of interdependent actions lies behind the placing of any packaged commodity on the shelves of the supermarket. This involves financing at every step of the way, communication and transportation, advertising and marketing, as well as the actual physical and mechanical labor of numerous specialized persons. A complicated system of interdependent actions must also occur before the customer has money in his hand with which to purchase the product.

While economic processes are a good example of complexity, one should not forget that a complex society is complex in all its major groups and institutions. The following is a brief indication of the fact that complexity pervades the whole American society:

a) The political groups in our society, especially the federal government, exhibit a tremendous amount of complexity. Efforts at simplifying the government have been directed toward the elimination of so-called fringe functions and the co-ordination of various bureaus. The term "bureaucracy" is usually applied politically, although it exists in all the major social groupings. The need to guide and to regulate the giant associations and structures of our society has itself resulted in a supercomplexity of government.

b) The economic groups are so obviously complicated that they hardly require a demonstration here. The division and interdependence of labor in the processes of gathering raw materials and manufacturing and distributing them to the consumer have become more and more specialized and detailed. The complicated problems of the giant corporations are matched by those of the giant labor unions. Plans for the future and files on the past are essential adjuncts to a capitalist economy, and they add also to its complexity.

c) The educational system in the American society is also highly complicated. New means of socialization—television, radio, and printed materials—as well as the shifting and expansion of youthful peer groups have added to the problems. Specialization reaches down into the elementary schools, is seen in the variety of curriculums in high schools, and achieves its most complicated forms in the university and graduate systems. The various associations of schools and colleges and of profesisonal educators and the development of technical, trade, and adult systems present a bewildering array of educational groups.

d) Recreation, which on the surface appears a simple matter of relaxing and having a good time, is also increasingly complex in the American society. The great variety of commercial entertainment implies an intricate system by which this is presented and sold to the public. The attempt to distinguish between professional and amateur athletes presents problems even in the field of collegiate sports. The practice of leaving home for a two- or three-week vacation involves tremendous competition among resort places in attracting travelers and vacationers.

e) The religious bodies, peculiar in their numbers and diversities in the American society, are also highly complex. The number of different cults, sects, denominations, and churches is greater than in any other major society in the world. Systems of worship range from the simplest to the most elaborate. The problems of internal administration in the largest religious bodies have become so numerous and complicated that they require trained, scientific management.

f) It is a commonplace that life in the American family has changed tremendously since grandfather's day, moving from simplicity to complexity. The multiple common functions once performed as a group in the large kinship circles are now performed by individuals, many of whom are agents for parents. Tensions and strains in the conjugal family come largely from the increased demands placed upon the individual by economic, civic, recreational, and other agencies. There are many complicated decisions that must be made concerning children in their schooling, extracurricular activities, physical training, and choice of vocation and occupation. Various social relations and functions must be constantly maintained with persons outside the family.

This brief survey is a mere indication of the tremendous complexity of American society as a whole. Complexity is not synonymous with confusion; American society tends to take a deliberate and scientific approach to the individual functions and structures. There is a general recognition by Americans that multiplication and differentiation must be accompanied by interdependence and co-ordination. A serious breakdown in one major group, like the economic depression of the thirties, affects drastically all the other major groups. Thus, complexity is not something random, haphazard, or confused. It is orderly and intricate and requires social competence, adaptability, and knowledge on the part of Americans.

DISCUSSION QUESTIONS

1. Is the term "world society" technically correct? Explain.
2. Distinguish between a secondary group and a society.
3. Give and explain the complete definition of society.
4. Distinguish between the general and the specific functions of society.
5. What is the difference between structure and function of society, and how do these relate to the dynamic and static aspects of society?
6. List the various bases upon which societies can be classified.
7. What is meant by classification by literacy? By dominant group?
8. List the characteristics of the communal type of society.
9. Why is there not in every case a sharp contrast between the communal and the associational types of society?
10. Give some examples of, and explain, the erroneous use of the term "community."
11. In what sense is community synonymous with social neighborhood?

12. Why have American social scientists made little study of religious bodies?
13. What is meant by the "unique relationship" between religion and society in America?
14. Explain the elements contributing to the rapidly changing picture of American regionalism.
15. How do the sociological and non-technical meanings of "society" differ?
16. What are the distinctive features of "society people" in America?
17. What items highlight the position of America in relation to other large societies?
18. Discuss: "Modern life has become more simplified, but modern society has become more complicated."
19. Give the major evidences that the American society is highly complex.

SUGGESTED READINGS

BENNETT, JOHN W., and TUMIN, MELVIN M. *Social Life, Structure and Function.* New York: Alfred A. Knopf, Inc., 1948, chap. xi.

BOGARDUS, E. S. *Sociology.* New York: Macmillan Co., 1949, chap. iv.

HERTZLER, J. O. *Society in Action.* New York: Dryden Press, 1954, chap. ii.

ODUM, HOWARD, and MOORE, HARRY. *American Regionalism.* New York: Henry Holt & Co., 1938.

SANDERS, IRWIN T. (ed.). *Societies around the World.* New York: Dryden Press, 1953.

WISSLER, CLARK. *An Introduction to Social Anthropology.* New York: Henry Holt & Co., Inc., 1929, chap. ii.

The previous section has given us only a partial view of group life. Sociology would be a static science if it studied only what social persons *are;* it must study also what these persons *do.* One must be able to abstract and generalize the patterns of behavior performed by the people in the society. In this part we proceed from the minimum unit, the culture pattern, through the various ways in which it is combined with other patterns to form the total culture.

We study first the observable, measurable, and external patterns (chap. vii), then the covert, conceptual patterns (chap. viii), and the various types of human relations and processes (chap. ix). Then we analyze the manner in which patterned behavior combines into roles (chap. x), develops further into various institutions (chap. xi), and finally constitutes the total culture itself (chap. xii).

PART **II**

Patterns and Culture

CHAPTER SEVEN

External Behavior Patterns

The study of sociology as a science is possible only because people in society think and act in certain similar *patterned* ways. A pattern is anything shaped or formed to serve as a model or guide in forming something else. The behavior pattern is shaped or formed through the constant repetition by many people of the same item of behavior. A personal habit is formed when an individual constantly repeats the same act in the same way. Analogously, we may say that when many people in a society do the same thing in relatively the same way over a long period of time there develops a "social habit." This repetitive way of thinking and acting is a cultural pattern.

People go to church on Sundays, they eat three meals a day, they buy automobiles on the instalment plan, they stand at attention when the national anthem is played. These are a few of the myriad patterns of behavior that constitute the total culture. The people keep doing these things in the same way because that is the way they learned that these things should be done. We define the behavior pattern briefly as a uniformity of acting and thinking that regularly recurs among a plurality of people. It is the basic and irreducible unit of roles, institutions, and cultures. It is the generalized, standardized, and regularized behavior of people that serves as a model or guide for what is acceptable and what is not acceptable conduct in any society.

For a meaningful analysis of patterns of behavior it is necessary to make the distinction between overt, directly observable patterns, which we discuss in this chapter, and covert, indirectly observable patterns, which we discuss in the next chapter. Sometimes the former are called behavioral or action patterns and the latter, mental or attitudinal patterns. Since the human being is a whole person, it is often difficult to make clear-cut distinctions between his "inner" and his "outer" behavior. His conduct is the behavior of the total person, and it is only for purposes of analytical understanding that we distinguish between external and internal patterns of behavior.

Patterns and Persons

The sociologist is directly concerned only with the patterned regularities of human conduct and not with those of subhuman or brute animal beings. Instinctual regularities of the so-called gregarious behavior of animals do not serve as a model or preview of human behavior patterns. Culture exists nowhere except among human beings. The ability of even highly trained animals to perform a repetitive pattern of tricks is at best a mere caricature of the ability of human beings to participate in social behavior.

We have said that the person is the irreducible unit of groups and societies and that the behavior pattern is the irreducible unit of institutions and culture. We do not find patterns in existence except where there are persons enacting them. Persons and patterns are essentially linked, but it is necessary to abstract from the concrete situation and to analyze them separately. We have already done this in our study of persons, categories, groups, and society. Similarly, we analyze behavior patterns independently of the individual persons who perform them.

It can be said that the individual human being "comes and goes," while the culture endures. The sum of the behavior patterns in any society forms a kind of cultural heritage into which the newborn infant enters and which the individual leaves behind him when he dies. If a whole society were wiped out, its culture would also die. Any particular culture exists only in and through human beings, but no particular human being is essential to the culture. Because the culture endures longer than any individual person, it is possible to speak of behavior patterns as though they existed independently of persons.

This abstraction from the concrete human being is further illustrated by the distinction between behavior patterns which are individual and those which are cultural. The social scientist is not interested in *everything* that the human being does. He studies only the nomothetic patterns, that is, the general and social regularities shared in by many, rather than the idiosyncratic patterns, the peculiarly personal habits of individuals. A study of the nomothetic patterns makes possible scientific generalizations, laws, and even predictions in social behavior.

There are many forms of behavior that become regularized and customary in the individual person but are not cultural patterns. Sleeping or eating is an unlearned biological pattern shared by all people, but it is not in itself cultural. Yawning, crying, laughing, perspiring, and similar patterns of behavior are frequently responses to the physical and cultural environment, but they are not the kind of social behavior we study here. There are also developed personal habits, such as sleeping on one's left side or one's right side, putting on the right shoe before the left, and eating one type of cereal or vegetable rather than another. These are patterned uniformities of behavior in the individual, but they are not cultural uniformities.

The external behavior pattern, more fully defined, is an (*a*) observable and measurable, (*b*) frequently recurring action, (*c*) shared in by many people, and (*d*) possessed of some social significance. For example, while sleeping is a physical necessity performed by all people, the use of beds, with mattresses and springs, and the custom of retiring before midnight are cultural patterns. Similarly, while eating is a common and universal human experience, using knives and forks rather than chopsticks, carrying food to the mouth with the right hand rather than the left, using napkins and placing them on the lap rather than around the neck are culturally developed patterns.

The Range of Patterns

Cultural patterns like ways of sleeping and eating are mentioned only for purposes of demonstration and clarification. There are vast differences in the social significance of patterned behavior; not all forms of social conduct are of equal importance either to the individual or to the society in which he lives. The degree of significance of any behavior pattern can be measured by three elements: *universality*, or the amount and degree of conformity; *social pressure*, or the degree to which society sanctions the behavior in question; and *social value*, or the importance the society places upon it. The person is greatly influenced to do those things everybody else is doing, the things society considers so important that it will punish those who do not conform and award those who do.

No one of these three elements is the sole index of the importance of a cultural pattern. For example, almost all Americans eat with their right hand and almost all Europeans with their left hand. While there is a kind of "pressure by example" to conform to the pattern, it is not so highly valued that a violator will be visited with dire penalties. Attending Sunday church services is a highly valued behavior pattern in Christian countries, but it is probable that less than half the adult Christian population performs this action regularly, and in general there appears to be no widely applied social pressure to do so.

Principal Types of Patterns

Social scientists have defined three rough categories of external cultural patterns and identified them by the terms "mores," "folkways," and "usages." These classifications are at best a rough division of behavior patterns ranging from the most important, compulsive, and universal, to the least important, compulsive, and universal. The dividing line among these three categories is often fuzzy because there are also variations within each category. Some patterns appear to overlap two categories when judged by the criteria that social scientists employ. Some changing or shifting patterns cannot always be exactly pinpointed on the continuum from the strongest mores to the weakest usages.

a) Mores are usually defined as the "must-behavior" of a society, the basic and important patterns persons follow because they feel obliged to do so. They are considered essential to the welfare of society. For example, acts of loyalty and patriotism are valued so highly in modern society that the traitor is looked upon with horror and loathing. The proper care and treatment of children are considered so important that the kidnaper, the molester of little children, and the mother who abandons or neglects her children are heavily penalized. Religious worship is so highly respected (even though many do not formally practice it) that the person who desecrates a religious site is considered guilty of a terrible crime.

b) Folkways are widely practiced patterns of behavior that are less obligatory than the mores. They are considered the "thing to do"; they are taken for granted as highly desirable cultural patterns, but there is no strict enforcement of them. For example, large numbers of weddings are performed at a church service and are followed by a reception for the bride and groom and by a honeymoon, but these three behavior patterns are not essential to the welfare of the society. The wearing of a wedding ring by a married man is perhaps becoming a folkway, while the married woman's wedding ring has almost the strength of the mores. The pressure that brings about conformity to folkways is usually a negative and informal kind, like ridicule, sneering, snubbing, and gossip.

c) Usages are the least compulsive of the external patterns of social behavior. Most of them revolve around the various etiquettes and conventions current in a society. They are proper and fitting rather than obligatory. Following are examples of cultural usages that have no great binding force but are widely practiced: the metaphorical reference to bodily functions, especially near children; the addressing of even casual acquaintances by first names; the tipping of the hat to adult women by men; and the shaking of hands among men.

Variations in Behavior Patterns

The study of external social behavior is complicated by the dynamic aspect of any culture. It is clear from what we have said about the indexes of universality, social pressure, and social value that there is no immutability or absoluteness about behavior patterns. We have seen that the intensity of each of these indexes varies in the range of patterns from mores, through folkways, to usages. There are other perspectives from which this relativity of cultural patterns can be viewed. These are the variations of behavior in the time, place, and social stratum in which they occur.

a) Temporal changes in cultural patterns are best observed in large dynamic societies. Mores are always durable and traditional, but even they show occasional additions and fluctuations. For example, driving a car on the right-hand side of the road was probably a folkway during the early days of the automobile, but orderly street traffic has become so vitally important that this practice has become one of the mores. A shift in the other direction is that of Monday washday, which has probably been reduced from a folkway to mere usage. Gainful occupation of married women, divorce and remarriage, buying on the instalment plan, extension of public education, and annual vacation with pay for wageworkers are all examples of shifting behavior patterns over a period of time.

b) Regional variations in social behavior indicate the presence of fairly well-defined subcultures within even a relatively well-integrated society. The term "local custom" alludes to this fact. It does not refer to the differences of culture between two places like Germany and Japan, or Ireland and Mexico, but to differences within the same society. Patterns of recreation differ regionally between rural and urban areas. Segregation of the sexes in high school occurs in some places and not in others. Patterns of racial segregation vary greatly from one place to another.

c) Social patterns also vary according to social strata. In general, it may be said that middle-class people in America, defined by the criteria we have already discussed, are those who best recognize, accept, and conform to standardized patterns of behavior. In considering class variations, however, the degree of conformity is not so important as the kind of patterns performed. For example, attendance at symphonies and concerts and operas is not a widespread behavior pattern in the lower strata of society. Playing golf and belonging to a country club are folkways among rising young business executives and upper-middle-class families.

Patterns Are Non-Rational

Patterned and repeated behavior of any kind is a convenient short cut in the conduct of human life. We are all "creatures of habit," and this simple fact adds tremendous efficiency to our actions. If there were no patterned conduct, personal and social, the whole process of living would be slowed down and would probably become psychologically unbearable. Cultural patterns are, as it were, "ingrained" in the people and do not require rational forethought or afterthought. They are the rote actions of the people. Children pick them up almost subconsciously so that when they mature they think of them as things that "come naturally."

This does not mean that cultural patterns are unreasonable or irrational. The term "non-rational" indicates that they are performed without much reflection or deliberation. People are aware of the proper modes of behavior, and elders in the society make a conscious effort to teach them to the youngsters. But the individual does not have to stop, reflect, choose, and invent the manner in which he is going to respond to every social situation. Cultural patterns are the ready-made responses existing in the society. The individual has learned them through imitation and suggestion; he respects them because there is weighty tradition and social authority behind them, and he performs them as though they were "second nature" to him.

We must repeat here that we are talking about external social customs, not personal habits. It must be obvious that these recurrent uniformities of behavior—mores, folkways, and usages—are in essence the customary patterns of the society. Unlike personal habits, they are regularized and standardized and shared by many people, but like personal habits they are learned, repeated, and developed. By and large it is almost as difficult for the person to change his social customs as it is to change his personal habits. Once they have been acquired by the individual in the society, they persist and endure. This persistence and durability are, of course, strongest in the mores and weakest in the usages.

Ideal and Real Patterns

All patterns of behavior are real in the sense that they exist, are recognizable, can be studied and analyzed. Nevertheless it has become customary among social scientists to define the "ideal" patterns as those that are *expected* of the people, and the "real" patterns as those the people *actually perform*. Everyone knows from his own experience that principles of conduct, the way things *ought* to be, do not always match up with the actualities of conduct, the way things *are*. This means that there exists social and cultural deviation. The expressed ideals of the society are not always and everywhere practiced by every member of the society.

The distinction between the ideal and the real patterns is not the distinction between internal, covert patterns and external, overt patterns of behavior. There are ideals on both levels, and we shall discuss this in greater detail in the chapter on social values. For example, among the covert behavior patterns in a Christian society there is the ideal and expected pattern of belief in monotheism; but there exist people in this society who hold a real pattern of belief in atheism, polytheism, or pantheism. Similarly on the level of overt, external behavior in a democratic society there exists an ideal and expected pattern of racial equality, but in this same society there exist people who practice patterns of racial discrimination.

The distinction between ideal and real patterns of behavior is not fixed and permanent. Custom reinforces custom. The real patterns of behavior that people perform over a long period of time are likely to become ideal patterns. This again is a question of social change we shall discuss in a later chapter. The subtle fact is that the expectations of behavior are contained in the behavior patterns themselves, so that individuals in society tend to conform to that which is done by large numbers of other people.

Patterns as Norms of Behavior

The terms "behavior pattern" and "behavior norm" are closely allied. Up to this point we have been stressing the fact that the pattern is something "shaped or formed" by recurrent actions of large numbers of people. The behavior pattern, however, is not only a form of conduct; it is also a rule, or norm, of conduct. The normative aspect of the pattern lies in the fact that it is used as a model or guide in "forming something else." It is an elementary fact of logic that the same object can be looked at from different points of view and can serve different purposes. The ways of acting are, from another point of view, the norms of acting.

This is no mere exercise in logic or play on words. We have already seen that the strength of the pattern, its permanence and durability, is measured by the three indexes of universality, pressure, and value. This variation of "strength," or importance, is also recognized when the pattern is viewed as a norm. The behavioral norm is, therefore, a rule, standard, model, or type according to which people are expected to perform repetitive actions in society. It is the standard against which any person can measure his social behavior.

The mores, which are the strongest patterns of behavior, are also the most important norms guiding social conduct. Folkways and usages are also standardized expectations of behavior but are not so imperative. In this respect, patterns are, or ultimately become, accepted norms of conduct, and they tend to become a large part of the normative system of any society. They are the rules of action to which most people subconsciously respond in doing what is right and proper in any social situation.

Explicit and Implicit Norms

The behavior pattern is, therefore, an *implicit* norm of conduct because its universal performance indicates universal, subconscious acceptance and brings about a social pressure so that people conform to it. These implicit behavioral norms, however, do not constitute the total system of regulations governing social conduct.

There exist also certain *explicit* behavioral norms in every large, modern society. These are found in the formal body of laws, promulgated and enforced throughout the society, and in the clearly stated formulations of ethical principles every society shares among its members. It would be a serious scientific error to suggest that these laws and principles are "nothing more" than ideal behavior patterns or that they simply evolved out of the institutionalized customs of the society. In many instances formal laws are promulgated precisely for the purpose of changing long-standing real patterns of behavior. In the United States, the so-called "labor laws" and the "race laws" are examples of this.

The principles of social conduct about which experts in ethics speak are based on what is right and wrong and not merely on the fact that large numbers of people have acted for a long period of time in certain similar ways. Unless a culture is seriously disorganized and a society on the verge of disintegration, there is always a certain consistency and co-ordination between the explicit legal and ethical norms of behavior and the implicit patterned norms of behavior.

The obligatory norms of social conduct must therefore be seen under a twofold aspect: (*a*) consciously formulated laws, principles, rules, and maxims that emerge from rational deliberation and are explicitly offered and identified as behavioral standards, and (*b*) non-rational and subconsciously accepted norms that are imbedded in the recurrent uniformities of action approved by the society. The latter more often and more deeply influence actual social behavior than do the former. All the informal, primary, face-to-face groups in any society operate on the latter, while the explicit laws and written regulations appear mainly in the larger, secondary associations of people.

Behavior Patterns Are Structured

It must be clear from what has been said that patterns of behavior are not just a list of random items that occur and recur with some regularity. Social behavior is structured or organized. The various items of behavior are interrelated and co-ordinated; they fit together. This structure is shown in the following explanations that may serve as both a review and a preview of the conceptual framework employed in this sociological analysis.

a) Behavior patterns are structured within any given social role. For example, all the separately recognizable parts of the mother's role, whether it is feeding the child, dressing him, planning for his nursery school, teaching him to walk and talk—all these are co-ordinated in the function of child care. The role is thus a sense-making combination of behavior patterns that must necessarily be internally co-ordinated and interrelated.

b) The so-called role relations also demonstrate the structure of behavior patterns. This structural aspect is seen in the relations of husband and wife, mother and child, teacher and student, employer and employee, doctor and patient, mayor and citizen, and others. If behavior were not co-ordinated within the social role of each person, and if the individual did not recognize, and reciprocate with, the corresponding behavior patterns, any systematic arrangement of social life would be unthinkable and impossible. The doctor who deals with his patient as an employer deals with his employee would soon have no more patients; the husband who treats his wife as a lawyer treats his client would probably soon have no wife.

c) The principal social processes or important types of social inter- action also show the structural aspect of behavior patterns. While it is true that social patterns are enacted by the individual, they are most often performed with one or more other persons. The social process of friendly co-operation illustrates this fact. There are certain minimum requirements, ways of acting and thinking, "rules of the game," which constitute friendship and which are already existing in the culture before two persons meet and become friends. Each person "senses" the expectations of these behavior patterns, realizes that they interlock, and if he wants to be a good friend he fulfils them.

Another illustration is that of competition, which is a highly valued social process in the American culture. Even competitors who are friends know that competition differs from friendship; and the differ- ence is found in the patterns of behavior which constitute each. The content of the competitive process is the combination of mores, folk- ways, and usages that are enacted by each competitor acting and re- acting to the other.

d) External behavior patterns are further organized and system- atized into institutions. For example, the various behavior acts that occur regularly at a religious worship service are co-ordinated with one an- other and are directed toward the goal of the religious institution. This is true even though many of the generalized actions and movements may not be fully understood by the participants. In the political sphere, campaigning and voting and law enforcement are institutionalized, and all the actions that constitute these three forms of political behavior are structured in a co-ordinated way.

e) Finally, culture is the organized total structure of all the behavior patterns of the people. The learned social behavior of a whole society constitutes a "pattern of living" of the people. Structure or organiza- tion is inherent in the very notion of behavior pattern. We shall study the larger aspects of this structure in subsequent chapters of this book.

AMERICAN ACTION PATTERNS

1. Some Political Patterns

Political behavior has become institutionalized in the United States. Politics in our country is much more standardized and regularized than most foreign observers realize. We are often called a "young nation," but our political system is older than that of most contemporary countries. Second, we have consistently been a country with only two major political parties. Third, the successful operation of political "machines" has become part of our national life. These three factors have added tradition and durability to the American political institution.

Certain political customs appear to be characteristic of American external behavior patterns. The most curious of these is political apathy. In a country where education is compulsory, the literacy level high, democracy greatly valued, and suffrage almost universally available, there is a relatively small participation of voters in elections. Apathy at the polls may be an expression of the freedom to vote or not to vote. No law compels Americans to vote, and there are probably many Americans who would not admit to a moral obligation to vote.

Voting behavior appears to follow several patterns; and the following statements are a rough summary of reliable research material about them. They are, however, a description rather than an explanation of voting patterns.

a) People of higher education tend to vote more regularly than those of less education. Better-educated people often have greater interest in and knowledge of the issues involved in elections. The act of registering and voting is in itself not complex and requires no higher education. This is especially true in an increasing number of urban places where voting machines have been installed.

b) People with higher incomes vote more frequently than those with lower incomes. While the vote of a poor man has equal weight with that of a wealthy man, it appears that the latter has a greater economic stake in his country and a greater incentive to preserve it. It is true, of course, that the higher the income scale, the fewer voters there are, and thus the numerical weight of lower-income votes is far greater.

c) Men vote more consistently than women. This is both proportionately and numerically true, even though there are more and more women of voting age as compared with men. The traditional notion that politics is not a "woman's business" is to some extent still prevalent. In spite of the enfranchisement of women and their wider participation in social and cultural activities, their interests are still for the most part non-political.

d) Urban residents vote proportionately more than rural residents. Education and income partially account for the difference, and also campaigns are more intensely waged and voting places more accessible in towns and cities. Political issues are more sharply drawn in the large centers of population, and a greater effort is made by the political parties to "get out the vote."

e) The majority of voters vote repeatedly and regularly for the same party. In national elections the Democratic party gets into power at one time and the Republican party at another time because there exists in America a relatively small number of voters who switch from one party to the other. These so-called independent voters are therefore an important minority category in the American population.

f) Party allegiance often "runs in families." A sort of tradition of voting exists in families and is handed down from father to son. As might be expected, husband and wife also tend to vote for the same party.

g) More than half the eligible voters do not exercise their franchise in state and local elections. It is only in national elections that the proportion of voters goes higher than 50 per cent. The proportion of nonvoters is extremely high in several southern states where many Negroes are prevented from voting, where the population is largely agricultural and the literacy rate and the level of education are low.

There are several other patterns of negative behavior that distinguish the American voting institution. Unlike many other countries, most American voters do not identify themselves with one major party because of their national background, religion, political philosophy, and economic status. Except in the Southeast, where the Democratic party is in effect the only party, neither major party can claim the allegiance of voters on these grounds. It is probably true that in some localities urban Catholic workers vote for the Democratic party and in other localities Protestant businessmen and farmers vote for the Republican party; but this is by no means a nation-wide phenomenon.

2. Patterns of Lawlessness

American urban society has become notorious for its widespread pattern of lawlessness, exemplified by delinquency, crime, racketeering, and syndicates. At this point we are not concerned with lawlessness as a social problem but with the fact that these practices appear to conflict with the basic statements we have made about normative patterns of behavior. The point of confusion for the beginning student is that criminal behavior, even though it is patterned, is inconsistent with approved norms and guides of social behavior.

Most Americans are law-abiding most of the time. People are conformists in most of their activities; if this were not true, an organized and orderly society would be impossible. The possibility of a continuing and functioning society is predicated on the fact that most people act and think in expected patterns. The patterns of habitual criminals and of people who commit occasional lawless acts are most of the time like those of everyone else in society. There are, however, certain consistencies of behavior that set the criminal apart from other persons. Some of these are as follows:

a) The criminal follows norms of behavior. He is lawless only in the sense that he consistently disregards some of the legal norms the society at large accepts and approves. In his world, he is expected to remain secretive about himself and others and to look down upon the police informer or "stool pigeon." He is expected to honor his word and to treat fellow criminals with respect and appreciation.

b) Only a small proportion of career criminals are lone wolves. In other words, crime is often socially organized. This organization is present not only in the large-scale gangs that traffic in dope and other illicit merchandise but also in the human relations which exist wherever two or more criminals work together. There is a reciprocity and interdependence among these people, even when they join only temporarily to do a single job.

c) The professional criminal specializes. He becomes successful and proficient in some kind of activity he has repeated many times. This is why it is possible for the police to "type" criminals and, ironically, to catch them more easily. Success in one line of endeavor creates certain observable consistencies that the police come to expect of the individual criminal. They do not search for a swindler among bank robbers and burglars.

d) From an institutional point of view crime is an economic pattern of behavior. The major incentive for the criminal is economic gain, a way of making a livelihood. Crimes resulting from the personal vice of habitual drunkards, dope addicts, and sex offenders are not included in this consideration of professional criminals. The explanation of the lawlessness of these deviants is probably found in psychological rather than in economic motives. Career criminals are therefore mainly identified by crimes against property and secondarily by crimes against persons.

e) Criminal behavior is a cultural product, the result of social experiences. Criminals exchange information, the young man learns from the veteran and expert; new ideas are generated and tested. Just as the normal, law-abiding citizen is constantly going through the process of socialization, so also is the career criminal influenced by his social and cultural environment.

These general patterns of behavior are characteristic of the professional criminal whose principal gainful occupation is the violation of other people's property. They do not account for all crimes, nor are they an explanation of the many variations among American criminals. Numerous studies have shown, for example, that the southern states have a higher crime rate of violence than other regions, that crimes against property are more numerous in urban than in rural areas, that age, sex, and intelligence differ according to the type of crime committed.

Whether Americans are less law-abiding than the people of other societies is a question which we cannot fully answer at this point. It is probably more accurate to say that the types of crime committed differ from one country to another. The social attitude toward the criminal, the competence of law-enforcement officers, the social status of the police, and the policies of punishment and reform are all variables that must be taken into account in the scientific study of criminal behavior patterns. The universal constant appears to be, however, that wherever professional criminals pursue their career, they follow standardized patterns of behavior.

3. Some External Religious Patterns

The sociological study of religious behavior has not been deeply pursued by American social scientists, although most introductory texts devote a chapter to religion, and several monographs have appeared treating religious institutions and groups generally. Religion in America continues to be considered both a personal and a sacred matter that must be handled with the utmost delicacy. Respect for the various religious convictions of people seems to have prevented most sociologists from making deep analytical studies of religious behavior.

The result is that many facets of this religious behavior are not well known to Americans. The great variety of churches and denominations and the differences in beliefs and liturgies have made it extremely difficult to speak of religious mores in the sense of external patterns that are universal, have high social value, and are accompanied by social pressure. Nevertheless, it seems possible to select some of the widest generalizations, not necessarily mores, of behavior that may be shared by most religious practitioners.

The following series of behavior patterns are variously practiced by many Christians in the United States. They are the most frequent patterns, learned in childhood and performed largely by rote. They are what we have called "non-rational." They contain deep meaning, but most people who practice them do so with little or no reflection. To some extent these things are done also by Christians in other parts of the world, but they are by no means universally practiced.

a) The wearing of a head covering by women while in a church is an almost universal pattern among the major Christian denominations, although it is probably not so widely observed in some other countries. This is an ancient pattern of behavior that goes back to the injunctions of St. Paul. Its symbolism is lost in obscurity, and most Christians have no explanation for it except that "it's the thing to do." Social pressure and tradition make it almost a must-behavior for females in certain denominations, even though its acknowledged social value is not high.

b) The use of the Sacred Scriptures is a varying but universal pattern among religious practitioners in the United States. In some religious bodies the ministers can recite the Bible almost word for word with reference to chapter and verse, and even the laity bases belief and practice entirely upon it. In the more liturgical religious groups excerpts from the Scriptures constitute an important part of divine worship. Bibles, prayer books, and missals appear to be increasing in importance among American churchgoers.

c) The singing of hymns is another widespread pattern of religious behavior. Most Protestant denominations include one or more hymns in all their formal religious services. This practice is relatively infrequent in the Mass but does occur in most other public services of the Catholic church. The fact that the congregation—and not merely the priest or minister—praises God through singing gives this religious pattern of behavior a significant collective aspect. Regular members are expected to know at least the most frequently sung hymns and to participate in them, even when their voices are not melodious.

d) The saying of grace at mealtimes is a traditional external practice used to some extent by all American religious bodies. This is a short formal prayer calling down the blessing of God before the meal and a prayer of thanksgiving at the end of the meal. In many instances only the former prayer is recited, while the prayer after eating is forgotten. The grace at meals is mainly a home and family behavior pattern, and its practice is decreasing as more and more Americans take some of their meals in restaurants and public places.

e) The sign of the cross is probably the most common external pattern that distinguishes Catholics from others. It traces the cross on the body with the right hand from forehead to chest, then to left and right shoulders. This sign is made before and after prayers, on entrance to a church, and in some places by people in passing before a Catholic church. It is also the form of the benediction or blessing given by a priest to which the laity respond.

f) Wearing of medals is an increasingly popular pattern of behavior by American Catholics. The medal is traced back to the early centuries when the Christian soldiers of the Roman army substituted them for medals of the emperor. The use of the St. Christopher medal, usually attached to automobiles, has spread beyond Catholic circles. Other medals are usually worn on a light chain around the neck.

It should be pointed out that certain action patterns are considered sacred in every culture and that therefore some of the religious patterns mentioned above are practiced in some form by all American religious groups. For example, chanting and singing and the use of prayers and sacred writings are clearly not limited to the Christian churches. The reading of religious periodicals, the giving of tithes or other contributions, and external marks of respect for the ministry are likewise repetitive patterns in all denominations. The custom of fasting seems to be widespread among orthodox Jews but is gradually decreasing among the Christian groups.

These examples indicate that there is a great variety of religious behavior patterns, that certain similarities might be found among them, and that this area of culture remains largely unexplored. It is quite possible that growing church membership and an increasing interest in religious affairs will provide further research data in religious patterns.

4. Recreational Patterns

The institution of recreation exists in every society, but the emphasis on recreational patterns differs enormously. In some societies full-time recreation is considered the prerogative of only children and the idle rich. The notion in some societies that work is evil and leisure is good is countered in others by the notion that gainful work is highly ethical and that leisure activities are morally suspect. It is obvious that the actual patterns of recreation in any society are influenced by the atti-tudes people take toward leisure and work.

In the American culture both work and leisure are highly valued. The shorter workweek has provided greater leisure time for more and more Americans, and the higher level of income has made it possible for Americans in general to pay for more recreation. This combination of leisure and money has helped to develop a number of distinctive features in our recreational patterns. In this analysis we omit consideration of creative work and hobbies and of literary and artistic activities, even though these are important patterns, and we discuss only the "play" aspects of recreation.

a) The commercialization of athletics has probably gone further in this country than in most other countries. Not only are the performing athletes full-time professionals, but large numbers of coaches, trainers, managers, and agents, as well as many subsidiary functionaries, make their living from sports. Recreation for them is business, and recreational patterns are economic patterns. Large profits accrue to the most successful participants in baseball, football, basketball, boxing, wrestling, and hockey.

b) The organization of so-called "big-time" athletics means that many Americans become spectators rather than active participants in sports programs. On many college campuses intramural teams are de-emphasized. The pattern of movie attendance and television watching is a further indication of the way Americans take their recreation as passive spectators. Just as the commercial aspect of recreation requires spendable income, so the spectator aspect requires leisure time.

c) The American attitude toward nature as a servant rather than as a mother has tremendously influenced various aspects of recreational patterns. Nature, in the form of mountains and plains, streams, lakes, and seashore, is something to be used and enjoyed, not merely to be looked at and revered. Even though the wanton exploitation of natural resources has given way to a national policy of conservation, the American attitude still remains a pragmatic one. Even the decorative aspects of nature must be useful to us.

d) The modern means of transportation have also had a tremendous effect on our recreational patterns. Americans are the most traveled people in the world, and their country has been called a "nation on wheels." This traveling has contributed to the formation of our recreational institution. Motels, roadhouses, and outdoor movies have developed from the use of the automobile. Vacations by bus, railroad, and airplane have brought Americans to places in our country that were once inaccessible. Our many kinds of transportation help to explain why, unlike most Europeans, we have never accepted hiking as a popular form of recreation.

e) Certain forms of traditionally masculine recreation, such as fishing, hunting, and camping, are now practiced by both sexes and all ages. They are a continuation of our pioneer, rural traditions and to some extent also a reaction to the confinement of city living. Values concerning better health, fresh air, and outdoor exercise are brought together in this form of recreation.

f) Social awareness of the benefits of recreation has resulted in the systematic organization of playgrounds and public parks. These are provided by the society as a means for healthy physical development and also as an antidote to delinquency. The emphasis on sports in America is not only commercial and professional. There is a social responsibility for the voluntary and amateur recreational needs of the people.

There are many artistic and literary aspects of the American recreational institution that we have not considered here. There is some question whether the serious pursuit of art can be analyzed as relaxation and recreation. In many ways these patterned actions reflect specializations in the American culture, and they probably require a separate analysis. They imply canons of good taste and merit about which there is much dispute, and they are on a level apart from outdoor play and sports that we have discussed here.

It is important for the beginning student of society to realize that recreation is not merely a by-product of a culture or an activity that people perform when they have nothing better to do. Recreation in some form or other is found in every society. It is one of the basic universal institutions. It constitutes an increasingly important institution of our culture as the American society continues to provide more leisure and a higher standard of material living for its people.

5. Patterns of Food Preparation

The American housewife is often considered the most fortunate woman in the world because the function of food preparation for her family has become "so easy." This has been caricatured by some apparently envious foreign women who state that the American woman needs only a can opener and an automatic stove. The facts are, of course, quite different, and intelligent interest in food preparation has increased in proportion to the extent that physical drudgery has been removed from it.

The point of interest to the student of society is the way in which these external patterns have been altered. Attitudes toward and values concerning food preparation have drastically changed. In previous generations it was a matter not only of necessity but also of pride that the housewife picked, cleaned, and preserved all kinds of vegetables and fruits, baked her own bread and cakes, cured and salted meats, and made sausages and other food supplies. All this hard work was valued for several reasons: it was necessary for feeding the family; it saved money; it assured the "homemade goodness" of the food; and it was the kind of work that any competent homemaker could be proud to perform.

These patterns of behavior that were once almost universal and highly approved in our culture are no longer practiced. This shift in the folkways of food preparation for the American family has been made possible through many factors operating outside the home, including the following:

a) The present system of food preparation is easier and more convenient for the housewife. Many preparatory steps of selecting, washing, and peeling food are now done by commercial processors. Ready-mixed preparations of all kinds are available. Fowl is cleaned and cut into ready-to-use sections. In other words, several preliminary steps in the preparation of food are done before the housewife begins her task.

b) Numerous devices have been employed to assure the wholesomeness of the product. The Pure Food and Drug Act, various organizations for consumer research, and the "seal of approval" by groups like the Good Housekeeping Institute have helped to guarantee that the food is as pure as that which "mother used to make." In fact, it may be much "purer" than the homemade items of a generation ago.

c) The diversity of food items available to the American family has also caused a change in the immediate patterns of food preparation. Commercial canning and packaging have advanced tremendously since the introduction of the deep-freeze process. The housewife must no longer adjust her menu seasonally, and the emphasis on "freshness" is no longer a problem.

d) The development of domestic appliances has paralleled that of commercial food-processing. Most homes have some form of refrigeration and many now have deep-freeze units. Time gauges and temperature controls have taken the guesswork out of cooking and baking. Stoves which burned wood and coal, with their intricate system of dampers and flues, have given way to an even and controllable supply of gas or electricity. The number and variety of "gadgets" available to the housewife are too great to enumerate.

e) Knowledge of the techniques of food preparation is now widespread. Instead of learning the particular technique of her own mother, the modern young housewife has the advantage of "tested" methods that are demonstrated in free cooking schools and on television and radio programs. In many places these schools and demonstrations are provided by the manufacturers of household appliances or by companies supplying electricity and gas. Home economics courses on both the high-school and the college level have also helped to generalize this knowledge.

f) Numerous publications for the American housewife have helped to change the old patterns. Cookbooks have become best sellers; the women's magazines contain both articles and advertisements devoted to the work in the kitchen. The accompanying pictures "glamorize" the housewife's task, while they show how easy and efficient it can be.

These factors indicate a general trend and are not universally present. Since ours is a money economy, and since many of these items are the result of commercial and technological changes, the performance of the newer patterns of food preparation is not found in many poor families. The general trend in any behavior pattern is, however, socially significant, and it is likely that these changes in the American housewife's task will become even more widespread.

DISCUSSION QUESTIONS

1. Give a full definition of behavior patterns and give examples.
2. Distinguish, with examples, between overt and covert patterns.
3. What is meant by saying that patterns are more durable than persons?
4. What is the difference between personal habit and cultural uniformity?
5. Explain the criteria for judging the range of patterns.
6. Define with examples mores, folkways, and usages.
7. In what sense are behavior patterns "non-rational"?
8. Explain the difference between ideal and real behavior patterns.
9. If patterns are the expression of behavior, how can they also be norms of behavior?
10. What is meant by explicit behavioral norms?
11. Show the principal ways in which behavior patterns are structured.
12. What is meant by the "pattern of living"?
13. Are patterns a component of culture or of society? Explain.
14. What factors contribute to the relative permanence and durability of the American political institution?
15. List the main patterns of voting behavior of the American people.

16. List the consistencies of behavior which characterize criminals.
17. If patterns are also norms of behavior, is it not a contradiction to speak of "patterns of lawlessness"?
18. List some external behavior patterns practiced by most American religious bodies.
19. Are recreational patterns necessarily limited to play and sports activities? Explain.
20. Why has the recreational institution increased in importance in America?
21. What factors have effected a change in the American patterns of food preparation?

SUGGESTED READINGS

BENEDICT, RUTH. *Patterns of Culture*. Boston: Houghton Mifflin Co., 1934.

BENNETT, JOHN W., and TUMIN, MELVIN M. *Social Life, Structure and Function*. New York: Alfred A. Knopf, Inc., 1948, chaps. xv, xvi.

CUBER, JOHN. *Sociology: A Synopsis of Principles*. New York: Appleton-Century-Crofts, Inc., 1955, chap. vii.

LINTON, RALPH. *The Study of Man*. New York: D. Appleton–Century Co., 1936, chaps. xvi, xxii.

OGBURN, W. F., and NIMKOFF, M. *Sociology*. Boston: Houghton Mifflin Co., 1946, chap. xxiv.

SUMNER, A. G. *Folkways*. Boston: Ginn & Co., 1909.

CHAPTER EIGHT

Conceptual Behavior Patterns

People in society not only act in similar ways, they also think in similar ways. We have been seen that the external patterns of behavior are the observable, measurable, overt customs of social persons. Now we turn our attention to the conceptual, internal, or covert patterns, the "mental customs" of the group or society. They are the shared ways of thinking and believing that are current in a culture and contain the creeds, meanings, values, and attitudes of the people. These recurrent uniformities of social thought cannot be studied by direct observation; they must be inferred from what people say and from what they do.

The term "pattern" may be generically defined to include both the "mental" internal patterns and the "behaviorial" external patterns. The human person performs always as a totality, and the distinction between internal and external patterns is abstract and analytical. We have seen in the previous chapter that a cultural pattern contains three definitional elements: (a) it is customary behavior in that it is repeated frequently; (b) it is performed in relatively the same way by many people; and (c) it acts as a guide, model, or norm for the people in the group or society.

We have said also that behavior patterns can be placed on a continuum from the culturally significant to the culturally trivial according to three qualifications. The pattern of behavior is considered important (a) if it is almost universal, that is, if large numbers of people perform it; (b) if social pressure and sanctions are applied for its performance; and (c) if it accords with the social values and if the people believe it is worthwhile and important. Both the generic definition and the measure of cultural significance are the same for both external and internal patterns.

In this chapter we are concerned only with those "ways of thinking" that are so frequent and so widely shared that they may be termed cultural patterns. They are the content of what is sometimes erroneously called the "mind" of a society or group. The individual and fully socialized member of the society is supposed to be characterized by these thought patterns. It is generally believed that people in the same society think alike, as is seen in such statements as "he thinks like a European," or "like an American," or "like a Southerner." The content of the judgment is often erroneous because of ignorance of other cultures, but the fact of "thought similarity" is a valid, scientific truth.

The Group Mind

Conceptual behavior patterns or cultural mental customs must be understood properly and used cautiously. They do not imply an objective and external "group mind" in the society. The term "group mind" is analogous only; it is a metaphor like the biological or mechanical analogies that illustrate sociological concepts. Individual mind communicates with individual mind in society, but they do not fuse or merge with one another to form a common mind. We say that a social action is performed by a group or that the social act is performed in a similar way by all members of the group, but we do not mean that the social group constitutes a single physical entity.

Common, everyday language contains many expressions referring to the group mind, and they are frequently used "as though" a mind of this kind actually existed. For example, one hears "My family thinks I ought to study to be a doctor," or "The Army expects every man to do his duty," or "The church teaches you to love your fellow man." We even speak of "states of mind," like pacifism, or pessimism, or pragmatism, that characterize a nation at different periods of history.

It should be obvious that this thinking, expectation, teaching, or state of mind does not actually exist in a collective mind separate from individuals. On the other hand, it is true that from the point of view of the single social person these conceptual cultural patterns are exterior to him. Other people also hold them and place pressure on him so that he conforms to them. Both action patterns and thought patterns of behavior are not found anywhere except in persons, but by a process of abstraction we analyze the common mental patterns of a group or society "as though" they existed separately.

Everyone has had the experience of being emotionally influenced and mentally moved by a social group. In certain respects he begins to think like the others. There are also many instances of a group or audience that is persuaded to think along the lines laid down by an orator, teacher, or preacher. The persuasive speaker reaches the minds of the audience and in some respects, at least temporarily, creates in them a similarity of thought. This is merely another way of saying that the individual minds separately make a similar response to the same influence. So the individual, too, makes a response to the combined influence of the other persons in the group.

Patterns and Consensus

While there is no evidence, empirical or inferential, of the existence of a social mind as a separate entity, the human person may be studied as both an individual and a social being. When many members of society think and feel in similar ways, they may be said to be "social-minded," and it is only in this respect that we may speak of the social mind of the individual person.

This sharing of conceptual patterns by many people is sometimes called "consensus," particularly when it refers to conscious agreement on decisions, values, and sentiments. That people should share the same ideas, that they should agree to the importance of the same values, is extremely important to the functioning of the group or society. Like-mindedness makes human co-operation easier, and we shall note later that consensus is an important factor in social and cultural integration.

The Range of Conceptual Patterns

The ideas of a society are not all equally important to the members of the society. Just as the external behavior patterns can be arranged on a continuum from mores to usages, so also can the conceptual behavior patterns be similarly distinguished. They, too, can be appraised —but with greater difficulty and less scientific accuracy—by the presence or absence of the same factors: the extent of conformity, the amount of social pressure, and the degree of social value with which they are held.

a) The conceptual mores are the social convictions, the must-thinking of the members of society, just as the observable mores are the must-behavior of external actions in society. These are conceptual patterns that involve values like national loyalty, monotheism, and monogamy, and their maintenance is considered essential to the welfare of society.

Conceptual patterns of the highest rank roughly parallel the external mores. People are expected to think according to these patterns; they are constrained to express the proper sentiments in conformity to them. The more seriously a social conviction is held in a society, the more cautious must any individual be lest he express a variant or contrary conviction. People are ostracized and sometimes persecuted, even in a liberal society, for going against the prevailing convictions. In a religious society the blasphemer jeopardizes his own safety, while in a secular society even an "insult" to the flag can bring heavy penalties.

b) The conceptual folkway is at a lower point on the continuum of covert patterns. The difference of degree of compulsion between the conceptual mores and the conceptual folkways corresponds to the difference between external mores and folkways. Everyone recognizes that certain ways of thinking, while taken for granted and considered desirable, are not strictly and universally enforced. The common ideas concerning adolescent males competing in athletics, avoiding noisy parties in the neighborhood, taking an interest in the children's school-work, and doing odd jobs for money while still attending school—all of these are conceptual patterns on a lower level than strong social convictions.

c) We may place the conceptual usages or "mere opinions" on the lowest level of this continuum of covert patterns. These are cultural patterns since they are held in common by numerous people, but they are less mandatory than convictions and conceptual folkways. They allow for differences of opinion mainly because the object to which the opinion is directed does not involve a significant social value. It does not matter very much to the society in general whether the individual person agrees or disagrees, but the well-socialized person is expected to conform. Mental conformity to the "correct" conceptual usages indicates "good breeding," and these ways of thinking in any society are usually found in the popular books on etiquette.

The empirical study of these categories of conceptual patterns is still in its infancy, but every observant member of society recognizes the difference between the concepts he *has* to believe and those about which a wide divergence is allowable. A preference for one brand of cigarette over another, for one type of television show, for one type of beverage, does not deal with the more important values of the society. On the level where wide differences of opinion are permitted we find the least important of the conceptual patterns of behavior.

Social Principles and Ideology

In this analysis of the conceptual patterns of society it seems necessary to make a further abstraction and consequently a further distinction. We have said that in the external patterns of behavior one can recognize the difference between the ideal pattern, which everyone is expected to praise as most acceptable, and the real pattern, the one people actually do perform. Similarly in the conceptual patterns of behavior there are ideal patterns expressed in the principles of social thinking. By a rather general consensus a society arrives at a body of meanings and beliefs that every "right-thinking" member is supposed to hold.

This body of meanings constitutes the "principles" of social thought and is frequently called by social scientists the *ideology* of a society. Sociologically speaking, we are not here concerned whether any of these principles are right or wrong, moral or immoral, but with their existence and the universality of their acceptance in any given society. These are the ideals, principles, and concepts people say "ought" to be held by everyone. This ideology may be more ephemeral than most people would like to admit, and the deviation between what people say they ought to think and what they actually think may be quite considerable.

In a liberal dynamic society it is probably true that the actual conceptual patterns become the conceptual principles, or ideology; while in a traditional, authoritarian society the ideology greatly influences the actual conceptual patterns. This rough generalization is subject to numerous exceptions. Every society employs devices to control and to "elevate" the thought patterns of its members. The educational, religious, and familial institutions are everywhere involved in the socialization of individuals, and their conscious and rational efforts are directed toward making the actual conceptual patterns conform to the acknowledged ideology.

This distinction between ideal and real patterns of conceptual behavior is an important analytical device for the study of culture. The two levels are never brought into alignment because the norms and standards of thinking change. The measurement of progress or regress in any society can be made by a comparison between the ideology the people proclaim and the actual patterns of thinking current among them.

Variations in Social Thinking

In numerous individual instances persons have been known to change their minds, to be converted to new social principles and ideologies that make a noticeable change in their subsequent external behavior. In the group or the society as a whole, however, it appears that conceptual patterns of behavior do not change as quickly as external patterns. Rural and agricultural modes of thinking "hang on" even for people who are busied about the actions typical of an urban, industrial society.

Ways of thinking are apparently more traditional and more deeply imbedded in the culture than are ways of acting. Liberals carry their convictions with them even when they are forced externally to conform to patterns of racial segregation. Conversely, convinced racists maintain their attitudes even when they are in places where discriminations are not legally tolerated. This tenacity of conceptual patterns is, of course, stronger at the level of social conviction than on that of social opinions, but variations occur according to the *times, places,* and *persons* under consideration.

The social thinking of the American people at the middle of the twentieth century is markedly different from that at the turn of the century. This change is more noticeable in the dynamic urban societies than in the relatively static agricultural societies. Attitudes toward collective bargaining in industry, social security for the aged, practices of child labor; beliefs concerning inferiority of immigrants or inherent differences of nationalities and races; opinions concerning the relation of the federal government to education, health, and welfare—all of these are examples of changed patterns of thought over the last half-century.

Obviously there are variations of social thinking from one region to another within the same country. The difference in thought patterns between the "down-easterner" and the Texan is apparent. Class position also has an effect upon one's patterns of thought. The difference of attitudes in the slums as compared to the better-class suburbs shows how the people in these places think about the various criteria of social status.

Thought patterns differ from one occupation to another, but one must be careful not to attribute the difference to the single factor of occupation. The ditch-digger and the doctor have different "outlooks" on life, but the distinction between their ways of thinking has been brought about by numerous divergent social experiences. This latter multiple factor helps to account for divergences of conceptual patterns in the individual. The general frame of reference resulting from the socialization process is adapted in slightly different ways by each individual, and this has a bearing upon his conceptual patterns of behavior.

Classifications of Conceptual Patterns

The patterns of social thought current in any culture constitute a most general category of covert behavior patterns. We have called them "mental customs"—covert, internal, conceptual patterns of behavior. We are using all of these terms synonymously. We have been able to make a rough classification ranging from the most compulsive to the least compulsive of these patterns and have seen that there are degrees of variation according to time, place, and social categories.

It is possible to study conceptual patterns from two points of view: as they influence the individual and as the individual participates in them. In the concrete situation, however, these two aspects tend to be simultaneous; for example, the person is not only influenced by public opinion, he also shares in public opinion in some way. He not only maintains certain attitudes, but he is also influenced by the shared attitudes of other people in his society.

Another classification social scientists have found useful is that of factual and fictional conceptual patterns. It is important to note that an erroneous concept shared by many persons is as much a social fact as is a correct concept. Widespread false stereotypes concerning certain categories of people are often more influential in social behavior than are the true judgments about the same people. The student of society, in striving for scientific objectivity, must learn to distinguish social fact from social fiction, and nowhere is this more important than in the area of patterned conceptual behavior.

Judgments and Prejudices

The difference between judgment and prejudice is that the former is based on evidence while the latter is made previous to the analysis of the evidence. Thus we are speaking here not of the intellectual and individual act through which the person comes to a correct or incorrect conclusion but about the conclusion itself. The content of the judgment is in accord with objective reality, while the content of the prejudice has not yet been tested to discover whether it is at odds with objective reality. Both judgments and prejudices are shared by many persons, and it is under this social aspect that they are socially significant.

Like other conceptual patterns, judgments and prejudices are often handed down from one generation to the next. They are part of the culture content, and no person can entirely escape them. A society that is rational and scientific in its approach to human behavior is hypothetically one in which prejudices decrease and judgments increase. Human beings everywhere have emotions as well as reasoning power, they have likes and dislikes; they are greatly swayed by what other people think. It is likely therefore that prejudices are, and will continue to remain, a universal phenomenon.

Attitudes and Stereotypes

Attitudes are conceptual patterns preliminary to and more basic than judgments and prejudices. An attitude is a tendency or orientation toward some socially significant object. This object is a person, group, or category, or it is some form of overt or covert behavior pattern. An attitude is usually considered by social scientists to be readiness to act externally in a certain way, but it must be distinguished from the external behavior itself. We say that persons have favorable or unfavorable attitudes toward other persons, and this means that they have a tendency to act positively toward some and negatively toward others.

All attitudes are learned behavior, but there are distinctions in both the manner of learning the attitude and the content of the attitude itself. Mere imitation of widely accepted attitudes in a society is quite different from the logical study that arrives at attitudes. Objective study helps to remove and to avoid negative and unfavorable attitudes. Thus the manner of learning the attitude has a direct impact upon the kind of attitudes held. Attitudes may also be specified by their content of superiority, inferiority, or of neutrality. Our social behavior with people toward whom we have an attitude of dislike is quite different from that toward people we like.

Stereotypes may be crudely termed "a combination of attitudes and prejudices." In other words, the stereotype combines an attitude of either favor or disfavor with a number of prejudices concerning the same person, or class, or category of persons. The result is a "mental picture" of others that is inaccurate both in its details and in its total generalization. We have seen that the stereotype is a mental habit by which we classify people by means of unverified social characteristics.

The stereotype is a preconception rather than a conception of a social category in the sense that it attributes to a whole category of people certain characteristics that are not really present in all. It is discovered most often in the traditional labels placed upon ethnic, racial, and religious categories of people. The label itself is usually a single term, but its connotation includes a series of flattering or unflattering—but usually untrue—generalizations. Popular concepts of the "national characteristics" of people of other countries are almost all stereotypes. In short, stereotypes are caricatures rather than true pictures of people.

Public Opinion and Propaganda

The scientific study of conceptual patterns of behavior has clarified and specified the two closely associated concepts of public opinion and propaganda. The term "public opinion" is frequently used to indicate a general composite of social thinking formed out of the opinions held by the several publics in a society. It is segmental; it never represents the thinking of the total adult population. An opinion poll never produces 100 per cent unanimity even of the people polled; it reports merely the percentage of the interviewees who think a certain way on a given question.

When one says that "public opinion will not stand for child labor," he really means that there is an appreciable number of persons who are opposed to it. There are many publics in any large society, but not all of them are interested in all public questions. There are times, however, when the social scientist attempts to discover the collective and general opinion on a question of public concern. On these occasions he observes what is at best a majority opinion, a kind of central tendency arising from the agreement of the representatives of the several publics.

Public opinion is merely an indicator, only partially accurate, of actual external social behavior. The answers to the questions "What do you think?" or "What would you do?" may not correspond to the person's subsequent action. Most often they do, but, whenever there is a time interval between the expression of an opinion and the actual external behavior, there are also numerous factors at work influencing action. Opinion polls predicting the voting behavior in a political election are more accurate the closer they are made to the actual day of election.

The fact that public opinion can be changed helps to account for the tremendous rise in the use of propaganda. Propaganda can be considered either a mechanism which gets us to accept certain patterns of thinking, or it can be considered for its content, that is, what the collective conceptual pattern is that it advocates. There is a kind of causal chain here. It is well known that most people prefer to conform to the thinking of people around them and to escape the negative consequences of non-conformity. Public opinion exerts pressure on us, and if the propagandist can influence and control public opinion, he can also exert pressure upon people.

Propaganda is simply the spreading of conceptual patterns by means of mass communication for the purpose of getting people to accept them. It differs from education in the broad sense because it deliberately attempts to induce attitudes and actions favorable to the person, group, or cause of the propagandist. The propaganda process is similar to indoctrination in that it produces results that can be traced to the influence and efforts of others.

All the forms of conceptual patterns may be altered by propaganda. This deliberate effort to change the thinking of people in society sometimes has a sinister connotation (a) because many people feel that it somehow interferes with their right and ability to discover and form their own ideas, and (b) because the sources from which the propaganda emanates are often concealed. For these two reasons people often conclude that the content of propaganda is devious and unreliable, and sometimes even downright false. The skilful propagandist, realizing this, attempts to have his ideas appear as scientific discoveries, genuine news reports, or unbiased editorials.

It is obvious that the content of propaganda, like that of social convictions and opinions of various kinds, can be either true or false. The canons of scientific inquiry can be employed here to discern the one from the other. The attitudes, prejudices, and stereotypes people harbor greatly affect their interpretation of propaganda in any given case. Members of the in-group, whether national, racial, or religious, who are active in spreading their own ideas, like to call this activity an "educational process" or an "information service." When an out-group tries to do the same thing, the members of the in-group often call it "mere propaganda," indicating that they consider it suspect, unreliable, and even false.

Wishes and Advertising

The fact that persons in society act in patterned ways for the achievement of goals makes the study of wishes important for the social scientist. It is probable that most of our wishes imply social relations and social goals. We are not concerned here with strictly personal desires and ambitions that do not involve other people. A wish may be defined as a conceptual pattern that affects present behavior by the anticipation of future behavior. Sociologically it is not mere "daydreaming" or fantasy.

The general wishes of most people are created and fostered in the cultural matrix. Most people wish to have those items that are highly valued in the society in which they live. The criteria of social status, which we have discussed in a previous chapter, provide a rough classification of cultural wishes. Some of these items, like "high birth" and beauty, are scarce and out of reach of many people, while others, like education and wealth, are attainable in varying degrees. Two elements, therefore, help to identify the principal wishes current in any society: the availability of the item and the social value placed upon it.

In modern society, propaganda has become the principal mechanism for influencing public opinion. Similarly, modern advertising has become the principal mechanism for creating, influencing, and satisfying wishes. The term "advertising" is usually associated with the commercial endeavor to make people favorably disposed toward certain commodities and services. Advertising is the business of making wishes come true, of demonstrating to people how they can achieve the satisfactions they anticipate and can pay for. Since advertising deals with purchasable items, it flourishes in a culture dominated by the economic institution.

It is sometimes observed that advertising first creates the wish and then fulfils it. The oft-repeated slogans advocating the use of this or that brand of whiskey, cigarettes, automobiles, or razor blades may become part of the folklore. The "reasons" given why the prospective consumer "needs" the product go far beyond the physical satisfaction of the item itself. Advertisers recognize and exploit the generalized wishes of the people. They indicate that social prestige, intelligence, beauty, good health, distinction, good taste, and various other desirable qualities are associated with the people who use their commodity.

Ambivalence

We have seen that there is a discrepancy between what is true and what is false in conceptual patterns but that both kinds exist as social facts. There is also a distinction between favorable and unfavorable attitudes. In general, negative and unfavorable prejudices and stereotypes arise from false information. There is usually a correlation between a person's lack of knowledge, or false knowledge, about others, and his unfavorable attitude toward others.

Ambivalence, however, is a state of mind in which a person has both favorable and unfavorable attitudes toward the same object. This is a psychological state with sociological implications. A person can, for example, have feelings of both love and hatred at the same time for the same person. Ambivalence appears to result most often from the inconsistencies of the demands of the social roles. Conceptual patterns tend to conform to the social role, which in essence consists of the combination of both external and internal behavior patterns.

Each social person is a composite of the various social roles he enacts, and these social roles are sometimes in conflict. The demands, wishes, and expectations of behavior of the business role may be inconsistent with those of the paternal role of the individual. An ambivalence results in the person, so that he appears to be a different person when he enacts different roles. These variations of behavior are to be expected since the external situations make different demands on the person, but the inconsistencies may cause difficulties in the person's internal conceptual patterns.

Ambivalence frequently involves a subconscious rationalization of the direction of one's wishes and interests. A typical example is that of pressure groups in relation to government. A group interested in control of offshore oil fields is likely to complain of the "monstrous expansion" of the federal government when it threatens to take control of the tidelands. The same group, however, is likely to favor federal aid to education and federal funds for flood control, local road building, and the erection of government factories and military sites in the areas adjacent to the tidelands. Variations of this ambivalent attitude are found in political parties, churches, and business corporations.

Ethnocentrism

A basic inconsistency exists also in the widespread pattern of ethnocentrism. This is a subtle and often undetected tendency in the individual to make value judgments about other cultures and societies. *Ethnocentrism* is a mental pattern, usually one of superiority, according to which we judge foreigners or members of the out-group by the norms, standards, and values to which we have become socialized. It is characteristic of the member of the in-group to be "loyal" to those patterns of behavior he has learned to believe in as "right." All others are for him to some extent "wrong."

Ethnocentrism is one of the greatest obstacles to scientific objectivity, and it is the source of patterns of prejudice, intolerance, discrimination, and stereotyping. It is an attitude not only toward other nations but also toward people of a class, race, or religion other than our own. In the latter sense ethnocentrism develops social distance even between people who may be in physical proximity. The ethnocentric attitude distrusts other people and their customs, considers them odd, and tends to belittle them.

Ethnocentrism refers to the centering of one's values and interests upon those of the group to which one belongs. The analogous personal habit is egocentrism, the tendency to center upon one's self, to believe one's self always right and anyone disagreeing wrong. These patterns of thinking become so strong and so completely imbedded that it is often extremely difficult to make objective judgments.

We must not assume that all the contents of the ethnocentric attitude are erroneous. As in the case of prejudice and stereotype, a person may be favoring values and beliefs that are demonstrably true as well as some that are demonstrably false. Ethnocentrism is displayed in the saying: "My country, may she always be right; but right or wrong, my country!" This is not patriotism, but ethnocentrism; it expresses an attitude of superiority over anything foreign and a basis of judgment that is strictly domestic.

AMERICAN THOUGHT PATTERNS

1. Patriotism and Ethnocentrism

Americans are becoming more and more conscious of their national existence; even naturalized citizens are proud to be Americans, and some who are only one generation removed from European ancestry develop a fiercer and more vocal patriotism than the descendants of old American families. The student who is himself a patriotic and loyal American is often puzzled by discussions of ethnocentrism and wonders whether he is being unfair to his own country in trying to develop scientific objectivity toward other countries.

Objectivity of attitudes requires a balance of judgment often difficult to attain. The important point to note is that the patriotic person need not be ethnocentric. One can appreciate the social values of another culture without giving up his own; at least he can attempt to understand these foreign standards of behavior without judging all members of the out-group as stupid and unintelligent. Most Americans pride themselves on being objective, fair, and reasonable—in fact, these are high values in our culture—but there are numerous ethnocentric attitudes expressed by Americans.

Following are a few of the many non-American cultural patterns that are derided by some Americans:

a) The lack of formal education and the extent of illiteracy that characterize the masses of people in most countries in the world are often confused with lack of intelligence. The high social value of universal, compulsory education in the United States is erroneously employed as a norm by which to measure the intelligence of those people in other countries who have not been so favored.

b) The relatively closed class structure existing in many countries is criticized as a defect by Americans who value upward mobility. We often assume that the ambitious efforts in social climbing constitute a kind of universal value and that there is "something wrong" with people who adapt themselves to a permanent social status. People who do not try to "better themselves" in an economic and material way appear somehow to have defective characters.

c) The practice of gesticulating when talking, which appears to be common among some Latin peoples, seems to many Americans ridiculous, if not uncouth. Because we have acquired the pattern of talking without using our hands, we come to the conclusion that this is the "best" way of carrying on a conversation. Similarly, we judge negatively the rapid talking and the excitable tones of voice frequently used by some non-Americans.

d) Americans consider the habit of tardiness among some peoples to be an affront and a sign of laziness. "Time is money" is a peculiarly American notion, and since we value time and therefore punctuality very highly, we find it difficult to understand people whose pace is unpunctual and leisurely.

e) Americans recognize many of the problems in their own family system but still criticize the parent-child relationship in many foreign countries. They feel that foreign children are often repressed and subject to inhuman restrictions, particularly if they are adolescent girls. Americans' belief in individualism, freedom, and competition influences their judgment of human relations in other countries. These values are used by Americans in giving sympathy to the children of foreign parents.

These are simple examples of American attitudes toward foreign culture patterns. They show that the American is often suspicious of what is strange to him. He distrusts foreign behavior patterns because he does not accept the social values according to which they are formed. He asks of foreigners, "Why don't they do things more *naturally?*" This question really means, "Why aren't they American in their ways?"

Americans are often surprised to find that foreigners have the same attitude of ethnocentrism toward us. This sometimes shocks us because most of us have assured ourselves that our patterns of behavior are the very best possible. This attitude is ethnocentrism in its severest form, and it is a characteristic of some people in all cultures. The ethnocentric person distrusts everything foreign and often even considers foreign culture patterns subversive to his own society. He greatly lacks scientific objectivity.

2. Fads in Conceptual Patterns

Fads are cultural patterns that are temporarily popular and then go out of style. They can be both internal and external behavior patterns. The conceptual fads in the thinking of the American people are ideas that attract attention for a while and then disappear. External fads, like extreme feminine hair styles, automobile models, and certain forms of recreation and types of dances, change more rapidly than the internal thought patterns.

A fad is different from a fashion because the latter is more often material and external, like fashions in dress and furniture. Changes in both fads and fashions are often advocated for their usefulness as though they really have a universally utilitarian basis. "Streamlining," for example, was ultimately applied even to stationary objects like refrigerators and stoves. More often, people conform to fads and fashions because they want the status that accompanies being "up to the minute."

These changes in the thinking of Americans give us a reputation for instability and restlessness among foreigners. They are, of course, a logical function of our dynamic culture. The student of society knows that our social and cultural system is constantly undergoing change. There are, however, many differences in the rate, kind, and direction of change. We here indicate only some of the more obvious conceptual fads that have occurred in the recent history of our country:

a) Pacifism was a very popular pattern of thinking in the twenties. The causes are multiple and include the reaction to the first World War as well as the general sentiment against "foreign entanglements" that has long been present in American thinking. Militarism, which appears whenever the United States is at war, is also an attitudinal fad. An interesting aspect of pacifism is that it runs counter to the aggressiveness, independence, and self-assertiveness that Americans value, and it has been actually practiced by only a relatively small number of conscientious objectors.

b) Economic discouragement is a state of mind that becomes a fad during recurrent periods of depression. People think that the frontier spirit has been lost, that economic opportunities are diminishing, and that we have reached the peak of our material development. This somber state of mind vanishes during times of prosperity. It goes counter to the popular conception of the optimistic American social personality.

c) Educational fads in the American culture do not affect so many people as the two previous examples. For a while, the educators emphasize the physical sciences; then there is a switch to psychology; then the social sciences become popular. These fads are part of the continuous search for simplified and effective "programs." There are extremists who fight for either the traditional or the progressive type of education and introduce minor temporary fads on both sides.

d) Fads in the patterns of child care in the American society are more volatile than those already mentioned. These fads appear especially in infant training, where the pendulum swings from one extreme of "mothering" and constant attention to the other extreme of rigid scheduling. In practice, the common sense of most mothers finds a compromise between the two extremes. The tremendous interest in this subject apparently stems from the hypothesis that the future personality is molded in earliest infancy.

e) Religious fads are numerous among Americans but affect relatively few people. Some of these fads are adaptations of oriental religions, but most of them are native American innovations. Some of them appear among people with liberal religious beliefs, but most of them are invented by fundamentalists. At various times individuals who claim to have special revelation and powers of healing have been able to gather many followers and disciples. Most Americans are unconcerned about these fads and consider the religious faddists to be quite unimportant.

The number of Americans affected and influenced by fads varies greatly. Most people accept them in the area of opinion rather than in that of conviction. Americans, like other people, are slow to change their deepest beliefs (and prejudices). This does not mean that the makers of the fad, the leaders of a faddist movement, are not deeply convinced. It means that their beliefs are in an area in which most people hold changeable opinions.

3. Opinion Polls and the American Public

The opinion poll, in its present form, is a peculiarly American mechanism. In other societies, both past and present, there have been inquisitive persons who tried to discover what other people thought. It remained for American social scientists to devise and improve sampling techniques, forms of questions, and methods of presentation through which they could investigate conceptual patterns. This does not mean that they have arrived at a perfect way of discovering people's opinions or that any of the pollsters claim complete accuracy for their work.

Nevertheless, the opinion poll is here to stay. Judging from their frequent publication in newspapers, from articles about polls in magazines, and from quotations from polls on radio and television, the American people are deeply interested in them and have a certain amount of confidence in them. A correct understanding of the validity and reliability of opinion polls requires a consideration of the following facts:

a) The opinion poll represents a sample of the personal expression of opinion by the individuals interviewed. It would be inconceivable that every man, woman, and child in the United States could be interviewed on any issue. Since our population is made up of many social categories, the poll tries to obtain a numerically representative sample from all of them. The most far-reaching poll is that of the national elections which involve somewhat more than half of the eligible voters and a much smaller percentage of the total population.

b) Opinion polls are static representations of thought patterns. They represent the opinion of those questioned at the time they were questioned. Polls taken in successive weeks on the same issue indicate that opinion shifts from time to time, but the change occurs usually in a relatively small percentage of the interviewees. Even with these shifts of opinion, however, it is possible to recognize definite tendencies of opinion in a population over a period of time.

c) Viewed with scientific objectivity, the opinion poll is not a prediction of future external behavior patterns. It is true that manufacturers make use of opinion polls as indicators of trends in consumption, but they depend much more heavily on the polls that study the actual use of their products, that is, the external behavior patterns of customers. We must carefully distinguish between the use of opinion polls as a propaganda and advertising device that attempts to persuade people to do certain things and their use as a precise instrument for the prediction of behavior. The latter is not fully reliable because all the variables cannot be known and controlled.

d) The validity of some opinion polls is questionable because of the tendency to give expected answers, especially when the questions concern important social values. Even people who indulge in extramarital relations are likely to give the opinion that they favor marital fidelity. Few atheists admit to an outright denial of the existence of God. Thus it is often difficult to distinguish between real opinion and "expected" opinion.

e) The results of opinion polls are always presented statistically, but the misinterpretation of these statistics sometimes gives a false impression. For example, if a poll registers 60 per cent with no answer, 10 per cent negative, and 30 per cent positive, it is an error to claim that "six out of eight answered affirmatively." This example could be multiplied by other misuses of statistics, none of them the fault of either the pollsters or their methods but of the people who interpret the results.

f) The validity and reliability of public opinion polls depend greatly upon the clear wording of the issue under consideration. For this reason the statements are almost always pretested and reworded so that they will not be either ambiguous or slanted. This has been done with great skill by experienced American pollsters, especially when they ask questions about major national issues.

The polling method is not, of course, the only or the best way to study human behavior. Even with all its refinement in the hands of experts, it is still a clumsy mechanism of research. Polls have been both extravagantly praised and thoroughly mistrusted. They are trying to measure what is not directly observable: the conceptual patterns of the people. It is safe to say that, when scientifically conducted, they are a helpful adjunct to the more reliable and direct methods of study such as participant observation, depth interviewing, and group tests of all kinds.

4. Propaganda in America

Americans profess a deep suspicion of propaganda, and many naïvely feel that it is a wicked weapon used only by subversives within our country and by dictators in other countries. When it is understood that propaganda is simply a method of informing people with the intention of persuading them, we realize it is all around us, especially in the economic, political, educational, and religious institutions. Through the mass media of communication we are barraged with counsel and suggestion to change and improve both our internal and external patterns of behavior.

This constant flood of persuasion deals primarily with conceptual patterns. We are asked to *believe* what the propagandist or advertiser is telling us. Judging from the measurable results of this type of appeal to our minds, it is a highly successful technique. The manufacturers who sell the largest volume of products hire the best advertisers, whose techniques of persuasion can be scientifically analyzed.

Following are the principal channels of persuasion employed by both propagandists and advertisers in their attempt to arouse interest and conformity:

a) The satisfaction of needs, actual or imagined, is one of the best selling points of the advertiser. If the listener, viewer, or reader can be persuaded that this product will make him healthier or more popular, provide greater comfort for him, help him to save money, or provide a symbol of his wisdom and intelligence, he may accept the product. If the propagandist cannot convince his audience of their need for his product, he has failed in the most important technique of persuasion.

b) The constant repetition of a slogan, trade mark, or key expression also appears to be an essential step in the persuasion process. After hearing of it many times, people can more easily remember a product or action. The trick of incorporating the slogan into music and jingles helps to preserve it in the minds of people.

c) Novelty is an important aid to persuasion. The claim that a thing is new, even "absolutely new," appears to have a strong effect, especially when it is presented in scientific terms. Since Americans value progress, this appeal is probably more powerful than it would be in less dynamic and more tradition-minded societies.

d) Trial offers have been found to be an effective means of persuasion. People are assured that once they try out this product they will never be without it. Free samples are distributed; a trial of ten days absolutely free of charge or a "money-back" guaranty is offered. This technique not only assures the buyer of the good will of the speaker and the worthiness of his product but also indicates that he is himself convinced of his claims. Somewhat similar to this trial offer is the use of illustrations and examples in the statements of politicians, teachers, and preachers. The illustration used is a "sample" of what they want people to accept.

e) The appeal to authority is one of the most widely used techniques of persuasion. The propagandist or advertiser tries to persuade people that he is not alone in his convictions. He does this by using the indorsement of experts or popular personalities and by giving the impression that "everybody is doing it" or that masses of people are in agreement with him. It is interesting to note that the testimonial need have no logical connection with the competence of the person to judge the value of the object or idea.

The term "propaganda" need have no sinister connotation. We have deliberately used the terms "propagandist" and "advertiser" interchangeably in this brief review of American techniques because both actually employ the same techniques. It is true that the advertiser is dealing with purchasable commodities and services while the propagandist is dealing mainly in the realm of ideas. It may also be true in certain instances that some propagandists are attempting to sell "good" ideas while others sell "bad" ideas. The educator is presumed to be a propagandist in the first category while the editor of a "hate sheet" belongs in the second.

There has probably never been a society in the history of the world which has exceeded our country in the extent and intensity of propaganda. From a sociological point of view this is an important phenomenon because it clarifies the way conceptual patterns of behavior originate and change. Beneath the surface the American people hold to a steady core of durable convictions, but even these convictions are appealed to through the various techniques of persuasion and propaganda. This is seen in the way politicians appeal to patriotic loyalty, and even to God and religion, in order to win voters to their side.

5. Prejudices and Discriminations

Fair play and justice, freedom and opportunity, and generosity and brotherliness are some of the social values Americans praise highly. In spite of these high ideals there is a recognizable amount of prejudice and discrimination among the American people. Perhaps our appreciation of high social ideals and values makes us more than ordinarily conscious of behavior that fails to meet these ideals.

Bias is probably inevitable in the human personality. Everyone entertains likes and dislikes, some of them based on objective reasons, others demonstrably irrational. We have seen that prejudice is an internal, conceptual, behavior pattern. It is a way of thinking accompanied by emotional overtones. Discrimination, on the other hand, is an external pattern of social conduct. They are closely related, and it is difficult to say in any particular case whether prejudice causes discrimination or discrimination causes prejudice.

The extent to which prejudice and discrimination are current in the American society indicates the extent to which we fail to live up to our expressed cultural ideals. The factual data in this regard are fairly well known, and the following are the principal areas in which prejudice and discrimination are most obvious in America:

a) Economic opportunities, which are ideally supposed to fit the competence of the job-seeker, are restricted in numerous ways. Fair employment practices are regularized in many states, but women are still sometimes denied the same wages as men doing the same work, or they may not be hired for some jobs at all. In some places there are strong economic prejudices against Jews and immigrants, and in most areas Negroes cannot get wages or jobs as good as a white person's.

b) In education, an unofficial quota system discriminates against the admission of certain minority category members, especially in private schools and colleges. Segregated schools, both private and public, are a demonstration of the belief that the Negro is inferior to the white and must therefore be separated from him. The gradual breakdown of this external discrimination is partly due to a decrease in prejudice and is expected to result in a further decrease.

c) Americans think of the familial institution as one in which personal choice and voluntary behavior are highly desirable. Yet there are many states that legally prohibit the marriage of Caucasians with Indians, Orientals, or Negroes, even when the person in the minority race has many Caucasian ancestors. In some state courts these laws have been declared unconstitutional just as the laws concerning racial segregation have been declared unconstitutional on the national level.

d) Housing restrictions in various localities are also clear evidence of prejudices and discriminations. In many instances they continue the pattern set by foreign neighborhoods and ghettoes established by the various classes of European and Asiatic immigrants. There are still many residential areas in which the people actually resist the "invasion" of other Americans who are of Mexican, Oriental, Jewish, Indian, or Negro descent.

e) The denial of both public and private recreational facilities is in many instances a demonstration of prejudicial and discriminatory patterns. Public parks, playgrounds, and bathing beaches, as well as resort hotels, restaurants, theaters, libraries, and country clubs, may be denied to certain minorities. There are certain social pressures, and even legal compulsions, that prevent association of people in leisure-time activities.

f) Political activities show a discrepancy between thought practices and external patterns. Women may vote but are usually not considered for anything more than a token political office. Although Negroes, both men and women, have the constitutional right to vote, they are kept from it in some states by extra-legal means. The leaders of the political parties are concerned with winning elections and staying in power, and the fact that they do not often propose Jewish, Catholic, Negro, and other minority members as candidates for public office is an indication that they recognize the prejudices of the masses of American voters.

g) The casual observer would probably expect to find little prejudice and discrimination among the religious groupings of any society. Yet most of the major churches in America have submitted themselves to patterns of segregation and discrimination. Sometimes their congregations are limited to or exclude a large racial, ethnic, or class minority because they serve a particular residential area. In other instances, however, a particular congregation, church school, or other religious organization deliberately excludes a social category.

This brief list of areas of prejudice and discrimination gives a static picture of a dynamic situation in the American society. Of all the institutional arrangements that are changing in the United States, these patterns of prejudice and discrimination appear to be changing the most rapidly. The trend is very definitely in the direction of their alleviation. Concentrated efforts are being made by most social agencies to remove external discrimination, especially the legal barriers against minorities. The removal of inner prejudices and the change of personal biases are much more difficult, but efforts are also being made to change them.

DISCUSSION QUESTIONS

1. Explain the definitional elements of a conceptual behavior pattern.
2. Give some examples of the non-technical meaning of the term "group mind."
3. Explain the range of conceptual patterns that corresponds to that of mores, folkways, and usages.
4. What is the difference between "ideology" and widespread conceptual patterns of behavior?
5. Why do conceptual patterns generally change more slowly than external behavior patterns?
6. Explain the various ways of classifying conceptual behavior.

7. Define the following terms and give examples: judgment, prejudice, attitude, and stereotype.
8. Is public opinion an accurate indicator of public behavior? Explain.
9. Why is propaganda sometimes thought of as sinister?
10. What is the connection between wishes and advertising?
11. In what ways are the social roles related to ambivalence?
12. Show the relationship between egocentrism and ethnocentrism.
13. Discuss: "The patriotic person need not be ethnocentric."
14. List some of the non-American patterns about which Americans become ethnocentric.
15. What is the difference between fad and fashion?
16. Give some examples of American fads in conceptual patterns.
17. What are the cautions to be made concerning the validity and reliability of opinion polls?
18. What are the principal channels of persuasion used by both propagandists and advertisers?
19. How does discrimination differ from prejudice?
20. What are the principal areas in which prejudice and discrimination are most noticeable in America?

SUGGESTED READINGS

ARNOLD, THURMAN. *The Folklore of Capitalism.* New Haven: Yale University Press, 1937, chap. vii.

CUBER, JOHN. *Sociology: A Synopsis of Principles.* New York: Appleton-Century-Crofts, Inc., 1955, chap. vi.

DAWSON, C. A., and GETTYS, W. E. *An Introduction to Sociology.* New York: Ronald Press Co., 1948, chap. xvi.

DOOB, LEONARD. *Public Opinion and Propaganda.* New York: Henry Holt & Co., Inc., 1948, chap. xi.

MacIVER, ROBERT M., and PAGE, C. H. *Society: An Introductory Analysis.* New York: Rinehart & Co., Inc., 1949, chaps. viii, ix.

QUEEN, STUART; CHAMBERS, WILLIAM; and WINSTON, CHARLES. *The American Social System.* Boston: Houghton Mifflin Co., 1956, chap. vii.

CHAPTER NINE

Roles

The meaning of a dramatic role that an actor performs in a play is familiar to everyone. The actor temporarily assumes the personality and behavior of a fictitious character and enacts his part in the play as though he were the person depicted. The concept of the social role is analogous to that of the dramatic role. The main difference is that in the social role the individual "plays himself." The social role is not fictitious or temporary; it has been learned in the process of socialization, enacted in the various groups in which the person participates, and has become part of the social personality of the individual.

We have seen that behavior patterns are the recurrent uniformities of social conduct, both overt and covert. Now when a number of interrelated behavior patterns are clustered around a social function, we call this combination a social role. For example, there are certain repeated patterns of behavior, actions and attitudes, duties and privileges, expected of each member of a family. In the performance of this behavior he or she is enacting the familial role. The social role is recognized and specified by the social need toward which it is directed and by the social group in which it is enacted.

We must not think that the person merely assumes a role for a while and then casts it off. Each person has many roles, but they are intertwined and deeply imbedded in his habitual ways of thinking and acting. The individual is simultaneously an actor and a member in the basic groupings of the society, and during the socialization process he tends to learn all the social roles simultaneously. Throughout his whole life he is expected to "play his part" as a member of society, and this he does in the enactment of his social roles.

Role and Social Personality

From the sociological point of view, the social personality is the sum of all the roles the individual plays. These roles are called social because they represent uniformities of conduct shared in by many people. The role can be studied scientifically, analyzed in detail, and observed in operation, because many people perform the same role in relatively the same way. The typical father role, or salesman role, or teacher role can be recognized among the people around us in society. If this were not true, the social scientist could not study organized human relations, nor could the society function in an orderly and systematic way.

The social personality is in essence the total role system through which the individual "deals" with society. Each person participates in numerous groups, and in each of these he plays his part or enacts his role. He does not invent the manner in which he will do it; he does it the way it is supposed to be done. A man may be the father of a family, a salesman in his business, a vestryman in his church, the lead-off man on a bowling team, a member of a parent-teacher association, a precinct worker in the local political party. He is the same single person, but he is playing institutionalized roles in the basic familial, economic, religious, recreational, educational, and political groups of his community.

It is important to note that although he is the same basic personality in whatever group he participates, he is expected to, and actually does, behave somewhat differently in each group. It is obvious that a man does not behave in exactly the same way at a religious service in church and at a golf tournament at the country club. The situation is different, and the function of the group is different in each instance. Thus, three elements combine—the *situation,* the *function,* and the *group*—to make the difference to which the individual must respond. In making the response to these elements, the person is performing his patterned social role.

In discussing the social person we have indicated that we leave the analysis of the individual personality to the psychologist. We are not suggesting that social personality replaces individual personality. Each individual is in some sense unique, and the social history of two persons, even of so-called identical twins, can never be precisely identical. When we analyze the social role and the social personality, we are abstracting from concrete individuals that which is common to them, shared by them, and culturally patterned.

Role and Status

There is confusion among students of society about the relation of role and status that is similar to the confusion that once existed in the concepts of institution and group. The latter has been clarified by the distinction that the basic unit of the institution is the behavior pattern, while that of the group is the social person. The terms "institution" and "group" cannot be used interchangeably, and we must also carefully note that the terms "role" and "status" cannot be used interchangeably.

As we have seen, status refers to the position of a person, class, or category in the social structure. Social status is a construct, an evaluation, arrived at by combining and applying the criteria of social values current in the society. It tells us *where* in social space the person is in reference to other persons. The social role, on the other hand, tells us *what the person does*. It is a functional and dynamic concept concerning the social performance of the individual and not the evaluation other people place upon him.

The distinction between role and status is clearer when we realize that the social role is one of the numerous criteria by which a person's social status is measured. Besides wealth, ancestry, sex, age, and the other criteria of status, the functional utility of the person to the society is also evaluated. This functional utility refers to that which he does in his social roles. In a pragmatic, dynamic culture where people want to get things done efficiently, the kind of roles which the person performs may be the principal criterion upon which his social status is evaluated. A person of high social status may be expected to perform certain roles in certain ways, but this is not the same as saying that his social status is his social role.

Roles and Relations

We have seen how social statuses are linked with one another in social stratification. The social status of any person is meaningful sociologically only when it is compared or related to the social status of other persons. Social status is interpreted in reference to the levels of superordination, co-ordination, and subordination on which persons are placed. In comparison with other persons, an individual has higher, similar, or lower social standing, and in this sense we may say that the relationship is *between statuses* rather than between persons.

It must be obvious also that social roles do not stand alone. It is meaningless to speak of them except in relation to the roles of other people. The various social roles the individual plays are related to one another within his own personality. But these roles are linked also, separately and collectively, to those of other persons. This linkage is what we mean by mutual and reciprocal social relations; and in this sense again we may say that they are *between roles* rather than between persons.

Ordinarily one thinks of social relations as a relationship among persons or groups of persons. This is, of course, a common-sense interpretation of the experience of people. But if we analyze the social relation more thoroughly, we see that social roles are the *intermediary mechanism* of social relations. People react to one another in and through their social roles. Mother and daughter experience a continuing personal relationship, but it is through the role of mother and the role of daughter that this relationship is carried out. Each acts and thinks in patterned ways, known, expected, and responded to by the other, and this is what we mean when we say that social roles must be reciprocal and related.

Content of Roles

The definition of social relations as the reciprocal relationship between social roles becomes clearer when we analyze the content of social roles. We have said that the patterns of behavior, centered upon a specific social function and directed toward a social goal, make up the content of the specific social role. The performance of the rights and duties consonant with the function is the core of the role; for example, the performance of the sacramental rites is the core of the role of the parish priest. Not all the behavior patterns associated with the role involve this strict moral connotation; for example, the time at which the priest recites his private prayers, or the manner in which he prepares his sermons, would not be equally important or equally enforced by social pressure.

The variation of patterns within the role is again an indication of the range of social behavior acceptable within the society. A mother who abandons her infant is guilty of an outrage against the values of the culture; she goes contrary to its mores and convictions and is condemned for failing in an essential duty of her role. The mother who loves, protects, feeds, teaches, disciplines, and in general takes care of her child is enacting her role in socially approved ways. But in the minor details of this performance much leeway is allowed.

The social role is made up of both overt and covert patterns of behavior. The doctor is expected not only to act like a doctor but also to think like and to have the attitudes, values, and knowledge of a doctor. There is a certain range of individual choices and of degrees of conformance, but this elasticity of role is socially permitted only up to a point. The doctor cannot behave toward his patient as he does toward his preschool daughter or his drinking companion. The patient and for for that matter the general public expect the doctor to enact his social role according to patterns that are fairly well known in society.

The content of any given social role is always related to that of other social roles. In the doctor-patient relationship, the patient is expected to take certain attitudes and to respond in certain ways to the doctor. If we analyze our own behavior in different groups and situations and in relation to various persons, we shall see that this is exactly what we do. One need merely examine the commonly repeated relationships, such as employer-employee, teacher-pupil, lawyer-client, priest-parishioner, parent-child, or the ordinary relations of friends and neighbors to realize that the content of one role must be consonant with the content of the other.

Expected and Actual Roles

We must not think of social roles as arbitrary, rigid, and automatic mechanisms of behavior that allow no choice of alternative patterns. Each social role is more or less generalized and standardized in any given culture. Certain behavior is expected in the roles of motherhood and fatherhood in every society, and the fact that most mothers and fathers conform most of the time to these expectations makes it possible for the sociologist to recognize and analyze the roles.

It is only when certain aspects of some roles are rigidly imposed, as in some religious rituals, some aspects of bookkeeping, and similar relatively automatic functions, that the social role becomes inelastic. But the human element—the ability to choose otherwise and the likelihood of making a mistake—is always present. Even in the relatively unchanging and traditional cultures there is not a complete and absolute conformity by everyone to the expectations of all role behavior. There is always room for at least slight variations, and in a rapidly changing culture these variations may be considerable.

As people become socialized, they do not learn isolated, unconnected, and irregular ways of behaving. They learn more or less complete roles by observing and imitating others and by being corrected and counseled by them. From this point of view it is the total role that is expected of the individual rather than any particular pattern within the role. As roles are repeated in relatively similar ways by more and more people, they become established and are expected of individuals. As we have seen, the expectation and the actuality are not always completely and perfectly realized. Knowledge of how he is expected to pursue a role, however, is often as influential upon a person's behavior as is the observation of the actual role enacted by others.

Examples of this influence of expected behavior are numerous. The local politician who is elevated to the position of federal judge tends also to elevate his patterns of behavior to those expected of one in his new position. The prejudiced person tends to restrain his most violent attitudes when he is in the presence of well-educated, intelligent, and liberal people. The man who is expected to tell lewd jokes to his drinking companions is expected also to refrain from this practice when he is in the presence of their wives, and he is usually able to shift his patterns of behavior to fit the circumstances.

Social Sanctions on Roles

The term "expectation," used above, means something more than mere anticipation. Social roles must be fulfilled if the society is to continue as an operating system. People must play their part, they must enact their roles in approved ways. The need of the individual to fulfil a social function is accompanied by the pressure of the society to see that he does it. There are social sanctions upon the enactment of the social role. The society approves of some things and disapproves of other things in the many possible ways in which a role can be performed.

The strength of social sanctions varies. Not all social roles of the person or within the society are equally important or compulsory. Nor is each segment of the role content as important as all others. The three elements by which one may distinguish the socially significant from the socially trivial in behavior patterns may also be applied to the social role itself. The significance of the social role depends on its universality, compulsiveness, and value to the society. These three elements will therefore account for the social sanctions exerted upon any social role.

The society judges each social role on several levels of behavior and applies pressures and sanctions accordingly. Within each social role there is (*a*) *required behavior* without which the role cannot be performed. For example, the role of the college student requires that he register for a sequence of courses, that he attend lectures, and that he submit to examinations. On another level the role involves (*b*) *allowed behavior,* about which the society or group makes no hard-and-fast rules. The college student may choose among extracurricular activities, read more than the required books, or write letters to the editor of the campus newspaper. There is also (c) *prohibited behavior,* against which the society employs penalties or negative sanctions. For example, the student is not permitted to incite others to a campus riot, throw chairs out of a window, or bring a jazz combo into the college chapel.

The degree to which the individual conforms to the requirements of the first level of behavior and avoids the last indicates the degree to which he is properly performing his social role. It also indicates the degree to which the society approves the enactment of his social role and to which the social sanctions of approval or disapproval are placed upon him.

The Formation of Social Roles

We have seen that the term "social role" is only analogous to the term "dramatic role." The latter role is the creation of the playwright. The dramatic actor imagines himself to be someone else and pretends to be performing the actions of the imagined person. The social role, on the other hand, is not the creation of the social scientist, nor is it an imaginary performance by the person. It is the creation of the culture in the sense that persons have performed it over and over; and while the principal roles exist everywhere, their formation has been somewhat different in each major society.

The existence and functioning of the basic social roles are necessary conditions without which there could be no social life. Like culture itself, roles are inherently present in societies, and they do not depend for their origin and existence upon the attainment of a certain level of development by a people. Primitive, preliterate, simple societies could not exist if the people did not carry out their social roles. In this type of society the roles are fewer in number but more rigid in required performance than in an urban, complex, industrial society.

One needs no more than a casual knowledge of the world's different cultures to recognize that even the basic social roles are not enacted in identical ways everywhere. Roles are molded according to the demands of the particular culture and society in which they are enacted. For example, some of the economic needs of a primitive society can be met through the relatively simple role of barterers. In a complex, commercial society this function is multiplied and specialized into the various economic roles of purchasing agent, discount clerk, salesman, advertising manager, copy writer, radio and television advertiser, and many others. The number, content, and kind of social roles existing in a society are the developed product of that society.

The varying influence of the major institutions in any culture helps to account for the emphasis placed upon the different basic roles. In a society where the economic institution is predominant, great stress is placed on the occupational roles; the main values center upon them, and their behavior expectations are quite exacting. In another society where the familial institution is predominant, the roles within the family and the kinship groupings become more refined and demanding. A still different direction and adjustment will be given to the social roles in a society where the political or the religious institution is pivotal.

Roles and the Individual

Every individual person is born into an existing culture in which the social roles have already been institutionalized. Since these social roles are very numerous and since no person can possibly enact all the existing roles, society must provide some mechanism through which role and person are brought together. We have pointed out that people acquire social status through ascription and achievement. They do not acquire roles this way. Strictly speaking, we cannot say that social roles are ascribed or achieved. Status is the result of a judgment in the minds of people; role is what one does. A person may have high achievement within a role, but he does not achieve the role itself.

Confusion in the use of these concepts can be avoided if we distinguish between preparation *for* and achievement *in* a social role. The mere fact that the role of elementary-school teacher exists in a patterned way in our society makes it possible for an individual to prepare for this role. The person knows ahead of time what the requirements of the role are, what kinds of abilities, knowledges, and skills will best fit him or her for the role of teacher. Certainly, work and study go into the preparatory steps, but this is achievement within the role of student and not, strictly speaking, achievement of the role of teacher.

A correct understanding of this relationship of the role to the individual requires a realization of their mutual influence. While a society may multiply the number and kinds of social roles, it is only in a limited sense we can say that the individual person creates even the partial content of the role. The social roles that function in any particular culture are a product of the experience and interaction of many people over a long period of time. Thus individuals have influenced and helped to shape particular aspects of roles. The individual enters upon existing roles, but he must in a sense "internalize" these roles, and in so doing he varies somewhat from other people in the performance of the roles.

On the generalized level of abstraction necessary in scientific study, we must say that the social roles are ready-made, pre-existing formulas of social behavior to which the individual accommodates himself. In a limited sense and in some aspects of the role there is mutual accommodation. There are two general ways through which this accommodation takes place, that is, through which the particular individual and the roles he will enact are brought together. The first is by assignment and the other is by assumption.

a) The assignment of the social roles means that the roles are given to the person from outside himself. Assignment is accomplished in two ways, depending upon the kind of social role under consideration. In some roles the assignment to the person is *automatic.* For example, certain familial roles like those of son, daughter, uncle, aunt, grandparent, and cousin do not depend upon the decision of the individual. This is true also of any aspects of social roles that the individual has from birth, such as age, sex, race, and ethnic background. Assignment of roles can also be *deliberate,* as when a child is adopted, or a girl is sold into marriage, or when an adult person is appointed to the role of sales manager, district judge, or church pastor.

b) A person acquires a role by assumption when he takes it on voluntarily, through his individual decision. For example, by the decision to marry, the contracting parties assume the roles of husband and wife. Similarly, roles are assumed when one decides to follow one occupation rather than another, to become a university student rather than to seek gainful employment, to strive for membership or office in any number of groups.

The distinction between assignment and assumption must not be oversimplified. In the complex situations of everyday life, there are many instances in which the deliberate external assignment and the voluntary personal assumption of the social role go hand in hand. There is co-operation on the part of those assigning the role and on the part of the person assuming the role. For example, the person who is willing to assume the role of godparent does not do so unless the parents of the child have deliberately assigned this role to him.

Classification of Roles

The social roles existing in a culture may be classified from many points of view. We have already seen that some roles are assigned and others are assumed, that some are simple and others complex. We may classify roles according to the degree of social value attached to them; some are held in low esteem and others are highly valued. Some have strict requirements, deep responsibility, and involve serious action, while others are relatively lax in their requirements.

Each person enacts at least as many social roles as there are groups in which he participates. These are the roles that gain the most attention from social scientists and are most readily recognized and understood from everyday experience. We have seen, however, that groups can be classified in many ways and that there is no completely satisfactory and all-inclusive arrangement of groups. The same difficulty faces us here, and we shall follow the same arrangement of social roles that we employed for social groupings.

We found that there are certain major groups of people in every society, and it is in and through these groups that the people are enabled to fulfil their social needs. Since the purpose of the social role is to function with other persons toward social goals and since each person participates in some way in all of the basic major groups, there exists a social role corresponding to each of these groups. Thus everyone at some time or other plays a social role in the familial, educational, economic, political, religious, and recreational groupings.

This kind of classification involves a distinction between major social roles and subroles. For example, within the major educational role, a person may perform the subrole of teacher, student, principal, dean; within the political role, a person may enact the subrole of ordinary voter and taxpayer or may have some appointed or elected function to perform. The complicated network of social roles within any of the major groups in society is, in fact, a related system of subroles. The person must be in either an inferior, an equal, or a superior role in relation to all the other roles; a man must enact the roles of father, husband, brother, son, cousin, or brother-in-law toward the other persons in the kinship system.

Key Role

We have said that each person has a key status that is the principal norm by which society esteems or disesteems him. Similarly, each person has a principal function and becomes identified with one of the major groups in which he plays out his main role. The identification of a key social role is simply a recognition of the fact that every individual is limited in time, talent, and opportunity and also of the fact that a certain degree of specialization of function is necessary in every society.

Like a person's key status, his key role tends to be measured against the pivotal institution in the culture. If economic groups and institutions absorb the most time, interest, and energy and contain the highest values of the society, the key role will be the economic role. Then when it is asked about a person, "What does he do?" the reference is to his occupational or economic role. It is obvious, however, that not every person in a society is gainfully employed, so that even in an economic-dominated society there are many people whose key role is non-economic.

While the most highly esteemed role in any society may be that through which a person performs his occupational function, the concrete situation may indicate other key roles. The key role of the adult may be economic, while that of his adolescent son or daughter is the educational role of student and that of his wife the familial role of mother. The professional politician, the full-time religious functionary, and the star athlete or entertainer gain their livelihood in the various major groups, and their key roles are considered political, religious, or recreational rather than economic.

The General Role

Although a person plays various roles in various groups and associations and enacts also a number of subroles, the social actor is a single person. Structurally and analytically, the sum of all his roles constitutes his social personality. This total social personality is a structure *in action* that performs many functions as a single individual. From this functional point of view, this person has a total, generalized role that is the combination of all the different roles we recognize when we think of the person as a whole human being.

This concept of the generalized role may be clarified by the example of the man who is said to "play an important role" in his community or society. We mean more than his contribution as a member of the political or civic structure. We mean his combined roles as husband and father, neighbor, voter, churchgoer, and businessman.

The general role, then, is not the same as the key or major role. Just as the various statuses a person occupies combine in his station in life, so also the various roles he enacts, when viewed as a whole, combine in his generalized role. This concept represents his total function or functions in the society, what he contributes to the society and what the society has become accustomed to expect from him.

SOME ROLES IN THE AMERICAN SOCIETY

1. The City Politician

The political party as developed in the American society has answered a social need not foreseen in any formal way by the Founding Fathers of our country. The people who first formed these parties did so in order to propose candidates to the voters, organize a system of support for them, and share in the power to which they were elected. The political party in the United States is an example of a social grouping that grew out of the needs of society and performs a social function. At the center of the party is the professional politician.

The "game" of politics has become mainly an urban game, and the most skilful and successful player is the city boss. He runs the city machine in the sense that he can "make or break" candidates. He can "deliver the vote" because he supervises an organization of people who are obligated to him for their jobs and for other favors. There are various kinds of political bosses in other countries, but the manner in which the social role of the city politician has developed in this country has made it a peculiarly American phenomenon. It can function more or less smoothly for two main reasons: first, most eligible voters are too apathetic to interest themselves in day-to-day politics; and, second, there is no other arrangement through which this necessary role can be performed.

The content of the social role of the urban machine politician includes the following patterns of behavior. These are the things that he does and that people expect him to do.

a) The city political boss acts as a middleman between the general public and the city administration. He is the informal go-between. On the one side are the citizens who want services and on the other side are the city officials who want votes. The city boss acts as a kind of broker who exchanges votes for services and services for votes.

b) In this capacity as broker he has to have a shrewd knowledge of exchange values. He usually asserts that anybody can come to see him and that he is willing to do favors for anybody. But in practice this is not so. The citizen who has many friends and relatives and is therefore in a position to influence many votes will usually get the preference.

The boss must also have a sufficient number of city officials under his influence and know which officials are able to perform which favors. The officials who are most obligated to him for their position will do the most favors for him.

c) The city boss must be able to obtain what are called negative services for some people. In some places he "handles" the tickets for traffic violators and puts in a word for other offenders to the judge or police recorder, and he may get police co-operation in order to allow certain illegal operations to continue. He can persuade health, fire, and building inspectors to interpret their respective codes in favor of a friend.

d) He must also be able to obtain positive services. He can get quicker garbage disposal and more frequent street cleaning for the areas where his supporters live. If a sidewalk needs repair or a tree must be cut down, he can "see to it." He can get jobs for people on the police force, in the fire department, in the city hall, and in the various other departments of city administration.

e) The boss usually holds no elected position, although there have been many exceptions to this in places where he almost completely dominates the city administration. In most instances, however, he obtains for himself an appointive position in the department that hires the most people. Often his income is supplemented and his organization gets financial support from funds contributed by protected people.

f) The city politician passes on the candidates for a party's election ticket. Prospective candidates know that his approval can win the nomination for them, and they are willing to make promises or at least to "have an understanding" with him.

The social role of the city boss seems to be a fairly permanent phenomenon in American city politics. It appears to fulfil a social need in providing an informal "short cut" through the legalistic and formal procedures of city government. The urban American wants to get things done without waiting in line and without going through a lot of "red tape." The city boss is able to get quick and efficient results.

This social role represents a position of power, and there is almost always a struggle for power going on in the cities. Seldom is the boss's position completely secure. The history of American cities is littered with reform movements. The boss who senses the coming of reform and co-operates with it has a good chance to stay in power. Most often he either fights it successfully or loses his power, only to be followed in his role by a "cleaner" city boss.

2. The Traveling Salesman

The itinerant peddler is part of the folklore of the American culture. From Colonial times on, he has traveled through the growing nation, bringing his wares to the people, cajoling them into buying, gaining a reputation as a charming man of the world and sometimes also as a clever swindler. He played a personal economic role in the distribution of goods in the days before the department stores, the supermarkets, and the chain stores.

The function of the traveling salesman is still the distribution of goods, but he is no longer simply the retail outlet for goods. There are still house-to-house salesmen in American cities, but the prototype of the traveling salesman is now a "manufacturer's representative." He is a wholesale merchant, the intermediary between the manufacturer and the retailer. The changing aspects of American urban and economic life have brought about changes in the social role of the salesman. Following are some of the main components of this role:

a) Most of the social relations of the traveling salesman are in secondary associations. He strives to build up primary relations with his customers, his fellow salesmen, and the employees of the hotels where he stops. Most of these people, however, remain outsiders to him, and he remains an out-group member to them. This is one of the reasons why the successful salesman tends to be exceedingly friendly and jovial, to get on a first-name basis with customers and acquaintances. He feels the social need to establish at least the fiction of primary relationships with strangers.

b) The traveling salesman spends most of his time away from his own primary groups—his family, neighborhood, parish, and local clubs. We have seen that primary group relationships are declining in America. The salesman is the outstanding evidence of this trend. The circus performer and the migrant worker usually travel with their families, but the salesman travels alone. He lives in hotels, eats in restaurants, and often whiles away his spare time in movies and bars.

c) The salesman is externally released from both the social support and the cultural pressures of his own community. In a sense, this may be called "abnormal" living because most people maintain a larger number of primary relations and because the whole society requires the functioning of primary groups. When he is moving outside these groups and relations, the salesman is not immediately and directly accountable for his social behavior. The known values of his intimates and friends, to which he tends to accommodate himself when he is at home, do not support him when he is on the road. This fact is the basis for the many shady jokes and stories told about the traveling salesman.

d) The successful traveling man must not only sell goods, he must also sell himself. Perhaps nowhere else in the world is the notion so widely prevalent that "personality" is the most important factor in selling. In spite of the social and cultural handicaps mentioned, the salesman must appear to be a charming, friendly, witty, and intelligent person. He must appear to be convinced that his product is better than that of his competitors in order to sell this conviction to his customers.

e) The functioning social role of the traveling salesman calls for an adaptive personality. There are certain generalized behavior patterns running through all his relations with his employers, his customers, his competitors, and others. Nevertheless the social situations into which he enters vary in different cities; he must be ready to adjust himself to them. His ability to adapt to these variations often means the difference between making and losing a sale.

The social function of the salesman's role must not be lost sight of in this descriptive list. In an industrial and commercial culture like ours, selling is the tremendously important link between mass production and mass consumption. The modern manufacturer cannot count on word automatically getting around that his goods are of high quality and low price. If he makes a better mousetrap, the world will beat a path to his door only if the salesman clears the way and points out the path.

The scientific methods of economic distribution require the co-operation of many persons besides the traveling salesman. Radio and television actors, announcers, and commentators have taken over much of the selling function. There are many other subroles performed in general distribution, but the traveling salesman remains the key person. His social role expresses the energy, drive, optimism, pragmatism, discipline, and expectations of the ideal type of what has come to be known as the American personality.

3. The Professional Athlete

There is probably no other society in the modern world in which the recreational institution affects so many people as it does in the United States. The functioning of a major institution and of the groups that accompany it requires large numbers of people whose principal social role is bound up in it. While this is true of many who are full-time agents in leisure-time activities, we are concerned here only with the modern American phenomenon of the professional athlete.

The professional athlete is not only a symbol of American affluence, a proof that Americans have the wealth to support their entertainers and the leisure to watch them in action. He also represents one of the high social values in our culture, that of competition as a good thing in itself. The competitive spirit, especially the idea of being a "good sport," carries over from the recreational field into business and politics, education and even into religion. The American is expected to be aggressive in everything he does but also to be a "good loser" when he fails.

Following are some of the components of the social role of the professional American athlete:

a) It is obvious that certain physical qualifications are basic to the athletic role. These are strength, agility, endurance, and skill. All these abilities require specialized training since the demands differ from sport to sport, for example, from wrestling to tennis. It is sometimes said that courage or "heart" makes up what is lacking in physical stamina, but this is highly questionable in the case of the full-time professional.

b) Athletic ability is an economic asset which is treated like a scarce commodity. The supply never seems to satisfy the demand. It is sold to the highest bidder, who is usually some kind of manager or enterpriser; and when the ultimate buyer, the public, no longer pays for the product, it is discarded. The athletes themselves recognize this fact, and they try to earn as much as they can while their abilities last.

c) As athletics becomes more complex and institutionalized, the athlete ceases to be an independent agent handling his own affairs. He has little to say about the time and place where he will perform; and even in the actual performance he follows the advice of trainers, coaches, team captains, and managers. In most other social roles, the higher the person rises, the more freedom of decision he has, but the opposite seems to be true of the star athlete. He is "valuable property" that must be handled with extreme care.

d) The social role of the athlete requires also certain patterns of behavior in relation to the general public. He is expected to be a model of propriety, a good example for the youth of the nation. He is helped a great deal by press agents and sports writers who extol the virtues of athletes and who usually cover up any but the most blatant breaches of conduct. This public responsibility is a further indication that sports have a moral connotation among American cultural values.

e) The demands of the social role of the athlete vary according to the different publics for which he performs. It is usually said that there is an unspecified "sports public," but this is an oversimplified generalization. Sports vary in their social status because they appeal to people at different levels of stratification. In a rough descending order of status the most popular American sports may be ranked as follows: tennis and golf, basketball and hockey, football and baseball, boxing, wrestling, and horse racing. The star tennis player plays for a different public than does the star wrestler.

f) Since sports are essentially competitive, the athlete must be on one side or the other and must have social relations with other athletes. In team sports, like baseball or hockey, he must be courteous and fair to opponents on and off the playing field. Even in individual contests like boxing, where the objective is to make his opponent insensible, the pugilist is expected to act "like a gentleman." The rules of the game govern this conduct during the actual performance, and the mores of professional athletics govern it outside the contest.

The professional athlete must play the role of public figure in America, but he is not esteemed at the same high level by everyone. To his followers and supporters he is an idol who is asked to sign autographs, put on benefit performances, and receive the acclaim of a hero. To the supporters of his opponent he is a "bum" who can be freely insulted and jeered at by the paying customers.

It is part of the social conditioning of the professional athlete that he must learn to be a target of both praise and blame. In the long run his actual competence does not depend upon popularity or unpopularity. His role calls for an equilibrium which can withstand either; and this is probably the ultimate reason why he is able to remain a professional.

4. The Elementary-School Teacher

America is unique among modern societies in its faith in formal schooling and in its willingness to maintain and expand its formal educational facilities. State laws exist, and are usually enforced, that fix the age limits up to which every child must attend school. The general level of formal schooling is rising far above these compulsory limits. More and more people are receiving higher degrees, and there appears to be no end to the number of special fields of learning in which an individual can earn an academic degree.

At the base of this ever growing educational structure are the elementary-school teachers. Unlike most other Western countries, in America more than three-quarters of them are females. At the present time the elementary teacher is in great demand; she is still earning a relatively low salary; and her social status is slowly rising. There are many stereotypes and caricatures of the teacher. The following list provides a partial description of her functioning social role:

a) The elementary-school teacher must often act as a parent-surrogate. Especially in lower-class neighborhoods where there is not much co-operation between parents and teacher, the mother "turns over" her child to the teacher. She often holds the teacher responsible for the behavior of the child. In many instances the teacher has to train the child in fundamental etiquette that she might normally expect him to learn at home.

b) The social role of the teacher includes patterns of leadership. As a matter of fact, she is the leader in all the classroom activities. The attempts to inspire leadership among the children and to instil in them notions of self-reliance and self-government still leave the teacher in the only adult and really superior role in the classroom. She originates, guides, alters, and directs the activities of the group under her control, assuming almost all the leadership functions.

c) The essence of the teacher's role, and that which gives it its name, is the function of instruction. The techniques that are used for imparting knowledge appear to be an almost inexhaustible area of research and experimentation in American teachers' colleges and departments of education. Many visual and auditory aids to teaching have been put at the disposal of the elementary teacher, and sometimes these techniques appear to be emphasized more than the content of instruction.

d) From the point of view of the total society the most important function of the teacher's role is the transmission of the culture. Children of immigrants, particularly, learn in the schools the American way of life. The teacher teaches not only reading, writing, and arithmetic, which are the tools of knowledge, but also American knowledge itself. She can hardly avoid doing this as an American talking about American things and in an American way. She socializes and Americanizes her pupils.

e) The teacher in many ways acts as an example of behavior for the children. Much of the informal education the child receives comes through perception and imitation of the teacher, who may be more impressive in her offhand remarks and her ways of acting than she realizes. The child does not imitate the teacher as much as the parent, but many adults recall vividly the attitudes and mannerisms of their elementary-school teacher.

f) In the American elementary schools the teacher often has to be an entertainer more than a disciplinarian. The theory is widely applied that the child's interest must be aroused and that it is somehow psychologically inadvisable to force him to do anything. There is no doubt that this makes great demands on the adaptability of the teacher in enacting her role. For most adults it is easier to dictate procedures to youngsters than it is to arouse their voluntary interests.

The teacher's social role is more dynamic in the American society than it is in most other contemporary societies. Its patterns are not so rigid because the experimentalism of our culture has entered upon them. The turnover of teachers—since many young women teach for only a few years before marriage—has also prevented the role from becoming too formalized. The teacher must be adaptive because the body of knowledge is constantly expanding, and the child is learning more and more from the various mass media of communication.

The elementary-school teacher is a pivotal person in the whole educational system, and the social role she plays is much more significant than most Americans realize. She represents the principal institutionalized channel through which our cultural heritage flows. She is an instrument for the maintenance and reproduction of our cultural values in each succeeding generation.

5. The Scientist

The American society is usually thought to have a secular culture in which the "explanation of the universe" has been taken out of the hands of the theologian and philosopher and placed in the hands of the scientist. Ours has been called an "engineering civilization" because the application of physical science has resulted in the significant control of nature. These results are tangible and measurable. They bring material comfort and social convenience to millions of Americans.

We are interested here in the social role of the person who makes these results possible, the scientist. The application of scientific knowledge is not the essence of science. The important point is the network of both conceptual and external patterns of behavior that explains the scientist himself. What kind of man is he? What are his ways of thought, his methods and procedures? It is possible to indicate some of the characteristics of the scientist that help to answer these questions:

a) The modern American scientist is a co-operative agent in research and not the lone wolf and queer genius of fiction. The importance of co-ordinating various aspects of a research project, of making cumulative and simultaneous advances, and of sharing and comparing results has been recognized. This does not mean that the individual scientist is less a genius because he co-operates with others. There is still room for the flashes of insight that accompany the greatest scientific discoveries.

b) The scientist is usually a man of disciplined diligence. He works long hours on a systematic procedure of investigation and verification. The demands of the scientific function eliminate the careless and self-indulgent person from the occupation. Exactitude and precision are characteristics of scientific research, and even the "small" error must be corrected by constant rechecking of the data.

c) The successful scientist is a man of dedicated faith in the value of knowledge. The common misconception that the scientist is completely "value-free" is belied by the repeated statements of scientists that what they are doing is really worth doing. It is obvious that he cannot know what the full consequences of his research will be when it is applied by others in the total society. His faith is a fundamental assumption, only partially demonstrated by society at large, that his findings can somehow contribute to the general and steady improvement of human life on earth.

d) Honesty is a conceptual pattern or virtue characterizing the American scientist. It is implied in the scientific way of life. The social pressure of fellow scientists and of the general public places heavy sanctions on scientific honesty. Any attempt to "force the data" in order to "prove" the desired results is ultimately detected, and the individual who does this pays with his reputation and his livelihood. Furthermore, the observed examples of this kind of dishonesty as practiced under totalitarian powers have made the scientist particularly wary of censorship and "thought control."

e) The role of the scientist is marked also by scientific skepticism essential in the search for truth. The scientist does not question basic knowledge or the validly tested uniformities of his field. The scientist is constantly working at the periphery of accepted knowledge, at the frontiers of the unknown, and his explorations require that he be tentative and open-minded.

The American treats his scientists with awe and respect; the term "scientific" is a value-loaded word in his vocabulary. The high social status of the scientist is sometimes transferred to areas in his life in which he has relatively little competence. In interviews with the press he is often expected to make pronouncements concerning public issues about which he knows very little. The published results have sometimes been ludicrous, as when the expert biologist gives his views of demography, the physicist answers theological questions, or the sociologist dabbles in medical questions.

In spite of these occasional aberrations, however, the scientist is playing an increasingly important "public role" in the United States. There appears to be a trend toward a broader concept of the utility of science for our society and culture. Prominent and expert scientists in both the physical and social sciences are assuming responsibilities for spreading factual information about their studies. This spreading of knowledge is a function of the gradual process of sociocultural integration that occurs in every maturing nation.

DISCUSSION QUESTIONS

1. Explain the meaning and content of the social role.
2. How does the sociological definition of personality differ from other definitions?
3. Show clearly the difference between role and status.
4. What is meant by the role relation?
5. Show by example that the role contains both overt and covert patterns of behavior.
6. How do behavior expectations influence actual performance of roles?
7. Discuss: "The strength of social sanctions on roles varies."
8. What is meant by saying that each social role has several levels of behavior?
9. Discuss: "Roles are universal but their formation is variable."
10. Why do we say that a person cannot achieve a role?
11. Show with examples the difference between assignment and assumption of roles.
12. What is the most common way of classifying roles?
13. What is the difference between key role and general role?
14. Outline the contents of the social role of the city politician.
15. How does the role of the traveling salesman differ from that of a clerk in the local retail store?

16. In what ways is the professional athlete a symbol and promoter of American social values?
17. What are the features of the key role of the American athlete?
18. Describe the role of the elementary-school teacher.
19. Why is the scientific role particularly valued in America?
20. What features characterize the role of the American scientist?

SUGGESTED READINGS

BROOM, LEONARD, and SELZNICK, PHILIP. *Sociology: A Text with Adapted Readings.* Evanston, Ill.: Row, Peterson & Co., 1955, chaps. iv, vi.

FICHTER, JOSEPH H. *Social Relations in the Urban Parish.* Chicago: University of Chicago Press, 1954, chap. x.

HERTZLER, J. O. *Society in Action.* New York: Dryden Press, Inc., 1954, chap. xx.

LINTON, RALPH. *The Study of Man.* New York: D. Appleton–Century Co., 1936, chap. viii.

MARTINDALE, DON, and MONACHESI, E. D. *Elements of Sociology.* New York: Harper & Bros., 1951, chaps. vi, xii–xiv.

YOUNG, KIMBALL. *Sociology: A Study of Society and Culture.* New York: American Book Co., 1949, chaps viii, ix, xxv, xxvi.

CHAPTER TEN

Social Processes

Human beings in society are interdependent and interrelated. Mutual interaction or reciprocal communication is so essential to both the individual and the group that without it the person would perish and the group would cease to function. People and groups can be and are related to one another in many ways, and the total society is a vast and complex network of social relations.

A difficulty sometimes arises in using terms like "relation," "human relation," and "social relation." Ordinarily one speaks of his relatives as persons who are related to him by birth, adoption, or marriage. The abstract term "relation" is sometimes personified, as when a person refers to the members of his family as his "relations." The sociologist employs the term in its most generic meaning as the link or bond that exists between persons and groups. In this sense it is not limited to family relations but includes all relations in factories, schools, churches, political parties, sports clubs, and every other kind of primary and secondary group and association.

We think of relations as personal relations, and it is true that two or more persons are always involved in them. In order to analyze the large network of relations in society, it is necessary to make certain abstractions from the concrete human beings involved. When we do this, we find that human persons and groups are related by virtue of status, role, and process. The first two of these we will review only briefly; the third forms the subject matter of this chapter.

a) Relation by status refers to the linkage of social positions we have already discussed in the chapter on social status and stratification. It is the relation of position or standing that individuals occupy in reference to one another. We have said that social status is meaningless if it cannot be referred to other statuses in subordinate, equal, or superior relations. This concept is applicable also to the relation of groups, categories, classes, and other pluralities to one another. The status relation, as the word implies, is a static concept. The kinetic or dynamic aspect is seen only when a person through social mobility changes from one status to another.

b) Relation by role refers to the functional, reciprocal interaction that occurs when people pursue their social roles together. This relation involves the expectations of social thought and behavior as well as the actual external performance of these role patterns. The role is the mechanism through which people carry on their mutual behavior, and so the roles of different persons meet and are related. These role relations are easily recognized in the mutual interaction of friend and friend, parents and children, salesman and customer, and in large numbers of other patterned mutual behavior situations.

c) Relation by process is a further analytical refinement, and on a level of abstraction different from that of the role relation. The social processes are a few basic, typable forms of social interaction that cross-cut all the numerous social roles people enact. The term "process" has been taken over into sociology from the general scientific meaning of a dynamic course, or repetitive series, of operations. In the mechanical analogy the process usually eventuates in a product, an achieved objective, but in social science we cannot speak of a "product" of social processes. In sociological terminology, the basic social processes are co-operation, accommodation, assimilation, conflict, contravention, and competition.

The social process is more than the link between two statuses or roles. Two persons who co-operate with one another or fight with one another are carrying on a social process that is something more than either their status relation or their role relation. Both the process relation and the role relation involve patterns of interaction, behavior by two or more persons that is *performed together* by both terms of the relationship, but the distinction between the two kinds of relations requires further analysis. The process transcends the role; the process of competition or contravention transcends the role of the salesman who engages in these processes.

Relations and Roles

We have seen that persons interact through the expression of their social roles and that the social role is composed of patterns of behavior surrounding a social function. When people fulfil the patterns of behavior consonant with their roles, they do so in relation to other persons. Since roles are always reciprocal—for example, the employer implies the employee, the child implies the parent—we may say that the actual performance of roles entails social relations. The social person and his roles function with, are *related to*, other social persons and their roles.

When father and son communicate in a social situation, the man is behaving like a father and the boy is behaving like a son. This example can be multiplied by all the social situations in which two or more persons interact. Just as social status makes no sense except in reference to other social statuses, so also the social role does not stand alone. The intercommunication and interaction of people playing their social roles constitute the role relation. This type of social relation refers to all the identifiable, repetitive patterns of social interaction in which two or more persons engage in the performance of social functions.

From the point of view of sociological analysis there are here three important elements which must be distinguished: (*a*) the numerous *patterns* of social behavior the individual performs that are co-ordinated and interrelated; (*b*) the *social role* that is a cluster of behavior patterns around an identifiable social function; and (*c*) the *role relation*, a functional pattern of social interaction that brings together the active roles people perform. Thus, we cannot say that the content of the social relation is nothing more than the content of the social roles as enacted between persons. The social relation is the link that brings together the roles and is not the combination of the roles as such.

The Content of Processes

On the abstract level on which we must discuss this complex question of human relations, we recognize that there are certain repetitive ways of behaving that run through all the types of human association people can have. The association of father and son, employer and employee, governor and governed, may be conjunctive or disjunctive. The people involved in these pairs may love one another or they may be antagonistic to one another. Thus the social process is not merely the static position one person holds in reference to another, or even the patterns of behavior that make up the role, but the ways in which these roles and persons reciprocally function.

The principal social processes are co-operation, accommodation, assimilation, conflict, contravention, and competition. These ways of behaving are patterned relations in every society. They are present to some degree everywhere, but the emphasis placed on one or the other of them is not the same everywhere. The characteristics of behavior patterns we have already discussed are also applicable to the description of social processes. They consist of both external and conceptual ways of behaving, frequently recurring in fairly similar ways, shared in by many people, and having some social significance. The content of the behavior pattern and of the social process can be analyzed "as though" it existed apart from other patterns and other roles.

The social process must always be analyzed as a way of behaving which involves a plurality. In other words, the content of the social process always includes the behavior *between* two or more people that is shared *simultaneously* by them. This important point—the distinction between the role relation and the social process—is clarified when we use an example. The pattern of competitive behavior between two brothers can be analyzed as a social process which is distinguishable from the fraternal relationship existing between them. The social role of brother contains many patterns of behavior that have developed in the culture. But the social process of competition is something more than—it is "added to"—the situation in which brothers enact their roles. Likewise, brothers in conflict still remain brothers, and the social process of conflict is not the enactment of the social role of brother.

Universality of Social Processes

The major patterns of social relations, like most human behavior in society, are largely standardized and routinized. The functional processes of interaction of group with group and of individual with individual have been observed in every type of group in which people associate. They appear to be fundamental to the maintenance of society in the sense that there are regularized and sanctioned ways in which these social processes are conducted.

The universal basic social relations are few. Some societies minimize one or more of these basic social processes, and other societies maximize them. A polar example is that of competition, which is highly emphasized in Western civilization and largely de-emphasized among the Orientals. Every society has developed standardized procedures through which accommodation and assimilation take place and through which even contravention and conflict occur. The cultural expression of these main forms of social relations differs quite broadly from one society to another. but they exist and are observable everywhere.

Classification of Processes

The broadest general categories of social processes are those that run in two opposite directions. The *conjunctive* processes are the patterns of related interaction through which persons are drawn together and become more integrated. The *disjunctive* processes are those in which people are pushed farther apart and become less solidaristic.

In some degree or other, the conjunctive processes are always expressive of the social virtues of justice and love, while the disjunctive processes are always expressive of the social vices of injustice and hatred. We use the terms "virtue" and "vice" not as moral habits but as patterned forms of social relations that include both external and conceptual patterns of behavior.

We do not classify these basic forms of social processes as either covert attitudes or as overt interaction, because each kind of social process must be presumed to contain both the measurable expression and the indirectly observable attitude. The disjunctive processes may be called *negative* to the extent that they reflect injustice and hostility among people, while the conjunctive relations may be called *positive* in the sense that they reflect mutual altruism and justice.

The three conjunctive positive social processes are co-operation, accommodation, and assimilation. Each of these is an identifiable form of social relation in which the participating persons achieve some objective considered beneficial or desirable to themselves. In so far as conscious motivation enters into these relations, they are an expression of the participants' self-interest, but in their actual operation they must be considered also of benefit to the total group or society. They help to perpetuate and maintain the society as a going concern.

The three disjunctive negative social processes are conflict, contravention, and competition. They, too, are social relations because they are ways of behaving in which two or more persons must participate. While the two parties may not always participate equally in the relationship, there is never a case in which one is active and the other completely passive. These processes are called negative because the people involved in them attempt to prevent others from attaining an objective which is considered desirable. They are called dissociative because the participants are at odds with each other rather than in harmony.

Co-operation

Co-operation is that form of social process in which two or more persons or groups act jointly in the pursuit of a common objective. It is not only the most common form of social relation; it is also an essential and indispensable requirement for the maintenance and continuance of groups and societies. Co-operation is, of course, a reciprocal relation. It cannot be "one-sided," although it is quite obvious that co-operation neither requires nor often contains an exactly equal amount of effort by each side of the relation. When we say that people act jointly, we mean that they are contributing effort together and more or less simultaneously for the achievement of an objective.

It is also often true that one party in the co-operative relation may achieve more of the desired goal than does the other party. We are speaking here, however, of the processes, rather than the fruits, of the co-operative action. Much of the success of co-operation is hardly noticed by people in everyday life because the practice of co-operation runs through all the major concerns of society. People assume that co-operation is the normal thing in doing business, providing material necessities, raising children, running the government. At times when the normal co-operative relation breaks down we are able to recognize more clearly its importance.

Co-operation is a social process that admits of kinds and degrees. It is, for example, much more intensive and continuous in primary groups than in secondary associations. The primary group assumes that its members will co-operate, while the secondary association often has to encourage and promote co-operation among its participants. The family appears to require and obtain more co-operation than do the other major groups of a society. The amount and kind of co-operation exercised in the educational, economic, political, religious, and recreational groups appear to depend upon the social values and the institutional dominance current in any particular culture.

The factors that account for co-operation are complex and numerous. The conscious desire for an objective, which may be ultimately reduced to self-interest, loyalty to one's group and its ideals, the fear of attack by an out-group, or the basic structural need for mutual dependence—all these factors function in varying degrees toward the continuing process of co-operation. Briefly we may say that co-operation is social solidarity in action, and these same factors are commonly described by sociologists as the factors of social integration, cohesion, and solidarity.

Accommodation

While co-operation is an essential and positive social relation highly beneficial to a society, accommodation is a kind of minimum working arrangement that enables people to continue their activities even when they are not in complete agreement and harmony with each other. The community, the factory, the school—almost any group in the society—strives for co-operation but may have to settle for accommodation.

In a complex society where the social person participates in various groups, he may find himself co-operating with one group and merely accommodating himself to another group. It is probably demonstrable that every large group has both levels of members, the co-operators and the accommodators.

Accommodation may be defined, therefore, as that form of social process in which two or more persons or groups interact in order to prevent, reduce, or eliminate conflict. Accommodation is also the necessary process that occurs after a conflict is over, in that the survivors learn to adjust and adapt themselves to each other. The objective of accommodation, however, is not merely negative. It is a means of living peacefully, of coexisting with one another, which may eventually lead to positive co-operation. It also is essentially a two-sided relationship, in which both parties, whether individuals or groups or whole societies, are participants in interaction. It is characterized by "give and take" in the sense that each side makes an alteration in its behavior patterns in order to accommodate the other.

There are many subtle shadings and degrees of the accommodative process, and these are fairly well recognized by any student of society. Mere toleration between persons or groups is the minimum amount of accommodation. Compromise goes further than this and is the process in which each side makes concessions to the other. Arbitration and conciliation are frequently used conscious forms of accommodation. There are also situations in which one party may be coerced by law, or threats, or physical force into accommodation with the stronger party. The consequent of international conflict has always been some form of accommodation between the victor and the vanquished.

Assimilation

Assimilation is a social process through which two or more persons or groups accept and perform one another's patterns of behavior. We commonly talk about a person, or a minority category, being assimilated into a group or a society, but here again this must not be interpreted as a "one-sided" process. It is a relation of interaction in which both parties behave reciprocally even though one may be much more affected than the other. Assimilation is not so much a result as a process, although the degree of assimilation achieved in any society is an index of its social and cultural integration.

The process of assimilation, a reciprocal relation, must be distinguished from socialization, which emphasizes the cultural effect upon the individual. It is true that every person must necessarily experience throughout his life the learning of behavior patterns. This is socialization, through which he constantly adapts himself to the culture and learns how to behave as a member of society. It is a general long-term procedure, emphasizing what the individual does and what the effects are upon him.

Assimilation is a specific process best observed in populations made up of divergent ethnic backgrounds. Here exist clearly discernible cultural traits coming from societies in different parts of the world. The varying patterns of thinking and acting meet and mingle. The people involved in this process do more than exchange cultural characteristics. They tend to adapt, adjust, and finally assimilate these traits to themselves. In this process the people also are assimilated to one another so that they now share similar patterns of behavior in a way different from that which previously existed in each party of the relation. For example, the cultural mingling of Moors and Spaniards is still discernible in southern Spain.

The degree and amount of assimilation that occur among people in any society depend upon a number of factors. The process tends to be slowed down where there are rigid lines of class and caste, where there is a reluctance or inability to share the highly valued cultural items. Differences in language, religion, education, and wealth are sometimes major obstacles to the process of assimilation. Ethnic minorities in Europe are historical examples of these obstacles to assimilation, like the Polish communities scattered through Russia and the long-established German minorities in Poland.

Conflict

Conflict is that form of mutual interaction through which two or more persons attempt to remove each other, either by annihilating or by rendering the other party ineffectual. Its most elementary form is armed warfare, in which large groups of persons meet in combat with the intention of destroying one another. The focus of attention and action in the process of conflict is always the parties involved in the relationship, but there is always present some other stated objective or purpose for which the conflict is waged. Conflict is interpreted as a means to an end. Deliberate conflict merely for its own sake is probably a rare occurrence even in so-called primitive societies.

The term "conflict" is used in many loose connotations, and it is necessary to specify it carefully. One hears of a conflict of ideas between the younger and older generations, of industrial conflict between management and labor, of a conflict of interests between political parties. Attempts to put someone out of business or to murder someone are sometimes called conflict. These meanings are not the same as the sociological concept with which we are dealing. As a social process, conflict is a reciprocal human relation in which both parties participate.

There can be no doubt that the preliminaries to conflict include various forms of disagreement. These are shown by words or actions of insult, abhorrence, rivalry, or contempt, or by personal and physical attacks, or by dishonors. Conflict often grows out of competition and contravention, and, unless the parties engaged in it are totally destroyed, it must be followed by some form of accommodation. Modern prize fighting, the purpose of which is to render one's opponent insensible, fits the definition of conflict; but it has also the aspect of a competitive sport, in which the combatants are striving for economic gain, a prize, or a championship.

Contravention

Contravention is a social process in which the opposing persons or groups try to prevent each other from attaining an objective, whether or not they want it for themselves. It is sometimes termed a polite and genteel form of conflict because it contains hostility and antagonism without head-on and direct attacks upon the opponents. It is necessarily a social relation because there are always two sides to the process, two terms of the relationship, which are not, however, always evenly matched.

Contravention often takes place alongside of, and even within, the co-operative process. Two or more segments of a national parliament or congress, who must ultimately find some form of general co-operation for the welfare of the country, frequently engage in the contravention process. The political parties are indispensable to one another and must in many ways co-ordinate their actions, but in other ways they contravene one another. Contravention takes many forms and is expressed in delaying tactics, in denouncing, thwarting, and frustrating others, and in spreading rumors and "smears" and conducting whispering campaigns. The use of the stereotype, especially one that emphasizes the negative qualities of a person or category, is a most common instrument of contravention.

Contravention is not sociologically significant if it is restricted merely to a person-to-person basis, as, for example, when two neighbors spread idle gossip about one another. It is often carried on in an organized manner between larger categories of the population, between different religious groups, social classes, and races, and between organized management and organized labor. There are many evidences of contravention between the majority and the various minorities in a society. All these examples are characterized by the efforts of each party to prevent the other from achieving an objective without either destroying the other or attaining the objective for one's self.

Competition

Competition is a social process in which two or more persons or groups are striving to attain the same objective. In the processes of conflict and contravention attention is focused primarily on the other party as such. In the process of competition both parties focus primarily on the objective that both want to achieve and only secondarily on each other. Persons and groups compete *for* an object, and the competition is always stronger when the object is short in supply and of high value.

Competition is carried out in a peaceful manner and is more formally regularized than the other disjunctive processes. There are conscious or unconscious "rules of the game" followed by the competing individuals and groups. Competition is considered a kind of game, with stakes that may be high, that must be played fairly; it is thought to be beneficial even though disaster may occasionally befall the weakest competitors, as when the smaller businessman fails to survive his stronger competitors.

The extent and degree of competition increase in a dynamic, open-class society in which opportunities are numerous and achievement is applauded. In fact, the competitive process may come to be valued almost as highly as the co-operative process. Generally people compete for the criteria of social status in any society. These are more numerous and more available in some societies than in others.

Complexity of Social Processes

Even the brief description we have given above of the various social processes indicates that these types of human relations must not be oversimplified. Several further considerations must be made here in order to relate these processes to the concrete social situations in which they are found.

First, it must be clear from what we have said that none of these processes is found, at least for any length of time, in a "pure" form. Conflict almost always has overtones of competition since the opponents are striving for something more than the destruction of each other. Long-term conflict and competition almost always involve contravention. There is a similar overlapping of the conjunctive processes of co-operation, accommodation, and assimilation. In spite of this complex interweaving of the various social processes, however, they are by no means synonymous, and they must for purposes of clarity and understanding be analyzed separately.

Second, the fact that the social processes transcend the specific content of role behavior is sometimes confusing to the beginning student of sociology. We have given sufficient examples to demonstrate that the specific content of the social role must be distinguished from the generic forms of social processes. The college student may enact his educational role in a competitive manner, or he may be going through an accommodative process, but he still continues to perform the patterns of his student role. He may be in conflict with his brother and very co-operative with the fellow members of his church, but through it all he is still performing the distinguishable familial and religious roles.

Third, the concrete operation of social processes sometimes appears complicated because the persons and groups involved may be performing two apparently contradictory social processes at the same time. This problem is clarified if we note the object about which the social process occurs. For example, two brothers may be competing for the love of the same girl but at the same time be successfully co-operative in a business venture. Two political parties may be contravening each other in the question of a farm policy, but they may also be in agreement on a bipartisan policy in foreign affairs.

Finally, the influence of the culture is an important factor in the ways in which the social processes operate in any given society. The significant social values of the people determine, for example, whether competition is emphasized more than co-operation or to what extent this or that social class or minority is allowed to participate in the social processes. The culture determines the rules and limits of the various processes and also the value of the objects over which the processes occur. A Bushman, for example, may understand competition and even conflict over food and hunting rights but not over oil fields, gold mines, and coal fields. The cultural values make the difference.

Conceptual Matrix of Social Processes

We have seen that the contents of social relations are both overt and covert patterns of behavior. In other words, when we analyze co-operation or conflict, we study not merely the external manifestations of behavior that accompany the process but also the internal attitudes, ideas, judgments, and biases connected with it. Competition is a "state of mind" shared by many people as well as a pattern of behavior externalized in interaction. The same can be said of the analysis of the other processes of accommodation, co-operation, conflict, assimilation, and contravention.

There exist also in every society more generalized conceptual patterns of behavior that act as a kind of conceptual matrix, or fulcrum, for the conjunctive and disjunctive processes we have discussed above. The principal ones for the conjunctive process are equity, justice, and love. These, too, are social relations because they involve reciprocal conceptual behavior and are not merely "virtues" or good habits that exist in the mind of the individual person. In fact, they cannot be realistically conceived except as a pattern of behavior between two or more persons who are equitable, just, and charitable to each other.

a) Justice is a social process in which the related parties perform the obligations due to each other. The relation of justice is a formal or informal contractual relation in which the rights of one person or group are met by the obligations of the other person or group. The concept of justice and the actual expression of the social process of justice are found in every society, even though the manner in which they operate differs vastly from one society to another.

We have seen that the mores are the most compulsive patterns of behavior in any society. This means that the obligation to perform them and to allow and to encourage their performance exists on the level of what the people in the society consider right and wrong. When a person deliberately violates the mores, he is jeopardizing the common welfare, he is "doing wrong" against the other people, and he is acting in an unjust manner. Society in other words claims the right to expect conformity to its most important behavioral patterns, and persons and groups who thus perform are enacting the social process of justice.

b) Equity is that social process which operates in the areas in which behavior patterns are not morally defined or strictly enforceable. People who do what "common decency" expects, rather than what the strict letter of the law and the rigidities of formal social sanctions require, are carrying on equitable social relations. It is the kind of relationship that arises out of social experience of what is the proper and fitting thing to do. Frequently the equitable relation occurs in situations that are not exact duplicates of previous situations, like that of an accident or disaster.

More frequently, however, the equitable relation is recognizable in the vast areas of folkways and usages when these patterns are performed between and among people. Here again we consider people dealing with one another under the aspect of general social goals and the common welfare, even though the equitable relation does not always consciously contain these objectives. The smooth flow of ordinary daily interactions is generally made possible by equity rather than by justice.

c) Social love is a broad, general process in which the interacting parties wish and do that which is beneficial for each other. It must be distinguished from romantic and conjugal love. Social scientists have begun to use the term "altruism" for this basic social process that implies a degree of self-sacrifice and makes greater demands on persons and groups than either justice or equity. It is in a sense the most fundamental social relation, more basic than any other, without which human groups and societies are inconceivable.

Social love does not operate under social pressure and it does not entail strict obligations enforceable by society. It is exemplified in many forms, and all of the valued social virtues like kindliness, neighborliness, generosity, and good will appear to be manifestations of social love. This social process is the antidote of egoism, ethnocentrism, and hatred, and it is obviously performed in various degrees by every social person in at least some of the social roles he enacts.

It must be remembered that we are considering these processes of justice, equity, and love from the sociological and not from the psychological point of view. We are not interested in how they are developed by, or how they affect, individual, personal behavior. We analyze them from the aspect of relations between and among persons and groups, and from this it is clear that these three processes underlie the positive and conjunctive relations of co-operation, accommodation, and assimilation. When they are deeply imbedded in the culture, they tend to restrain and temper the negative aspects of the disjunctive processes of conflict, contravention, and competition.

AMERICAN SOCIAL PROCESSES

1. The Value of Competition

Americans take it for granted that competition is a good thing, that "competition is the life of trade," that this social process has many positive values. A comparison with other societies shows that Americans actually put this concept into practice. The American politician who fails to win office in political competition does not flee the country in fear of his successful rival; riots do not ordinarily break out at the end of football and baseball matches; even beauty contests do not break up with the contestants clawing each other. Fair play and the rules of the game have become deep and traditional cultural patterns.

There is often a fine line between competition and conflict, and the American usually thinks of competition as a substitute for conflict rather than as a prelude to conflict. When the child is encouraged to be self-assertive and aggressive, he is not being told to defeat others but to improve himself. He must be courteously competitive, and if he loses his head in either winning or losing he is scolded for not being a good sport. The following list shows that the process of competition is encouraged by Americans in all the major areas of social activities:

a) Economic competition is to be expected in a culture that applauds initiative and freedom, makes available opportunities, and values the material criteria of success. Business competition is not free and haphazard; it is more and more regulated so that everybody gets a chance. Antitrust laws and antimonopoly suits have become part of our cultural tradition; and while regulations never work perfectly they do tend to preserve both the spirit and the form of competition.

b) Competition among young people in the educational institution is not an original American notion, but it has extended to a larger percentage of persons here than elsewhere. In an effort to decrease the frustrations of unsuccessful competitors some educators have proposed the removal of competitive tests and scorings. In a sense, this attempt "goes against" the culture. As long as competition is considered a value in itself, and as long as the system of grades and credits is employed right up through postgraduate studies, American youth will engage in it and be affected by it.

c) In the recreational institution competition is the "essence" of sports. Even the modified mayhem which characterizes professional boxing, wrestling, and football is applauded as the typical expression of the American competitive spirit. The "dirty" contestant who breaks the rules is penalized by the officials and often scorned by the audience. Sports are considered a very healthy activity with moral and psychological overtones; they provide an outlet for youthful aggressiveness; they keep the young person out of trouble. Sports competition is supposed to substitute for and to help avoid conflict with others.

d) The familial groupings in any society must necessarily be characterized by the basic process of co-operation among the members. Nevertheless, there are peculiar competitive aspects in the American system, especially in the premarital experiences of youth. The dating customs, and particularly the method of evaluating dates, involve the process of competition. Every college campus is the scene of competition among girls for dates with a popular young man, and vice versa; and the prized objective is most often not marriage but the exchange of high-school rings or of fraternity and sorority pins. In a sense, this competition too is a game, and the person who loses the contest has to be a good sport.

e) Competition in the political arena is a recurrent social phenomenon in the American society. This is not only competition between individuals who are vying for office but also between organized groups of people who are supporting the respective competing candidates. Except in rare instances in minor elections, the candidate who does not have an organization to support him cannot hope to compete successfully for public office. In order to keep elections fair, laws have been evolved to control campaign spending, the counting of ballots, and the watching of polling booths.

f) Among religious bodies the American society has gradually developed a system in which conflict has been replaced by competition. Churches are numerous, and no church contains more than a minority of the population. The result is that no one, with the exception of a few full-time church functionaries, thinks about "defeating" other religious groups or of "putting them out of business." This is not an armed truce among the churches. It is a typically American expression of competition for souls, for increased prestige, and for the prize of bigness.

These examples indicate that competition enters in some form or other into all of the major areas of American social life. Both as a conceptual pattern and as a pattern of external behavior it is an extremely important sociological element. It would be naïve to suggest that the processes of conflict and contravention are of no importance, but it is a fact that their effects have been minimized by an emphasis on competition. What appears to be unique in the American culture is the consideration of competition as a positive, associative form of social process instead of a negative, dissociative relation, as it seems to be considered in many other cultures.

2. American Teamwork

Americans are fond of boasting that co-operation is the most effective form of human relation. The primary proof of this assertion is the organized, co-ordinated, co-operative system of mass production and mass distribution that has made available to the people an abundance of commodities and services. The belief that *anything* can be done through teamwork pervades the American culture. "Let's all work together" is a slogan heard frequently everywhere in the country.

An analysis of the way in which social co-operation actually works requires some sober reflection and tends to temper boastful enthusiasm. Large-scale co-operation is thought of as the means for solving large-scale social problems. The American approach seems to be expressed thus: "Here's a big problem; let's get together and solve it." But still there remain tremendous unsolved social problems in the United States. Even if we grant that these problems *can* be solved by teamwork, what are the underlying conditions that assist or hinder co-operation?

In general it may be said that people will co-operate under three conditions: first, if there is concrete action to be taken; second, if the responsibility for performing the action can be fixed; and, finally, if the people agree that the action is worth performing. When there is general consensus on these three points, Americans tend to co-operate willingly and successfully. Let us demonstrate this generalization with several examples.

a) Americans usually co-operate readily, generously, and effectively when faced with a disaster. They give help to victims of fire, explosion, floods, and epidemics. People co-operate in the organization of relief. Those who can do so usually feel they should do something concrete—donate money and supplies or give immediate physical aid. The Red Cross is usually the co-ordinating agency for this relief, and when there is a major disaster, help comes from all over the nation as well as from the communities near the disaster scene.

The teamwork of Americans during the two world wars is the major example of the efficient handling of a disaster problem. Social co-operation reached a peak then and was more widespread and more effective than any attempts at organized peacetime co-operation. There were, of course, shirkers and laggards as well as some conscientious objectors and others who could not co-operate, but these people are present in every large society. By and large, the American people believed that winning the war was an extremely important objective; they made innumerable concrete contributions to it, from actually fighting to saving empty tin cans. They felt that each individual and group had a responsibility in the general war effort.

b) In the American society there exists an area of ambiguous social problems where there is a general lack of co-operation and where often the initial teamwork breaks down. A general feeling is that "something is wrong" and also that "somebody ought to do something," but there is no real consensus about the seriousness of the problem and no exact way of fixing the responsibility for co-operation on definite people. In these problems people often do not know what to do and leave the solution to others.

Most of these problems skirt delicately around moral issues and values. Juvenile delinquency in the urban schools and streets, the spread of pornographic and lascivious material in books and magazines, the known existence of commercialized vice of all kinds, police brutality and corruption in some places, organized interstate rackets—all these are examples of prevailing social problems that require social co-operation for their solution. Here and there effective but usually temporary "cleanups" have occurred, but in general, these problems show that "everybody's responsibility is nobody's responsibility."

c) A third type of social problem exists in which there has been only partial co-operation. Here one finds a general consensus about the values involved but much disagreement about what is to be done and who is to do it. Americans seem to agree that every family is entitled to a decent home, that every person should have adequate health care, that workers should receive sufficient income, that better highways are required, and that relations between races should be improved.

Many people fail to co-operate in the solution of these problems; in fact, there are instances of organized teamwork that contravenes the current attempts to solve the problems. A certain amount of improvement has been achieved, but effective opposition has often been based on the argument that the method of procedure is in some way "un-American." In other words, people are not in agreement on the values involved in the process of co-operation.

American teamwork, or social co-operation, is particularly interesting when we appreciate the high value Americans place on the competitive process. There is in fact no contradiction in the simultaneous existence of co-operation and competition as important processes within the same culture. An unusual characteristic of the American culture is the apparent belief that competition itself gets things done as efficiently as co-operation. The feeling is that competition stimulates social action and that co-operation within the group results from competition with other groups.

3. The Americanization Process

The "melting pot" is a popular figure of speech for what is more precisely termed the process of Americanizing people from all over the world. This assimilation is widely discussed in our country, and the large number of immigrants who have come to the United States has made the study of assimilation an important project for American sociologists.

Many Americans assume that assimilation has been a one-way process entirely; that America has "given," and the immigrant has "taken." We must remember, however, that assimilation is essentially a social relation, a form of reciprocal communication, and that both terms of the process are involved in mutual behavior. It is perhaps a valuable lesson in the prevention of ethnocentrism to analyze briefly some of the contributions made *to* our culture by foreign cultures. Some of these contributions are as follows:

a) The basic concepts of democracy, that is, of liberty and equality, came out of the philosophy of the Enlightenment in eighteenth-century Europe and have their origins still earlier in the social philosophers of Europe. The legal system that surrounds and protects the application of democracy is a cultural debt to England.

b) The central religious ideas of Christianity are also a European importation. Although the actual practice of Christianity has taken numerous and sometimes bizarre forms, the underlying beliefs in the redemption from sin, in the brotherhood with Christ and the fatherhood of God, have been widespread influences in the social relations of Americans. During the years of highest immigration, ministers and priests accompanied their countrymen to the United States. Catholic Brothers and Sisters have immigrated by the thousands to help preserve their faith and to do missionary work among Americans. They have impressed their own ethnic traits upon the people.

c) The most obviously borrowed cultural pattern Americans have assimilated from foreigners is the English language. The changing pronunciation, the abandoning of old words, and the coining of new terms have brought numerous accidental variations in the use of the "mother tongue"; but our language is still basically an importation from England, and changes are frequently imported from other countries.

d) Little of the food we enjoy is originally or typically American. Every large city is dotted with restaurants offering the food specialties of different nationalities: Armenian, Chinese, French, Italian, Mexican, and many others. Even the eating utensils we use are of foreign origin. An interesting aspect of assimilation in these restaurants is that the "foreign" eating places are owned, operated, and patronized mainly by Americans.

e) Most of our clothing styles are of foreign origin, and, until the invention of synthetics, so were most of our materials. Paris fashions for women and Hawaiian shirts for men are merely two of a long list of foreign styles adapted by Americans for their own use. Even the "natural" difference between male and female clothing, which makes the appearance of Americans so different from that of Asiatics, is in reality an imitation of European customs.

f) The architecture of American public and semipublic buildings imitates styles from ancient Greece and Rome and from medieval Europe. Even the newer, so-called "functional" designs, employing steel, glass, and concrete, had their origins outside the United States in, for example, the *Bauhaus* group in Germany. Many of the household conveniences used everywhere by our people are not original American inventions.

This is a meager list of innumerable cultural items, physical objects, and conceptual and behavior patterns that our people have Americanized through the process of assimilation. Many aspects of our school system, our religious practices, and our family customs have their roots in the non-American world. We must realize, however, that, because of the time perspective and the relations we now have with foreigners, the assimilation process is slowing down. America is developing its own cultural characteristics.

The further we are removed in time from the large flood of immigrants, the less significant becomes the original impact of assimilation. This is as applicable to the native American as it is to the immigrant himself. Also the immigrants of recent decades have had better education and less need to be accepted and assimilated—some are "intellectuals"—and are of higher social status than those who came at the beginning of the century. Since they are fewer in number and since Americans now have much greater self-confidence and less need for the culture of other countries, the contribution to the American culture from foreign immigrants is gradually lessening.

4. Examples of Contravention

In the development of the American culture there has been a peculiar emphasis on two negative social processes. There has been an encouragement of fair competition on the one hand and an attempt to lessen conflict on the other. Little attention has been paid, except by the social scientists, to the process of contravention, which may be called an intermediary form of opposition. Yet this process is actually widespread.

Contravention is a recognizable social process, but it appears to be misinterpreted because it is often employed as a substitute to avoid conflict or as an aid to better one's chances in competition. People contravene (oppose the goals of) one another because they are competitors who are unwilling to become outright enemies. Contravention occurs in all types of human relations, institutionalized situations, and social groupings.

The following are examples of contravention commonplace in American life that are recognizably distinct from the social processes of conflict and competition:

a) In competitive business, especially in advertising, contravention is frequently practiced. When one manufacturer boasts that medical doctors have proved that his cigarette contains fewer throat irritants, another manufacturer counters with the statement, "We are tobacco men, not medicine men." One advertiser sells a cigarette on the basis of its "filter tips," and another contravenes with "Enjoy the fresh unfiltered flavor of our brand."

b) Contravention has been a frequent weapon in labor-management relations. The employment of labor spies to report on union activity and the use of yellow-dog contracts to prevent unions helped management to contravene labor. Tying up the telephone switchboard of a plant and using the slow-down technique on the assembly line were among the methods used by the workers.

c) Legislators and lawyers are adept in the use of contravention techniques. Opponents in Congress are hindered by the tabling of motions or by the burying of resolutions in various committees. Lawyers in the courtroom sometimes use stalling tactics in favor of their clients.

Insurance companies are sometimes reluctant to settle large cases, and they use various legal court procedures and administrative practices for hindering the success of claimants.

d) Contravention is sometimes used to prevent members of minorities from voting or holding office. The requirement that people may register to vote only after having read and interpreted the Constitution of the United States is applied in some states only to Negroes. In some instances a Negro who becomes active in politics is denied banking facilities and credit in business places. There are numerous other tricks of contravention in this area.

e) The striving for a higher class status is contravened in many subtle ways, usually by women. Those who can control the invitations issued for dinner parties, balls, and similar leisure-time activities may see that certain people do not receive one. Some people are kept from membership in clubs and attendance at exclusive schools not necessarily by formal rules but by a deliberate and informal hindering process.

Contravention is common in the ordinary, everyday life of people in our society. The differences of opinion, the arguments between the older and the younger generation, are all indications of this social process. The so-called "battle of the sexes" is essentially contravention rather than conflict and is seen in derogatory remarks made by men or women against the other sex; in ways of frustrating the ambitions of women in careers that men call their own; and in the negative gossip of some older single women against men in general.

This process is at work also among the many minority categories of the American population. These people's strivings for higher social status, for economic gains, and for political participation are often thwarted by others. The small farmer and businessman, the immigrant and ethnic groups, the domestic and migrant workers, and many others experience contravention in many ways. Some of the competition among the major religious bodies in our country is aided by subtle forms of propaganda, stereotyping, and name-calling that may be called contravention.

The most notable national example of contravention in recent years is that employed in the investigation of subversives. Many honorable persons who were once connected with Communist groups have been seriously thwarted in their careers and other pursuits because they are considered to be presently guilty of previous association. These people are denied certain kinds of employment and the accompanying status because others tend to generalize and label them "subversive." The accused individuals are not destroyed; destruction would be the outcome of conflict.

5. Minimizing Conflict in America

While the American population is gradually becoming more integrated by the assimilation process, we must remember that there are still many diversities among our people. The great variety of peoples who originally formed the population and the differences of interest that motivated them have constituted in the past an area of social conflict. Sectional, religious, racial, and ethnic differences have at times exploded in violent riots or in genuine economic and political conflicts.

In recent years many factors have been at work to alleviate and to prevent these conflicts. These problems constituted a challenge to the administrative and the social authorities in all the major groupings. The pragmatic and rational approach characteristic of our culture has fostered a conviction that they can be solved. The threat of external power in two world wars, the moral pressure of the American ideology, and, not the least, the contribution of the social sciences have all been factors in the minimizing of conflict.

It may be helpful to list some of the forces presently at work in the attempt to remove conflict and to encourage co-operation among the divergent elements of the population.

a) College courses in social science have presented an analysis of the factors of intergroup conflict, and they provide, at least by inference, some of the social possibilities of programs for avoiding conflict. These academic courses reach only young college students in our society, and only a limited number of these. Nevertheless, if it is true that college graduates will have in later years an increasing influence upon social relations, these courses are of great value.

b) Intergroup programs specifically designed for the alleviation of conflict and the promotion of co-operation are increasing. These programs take the form of workshops that may meet for several weeks during the summer, of annual conferences for experts in the field, and of various kinds of meetings sponsored throughout the year. The annual celebration of Brotherhood Week provides an opportunity for concentrated attention by Americans upon the techniques of social co-operation.

c) Various mechanisms have been devised for the reduction of industrial conflict. The widespread use of collective bargaining, the facilities of the National Labor Relations Board, and the techniques of arbitration and conciliation have all helped to bring about relative order and peace in labor-management relations. This is an area in which there was actual conflict and bloodshed during the 1930's. In some sections of the country these mechanisms are still opposed, but large-scale industry has accepted and often even promoted their use.

d) A number of effective organizations have been at work to reduce tension and remove conflict in race relations. In spite of sporadic and much-publicized attempts to halt the trend toward improved race relations, remarkable progress has been made in this field of human relations. Besides the organizations professionally dedicated to this work, there are large numbers of interracial committees and groups working toward this end in religious, political, and civic affairs, in military and veterans' organizations, in women's clubs, in labor unions, and in other associations.

e) Efforts are made also to remove religious conflict, not only in national organizations of Christians and Jews and in federated Protestant churches, but also within most of the major religious bodies. The latter groupings take various forms of social action through which they are indoctrinating their own members on the importance of social virtues. The theological differences still remain in the various religious bodies, but co-operation and unity on non-religious levels are stressed.

One of the most encouraging aspects of all these efforts to reduce conflict lies in the fact that they are deliberate and intelligent. Most of the people active in them repudiate the notion that "things will somehow work out by themselves" or that "time will cure the problems." The leading and most influential persons in large communities and large organizations appear to be convinced that internal conflict can be consciously avoided. The techniques of co-operation are constantly being refined, and intelligent appraisals of them continue to be made.

The population of the United States provides a laboratory for experimentation in these programs. The assumption that every society, no matter how advanced, always contains the potential of social conflict beneath the surface has been neither proved nor disproved. This potential appears to be reduced when the major divergences are reduced; but the American people seem to be intent upon demonstrating that conflict can be minimized even while important differences remain among the population.

DISCUSSION QUESTIONS

1. What is the difference between status relation and role relation?
2. Show by examples that the role relation is not the same as the social process.
3. In what ways do the universal social processes differ from society to society?
4. What is meant by the terms "conjunctive" and "disjunctive"?
5. Why is "one-sided" co-operation an impossibility?
6. Describe the principal forms of accommodation.
7. How does assimilation differ from socialization?
8. What are the most common preliminaries to conflict?
9. How is it possible that contravention sometimes takes place within the co-operative process?
10. Under what conditions does competition increase?
11. Why is a social process seldom found in a "pure" form?
12. If justice, equity, and love are moral virtues, how can they be analyzed as conceptualized social processes?
13. Why is competition highly valued in the American society?
14. Describe briefly the process of competition in the major groups.
15. Under what conditions do people tend to co-operate best?
16. Describe the various levels of social problems and the differential degree of American co-operation in them.
17. Discuss: "America is the melting pot of nations."
18. What common cultural items are accepted by people assimilated in the American culture?
19. Give examples of contravention in America and show that they are distinguishable from competition and conflict.
20. What forces are at work to minimize conflict and maximize co-operation in the American society?

SUGGESTED READINGS

CUBER, JOHN F. *Sociology: A Synopsis of Principles.* New York: Appleton-Century-Crofts, Inc., 1955, chaps. xxxii, xxxiii.

HILLER, E. T. *Social Relations and Structures.* New York: Harper & Bros., 1947, Part III.

MAY, MARK, and DOOB, LEONARD. *Competition and Cooperation.* New York: Social Science Research Council, 1937.

MERRILL, F. E., and ELDREDGE, H. W. *Culture and Society: An Introduction to Society.* Englewood Cliffs, N.J.: Prentice-Hall, Inc., 1955, chap. xxv.

MURRAY, RAYMOND. *Sociology for a Democratic Society.* New York: Appleton-Century-Crofts, Inc., 1950, chaps. xvi, xvii.

SUTHERLAND, ROBERT, and WOODWARD, JULIAN. *Introduction to Sociology.* Chicago: J. B. Lippincott Co., 1940. Part V.

CHAPTER ELEVEN

Institutions

Like several other terms that have a technical, scientific meaning in sociology, the word "institution" is often used in a non-sociological sense. One hears that the village drunk has become an institution, or that a college is an institution of learning, or that an orphanage is an institution for the care of children. It is true that these usages are correct in the informal context in which they are employed, but they are not correct according to the strictly scientific definition of the term.

Definition of Institution

Sociologically speaking, an institution is not a person or a group. It is part of the culture, a patterned segment of the way of life of a people. As we have seen, overt and covert patterns of behavior build up into social roles that persons enact and into various kinds of social relations between and among persons; chief among these relations are the social processes. Social relations and social roles form the major elements of the institution. An institution is a configuration or combination of behavior patterns shared by a plurality and focused upon the satisfaction of some basic group need.

The definition of the institution may be better understood when we list and describe its characteristics. The following are the essential characteristics of the institution:

a) Institutions are purposive in the sense that each has as its objective or goal the satisfaction of social needs. They are ways of behavior through which people in association with one another get things done.

b) They are relatively permanent in their content. The patterns, roles, and relations that people enact in a particular culture become traditional and enduring. Like any man-made object, they are subject to change, but institutional change is relatively slow.

c) The institution is structured. The components tend to hang together and reinforce one another. This follows from the fact that social roles and social relations are in themselves structured combinations of behavior patterns.

d) Each institution is a unified structure; it functions as a unit. No institution can be completely separated from other institutions, but it does function as an identifiable series of human behavior.

e) The institution is necessarily value-laden in the sense that its repeated uniformities become codes of conduct, some of them written into rules and laws but most of them subconsciously exerting social pressure.

From these characteristics we may form the following more complete definition: an institution is a relatively permanent structure of social patterns, roles, and relations that people enact in certain sanctioned and unified ways for the purpose of satisfying basic social needs.

Institution and Group

One of the most common errors of the beginning student in sociology is in confusing the terms "group" and "institution." It is well to emphasize again that these terms are not synonymous. The concepts they represent are distinguishable, and the objects they conceptualize are quite different in the real order of existence. The concept of institution is, of course, an abstraction, but the institution itself is as real as, and far more significant than, any material object of culture.

An institution is not a group of people. We have seen the importance of distinguishing between persons and the behavior patterns they perform. What the person does or what people do is distinguishable from what the group is. Patterns of behavior, processes, and roles are institutionalized, but persons and groups are not. The group is a plurality of persons who enact institutions. The college is essentially a group of people who are following an orderly system of behavior called the educational institution.

The internal attitudes and the external customs of a group of people are focused upon the collective satisfaction of basic social needs. The mores, folkways, and usages are institutionalized ways of doing things together. They are not merely random and haphazard bits of human conduct. They are channeled toward recognized and valued goals. The people link them together in the performance of their roles and processes, and all of these taken together are an institution.

The Functions of Institutions

What does the institution "do" for people in their group life? In order to answer this question we must make certain distinctions. (*a*) The objective, goal, or purpose of an institution is the same as that of a group. The economic, religious, and political groups strive for economic, religious, and political ends. (*b*) The functions performed by the group are the conceptual and external activities performed in patterned ways by the people. They are what the people actually do in their social roles and relations, and they constitute the main content of the institution. (*c*) Finally, besides the specific objectives and the patterned activities of the group, there are certain generalized functions that all institutions perform for the people.

It is only these generalized functions of institutions that we discuss here. From the point of view of the individual person, some of them may be termed *positive* and some *negative*. Some functions of institutions bring about a higher level of integration and co-ordination in groups, while others do not.

a) Institutions simplify social behavior for the individual person. The ways of thinking and acting have become largely regularized and prearranged for the individual before he enters the society. He does not have to stop and learn or invent his own way of doing things, because the institutions to which he has become accustomed during the socialization process provide a way. We have seen that much social behavior is non-rational and almost automatic for the individual; this happens because the behavior has been institutionalized.

b) As an extension of this function, the institutions also provide ready-made forms of social relations and social roles for the individual. The principal roles and relations are not "invented" by individuals. In most instances the person "knows ahead of time" what the expectations of behavior are in relations with other persons and in the enactment of roles. The institutions provide pre-existing roles in which the individual can develop his own special abilities and wishes. Since he knows or can find out what is expected and what actually occurs in the role of business executive, lawyer, husband, baseball player, and so forth, he is able to "fit himself" for the performance of the role.

c) Institutions act also as an agency of co-ordination and stability for the total culture. The striving for consistency is a logical tendency in human society and is aided by institutions that stabilize and harmonize the behavior of the people. Ways of thinking and behaving that are institutionalized "make sense" to people. They provide a means of security because they become the normal and proper ways of which the great majority of people approve. While segments of an institution may change in a dynamic culture, the major institutions continue on in a stable and enduring manner.

d) Closely allied with the function of stability is the fact that institutions tend to control behavior. The institutions contain the systematic expectations of the society. Because institutions exist, the individual person knows how he should act and think among other persons. Group behavior is often subconsciously fixed through constant repetition, and when there is need for planning, the group can easily ascertain from its institutions the normal modes of procedure. Individuals and groups find it easier to conform than to deviate from the institutions. Social pressure is maintained even on the prospective deviant groups by the mere existence of institutions.

Besides these positive functions of institutions there are certain *negative* aspects to be taken into consideration. Since no culture operates in all its segments to the optimum benefit of all the people, it is to be expected that certain difficulties arise through the functioning of institutions.

a) In general, the major negative function of institutions is the way in which they sometimes obstruct social progress. Because institutions conserve and stabilize social behavior, they tend to be rigid and discourage change. This conservatism is a twofold function. The institutions sometimes conserve patterns of behavior even when the values represented by this behavior have become outmoded. On the other hand, they sometimes conserve social values that are quite inconsistent with the external behavior of the majority of the people. This resistance to change is implicit in the notion of the institution as the "cake of custom" or in the notion that it rules with the "dead hand of the past."

b) Similarly, institutions sometimes serve to frustrate the social personality of individuals. People who do not fit into the culture and who try to resist the control of institutions are considered odd. They may be misfits because they are unwilling to allow the institutions to hold them down too rigidly. These people often become deviants of one kind or another, attempting reform movements, committing criminal and delinquent behavior, or acting in ways others consider culturally abnormal. Absolute individual freedom does not exist in any society, but personal frustrations readily occur where individualism is a high ideal, on the one hand, and institutions force people to conform, on the other.

c) Another negative function is the diffusion of social responsibility. Customary ways of behaving that are completely out of date, that harm some individuals and groups, and that require reform are sometimes permitted to continue because no one takes the responsibility for changing them. This diffusion of responsibility is evident when people complain about "the system" or when they justify their behavior on the grounds of established custom. An institution may work injustice upon people, but the fact that it is long established gives it a sanction. In some instances, people who are fearful of change are also willing to accept the discomforts and inconveniences of established routine.

Universality and Variability of Institutions

We have seen that patterns, roles, and relations, which are the ingredients of institutions, exist in every society. It is likewise true that they are everywhere systematically arranged into institutions. Not only is social behavior always institutionalized, but the major institutions are necessarily present everywhere. The basic universal social needs are satisfied in some culturally approved systematic way in every society. These basic institutions—familial, educational, economic, political, religious, and recreational—are so essential to a culture that without them social life would be unthinkable.

Anthropologists have never discovered a primitive, contemporary, or historical society in which these basic institutions did not exist. This fact obviously argues to the basic necessity for these institutions. But anthropologists have also found a tremendous variety in the way these institutions satisfy minimum basic needs. Anyone who has a smattering of knowledge concerning people outside his own culture recognizes that family customs, religious mores, recreational trends, and the other institutionalized patterns differ considerably. The ways of conducting educational, economic, and political affairs show great variation from culture to culture.

This combination of universality and variability should not be puzzling to one who recognizes the plasticity and potentiality in social behavior. Several factors of variability must be considered: First, human beings have demonstrated great ingenuity and adaptability in satisfying their social needs. Second, a certain degree of choice and decision is involved in the selection of alternative ways of doing things. Finally, the geographical environment in which people live differs widely and has a certain degree of influence on social behavior.

Classification of Institutions

We have seen that there are many ways of classifying social groups because there are many points of view from which groups can be studied. Similarly, institutions lend themselves to classification from different points of view. Some institutions are strongly compulsive, others place little obligation on people; some are as wide as the society in their application, others are relatively local; some involve high social values, others deal in a lower order of values.

For purposes of clarity, the most fruitful general classification of institutions is the twofold division into *major* and *subsidiary* institutions. This distinction is made on the basis of three characteristics: universality, necessity, and importance. The major basic institutions are those that the largest number of people participate in, that are essential to the society, and that are considered most important for the individual and the common welfare. These are the familial, educational, economic, political, religious, and recreational institutions.

The subsidiary institutions do not have these characteristics. They are the numerous, minor, and variable institutions that are contained within the major institutions. Every subsidiary institution can be classified under one of the major institutions, although in the concrete life situation it may partake of the aspects of several major institutions.

Following is a brief description of the major institutions, with some indications of the subsidiary ones that are found within them. We must recall here that patterns, roles, and relations are contained within the institutions and that these are the instrumentalities social persons use in the conduct of social life.

a) The familial institution is the system that regulates, stabilizes, and standardizes sexual relations and the reproduction of children. Its most widespread form is the monogamous union of male and female living together with their children in a household. The subinstitutions of courtship, marriage, child care, in-law relations, and many others are contained under this main institution.

b) The educational institution is basically the systematized process of socialization occurring informally in the home and in the general cultural environment and formally in the complex educational arrangements of the society. Within the framework of this institution are the subsidiary arrangements for grading and testing, graduations and degrees, homework, and the honor system.

c) The economic institution is the configuration of patterned social behaviors through which material goods and services are provided for the society. It involves fundamentally the production, distribution, exchange, and consumption of commodities. There are many subsidiary institutions like credit and banking, bookkeeping, advertising, collective bargaining, and seniority systems.

d) The political institution functions primarily to satisfy the need for general administration and public order in society. There are many subinstitutions within it such as the legal, police, and military systems, the forms of appointment and election to public office, and the diplomatic relations with foreign countries.

e) The religious institution satisfies man's basic social need for a relationship with God. It is expressed in creeds and in forms of worship people perform together. It always includes moral and ethical systems indicating the rightness or wrongness of both external and conceptual patterns of behavior. Subsidiary institutions are the lay-clerical relationships, the systems of prayer, and the arrangements for divine sacrifice. Practices of magic and superstition are in some places institutionalized by religious groups.

f) The recreational institution fulfils the social need for physical and mental relaxation. It includes numerous subsidiary institutions such as games, sports, and dancing as well as the aesthetic systems of art, music, painting, and drama.

Network of Institutions

The co-ordinated network of interdependently functioning major institutions is vital to the continuance of the culture and the society. No institution can exist by itself; each influences in varying degrees all the others and is in turn influenced by them. The whole configuration of major and subsidiary institutions is articulated through the social relations and roles enacted by persons and groups.

The interdependence of institutions is demonstrated in many ways, especially in large, complex, and industrialized societies. For example, impairment of the orderly functioning of the economic institution would have grave effects upon all of the other institutions. The clearest historical example of this is a major economic depression that has repercussions and brings about changes in familial, educational, political, religious, and recreational institutions. Major changes in the patterns of family living, or in the political institution, seriously affect the other institutions.

This very interdependence sometimes makes it difficult to assign every subinstitution clearly to one of the major institutions. Since man is a total personality, his behavior patterns overlap the institutions. Furthermore, although there are many inconsistencies, the institutions co-operate and dovetail with one another. For example, some forms of athletic sports are subsidiary institutions that may be considered both recreational and economic but are also often performed within the framework of subsidiary educational and religious groups.

There are many other examples of this complexity, all indicating that no social group can purely and exclusively perform the patterns of only one institution. A religious group, identified by the fact that it pursues primarily the function of the religious institution, performs also other institutionalized functions—educating children, providing recreation, and raising and spending money. Similarly, the state does not necessarily "invade" the rights of individuals and groups when it promotes the welfare of familial, economic, educational, and other institutions. This is simply an example of the basic fact that no person or group can be purely political.

In spite of the fact that the different institutions are interwoven in the web of culture and are necessarily interdependent, they are not always in harmony with one another. There are instances of institutionalized patterns working at cross-purposes or at least being to some degree inconsistent. An easy example of this inconsistency is seen in the economic and religious institutions. If a prime motive of the economic institution is the pursuit of profit and if that of the religious institution is selfless service of God and humanity, there is an incongruity for the person who is endeavoring to fulfil the expected roles in both institutions.

While it is true that the social person may choose from many alternative patterns within any given institution, he tends to follow those that are most standardized and approved. The man who is by all norms an exemplary husband and father may also be persuaded that it is "good business" to extract exorbitant rents from slum tenants. The church warden who attends religious services on Sunday morning may also take his out-of-town guests to a lewd performance at a night club on Sunday evening. These internal inconsistencies of role behavior are not always recognized by individuals because the external inconsistencies of institutions have come to be taken for granted as approved and expected modes of behavior.

Institutions and Social Sanctions

We have seen that persons can be ranked according to higher or lower status and that roles have differential esteem in the society. In other words, not everybody or every function is treated with equal esteem; some persons and some behaviors are approved and others are disapproved. From this it follows—and it is also an empirically demonstrable fact—that in any culture the institutions are ranked in order. The major institutions are more important than the subsidiary institutions.

The *pivotal* institution, however, is most important of all. We have seen that among the numerous social roles the social person enacts there is his key role, which is recognized by other people as being the most important and influential. The pivotal institution is to the culture what the key role is to the individual. Historical examples of pivotal institutions are numerous. The Roman culture was dominated at one period by the political, the Chinese by the familial, the Indian by the religious, and the American by the economic institution.

The rise of the pivotal institution to its place of prominence must obviously have the positive sanction of the people in the society. This means that the values expressed, the functions performed, and the roles enacted in that institution must have the general approval of the people. The person therefore "sacrifices" certain aspects of his role in the other institutions because of the expectations and demands of the pivotal institution. This is further evidence of the interdependence of the major institutions; when the people center so much attention upon the pivotal institution, any serious disturbance of this institution has far-reaching consequences throughout the culture.

Despite the high esteem in which the pivotal and other major institutions are held, there continue to exist in every culture certain subsidiary institutions that are sanctioned with penalties. For example, patterns of criminal behavior develop mainly as a subsidiary economic institution even though crime is negatively sanctioned. Gambling is a recreational institution that is widely disapproved. Ticket-fixing and police brutality are institutionalized in some places despite the general disapproval of this kind of behavior. The study of the extent to which these forms of behavior become social problems must be taken up elsewhere.

Institutional System as a Total Culture

The major institutions are conceptualized as a complete and continuous network in which both the total and all its segments are a functioning system. This we call the culture of a society. In order to visualize this total institutional system more clearly, it may be helpful to note the following:

a) Once the pivotal institution is recognized, the position of the remaining major institutions can be conceptualized as clustering around it. Within each of these may be placed the subsidiary institutions, some of which are closely integrated and others which are incidental or even partially inconsistent with the major institution.

b) The major institutions can be identified by the objectives they are pursuing, but their relative position of importance in any culture can be judged by other criteria. Thus, the "power position" of a major institution can be judged by the degree of control and dominance it exerts over other institutions, the extent to which it "invades" other institutions, and the strength of its affiliation with them.

c) Since patterns, roles, and relations are institutionalized around certain central objectives, they can be studied from the point of view of the person in action. The position and importance of any given institution can be evaluated according to the degree of interest and the amount of time and energy people employ in it.

d) Social values are involved in all institutions, and one may say that the position of any institution depends largely upon these values. This again requires a knowledge of the persons who perform institutionalized behavior. If the persons of high social status in any society gain this prestige through the economic rather than through the religious institution, this reflects the importance of both the economic values and the economic institution.

It is important to remember that the institutional system operates for and through people. It can never be conceptualized as either internally or externally static because it grows and changes through actual human behavior. Sometimes a minor institution stays on in a culture long after it has ceased to be useful. Sometimes institutional changes are induced through legislation and other deliberate effort. At any rate, institutions do not exist unless they are used by associations of people, and the fact is that institutions need people as much as people need institutions.

ASPECTS OF AMERICAN INSTITUTIONS

1. The Pivotal Institution

A key to the understanding of any culture is a knowledge of its dominant major institution. It has been said that the American society has a "businessman's culture," that all human relations have been reduced to dollars and cents, that what has made America "great" is its system of free enterprise. Statements of this kind are, of course, crude exaggerations made by the misinformed, the disgruntled, and perhaps the envious. A quick judgment about a whole culture is easy, but it is also usually erroneous, especially if it is the result of an ethnocentric attitude.

Nevertheless it is true that a total culture is colored by its dominant institution and that in the American society all the major institutions are influenced by the economic institution. Americans usually think that this is logical and "natural," since preparing for one's lifework, making a living, providing for a family, getting ahead, and getting a raise and a promotion are all extremely important things. Not every society, however, considers these matters so important as we do. Furthermore, while we may believe that the religious institution is on a higher plane of values than the economic, or that economic activities are basically merely a means for better familial and recreational life, objective analysis shows that in our culture these institutions are also greatly influenced by the economic.

The following give a brief indication of the ways in which economic patterns and values have invaded and influenced the behavior of Americans in other institutions:

a) In the educational system in America a great deal of lip service is paid to the importance of the humanities—literature and the other so-called "cultural" subjects—particularly on the college level. The fact is, however, that the overwhelming majority of male students and a good many female students concentrate on "useful" subjects. They know that graduates with specialized training get the better jobs sooner, and their parents know it too.

b) The peculiar American pattern of religious institutions, in which each church has to fend financially for itself, has put a strong emphasis upon economic activities. The pastor who is a good businessman, gets contributions, pays the debts, and maintains a large assemblage of buildings is the man who receives wide approval. The United States is probably the only country in which a biography of Christ depicting him as a successful businessman could be a best seller. The parable of the talents is often interpreted to mean that a man is morally obligated to use his abilities for economic and material advancement.

c) The commercialization of recreational activities shows the way economic patterns have invaded this institution. Other societies have rewarded their athletic heroes with ivy crowns and feasts and medals, but in our society they are professional heroes who expect and receive high financial rewards. The stage is not subsidized by the community; it has to be a profitable enterprise or it ceases to function. The same can be said of other media of entertainment and of many other leisure-time activities.

d) The political institution has been affected by the fact that government has become "big business." Although there is no political compulsion by which the government should show a profit or balance the budget, there have been frequent demands that we should have a businessman in the White House. Lack of success or experience in business has been used as a campaign argument against presidential candidates. The fiscal policies of the government, the direction of federal banks, the raising and spending of tax money, and the problem of controlling inflation and preventing depression are all examples of economic patterns entering the political institution.

e) In the familial institution economic demands have altered patterns, roles, and relations of Americans. The amount of time a man can spend with his family, the type and amount of commodities the family consumes, the employment of women outside the home, and the movement into cities and suburbs are all examples of the way in which the economic factor invades the home. The gainful occupational function has limited, if it has not replaced, family and ancestry as the most powerful of the criteria of social status. Economic values have added steady pressure to the rising material standards of family living.

In a brief description of this kind we must be careful not to fall into the fallacy of single causality. It would be an error to assume that all the institutional problems which face Americans are fundamentally economic and that, if the economy can be straightened out, all will be well in our society. We have sufficiently illustrated multiple causality and institutional interdependence to show that all the institutions are fundamentally important. To point out that the economic institution is the pivotal institution is not to say that this institution is the total culture.

2. The Changing Marriage Institution

The European who visits the United States is often fascinated by the institutionalized aspects of American marriage and family life. The visiting Oriental is often shocked by them. The reaction of these foreigners indicates that the American marriage institution is quite different from that found in some other cultures. It also indicates that ethnocentrism—judging a strange culture on the basis of one's own cultural values—is universally exercised.

The familial institution is an integral segment of the American culture. Because we have been so thoroughly saturated with our own culture, Americans find it difficult to stand off and view this institution objectively. We often fail to realize that many of the so-called "family problems" are a logical part, and perhaps a necessary consequence, of the marriage institution. In our dynamic culture this institution has changed considerably from the forms which it took in early America and even more from its original European counterpart. Following are some of the more significant conceptual and external patterns of behavior that highlight institutional change.

a) The sacramental character of marriage has been almost completely ignored in many American families. The notion that marriage implies a sacred promise to God, as well as to one another, has often been overlooked even among couples who practice a religion in which this notion nominally prevails. A church is the most popular place for a wedding, but the inner significance of a divine promise, mandate, and relationship is usually ignored.

b) The marriage contract and the subsequent bond upon which family unity is built are things of the heart. The emphasis upon romantic love as the essential foundation of family life has been so thorough among Americans that we are shocked at the notion of a marriage of convenience, of marriage brokers, or of marriage for reasons of financial and social status. In many instances the marriage contract lasts only as long as the heart is in it, and the most desperate requirement of the married couple is that they "stay in love." Unlike a financial contract or a political commitment, the marriage promise in this context allows for a change of heart and mind.

c) The contractual aspect of the husband-wife relation is reflected in the concept of partnership marriage. The notion that the husband has the general management of the household while the wife is his chief lieutenant is not an acceptable one between the equal partners. The emphasis in American marriage appears to be on co-operation on an equal plane rather than on co-operation between two persons of unequal authority and differing responsibility. While the concept of duty is involved in all contractual arrangements, there is a notable emphasis here on the equal and independent rights of the two individuals. Here again the focus is upon personal happiness which every American marriage is supposed to bring to the partners.

d) Since each family is expected to make its own way, dowries and family fortunes do not supply the financial foundations for marriage.

Inheritance taxes have decreased the latter and custom has banished the former. The newly married American couple receives many gifts and household appliances, but these are a kind of loan that has to be paid back when other friends and relatives marry. The family's necessity to fend for itself, together with the social pressure for higher standards of living, places a great strain upon human relations within the family.

e) The discontinuity of generations, and therefore the loosening of traditional kinship ties, is evident in the separate households that newly married couples establish. This separation from the parental home, the result of job and territorial mobility and upward social striving, is more than a spatial removal from the old homestead; it is also an aspect of the decline of primary group relationships. The young couple loses the cultural support of the kinship group, has to develop new social relations that are not kin-based, and must depend more heavily on the husband-wife relationship. They also lose the social benefit of stability that accompanies attachment to a territorial community.

f) In the light of the above it should not be surprising that tandem marriages have been widely accepted among our marriage patterns. The lack of traditional stabilizers has not made us lose faith in marriage. On the contrary, more Americans marry, and marry younger, than the people in any other Western country. But the American has a moral scruple about taking more than one spouse at a time, and the pattern of keeping a mistress or of having a lover is a violation of the general code of marital standards. There is no cultural compulsion for this kind of conduct since divorce and remarriage are so easily arranged and so widely accepted.

g) The extent of child-spacing and the effect it may have on the marriage pair have not been sufficiently studied to warrant extended comment. The birth rate was consistently high during the decade following the war, but the average family size is smaller than it was two generations ago. The movement for planned parenthood has introduced pragmatic rationalism to the marriage relation, not only in spacing and limiting the number of offspring, but also in promoting research to increase the fertility of childless couples.

This list of institutionalized patterns in American marriage must not lead to the negative conclusion that marriage has lost its importance as an institution or that Americans despair of its basic and successful social functioning. The fact is that in no other society has this institution been so thoroughly studied; nowhere else are there so many marriage counsellors and clinics, so many statistics gathered and books written, or so many lectures and academic courses devoted to this subject.

It should be noted also that the patterns described above are integrally related to the total American culture. They reflect the patterns of other institutions, are logically interwoven with them, and are behavioral expectations in the kind of culture we have. Indeed, it would be surprising, in view of the major institutions and of the total culture, if the marriage institution did not have these characteristics in our society.

3. Aspects of the Political Institution

Americans boast of the great advantages of political freedom, of the high ideals of democracy, and of a political institution that has endured while many others have collapsed. Often, however, the same Americans decry politics as a "dirty game," complain about "cheap" politicians, and call for a reform to "clean up the mess." There is, of course, a vast difference between the idealized version of the American political institution and the practical everyday patterns of political behavior. A realistic appraisal of the ways in which our institutions function relieves us of either pessimism or idealism.

There are certain patterns within the American political institution that appear to be characteristic of our culture. They are present to some degree in the political institutions of other societies, but they do not play so important a role there as in our own. These patterns are typically American only in the sense that they are in widespread use here and they help us to understand the operation of the total institution of politics.

a) The spoils system is not an American invention, but it is worthy of note because many Americans resent it and many foreigners are surprised to find it here. In essence it means that the winning party in an election assumes the right to assign jobs and patronage to those who have helped to win the victory. No one questions the President's right to select his own cabinet and other officials, since he obviously requires co-operative assistants of his own choosing. There are many other jobs, however, directly or indirectly political, that the winning party, from the top federal level to the small town and county level, has the right to assign. The civil service system has gradually and persistently decreased this practice, but the spoils system still flourishes.

b) In general, upper-class persons are unwilling to serve in the political system. Except for the top-level jobs in the diplomatic service and in Washington, most of these people prefer to be served rather than to serve. The political apathy of the masses in America is matched and reflected by the apathy of people of high social status. This is partly because of two cultural phenomena: first, the belief that one somehow "soils" his hands by mixing with politicians; and, second, the fact that the political institution is not the dominant institution of our culture.

c) Closely allied to this pattern is the low esteem of political servants. Even in those cases where the political office itself holds high prestige—as the presidency, cabinet membership, ambassadorships, and to some extent congressional and gubernatorial posts—the incumbents of the office are often criticized for being "mere politicians." It appears to be the right of people in a democracy to excoriate and to calumniate their public servants. Even though successful politicians are always surrounded by groups of loyal and devoted followers, they are almost always subject to vilification by still larger numbers of people. This conceptual pattern of low esteem appears to be bound up with our political institution.

d) It appears that the successful politician is often obliged to pose as the defender of the people, a homespun man who shares the interest of the people. This pose has deep moral implications because it often means that political expediency, that is, giving the people what they want, takes precedence over political statesmanship, that is, acting on the basis of social and moral principles. The pattern requires that the politician identify those dangers from which he is defending the people: the international bankers, the munition manufacturers, the labor racketeers, the ruthless employers, and, especially of late, the "subversives." All of these opponents are pictured as dangers to our American way of life.

e) The American political institution lacks radical elements. The politician who wants to serve the majority of the people and to win the next election cannot afford to be a proponent of either the extreme right or the extreme left. The United States is remarkable for the fact that it contains a greatly diversified population and at the same time does not have a multiplicity of political splinter parties. The political philosophy of even the two principal national parties is often indistinguishable. They are competitors for the people's favor more often than they are opponents, and the party in power tries to imitate the successes and avoid the failures of the preceding administration.

Many other patterns of thinking and acting exist within the American political institution. Those we have discussed tend to be informally institutionalized yet extremely effective patterns. The sociological study of the actually functioning institution requires a knowledge beyond the formal and idealized norms and regulations of the institution. If we are interested in the manner in which an institution actually works, rather than merely in how it ought to work, this kind of insight is necessary.

We must repeat that the American political institution "fits into" the total American culture. Much of what goes on within it can be objectively understood only when interinstitutional relationships are recognized. Even though there are certain inconsistencies, especially in institutional values, the major American institutions have reciprocal influence.

4. Increasing Institutionalization

It is commonly observed in sociological literature that America is shifting from the communal to the associational type of society. Secondary groupings are more emphasized; more groups with specialized functions are arising; and casual contacts are replacing primary relations. In general our society is becoming more and more adaptive, stratified, multiple functioning, loosely structured, and rapidly changing.

A necessary concomitant of this kind of social development is the increase of institutionalization. The components of the institution—behavior patterns, social roles and relations—are becoming more specialized, formalized, and regularized. In spite of our insistence upon the importance of freedom and self-direction, we Americans are being more and more forced into formal routines of behavior. Increasing institutionalization is part of the personal price we pay for the advantages of a highly developed, complex, industrialized society.

Following are some of the indications and examples of this process of institutionalization in our culture:

a) The red tape in the social system is irksome to many Americans when they fill out job applications or tax forms, register for school, or apply for public welfare assistance. They find that "everything has to be in triplicate." There are so many "steps" to be taken, so many individuals to consult, that people become exasperated. The number of formal requirements is increasing; more records are being kept; and behavior is often regulated on the basis of records and requirements.

b) The underlying motive for institutionalization appears to be the

American drive for efficiency. The required actions are often time-wasting and inefficient from the point of view of the individual, but the focus is on the efficiency of the larger association, the total institution and system. To get things done in a rational and orderly way requires that large numbers of people perform the same act in the same way. There is probably a point of "diminishing returns" at which the devices of efficiency become cumbersome and wasteful, but it is not easily recognized if the patterns have become highly formal.

c) Institutionalization is seen also in the rigid routine of roles. As performance becomes more specialized, particularly in gainful occupations, the component patterns of the role become more automatic. There are many jobs, even relatively high in the occupational structure, where originality and ingenuity are discouraged. The crude statement of the employer that "We don't pay you to think" is not really replaced by the encouragement of an employees' suggestion box. The most valuable suggestion is one that can increase efficiency, and, if it is accepted, it will usually further routinize the occupational role.

d) The multiplication of roles within any major institution and group logically accompanies the specialization of functions. The discovery in industry that total productivity could be increased when each operation was reduced to its smallest, repetitive, unit act has been carried over into the political and educational institutions and in some degree to the other institutions. The consequence of the simplified role is the multiplication of roles. This is not essentially a matter of "making jobs" for the sake of keeping everybody busy but of getting the total operation completed more efficiently.

e) Bureaucracy has increased along with institutionalization in the major groups of American society. To organize social behavior effectively so that people's roles and relations function efficiently has been the objective of larger and more numerous bureaus, boards, panels, and committees in government, business, churches, schools, and other groupings. The red tape and the inconvenience individuals suffer through increased institutionalization are not the result of casual and arbitrary decisions but of an attempt to decrease the complexity of administration at the higher levels.

f) Institutionalization always occurs with the increase of the importance of secondary associations. The primary relations are informal, intimate, and adaptive. The individual in the primary groups may be a relatively rigid and traditional personality, but his patterns and roles can be adapted to him. In secondary associations by contrast the patterns, roles, and relations must be formal, mandatory, and fairly rigid; and the individual must learn to adapt himself to them. Thus, it may be said that these larger groups are operated and regulated by institutional forms rather than by the personalities who constitute them.

Finally, it must be pointed out that every society is in some degree institutionalized. All people must necessarily use behavior patterns, and all groups must use institutions. When we say that the American society is becoming more institutionalized, we mean that the institutions are becoming increasingly important, more formal and rigorous, and are affecting more people in many more ways than ever before. In this kind of society the universal fact that we are "creatures of our culture" takes on new meaning.

5. Institutional Inconsistencies

We have said that in general the term "institution" implies a related network of social behavior integrated around social needs. But at the same time there are also inconsistencies and lack of integration within institutions. The fact is that no culture is entirely integrated; no culture has all its components in consistent co-ordination with one another. There are parallel lines of social behavior in minor or subsidiary institutions that appear to be inconsistent with each other.

In the American culture there are numerous irrelevancies that are *cultural residues* rather than outright inconsistencies. For example, the wearing of ties by men, the buttons on a man's coat sleeve, the construction of open fireplaces in apartments that are centrally heated, the purchase of candlesticks, and many other patterns are now ornamental rather than functional. These are residual from earlier stages of the American culture, and though they exemplify the endurance of traditional usage, they cannot be considered examples of major inconsistencies.

Institutionalized ways of behaving can never be totally inconsistent or in total conflict with the culture. Even the major examples of institutional inconsistencies in the American culture include some elements that are consistent with some other elements. A conclusion about the inconsistency of an institution depends upon the vantage point from which it is viewed and upon the particular other institutions to which it is compared and related. Let us illustrate this fact with several well-known and widespread instances.

a) Institutionalized bribery is relatively common in many areas of American public life. Some of it is "polite" and just within the law, but much of it completely and directly violates the law, to say nothing of the ideals of public honesty. The word "graft" is colloquial in the United States, and it is defined as the "illegitimate receipt of money through and by official service." Here is a practice that has become smoothly patterned; it has become institutionalized, and it may well be called inconsistent.

From another point of view, however, it is highly consistent. As a matter of fact it is possible only because there are large segments of our population that demand the kind of services obtained through bribery and graft. The outstanding example of such services in our recent history was the bootlegging of illegal liquor. Other current examples in some places are: houses of assignation, of gambling and lewd performances, the traffic in narcotics and other illegal commodities, the maintenance of buildings that are fire hazards, and the suppression of organized labor.

b) Nationally the divorce system has been termed a "legal jungle" because of its internal inconsistencies. The causes for divorce and the requirements of legal procedure differ from state to state; but still more confusing is the fact that the majority of divorces are based on collusion between the interested parties, a practice that is strictly illegal in all divorce courts. And, of course, divorce is inconsistent with the traditional institution of permanent and monogamous marriage.

On the other hand, the divorce system is consistent with a number of strongly intrenched and often misinterpreted American behavior patterns. It conforms to the widely accepted notion that marriage is primarily an instrument for the happiness of the partners and to the emphasis on personal freedom and equal rights. Even the subsidiary pattern of allowing the wife to file for divorce and of favoring her in the divorce settlement indicates that at least this aspect of chivalry is not archaic.

c) Institutionalized racial discrimination is a major inconsistency in the American culture. In fact, the racial pattern has been termed the great contemporary American dilemma, because it is patently at odds with the stated values of democracy and Christianity.

Nevertheless, it conforms with the long-term Anglo-Saxon attitude of superiority toward the colored peoples of the world. It is an instrument also for maintaining social class and caste by many whites who do not possess enough of the other criteria of social status. By attempting to treat Negroes like immigrants, it continues America's century-old tradition of utilizing and exploiting the newest and lowest stratum of society. Even local autonomy and states' rights have been invoked in some areas to justify the pattern of racial discrimination.

From the point of view of ultimate cultural values of the American people it is probably true to say that much of the explanation for institutional inconsistencies is a mere rationalization. Often false reasons, self-interest, and values of a lower order are employed to justify inconsistent social behavior. Rationalization, however, does not lessen the social reality. It does not make it less a social fact that the inconsistencies actually exist.

DISCUSSION QUESTIONS

1. Explain the technical definition of the term "institution."
2. What is the essential difference between group and institution?
3. What is the difference between the goal of an institution and its specific function?
4. How do the positive functions differ from the negative functions of institutions in general?
5. Explain why institutionalization is both universal and variable.
6. What are the bases of distinction between major and subsidiary institutions?
7. With an example demonstrate the function of each major institution.
8. If the major institutions are interdependent, why are they also sometimes inconsistent with one another?
9. In what way does the pivotal institution lend positive and negative sanctions to social behavior?
10. Demonstrate the chief aspects of the culture as a system of institutions.
11. What is meant by saying that the institutional system operates for and through people?
12. In what sense is a total culture colored by its dominant institution?
13. Demonstrate the ways in which the economic institution influences the other major American institutions.
14. What present-day factors help to account for the changing marriage institution?
15. Discuss: "Marriage has lost its importance in the American culture."
16. What institutionalized patterns may be called characteristic of the American political system?
17. What is meant by "increasing institutionalization"?
18. Discuss: "American culture is becoming more institutionalized."
19. What is the difference between cultural residues and institutional inconsistencies?
20. How are bribery, divorce, and discrimination both consistent and inconsistent within the American culture?

SUGGESTED READINGS

BENNETT, JOHN, and TUMIN, MELVIN. *Social Life, Structure and Function.* New York: Alfred A. Knopf, Inc., 1948, chaps. xii, xiii.

BROOM, LEONARD, and SELZNICK, PHILIP. *Sociology: A Text with Adapted Readings.* Evanston, Ill.: Row, Peterson & Co., 1955, chaps. ii, vii, xi.

HAAS, F. J. *Man and Society.* New York: Appleton-Century-Crofts, Inc., 1952, chaps. iv, vi, ix.

HERTZLER, J. O. *Social Institutions.* New York: McGraw-Hill Book Co., 1929, chaps. i–iv.

LAPIERE, R. T. *Sociology.* New York: McGraw-Hill Book Co., 1946, chaps. xiv, xv.

TIMASHEFF, N. S., and FACEY, P. W. *Sociology: An Introduction to Sociological Analysis.* Milwaukee: Bruce Publishing Co., 1949, chaps. iv–vi.

CHAPTER TWELVE

Culture

Culture is another strictly technical term in social science that is widely used in various non-technical meanings. We sometimes hear that a cultured person is one who has refinement and good manners, who recognizes and enjoys the finer and aesthetic things of life. In this restricted meaning, culture can be possessed by the relatively few persons who have the leisure, wealth, competence, and interest to indulge in these patterns of refinement.

The sociological fact is, of course, that every normal person in the society "has culture." As we have seen, every person goes through the socialization process. From infancy he begins to learn to accommodate himself to the conceptual and external patterns of behavior that are socially acceptable. He gets training in the pursuit of social roles; he is always in the midst of social relations. *Everyone is a cultured person* and must necessarily be one as a participant in groups and in the total society. Thus, the scientific definition of culture cannot be applied only to the fortunate few in the upper strata of society.

What Culture Is Not

Culture is not the group or the society. To use it interchangeably with these terms is to miss the whole distinction between people and their patterns of behavior. People in group life have a behavioral system; they make use of institutions; they possess a culture. One cannot identify the possessor with the thing possessed. There must be an equally clear distinction between the society and its culture.

There is also sometimes a confusion of meaning between the terms "culture" and "civilization." Whatever definition one may give to the word "civilization," it is certainly not the same as the definition of culture. Those who speak of culture as the more highly developed use of the finer things of life limit civilization to the technical and utilitarian aspects of social living. In this conceptual framework, civilization is technological while culture is social refinement.

In precise scientific language one speaks of primitive cultures and civilized cultures, the latter being more complex and developed than the former. There is an arbitrary line that divides one from the other, and it is often difficult to determine the basis upon which this line is drawn. The word "civilized" seems to be as good a starting point as any. It is derived from the Latin words *civitas* and *civis*, meaning "town" and "town dweller," and it implies a people who are sedentary, literate, and complex in their behavior.

In a civilized (as compared to precivilized) society, the people live in large, permanent aggregates rather than in nomadic tribes. They have a written language for recording their history that is of great educational value. They develop a diversification of functions and a specialization of labor. Their behavior is more formally institutionalized and their whole culture is more complex than that of precivilized people. Even though we make a distinction between precivilized and civilized cultures, however, we must realize that these characteristics are a matter of degree. Thus we may recognize among the world's contemporary societies cultures that are highly civilized and cultures civilized to lesser degrees.

Definition of Culture

We have seen that the irreducible basic component of the culture is the recurrent pattern of social behavior. We have seen also that these patterns combine into various social roles, human relations, and social processes. These again are the components of the numerous institutions, major and subsidiary, that are present in every culture. Thus, we may say that the largest segments of the culture are the institutions and the smallest segment is the behavior pattern.

Briefly, then, culture is the total configuration of institutions that the people in a society share in common. The term "configuration" refers to the web, matrix, or network, in which the related and co-ordinate institutions function as a whole system. The people share this cultural system, but not in the sense that every individual and group participates equally or does everything in exactly the same way. There are some social roles that cannot be enacted by some persons. There are some institutions that demand much more participation than others.

Cultural Heritage and Environment

From the point of view of persons and groups it is essential that the total culture be conceptualized as both hereditary and environmental. This is important because culture is both taught and learned and is derived by the individual from both his elders and his contemporaries. The socialization process is the channel through which the individual becomes assimilated to his culture and his society.

When we say that the culture is *hereditary,* we mean that the institutionalized ways of behaving are symbolically transmitted from one generation to another. The particular institutions are built up by the accretion of many people's experiences over a long period of time. Individuals come and go, but culture persists; it must be handed down in some form or other. The "cultural heritage" has nothing to do with physical generation or biological transmission. It is handed on by a process of learning. When we say that some ancient culture has entirely disappeared, we mean either that the whole people using it were wiped out or that it gradually merged into some other major culture.

When we say that the culture is also *environmental,* we mean that each person is born into, and grows up in, a society in which a culture already exists. The culture that each generation inherits from its ancestors is the one that each individual has to learn to live with. It is obvious but extremely significant that an American grows up to be an American and an Italian grows up to be an Italian. This is the cultural environment in which he lives and develops and which he leaves behind him when he dies.

It is not a contradiction to remark that while people are the ultimate creators of the culture, they are also in large measure the creatures of their culture. A person may escape society for a while, but he can never escape culture. The cultural environment is probably the strongest single influence upon the social behavior of the great majority of people. Even in isolation, where the person tries to "get away from it all" temporarily, he thinks and acts according to the patterns of behavior with which he grew up. The institutions of his culture have formed his social personality and have made him the kind of person he is.

The pervading influence of the cultural environment is seen most dramatically in those who visit or who immigrate to a society with a culture different from their own. The language barrier is often an obstacle to understanding the foreign culture; but a much more significant obstacle is that the customs of the people are strange. The ways of thinking and doing things, the cultural values and forms of relationship, are difficult to understand and to accept. Whole generations of immigrants have remained culturally "marginal" persons to the end of their lives. A foreigner seldom if ever completely loses the traces of the culture in which he was originally socialized.

The total culture necessarily contains the basic major institutions—familial, educational, economic, political, recreational, and religious. Since every total society must have the major groups of people who associate for the satisfaction of these basic social needs, these groupings necessarily use institutionalized ways of behavior. The subculture, in its broadest sense a large variation within the major culture, also contains these basic institutions.

Culture Areas

The term "culture area" refers to a limited geographical territory in which a recognized culture, or subculture, exists. It does not always refer to political or national boundaries, although some of the larger and older countries more or less correspond to separate culture areas. There are, however, some instances where a major cultural institution is pursued in relatively the same way in two or more large societies. For example, the economic institutions of Canada and the United States, and the religious institutions of some of the South American countries, show great cultural similarities. In these examples we identify an "area" of economic culture and of religious culture.

More frequently, however, the culture area is a relatively small territory in which the people share similar patterns of behavior somewhat different from those of the large society. The different regions of a large country, especially if they have ancient traditions, represent culture areas or subculture areas. The concept of the culture area is particularly useful in the study of primitive peoples and in the historical analysis of ancient tribes. Through this latter study it is possible to trace the origin and diffusion of particular aspects of culture.

Culture Complex and Culture Trait

The terms "culture complex" and "culture trait" are commonly used in social science literature, especially in anthropological writings. The word "trait" is synonymous with "characteristic"; therefore, something characteristic of a culture is called a "culture trait." It refers, however, only to single, small elements that are found in a society and are an index or symbol of behavior patterns. Thus, a material culture object, like a baseball bat, a stone ax, a writing quill, is a culture trait and an indicator of the broader behavior patterns surrounding its use. In an earlier day, anthropologists defined the culture trait, both material and non-material, as the smallest unit of the culture, but this usage seems to have been discarded.

The meaning of "culture complex" has also changed. Its first meaning was that of a cluster of culture traits surrounding some particular institutionalized social functions, but we now use it synonymously with the term "subsidiary institution." One could speak of the tobacco complex among primitive peoples, indicating not only the cultivation of this product but also its various social and ceremonial uses. In modern industrialized society one may speak of the automobile complex, the social security complex, the garden club complex. In so far as these complexes are made up of institutionalized patterns of behavior, social roles, and relations, they are nothing more than subsidiary institutions.

Material Culture Items

Up to this point in our study we have studiously avoided the inclusion of material items as component parts or segments of the culture. The logic of definition requires that only similar things be placed in the same category. If behavior patterns are the irreducible components of the culture, and if these combine into roles, relations, and institutions, it would be illogical to include among them items like baseballs, refrigerators, prayer books, and atomic submarines.

We speak here of material things that are culture items, but this "mere" materiality does not make them unimportant. They are bound up with the lives of persons and groups, and they cannot be left out of the scientific considerations of the student of society. There are four reasons why these culture items should be studied. They are certainly *products* of the culture, in the sense that the people in the society have invented and fashioned them in response to their social needs. They are also *instruments* that the people utilize in carrying out their behavior patterns. They may also be called *vehicles* of the culture that carry much of the physical load of the social functions. Finally, these material items are also *symbols* because much of the culture can be interpreted from the kind of objects used by the society.

The techniques of behavior associated with the making and using of cultural products are in themselves part of the culture. The objects themselves vary tremendously from one society to another. An igloo differs from a city apartment hotel, a stone cathedral from a rural church, a machine tool from a weaving loom, but all these are similar in the fact that they are the products and the expression of the culture. These things constitute a man-created artificial environment interposed between people and the natural environment that tremendously affects the patterns of behavior. When studying prehistoric cultures these extant objects are often the only items from which the culture can be "reconstructed."

Culture Lag

We have seen that although social behavior shows regularity and order, it is also a functional, dynamic, or kinetic thing. A total culture is always in movement, both in relation to its internal components and in comparison with other cultures. But all the segments of a culture do not move at an equal rate, and this difference of movement of the parts of the culture is known as "culture lag."

An adequate concept of culture lag requires the establishment of some norm according to which the lag can be judged, and this constitutes the central difficulty in the measurement of culture lag. Which institution is leading and which is lagging? It is impossible to have complete stagnancy, security, and perdictability of human behavior, and it is apparently also impossible to have the same rate of movement by all people in all institutions. The same person may be quite "progressive" when he enacts his role in the economic or recreational institutions and yet be quite "backward" in his political and religious behavior.

The term "culture lag" almost necessarily involves value judgments. It usually indicates a negative aspect of social behavior. If one can decide what constitutes social progress in any given culture, he may be able to judge which institution is lagging behind the others. On the other hand, if mere change, or rapidity of change, is used as a norm, the negative connotation of the lag is lessened. For example, in most Western countries, very rapid change has occurred in the development of technological, industrial, and mechanical techniques. This means, in general, that the economic institution has been the fastest-moving part of the culture and that the varying "space" between it and the other institutions constitutes culture lag.

Classification of Cultures

If we think of the total culture as being the possession of a single society, it is obvious that there are as many cultures as there are societies and that they can be classified in a similar way. Thus, one may speak of a continuum of cultures from the simple to the complex, from the least dynamic to the most dynamic, from the partially developed to the most highly developed. We have already distinguished between primitive and civilized cultures.

It appears to be most useful for the sociologist to specify the culture by its most dominant institution. There are cultures identified as commercial and industrial because of their important economic institutions. Other cultures have been characterized by their familial institution, as prewar China; or by their political institution, as ancient Rome; or by their religious institution, as medieval Europe. The dominant or pivotal institution gives meaning to the interpretation of a culture and provides a helpful insight into both the values and the practices of the society.

We have already indicated that a culture area can sometimes be identified as a certain region of a country that is the location of a subculture. Just as one finds subgroups within a society, one can also classify a number of subcultures within the larger total culture. A common distinction is made between urban and rural culture, and in some rapidly increasing populations there is also an emerging suburban culture. The culture of a mountainous region may differ somewhat from that of the plains or the seacoast. As the total society's control over its physical environment becomes more complete, these purely topographical influences become less important as denominators of subcultures.

Adaptations of Culture

While it is possible to delve historically into the origin of this or that culture pattern, the origin of culture as a whole is simultaneous with the origin of society. Culture is the necessary concomitant of society and has existed wherever human beings have lived in group life. Nevertheless, cultures vary greatly from one society to another, from one period of time to another, and to a lesser degree a culture may vary internally from one institution to another.

Man is one, but cultures are many. We have seen that many factors are at work in this multiplication and differentiation of culture, from the geographical environment to man's ingenuity in doing things in many different ways. These multiple factors must be subsumed here in the discussion of the four principal ways in which culture adaptation occurs. Besides the major basic and universal institutions, one may discover a similar culture pattern in two dissimilar cultures. There appears to be no single, complete explanation for this fact, and the following explanations overlap:

a) Parallelism refers to the independent development of a culture characteristic in two widely separated cultures. There is no historical evidence that the use of the wheel, or of the arch in buildings, or of domesticated dogs, pigs, and other animals was originated by one people in only one place. Even in the modern world the same mechanical invention or scientific discovery occurs in places that are very far apart.

b) Diffusion is the much more common process of patterns and traits passing back and forth from one culture to another. The examples we have given concerning the importation and adaptation of behavior patterns, of food customs, and of religious practices give ample evidence of this diffusion of culture.

c) Fission is a process that can be traced historically when a long-established society breaks up into two or more independent units. The various tribes of North American Indians, the Eskimos, and the Appalachian hill folk are examples of people who have broken away from their cultural origins and have developed different internal cultural traits. But they retain also some of their ancient patterns relatively unchanged.

d) Convergence is the fusion of two or more cultures into a new one which is somewhat different from its predecessors. The Norman invasion of England, the fusion of the Moorish and Spanish cultures, and the convergence of Roman and Germanic traits are well-known historical examples of this cultural adaptation.

Diffusion and convergence of culture are the two forms of adaptation most important in the modern world. The physical intermingling of people from different backgrounds has increased tremendously because of both forced and voluntary migration. People transport with themselves the behavior patterns from their original culture. More important than physical intermingling, however, is the rapid communication of ideas from one culture to another.

Functions of Culture

A culture exists in order to systematize the satisfaction of the social needs of people; the means for this satisfaction are the various major and subsidiary institutions that constitute the culture. The culture as a whole, however, performs a number of functions distinct from the objectives of the various institutions. We have already noted the generalized functions of the institution: simplifying behavior, providing roles and relations, and exerting social control. To some extent these institutional functions are also the functions of the total culture, but there are additional functions that can be attributed to the culture:

a) The culture serves as a "trade mark" that distinguishes one society from another. It characterizes a people more meaningfully and more scientifically than the color of their skin or any other physiological marking. It provides for the student of society a basis for distinguishing peoples that is much more realistic than territorial and political boundaries and so-called national characteristics.

b) The culture brings together, contains, and interprets the values of a society in a more or less systematic manner. It is through the culture that people discover the meaning and purpose of both social and individual living. The more thoroughly the person understands the culture the more he realizes that it "hangs together" in a kind of design for living. Meanings and values become integrated in and through the culture.

c) The culture provides one of the most important bases for social solidarity. It inspires loyalty and devotion to associates and to the society in general. A love of one's country, or patriotism, is in effect, at least, an appreciation of its cultural characteristics. The definition of culture includes the essential notion that the people of a society function together for the attainment of worthwhile objectives. This cooperative effort both contributes to and follows from social solidarity.

d) The culture provides a blueprint of, as well as the materials for, the social structure. It systematizes social behavior so that the person participates in society without the necessity of constantly relearning and inventing ways of doing things. Culture relates and co-ordinates all the various segments of the behavior of individuals and groups.

e) The culture of any society is the dominant factor in establishing and molding the social personality. While there is a variety of unique differences among the persons in a society, there is also a kind of cultural stamp on the personality that no one can escape. Obviously the self-directing person has the ability to choose and to adapt, but his social personality is by and large the product of his culture. It is therefore possible to speak of the typical American, or Frenchman, or Italian.

An analysis of these functions will readily indicate the tremendous importance of culture not only for the individuals and groups within a society but also for the relations of one society to another. It can be said that a society is what its culture makes it, even though the obverse is also true: a culture is what the society makes it. Culture and society are inextricably bound up with one another, and people and cultural patterns are constantly influencing each other. There is a constant process of adaptation between them.

DISTINCTIVE FEATURES OF AMERICAN CULTURE

1. American Negro Culture

It is commonly observed in social science that distinctive cultures develop when a large plurality of people is sufficiently separated from other organized people. An isolated society that has little contact and communication with other societies tends to develop certain distinctive cultural characteristics. We have seen, however, that it is possible for a cultural pattern to develop in parallel ways in two widely separated societies. It is possible also for it to continue its development when a single culture separates into two different systems or when two cultures merge into a new one. Finally, the process of diffusion allows for an interchange of cultural traits between two distinctive cultures.

The case of the American Negro does not fit any of the four classical forms of adaptation: parallelism, fission, convergence, or diffusion. For the foreign observer the American Negro appears to have a kind of imported subculture in the sense that immigrant minorities like English, Irish, Germans, Italians, and others have maintained subcultures within the American society. For the American who approves of racial segregation, the Negro not only has but should have a self-developed, original, and non-white culture.

The social facts in the American scene indicate that both these views are erroneous. The migration of Negroes to America and their socialization here were almost totally different from the experiences of white European minorities. In the latter part of the last century it was thought that through "equal segregation" a distinctive Negro society and culture could develop, but this theory was sociologically unrealistic, and this development has not come to pass. The fact is that at the present time both white and Negro Americans share the same American culture.

This American culture of course contains traces of African culture. As we have seen, the American culture has borrowed from almost every culture on every continent of the earth. Cultural borrowings occur wherever there are contact and communication among societies. But although we have borrowed the use of glass from the ancient Egyptians, the use of coffee from the Arabs, and the use of waffles from the

Scandinavians, we do not identify Egyptian, Arabian, and Scandinavian subcultures in American society. Similarly, the working of bronze and the manufacture of enamel, which we have borrowed from Africa, are not signs of an African subculture.

The culture of the American Negro involves much more than an occasional historical borrowing of culture traits. When the slave trade began, there existed many separate societies and cultures with different languages on the African continent. Large tribes had a stable, highly developed way of life, with all the major systematized cultural institutions. Large-scale invasions by the slave hunters disrupted and in some cases destroyed these societies. Thousands of Negroes were separated from their various established cultures and transported to America, many of them coming via the West Indies.

The difference between the European and the African migrant and the reasons why Negro Americans have not developed a separate culture are as follows:

a) The African was deliberately separated from members of his own tribe precisely in order to prevent social and cultural unity among the slaves. This separation process was begun in the actual slave-hunting, was continued in the slave markets both abroad and here, and was completed by the selective purchase and distribution of slaves to different plantations. It was thereafter only by chance that an individual African would have contact with a fellow member of his own original society.

b) From the point of view of the African this meant that he was an individual migrant, a cultural isolate. He was forced to adapt himself to other similar, culturally isolated individuals. Even though he may have been in the physical presence of dozens of other fellow Africans, they were strangers and foreigners to him. Culture shock was multiplied for him in a way that the loneliest white European migrant never experienced.

c) From the point of view of the group this isolation meant that no single African subculture was able to take root among the slaves; none could predominate and no new culture could emerge. If the Africans could have migrated as a cohesive social group or could have joined with others who shared their language and customs after they arrived, as the white European migrants often did, there would have been a possibility of a separate and distinct subculture.

d) Although there were always many free Negroes in America, it must be remembered that the great majority were forced migrants remaining here under duress. If their owners were lenient, they were able to form primary groups, but they never formed a society in the strict sense of the term. They were never independent and separate from the dominant whites, and the necessary consequence was that the latter imposed cultural patterns upon the Negroes. Thus, from the beginning, the American Negro was forced to adopt the permissible patterns of overt and covert behavior he found in America. For these reasons he became acculturated much more rapidly than most of the later European immigrants.

e) The notion that the Negroes now have a separate subculture because they have been a segregated people is historically and scientifically erroneous. If the American Negroes had had the forced separation of the American Indians on reservations, or the voluntary separation of some of the white hill folk, it might have been possible for them to develop a distinctive society and culture. But this has never been the case; they have always participated in the American culture, and the possibility of a separate Negro subculture has completely faded from contemporary American life.

Even though the Negro has suffered discriminations and exclusions in various degrees in wide areas of American life, his basic cultural patterns are American. He knows no other major institutions except those of the American culture. His family patterns are those of other Americans; his religious and economic activities are similar to those which exist in the general cultural environment. As his opportunities expand in the educational, political, and recreational groupings of the American society, he does not invent or import different institutional patterns.

The system of racial segregation does not work when there is close cultural similarity between the peoples to be segregated. An effective segregation system cannot be based on the relatively superficial distinction of physical characteristics. It requires a difference or a cluster of differences in the culture base, in language, religion, family, and politics. It can exist, at least temporarily, only if one people is completely subjugated to another.

All Negroes can trace their American ancestry back further than the great majority of white Americans. Very few Africans migrated to this continent after 1800; but the large flood of white Europeans did not begin to arrive until later in the last century. By that time the Americanization of the Negro was completed. The attempt at "legal but equal" segregation of the races at the end of the last century came much too late to achieve any effective cultural fission between American whites and Negroes. The result is that at the present time there is no identifiable American Negro culture.

2. Some American Culture Lags

The theory of the culture lag has been criticized mainly because of the difficulty of deciding upon the norms according to which the lag is measured. If a person declares that American material patterns of economic production are far ahead of non-material patterns (ideas, attitudes, and values), he could find many examples to prove this culture lag. He could also demonstrate with as many examples that many of our ideas are far ahead of our practices and that some material patterns lag behind the non-material.

Americans tend to use one institution, the *economic*, as the norm by which to measure the progress of our other institutions. The success that Americans have had in the production and distribution of goods and services has been so spectacular that it draws wide attention both here and abroad. Furthermore, this kind of success can easily be enumerated, measured, and compared with scales and graphs. The familial, educational, political, and religious institutions should not, however, be underrated simply because they have not adapted themselves in the same way, or have "lagged behind" the pace of the economic institution.

To understand the culture lags in America, it would be fruitful to select other norms of evaluation and measurement. Instead of comparing the material with the non-material patterns or the economic with the other institutions, we may use as a norm the current knowledge and resources at the disposal of the American people for the improvement of their institutions. There are institutions in which we have the "know-how" and the physical equipment to make improvements and progress but have not done so. In determining cultural lag, actual improvements should be measured against realistic potential ones, that is, those that could be made with the knowledge and resources *now* at hand.

Following are some of the most striking examples of American cultural lag in areas where the potential and the actual have not been brought together:

a) A significant percentage of American families are living in inadequate housing. The mass production of housing has not achieved and probably cannot achieve the refinement of techniques employed on the assembly line for the production of movable units. However, our national wealth is more than sufficient to provide decent housing for everyone, and our experience in public and low-income housing has been extensive enough to build the needed dwelling units without delay. This is an example of cultural lag because we have both the material and the knowledge to fill the gap.

b) There are people in the United States who suffer from hunger, whose diet is insufficient and improper. Whatever the immediate personal and social reasons why individuals and families suffer from malnutrition and inadequate food, the fact is that we Americans possess superabundant food resources and the knowledge of ways to distribute them. The fact that numbers of Americans are not well fed, that we actually do not bring surplus food and hungry people together, is an elementary example of cultural lag.

c) Another lag in our culture is seen in the lack of medical care for many Americans. Medical science has made tremendous advances in our times, and the country is wealthy enough to provide all the physical instruments of healing for all the people. Americans experience many curable sicknesses and needless deaths every year because medical science is not actually made available to them. While death is inevitable for every individual and some diseases are still incurable, the lag between the potential and the actual is tremendous.

Many Americans do not have equal access to recreational and educational facilities. Others receive unequal treatment from the police and the courts. Still others find themselves thwarted in their political and religious aspirations. In many instances these situations may be due to personal incompetence and irresponsibility. They must, however, also be termed examples of cultural lag, even though they are often pointed out as the "price one pays" or the "risk one assumes" in living in our dynamic, progressive, and adaptive culture.

We have selected only three instances of cultural lag because these three are the most apparent. They are also the least controversial from a factual point of view. It is a demonstrable social fact that many Americans suffer ill-health and are ill-fed and ill-housed, even though this land of plenty is capable of remedying these deficiencies. These problems are present all over rthe United States; but there are also local and regional examples of other cultural lags in economic, political, and other institutions.

Pointing out the lag between the potential and the actual does not indicate the reasons why these lags persist in a dynamic, progressive, and pragmatic society. It is likely that the causes lie deeply rooted in certain traditional American cultural values like free enterprise, private property, the profit system, or inviolability of the home and family, or in characteristics like the political inertia of the masses. Most of these are part of the philosophy of individualism, which is itself an enduring pattern of our culture.

3. The Changing Rural Culture

The United States is one of the least rural nations, but it is also one of the most successful agricultural nations in the world. The 1950 Census showed that less than one-sixth of our population actually lives on farms, and less than 12 per cent of our gainfully employed workers are farmers. At the same time we have tremendous surpluses of agricultural products, billions of dollars worth of extra foodstuffs, that we cannot possibly consume. The trend continues in opposite directions: a decreasing number of farmers and an increasing quantity of agricultural products.

This is a situation unique in the world's history. Mankind has been predominantly rural and agricultural for as far back in time as we can trace human history. Most human experience has been enacted in rural society with a rural culture; and this has been true up until recently in the Western world and even in the United States. Rural traditions run deep in our culture.

The present transitional phase of American rural culture is characterized by a number of elements that have not previously appeared in the same combinations. There were periods of time, and there are societies, in which a relatively clear distinction could be made between the urban and the rural culture. Not only did the institutional functions differ in the two areas of the same society, but the urban and rural people were physically and socially separated from one another. In the present American society the two have been brought into contact through the media of transportation and communication.

Following are the most significant changes that have come to the rural areas. Taken in combination, they represent an important trend in the cultural patterns of the American farm population.

a) Urbanism has invaded the rural way of life. Generally, this means that the city has been brought to the country. We think of urbanization as a process of migration from the rural to the urban areas or as a concentration of many people in a limited territory. There has been much urbanward migration, but the farm and the ranch have become mechanized, and the rural people have more and more accepted urban patterns of behavior. Physical isolation in which distinctive cultural patterns may develop and endure loses its cultural influence as radio and television programs and newspapers from the city reach the farm.

b) The most spectacular alteration in the American rural culture appears to be that of the familial institution. The farm is changing from a family enterprise, in which each member makes a valuable economic contribution, to a large business operation, in which skilled labor and expensive machinery do the work. The functions, roles, and relations that traditionally characterized the farm family have had to take new directions and new forms. There is more leisure for the mother to pursue non-economic functions and for the children to obtain a greater amount of schooling. The rural home is no longer the center for the recreational, educational, or religious functions.

c) The primary relationships in the old rural neighborhoods are declining. Although the farmer has always been conservative and individualistic, there is no longer the need for the kind of co-operation that once existed. This co-operation took the form of economic help in gathering harvests, borrowing and lending implements, and building barns and fences. Congeniality patterns of the past, like all-day visiting, church dinners and festivals, and barn dances, have gone out of fashion. Rural people range farther afield for their recreation even while they have become more self-sufficient in their economic activities.

d) Economic relations with the city have multiplied as the mutual dependence of city and farm has increased. Obviously, urban people have always depended upon agriculture to supply their food. The financial dependence of the farmer upon the city centers has now become greater than ever. Gasoline and oil, fertilizers and tools, field machinery, and barn equipment cannot be obtained through barter. The cost of the farmer's operation and the price he receives for his products are both governed largely by factors outside his control.

e) The development of numerous secondary associations has broadened the cultural milieu of rural people. Participation in these larger groupings has had a manifold increase. More young people participate in organizations like the 4-H clubs and Future Farmers of America and more adults in co-operatives, marketing associations, and various programs sponsored by county and state farm bureaus. The growth of secondary groupings in the rural areas has followed at a slower pace the pattern of larger, formalized groupings in the cities.

f) The political institutions of the rural culture have been altered by the farmers' new relations to federal and state governments. Price supports, crop control, import taxes, and credit restrictions cannot be handled by the local government. The farmer's political needs go beyond the local township or county and include national and even international issues. Since he is also part of this total complex society, the farmer has necessarily had to widen his horizon, and this is simply another way of saying that the rural American culture has decreased the difference between itself and the more typical American urban culture.

This list of items must not be interpreted as a universal change applicable in all rural areas of the United States. There has been an unevenness in rate and kind of change in different parts of the country. The most widespread change has been from the small family farms to so-called factory farms. The latter have been most often gigantic operations existing in all the farm states and owned by food-processing corporations. Unorganized migrant labor has been introduced in some of these places; and social conditions exist that were unknown on the traditional, stable family farm.

4. The Southeastern Regional Culture

The region known as the Old South, comprising the eleven southeastern states, has been both romanticized and vilified. Equal misrepresentation has been made in the name of realism and in the name of poetry. To most Americans, the southeastern region is a culture area distinct from the rest of the country. The people act differently; they speak with a drawl; they move more slowly than other Americans. They have traditions of hospitality and gracious living; they even have food patterns and religious practices peculiar to the region.

Society and culture are changing very rapidly in the Southeast. Mechanization of the farms has pushed people into the local towns, into midwestern and northeastern cities, and into the Southwest and the far West. The growth of cities and the increase of industry have quickened the pace of living. Facilities for health and education are improving. Patterns of political behavior are shifting. Even the traditional relations between upper and lower class, between Negro and white, are changing gradually.

Although this transition is relatively rapid at the present time as compared with a generation ago, it is still possible to capture the main elements that gave the Old South a distinctive subculture within the

American total culture. The rest of our society is also changing, and in many ways more rapidly; but in spite of this fact the southeastern culture is tending to merge with the total culture. It is, in this sense, becoming more American. Traditional cultural differences still endure, but they are fading in importance. Contemporary southeasterners do not take them as seriously as their grandfathers once did.

One of the most significant facts, which is frequently overlooked, is that the Old South has become the New Southeast. For a long time it has been unrealistic to maintain the fiction that the United States is divided into only two sections, the North and the South, although this regional view still persists among older people in the Southeast. The United States has expanded tremendously in area and population since the Civil War, so that a double process of shrinkage and of Americanization has been going on in the southeastern region.

Following are some of the main factors that help to account for the residual regional differences of culture in the southeastern states:

a) The composition of the population gives one of the main clues why this subculture differs from the total American culture. The immigrant stock, both white and Negro, has a longer continuing history than that of the other parts of the country. The Old South was practically untouched by the successive waves of European migration from the 1840's until the first World War. While these immigrant peoples were spreading across the northern states, the southerners continued to reproduce themselves and in later decades were able actually to "export" persons to other parts of the country.

b) It must be noted that this lack of immigrant stimulus was an important factor in maintaining regional cultural forms. Foreigners did not come to America merely as physical entities. They brought with them cultural patterns, ideas, attitudes, and values, which fused with the dynamic and receptive total culture. Most of this cultural influence bypassed the southern people. The Southeast, therefore, became "Americanized" more slowly than the rest of the country, and there is still today a residual ethnocentrism and even resentment against "foreign" ideas. The traditional, conservative ethos of the region was formulated over this long period of time.

c) Much can also be made of the fact that this region has been mainly agricultural and rural. Patterns and institutions change more slowly in the rural environment; and the type of farming adopted also helped to slow down change. The South was not a land of numerous, independent, vigorous farmers who managed their own small holdings.

The dominant agricultural pattern was that of the large plantation, concentrating on single money crops and paying minimum attention to conservation of natural resources.

d) The plantation system was also a system of human relations, and it is in this area that a great hindrance to cultural development existed. The fact that the middle class was practically non-existent marked off the Old South as being non-typical in middle-class America. The mass of Negro workers, both during and after slavery, and the attitudes the dominant whites took toward them constituted a distinctive non-American feature of southern culture. Freedom of movement, of work and opportunity, of upward mobility, is a basic ingredient of the American culture, and formalized restrictions hampered this freedom everywhere in the regional culture.

e) The segregation system, the studied practice of keeping the masses, especially the Negroes, on the lowest rung of the social structure, has affected all the major institutions of the Southeast. It has affected the family by a peculiar combination of strict marriage prohibitions, illegitimacy, and loose sex relations. It has accounted for the low rate of literacy and the inadequate educational system. It helps to explain the religious practices arising from literal fundamentalism. It affected the antilabor attitudes of both business and professional persons and helped to maintain an archaic political philosophy.

It is no oversimplification to point to these elements—the composition of the population, the type of agricultural system, and the structure of segregation—as the principal factors in the development and maintenance of the old southern subculture. The extent to which these have differed from the general patterns of the American culture, and the extent to which they are now changing, mark the progress of the Americanization of the southeastern region. There will probably remain an identifiable regional subculture as long as minor institutional patterns endure. Rapid change, however, is now occurring in the major factors mentioned above; and this necessarily implies the emergence of behavior patterns in the New Southeast that more closely resemble those of the total American culture.

5. The Suburban Culture

The vast development of the residential areas adjacent to large cities is a relatively new American phenomenon. The rate of growth of large cities has gradually decreased while that of the suburbs has rapidly increased. The rural-urban trend of population migration continues, but a parallel trend has been the movement of people out of the cities into the suburbs. The source of the suburban population is therefore not the farm but the city.

At least in some respects, the suburban population is developing a new way of life, that is, a kind of American subculture. This culture has its roots in the cities. It is an evolution of some of the culture patterns that have existed among the urban people. While the expressed motivation for the suburban migration is in many instances the desire to "get away from the city," it is not necessarily an attempt to "return to the fields." The contemporary suburban culture is so different from the typical older rural culture that the two can hardly be compared.

Some of the characteristics of the suburban culture are as follows:

a) The general term "middle-class mentality" may be aptly applied to the people in many of the newer suburbs. While this mentality is more or less characteristic of the American population, it appears in a "purer" type among the suburban dwellers. They are the people who have moved not only outward but upward. They are the management, professional, and white-collar people who are distinguishable from the masses of industrial and service workers. They constitute the class that best represents the style of life for which millions of Americans are striving, and, to some extent, they "set the tone" for that level of living.

b) The suburban way of life exhibits standardization of many material items of culture. The size of dwellings, their material equipment— like picture windows, combined living and dining rooms, breakfast nooks, and modernized kitchens, and in addition the family's automobile, television set, and limited expanse of lawn—all are similar items characteristic of the suburban home. Here again the "best" of the mass-production system is exhibited. These people do not have the luxury items of the very wealthy, but they do have things that the masses cannot afford.

c) The suburbs are relatively new population aggregations, and they have attracted large numbers of young married people. They are not places of retirement for older people. Suburban youthful vigor is reflected in the spirit of the community. These young couples have young children; they share many of the same interests and problems. In spite of their basic middle-class conservatism, they are in many ways imaginative, pragmatic, and progressive. To some extent they even have a trace of the "pioneer" attitude of people who are venturing into a new area of life.

d) One of the outstanding features of the new suburbs is the increase of primary contacts among individuals and groups. The whole social and physical setting makes possible the immediate, face-to-face relations that are difficult in the city. The characteristic urban anonymity is replaced by religious and recreational groupings of friends and neighbors and by personal contacts in schools, playgrounds, clubs, and stores of the community.

e) The restoration of community appears to be one of the more significant aspects of the developing suburbs. People who function together, hold relatively the same values and have similar social backgrounds, are also people who tend to form a genuine community. The amount of conformity and the degree of social pressure in the suburbs are helping to develop a recognizable cultural system. Social solidarity among the residents brings back some aspects of old-fashioned neighborliness.

f) The suburbs are economically dependent upon the adjacent large city. The great majority of suburban families receive their income from the urban occupation of the husband and father. This means, of course, that at least one member of the family is in continuous and direct contact with much of the urban cultural milieu. In fact, this economic contact with the big city makes possible the essential physical and material base of the suburban community.

There are of course many fringe areas of big cities that are not the suburbs of this description. Industrial and commercial areas, railroad yards, stockyards, and similar enterprises make these places undesirable for residential use. These tend to become slums or near-slums characterized by the social disorganization of the more densely crowded urban areas. The typical emerging suburbs are more distant from the city.

The suburban culture appears to be a permanent and increasing phenomenon in American life. As the material standard of living rises, the means of transportation improve, and the need for farm land decreases, it is likely that the American culture will become predominantly suburban. It appears that our society will continue the trend from rural to urban culture with a further step to the suburban culture. This change of major significance requires continuing study and analysis by the social scientist.

DISCUSSION QUESTIONS

1. Explain: "Every normal person has culture."
2. How does culture differ from society and from civilization?

3. Explain the statement that culture is both hereditary and environmental.
4. If people create the culture, how can people be creatures of culture?
5. What is the difference between culture area and culture complex?
6. What is the significance of studying material culture objects?
7. What is the central difficulty in the measurement of the culture lag?
8. How does the dominant institution help to classify cultures?
9. Explain the principal ways in which culture adaptations occur.
10. What are the main functions of a total culture?
11. Do the American Negroes have a distinctive subculture? Explain.
12. List and explain the differences between the African and the European migrant to America.
13. What substitute can be profitably used for the material culture as a measure of cultural lag?
14. List and discuss some of the more obvious examples of American cultural lag.
15. How can the United States be one of the least rural but also one of the most successful agricultural nations in the world?
16. What are the most significant changes occurring in the rural culture?
17. Mention the more obvious stereotypes of "Southern culture."
18. Explain the principal factors preventing the Americanization of the southeastern region.
19. In what sense can the suburbs be said to have a distinctive culture?
20. To what extent is it likely that the American culture will become predominantly suburban?

SUGGESTED READINGS

GILLIN, JOHN P. *The Ways of Men*. New York: Appleton-Century-Crofts, Inc., 1948, chaps. xxii–xxv.

GREEN, ARNOLD. *Sociology*. New York: McGraw-Hill Book Co., 1952, chap. v.

HILLER, E. T. *Social Relations and Structures*. New York: Harper & Bros., 1947, chaps. ii–v.

LINTON, RALPH. *The Study of Man*. New York: D. Appleton–Century Co., 1936, chaps. xvi–xxii.

OGBURN, WILLIAM F., and NIMKOFF, M. F. *Sociology*. Boston: Houghton Mifflin Co., 1950, chap xxv.

ROSS, EVA J. *Fundamental Sociology*. Milwaukee: Bruce Publishing Co., 1939, chap. iv.

The previous sections have given us a conceptual framework and some scientific insights into the parallel analysis of patterns and culture, of persons and society. In this section these two separate lines of analysis are brought together into the study of various sociocultural phenomena.

The essential study of the meanings of group life and cultural habits is done through an analysis of values (chap. xiii). Social persons are both the subjects and the agents of mobility (chap. xiv). The total systems of culture and society are in the process of change (chap. xv) and are influenced through various forms of control (chap. xvi). The norms and values of people are sometimes violated so that there is deviation (chap. xvii), but there exists also a necessary degree of sociocultural integration (chap. xviii).

PART **III**

Culture
and
Society

CHAPTER THIRTEEN

Values

Perhaps no other subject has caused so much controversy among sociologists as the study of values. Their attempt to act as "value-free" scientists has sometimes led to the suggestion that they believe social values have no reality, cannot be studied without the involvement of one's personal values, or are purely psychological and ethical entities outside the orbit of social science. At the present time, however, it is generally agreed among sociologists that values are important *social facts* and that they can be submitted to scientific study and analysis.

Definition of Value

The use of a descriptive definition instead of a strict logical definition has caused confusion in the discussion of social values. Descriptively we may say that everything that is useful, desirable, or admirable to the person and group "has a value." Must we say, therefore, that the thing itself is not a value but that it merely contains a value? For example, is education itself a social value, or does its value lie in the capacity it has for satisfying certain basic social needs? The fact is, of course, that the importance an object has transfers to the object itself, so that education is not only socially valuable, it is a social value. The sociologist finds his data among people in society, and he finds that in the minds of the people a certain "worth" is attached to education.

We have, then, three elements that must be considered in the discussion of social values: (*a*) the *object itself*, which is a value, (*b*) the *capacity of the object* to satisfy social needs, and (*c*) the *appreciation of the people* for this object and for its capacity to give satisfaction. We may recall here that the same object can be given different definitions according to the different aspects from which it is viewed. We have seen that repeated uniformities of behavior can also be viewed as norms, or models, of behavior. Similarly, we may say that certain "worthwhile" objects, as judged by the people in a society, are both social values *and* the criteria of social values.

Sociologically, values may be defined as those criteria according to which the group or society judges the importance of persons, patterns, goals, and other sociocultural objects. We are not directly concerned here with either the intrinsic worth of these things or with the specific personal valuation made of them by any particular individual.

Criteria of Valuation

Values, therefore, are the criteria that give meaning and significance to the total culture and society. More fully described, the values of concern to the social scientist have the following characteristics. They are *shared;* they are agreed upon by a plurality of people and do not depend upon the judgment of any particular individual. They are *taken seriously;* people connect these values with the preservation of the common welfare and the satisfaction of social needs. Values involve *emotions;* people are moved to make sacrifices, even to fight and die for the highest values. Finally, since values require consensus or agreement among many people, they may be conceptually *abstracted* from the various valued items.

We have already seen that every society employs criteria by which it determines the social status of persons and by which it places pluralities of persons on a higher or lower rank of appreciation. These criteria are called the determinants of social status and class. The people consider these more or less objectively measurable determinants to be worthwhile: family and ancestry, wealth, functional utility, education, religion, and biological characteristics.

When we inquire about the social status of an individual, we are really asking about his social value as measured by these criteria—the objective esteem or disesteem, approval or disapproval, attached to him. The manner in which people evaluate one another and the kind of cultural object they hold in high or low esteem are of great basic importance to the functioning of the society. Value judgment, or social evaluation, necessarily implies a comparison of what is better or worse, higher or lower, in esteem and approval. These judgments are, of course, sometimes false, as in the case of extreme ethnocentrism.

The Source of Values

It is an oversimplification to say that values are important because people are important. It is true, of course, that values have no scientific meaning for the sociologist except in so far as they are connected with human beings. The social person and his behavior patterns are the starting point of the study of sociology. What makes some people (and their behavior) more important and more highly valued than others? Why do all social and cultural phenomena have value only because they are related to human beings? We are seeking here the answers to these questions in the sources of values, and these sources may be analyzed on two levels.

a) We have already seen that social status (that is, the evaluation of the person by others) comes to the individual by ascription and achievement. The social consensus of high or low status is based on the individual's possession of those items that are highly valued in the culture. They are circumstances and conditions the value of which the individual cannot control. Stated briefly, this means that this source of the values is external to the social person.

Social esteem comes to a person of good family, not because of the person himself, but because good family is a criterion of high value in his society. The merit is, as it were, transferred to him from outside himself. Similarly, the high value of the wealth he possesses and the religion he practices is transferred to him. The social esteem attached to his functional role, to the type of education he has, and even to some extent to the physical qualities he possesses has its source in his cultural environment. All these valued items are part of the culture content surrounding the individual.

b) On another level of abstraction, however, there is also a source of values internal to the social person. The human dignity of the individual entitles him to respect. The mere fact that he is a person accountable for his behavior, praiseworthy for his good deeds and reprehensible for his evil deeds, is a basis for social evaluation. The moral right to personal inviolability is centered on the fact of humanity itself. This inviolability, responsibility, and dignity are not originated by the society and then handed over to the individual.

The fact that society recognizes and appreciates this inner source of evaluation is historically demonstrated by the exceptions taken to it Whenever men have enslaved other men, degraded their dignity, or shamefully exploited them, they have justified their actions by the argument that the victims were somewhat less than human. The abused race or category of people had to be considered as a lower order of being, without human rights and dignity, irresponsible and violable, in order to justify their enslavement. The attempt had to be made to remove the inner source of evaluation because societies everywhere have recognized the validity of these inner values.

Values and Behavior Patterns

The fruitful study of patterns of behavior, both overt and covert, requires an understanding of the values current in a society. These patterns do not have equal importance; mores are more compulsive than mere usages. One of the reasons we often cannot "make sense" out of the behavior patterns in foreign cultures is because we do not know and understand the values of the culture. The behavior that seems insignificant or absurd to us in a primitive culture may have great importance and value to the persons who perform it. Similarly, a lack of conformity to the patterns in one's own society often implies a lack of knowledge of the important social values.

It is the high value attached to monotheism, patriotism, and monogamy that places the patterns of religious, patriotic, or marital behavior among the mores. The philosopher may point out that God is intrinsically of higher value than human beings and that man is intrinsically more valuable than inanimate objects. The social scientist, however, operates in the extrinsic order, and it is through a knowledge of social values that he comes to judge whether a behavior pattern is trivial or essential to the people in the society. Behavior patterns that have the highest social value are also accompanied by the widest conformity and the strongest social pressure to conform.

Values and Social Roles

We could not speak of the values attached to behavior patterns were it not for the persons who perform these patterns. Values exist only because there are persons worthy of evaluation and competent to evaluate other persons and things. Just as the person-in-action is the irreducible component of society, so also is he the ultimate focus of values. The principal mechanism through which people express and symbolize values is the social role.

We have seen that patterns of behavior combine into social roles through which people function toward desired social goals. Within the role patterns are variously evaluated on a continuum from the most to the least important. The college student knows that the existing series of behavior expectations within his own educational role is not of uniform social value. Studying for an examination is of greater value than attendance at a fraternity meeting. Writing a term paper is more important than having lunch in the college cafeteria. The person is expected to know the varying degrees of value attached to the different patterns within his role and to concentrate on the more important ones.

In the total society the multiple social roles of the person also differ in value. This again depends upon the dominant institution of the culture and to some extent also upon the age, sex, and other circumstances of the individual. While it is true that the economic, the familial, or the religious role may have the highest social value in any particular culture, it is also true that any given individual may have a differing dominant role. For the wife and mother, the familial role has the highest social value in any culture. A bishop is expected to place his religious role above his economic, political, or any other role. Society, in other words, invests social roles with degrees of social value, and the behavior patterns of individuals must be in accord with these values.

Values as Behavior Sanctions

We have said that wide conformity, social values, and social pressure are objective indexes by which we can determine mores, folkways, and usages among the behavior patterns. Ultimately, however, the social value attached to a set of behavior patterns exerts strong pressure on people so that they conform to the value. This means that social values act as norms or standards of behavior patterns. When the society in general approves or disapproves a certain course of conduct, it is in effect saying that the behavior in question is right or wrong, correct or incorrect.

The social sanctions, that is, the rewards and penalties the society visits on the person because of his behavior, are intimately bound up with the ways in which the people evaluate that behavior. The hero and the public servant are honored and rewarded; the criminal and the racketeer are despised and punished. In both cases, however, the strength of the sanction is usually commensurate with the value attached to the behavior. For example, the penalties attached to the various types of criminal behavior are graded from light to severe on the basis of the way in which people grade the behavior itself. Capital punishment or life imprisonment is the sanction on first-degree murder, while a small fine is the sanction for a parking violation.

The system of rewards and punishments employed by a society has its ultimate basis in the value system. If there were no values in a society, and if these values were not known to differ in degree of importance, the society would lose its strongest instrument of social control. Although the system of values is the result of the accumulated wisdom of human experience, these values have a direct effect on contemporary human experience. They determine what is required of people and what is forbidden, what is praised and rewarded, and what is censured and punished.

Values and Social Processes

We have seen that people in society are related to one another most significantly through the reciprocal performance of their social roles. This relationship of person to person and of group to group is largely regulated and controlled by the values of the society. The whole network of status relations, superordinate, co-ordinate, and subordinate, could not operate if the people did not recognize and agree upon a body of social values. For example, the relationship between parent and child can be analyzed not only from the behavior of the roles themselves but also from an evaluation of the relationship itself.

The generic social relations, or social processes, in organized society are patterned according to relatively few basic types, some of them conjunctive and others disjunctive. Social values are involved in the actual functioning of these relations. The processes of co-operation, accommodation, and assimilation are usually highly valued because they promote harmony, good order, and social peace. The patterns of behavior and the roles people enact in these processes are oriented toward the higher values, the approved and esteemed modes of conduct. The reasons why people co-operate, the functions they perform, and the co-operating participants themselves are all measured on the criteria of higher social values.

The disjunctive processes are usually ranked lower in the scale of values, but the actual participation in these negative relations is often motivated and justified by higher social values. For example, the process of conflict as such is usually abhorred by the people in the society, but when the process is invested with other criteria like patriotism, heroism, justice, protection of the home, or personal and national honor, it becomes highly valued. Under similar conditions and with similar motivation, the process of contravention is also raised to a higher rank of evaluation. In some cultures, the process of competition, though ordinarily a negative relationship, is often praised and encouraged on the assumption that it has value "in itself."

This discussion of social processes indicates that social values are not merely norms of behavior but are also often used as a basis of *motivation of behavior*. If certain criteria of approval and disapproval exist in a culture, it is logical that people appeal to them as a justification of their own behavior. Nowhere is this seen so clearly as in the network of social relations. It is a fundamental need of the normal person that he have social status, that he be thought well of by others, and even that he think well of himself. The individual cannot successfully deal with others if he does not conform to the expected and approved ways of behaving, and this is another way of saying that he conforms to a system of social relations because they are invested with social values.

Classification of Values

Social values are closely related to patterns of behavior, social roles, and social processes, as well as to the whole stratification system of a society. Any one of these social phenomena could serve as a starting point for the classification of values. For our own analytical purposes, however, we here employ three bases of classification—the social personality, the society, and the culture. Although we are thus classifying values from three points of view, we must remember that the values discussed combine and overlap in all three.

a) The degree of compulsiveness provides a continuum on which social values may be conceptually arranged, that is, arranged according to the degree by which they affect the social personality. At one extreme are the morally strongest and internalized values the person accepts as a matter of conscience. The violation of these values would result, in the normal person, in feelings of guilt and shame. He feels compelled in conscience to comply with these values, and the society makes intense efforts to assure compliance. At this pole are the most rigid commandments, and, no matter how they are worded, the values imply both "thou shalt not" and "thou shalt." For example, the positive values of monotheism, patriotism, and monogamy imply the negative criteria of polytheism, treachery, and polygamy.

The social values that imply the highest moral and ethical compulsion tend to be the moral core of the individual's own personal ethics. From this high point the continuum shades off to the less important and the less compulsive values. This does not mean that there is always less conformity to these lesser values by the members of the society, but people often conform to them from convenience and habit rather than from an intense conviction of their values. There are obviously many patterns that are less compulsive because they are clothed in lesser values. For example, conventional forms of etiquette, norms of convenience and efficiency, and matters of aesthetic taste can be violated without a feeling of guilt and without serious social reprisals. At this end of the continuum of values, the moral quality of the behavior is not emphasized.

b) Social values may also be arranged on a continuum of associative functioning, as we have seen, in speaking of the social processes. Some social values are more important than others in getting things done in the society and in achieving co-operative efforts among persons and groups. These highest values indicate what is desirable and even essential for the continuance of society and for the common welfare. In this area the social relations of justice and love are most operative, and also there is a balance and relationship of high values like personal freedom and social authority. Briefly, whatever contributes to co-operation, accommodation, and assimilation may be said to be of associative value.

At the other pole of this continuum are the negative or antisocial values. They constitute an area of value conflict and emphasize the confusion between personal and social obligations. It cannot always be said that what is good for the society is good for the individual, and vice versa. Values that are negative and dissociative from the point of view of the total society may be highly esteemed by an individual person, an interest group, or a pressure group. Nevertheless, any value, whether it is racial superiority, business loyalty, or religious beliefs, which promotes the negative social processes must be termed a disjunctive value.

c) Values may be classified most meaningfully according to their institutional function in the culture. This classification agrees with the common usage of terms; we frequently identify separately values that are religious, political, economic, and so forth. Here we do not speak of a continuum from higher to lower, compulsive to permissive, positive to negative, although within the major institutions each of these sets of gradations can be recognized.

The systematic analysis of social values in a culture reveals that there is a set of values employed in each of the major institutions. People who perform their functions in a corresponding major social grouping such as the family recognize that there are certain major values to which they must adhere in their family life. The political and the economic groupings are also governed by distinctive social values. There are also important values in operation in the religious, educational, and recreational groupings of any society.

In this sense it may be said that social values, like patterns, roles, and relations, become "institutionalized." Values attached to certain cultural behavior for a long time simplify and ease the functioning of the institution. They become closely identified not only with the behavior itself but with the behavior in this or that institution. The longer the value and the behavior endure together and the more closely they are identified, the more likely is it that the combination will be institutionalized. That is why in traditional, slowly changing societies there is a tendency to say that there is *only one way* to bring up children, to plant crops, to conduct a church. The institutional value has merged with and reinforces the accepted institutional pattern.

Functions of Values

It is fairly clear, from the definition of the term, what the purposes of values are in a culture. We have seen that values are conceptually recognized, emotionally involved, shared in common, and taken seriously, and that they act as norms of judgment. It is also clear that values as such are not goals or objectives of social action and thought. They are not the things sought, but they are what gives the sought-after things importance. People use them as norms and criteria that point the way to goals and objectives.

In more detail we may here indicate that the mere presence of social values brings about certain social consequences. The actual pursuit of these social results may be termed the general functions of social values.

a) Values provide a ready-made means for judging the social worth of persons and pluralities. They make possible the whole system of stratification that exists in every society. They help the individual himself to "know where he stands" in the eyes of his fellow men.

b) Values focus the attention of people upon material cultural items that are considered desirable, useful, and essential. The item so valued may not always be "best" for the individual or group, but the fact that it is a socially valued object makes it worth striving for.

c) The ideal ways of thinking and behaving in any society are indicated by the values. They form a kind of blueprint of socially accepted behavior so that people can almost always discern the "best" ways of acting and thinking.

d) Values are guideposts for people in their choice and fulfilment of social roles. They create interest and provide encouragement so that people realize that the demands and expectations of the various roles are functioning toward worthwhile objectives.

e) Values act as a means of social control and social pressure. They influence people to conform to the mores, encourage them to do the "right" things, and give them a feeling of merited esteem. On the other hand, they act as restraints against disapproved behavior, indicate certain prohibited patterns, and make intelligible the feelings of shame and guilt coming from social transgressions.

f) Values function as a means of solidarity. It is an axiom among social scientists that groups cluster around and are united by common shared values of a high order. People are attracted to others who cherish the same values; and it may be said that common values are among the most important of the factors that create and maintain social solidarity.

Conflict of Values

Although the general values that are widely accepted in a culture have an integrating effect on the people, social problems may in some instances develop from social values. These problems arise primarily in two instances: first, when there is a discrepancy between the expressed values of the culture and the actual behavior of the people; and, second, when the values of the various subgroupings in the society are in conflict.

a) A social problem may be roughly defined as the disparity between the level of social values and the level of social behavior. If the people did not have high values, strong beliefs, and expressed ideals, there would be no norms against which behavior patterns could be measured. If there were no high values attached to persons and property, there would be no sanctions on their violation, and there would be no crime problem in society. Similarly, substandard housing, sexual promiscuity, racial discrimination, child labor, and all other social problems could not be defined unless there were value norms against which this kind of behavior could be judged.

The ranking of social values becomes important in this respect. As it achieves successive, subsidiary goals, the progressive society constantly revises and raises its standards. Social values are not absolutes, but they are always out of reach of the people. The gap between behavior and values is never and can never be entirely closed. The fact that human beings in the aggregate aspire to more than they can achieve means that there will always be social problems, and in this sense social values "cause" social problems.

b) Even though a culture is meaningfully integrated by the general consensus concerning the highest values, there are many instances within a society in which one set of values is in conflict with another. We have already discussed this aspect of institutional inconsistency. Conflict occurs when the values of the familial institution, for example, are not congruous with those of the economic institution, or when the values represented in the educational role are inconsistent with those of the home. The values of the church sometimes clash with those of the state or of the business world.

This clash of values is most apparent in a pluralistic society in which large numbers of diverse groups are striving to bolster the loyalty of their members and to make their influence felt in the larger society. The interest groups and the pressure groups are value groups. In a democratic society, the right to maintain and to express diverse values is protected, and there are usually some useful mechanisms through which compromise of values is possible. Nevertheless, most of the major social problems can be stated in terms of a clash of values.

This value diversity necessarily has an effect on the social personality. In an industrialized, urban society few people can spend their whole lives isolated in the groups that have congenial values. Their contact with other groups and their experience in other social situations highlight the contrast of social values and norms of behavior. Institutional inconsistency, the value expression of social problems, is translated into role inconsistency, the value expression of personal problems. The adaptive personality is most often able to override this difficulty, but for others it causes frequent and painful self-compromise.

Ultimate Values

The social scientist does not study immutable and absolute values. In so far as these exist, they are analyzed by philosophers, theologians, and students of ethics. Mutability is an essential characteristic in all societies and cultures. Change is characteristic also on the level of social values that are nowhere completely fixed, rigid, and immutable criteria of behavior. The fact that *value systems differ* from one culture to another, from one time to another within the same culture, and even from one region and class to others within the same society demonstrates the flexibility and mutability of values. This means, of course, that the criteria of judgment for what is good or bad, right or wrong, and correct or incorrect vary considerably in the minds of men.

In the light of this universal mutability and variation of social values, it is obvious that the term "ultimate values" must be used with scientific caution. Nevertheless, this concept has been formulated and used by social scientists in a relative, or "semi-ultimate" sense.

It can be demonstrated that the people in any particular society accord general consensus to a *core of important social values*. These are the ultimates for this society, the relatively few basic values against which the people measure their behavior and which characterize a culture and differentiate it from other cultures. These core values are seen most easily within the institutional framework, each major institution containing one or more of the most important social values. The ultimate social value may be expressed affection in family life, democratic procedures in the political system, monotheism in the religious institution, and other similar basic principles.

The concept of ultimate values may refer also to the *minimum consensus* found in all societies concerning certain "principles" of behavior. Although they vary in their interpretation and application of these ultimate social values, all societies everywhere put prohibitive sanctions on incest, murder, blasphemy, lying, and stealing. All societies place a high value on fidelity, friendship, love, and justice. This is another way of saying that the psychic unity of mankind is exhibited not only in basically similar human intellects and wills but also in a minimum similar social conscience.

ASPECTS OF THE AMERICAN VALUE SYSTEM

1. American Materialism

It appears to be almost inevitable that a society's values become most important in that area of behavior in which the society has been most successful. The American society has had its most dramatic success in its mastery over the physical environment. Americans have dealt with matter in a skilful and ingenious way that has probably never been surpassed in the history of humanity. This success in handling and mastering matter has eventuated in a tendency to use material criteria even in the judgment of spiritual and humanistic achievements.

Materialism is a question of degree, and the statement that American culture emphasizes materialistic values must not be interpreted to mean that it contains no spiritual values or that spiritual values are completely irrelevant. We are speaking here of a tendency to, and an emphasis on, quantitative measurement. The emphasized norms of judgment in the American culture are the characteristics of matter: size, numbers, frequency, and speed. The sensate qualities of matter are emphasized when it is said that a product looks, feels, and tastes "better," that it gives more comfort, pleasure, and convenience.

Foreign observers have sometimes made the exaggerated statement that in the American society all behavior has been reduced to a "question of dollars and cents." They are misled because in America some values have been expressed in pecuniary norms. Many Americans feel that the most successful father is the one who "best provides" for his family, and this provision is measured by the amount of money income he brings home to his family. Movie fans watch expectantly for the yearly announcement of earnings by their favorite actors and actresses to find out who have been the "best" entertainers.

It is commonly assumed that the most successful clergyman is the one who draws the largest crowds to his pulpit or to his radio or television program. The pastor or minister who runs his congregation in a "business-like way" and who has paid off the debt on a church building is highly praised. Similar criteria are often employed in judging the function of college and university presidents, who tend to move off the academic level and into the ranks of business managers. The mayor, governor, or president who is seeking re-election spends much of his campaign convincing the people of his fine record in financial and material achievement and improvements.

All these roles are also measured by non-material and non-pecuniary criteria. The political functionary, the educator, the clergyman, the entertainer, and the parent are also appraised according to the major values current in their corresponding major institution. This is to be logically expected, and probably cannot be omitted, in any society. Thus, it is not true that these institutional values have been converted into, or absorbed by, financial and quantitative norms of measurement. What has happened is an invasion of the major institutions by a set of values that apply properly in the economic institution.

In a materialistic culture like ours there exists also the vague assumption that spiritual and humanistic gains almost automatically flow from material success. There is, of course, the demonstrable fact that cultural values often suffer when people fall below a minimum standard of material living. Peace of mind, cultural interests, and normal social relations require something more than material subsistence. This, however, is quite different from the notion that the more material success a person has, the happier he will be, or the notion that all social problems will disappear if poverty is abolished, or the notion that material success is an index of divine blessing.

The vigorous young American culture stands in contrast to traditional, slow-changing cultures. We emphasize objects that are the "biggest and the best"; they emphasize those that are the "oldest and the best." We logically stress those matters in which we have achieved the most success: the longest bridge, the widest highway, the tallest building, the fastest airplane—all these are quantitative. It is characteristic of the American society to look forward to the near future when it can surpass even these superlatives.

It would be a great error to conclude that the American culture is pervadingly materialistic simply because Americans find measurable symbols the handiest way of expressing the numerous non-material functions and values. Because the father's job and salary are used as an index of his affection for his family, this does not mean that paternal affection is weak or absent. Because material symbols are employed to measure success in religious, economic, and political institutions, this does not mean that religious motivation, business loyalty, or concern for the common welfare have decreased in these institutions. Materialism has not supplanted non-material pursuits and functions. Indeed, it can probably be demonstrated that the pragmatic, down-to-earth use of measuring techniques has been an incentive to further and better effort on the level of non-material activities.

2. Increasing Concern for Humanitarian Values

The term "materialistic culture" is a relative term, and in the American society material achievement is not generally considered an end in itself. To lust after wealth for its own sake is characteristic of the miser but not of Americans in general. Wealth is considered a means to produce or consume more commodities and services. No American is willing to admit that he is accumulating wealth as an end in itself. Even if he is doing this, he rationalizes his conduct with more worthy explanations.

The father of the family may spend his time and energy in business activities, and he explains that he is doing this for his wife and family. The college president who pursues the alumni for contributions and seeks to build up the endowment fund explains that higher education is now a costly business. These examples indicate that while material achievements come to be used as a norm of success they are also used as a means for the fulfilment of higher goals. There is nothing inherently illogical or incompatible in this combination.

It is in the light of this fact that the American culture demonstrates a concern for both material success and humanitarian values. One may say that both these concerns are increasing along parallel lines, and there may be a kind of mutual causality between the two. As we realize more and more the tremendous potential of our natural resources in terms of material benefits to the masses of people, we tend to realize also the importance of extending and protecting the higher values.

Following are a few of the more obvious examples of persons and categories who are benefiting from, as well as participating in, the development of the American social conscience.

a) The increasing concern for humanitarian values may be seen in the extension of the rights, privileges, and potentialities of the American culture to more categories of Americans. For example, the high value of participation in the political institutions was extended to include women after the first World War. Some Americans objected to this move, but there were also many suffragette and equal-rights groups that had maintained a consistent campaign in its favor. It was an almost inevitable cultural trend that women should get the vote.

b) Another example is that of the child labor laws, to which there was also a certain amount of opposition. They were made to protect children against exploitation, and although they are sometimes still violated, the general principle that society must protect children is now accepted in the American culture. The right of labor to organize and to bargain collectively is now written into our laws. The promotion of fair employment practices that attempt to remove discrimination against minority peoples has been accepted in some states and will probably eventually spread to the entire nation.

c) The concerted efforts to protect religious and racial minorities in the American society are symptomatic of this growing concern for humanitarian values. This protection has been pursued more vigorously than ever since the end of the second World War. There are still racial and religious bigots in America, and there probably always will be, but the trend toward the removal of external abuses is unquestionable. The conscience of the society has expressed itself not only in new

laws and in a humane interpretation of old laws but also in the large
numbers of voluntary groupings that support this change.

d) People who are handicapped in various ways are also receiving
more attention in the numerous programs of social and humanitarian
welfare. Polio victims, children with speech and hearing defects, illegitimate and orphaned children, dependent mothers, the aged, the unemployed, and many others represent categories of persons who cannot
solve their problems unaided. The sporadic philanthropy and voluntary
charity of the past are being supplemented by efficient and organized
campaigns for funds, as well as by the official commitment of funds
and services by local, state, and federal governments.

An interesting aspect of the practical application of humanitarian
values is the kind of opposition it almost always meets. Before the
change is made the people generally give lip service to the ideal but
object to the particular practice proposed. After the change is made
the people learn to accommodate themselves to both the ideal and the
practice. Hardly anyone argues now against women voting, or against
the laws protecting children from exploitation, but there are still
people who fight bitterly against fair employment legislation and
against equal rights for Negroes.

The opposition is invariably and curiously based on the argument
that the extension of rights to others is an invasion of private rights.
There is merit in this argument only in so far as the formal obligations
of the individual increase when he must observe the rights of others.
Rights and obligations are correlative, and it is to the credit of the
American culture that this fact is more and more accepted in the social
conscience. There is nothing inevitable or absolute about this cultural
trend, and its social causes and conditions are numerous, but it is a
demonstrable fact of contemporary American society.

3. Ultimate Core of American Values

The American society contains so many diverse groupings and categories, and the American culture contains so many diverse value orientations, that at first glance it would appear impossible to find a core
of values on which all Americans agree. Nevertheless, there are certain
ideas and beliefs that are widely manifested in external patterns of
behavior. If we abstract from these, we find that which is considered
important by the majority of our people. This is the value system.

In spite of the differences in religion, race, ethnic background, economic status, and regional subcultures, most Americans would sub-

scribe to these values. This is what we mean by an "ultimate core" of values, a series of major themes running through the culture. In combination, they are typically American, although each will be found to some degree in other cultures also. They are ultimate, not in any absolute sense, but in the sense that they are the highest common denominators of what the people consider valuable.

a) The value of a rational approach to life is almost universally accepted among Americans. This is seen in the constant endeavor to reexamine concepts and practices of the social system and to seek more reasonable, time-saving, and effort-saving ways of doing things. We have been called an engineering civilization, intent on applying science to the control of nature and to the solution of all problems. There is still, of course, much folklore and superstition and many irrationalities and inconsistencies in our culture, but the dominating approach is a scientific one.

b) Closely allied to the rational approach is an emphasis on the value of progress. A belief in the perfectibility of society, culture, and personality has been a kind of driving force in our history. Americans have faith in the future, not as the simple evolutionary passage of time, but as a period in which human effort can be successfully applied to the solution of problems. The important aspect here is the American state of mind, willing to accept change and experimentation; it is a kind of national attitude that change induced by intelligent effort is bound to be good.

c) The value of individual success is greatly stressed as an accompaniment of the rational approach to progress. We have seen that success is often measured by material and pecuniary rewards, but this does not mean that success is valued only when it is achieved through business and economic efforts. The so-called self-made man or woman may be a physician, an athlete, or a beauty queen as well as a biochemist or physicist. For the most part success is valued as the result of achievement, but there is also a wide acknowledgment that the "breaks" play a part on the road to success.

d) A high value is placed upon work in the American culture. One of the principal criteria of a man's worth is "what he does," that is, his functional utility to society. The drive to work has in the past amounted almost to a compulsion among Americans. With the national increase in material comfort, success, and leisure this compulsive aspect of work has lessened somewhat in the individual, but there is still a general emphasis on activity, on "getting things done." The foreign observer is always struck with the hustle and bustle of American cities.

e) One of the few traditions of the relatively young American culture is its emphasis on the value of freedom for the individual. The recognition of the intrinsic qualities of man—his moral responsibility, his inviolability, and his dignity as a creature of God has been typical of our value system. Freedom no longer means merely a release from political restraints and economic coercion. Freedom for both the individual and the society is almost universally accepted as a value among Americans even though it is sometimes violated.

Many other facets of American social behavior also give a clue to our core of ultimate values, but most of them appear to be correlated with those we have already mentioned. The curious combination and balance of the two central values of materialism and humanitarianism indicate the American faith in both physical and social perfectibility. They show also the intention of a free society to work hard, successfully, and scientifically to achieve progress.

4. American Liberalism and Values

Liberalism is a general term that appears to fit in nicely with many of the highest values of the American culture. The liberal likes to think of himself as a scientific, progressive, rational, and enlightened person who insists above all that the human spirit must be free. But it is the concept of freedom and its interpretation in terms of human behavior that causes great confusion among liberals. Like other generalized core values—loyalty, belief in God, pragmatism, ambition, and neighborliness—it suffers when it is submitted to analysis and definition.

a) The central problem of liberalism lies in the question of limitations on freedom. Only the naïve and immature can think of freedom as an absolute value. Like all other sociological concepts, freedom is relative. One need go no further than his own experience to realize that concrete social behavior and "untrammeled" freedom are contradictory. Our daily social life shows clearly that we are at every turn influenced, determined, pressured, and conditioned. This does not make us cultural puppets, for we are often permitted, and even forced, to make choices between alternative courses of action and to "take a hand" in the determination of our own and others' behavior. Even on this level we often want to do what we have to do.

b) A more subtle, but equally naïve, type of liberalism allows limitations on freedom only in those areas where the proposed action is harmful to others. According to this view there is no other kind of moral evil except that which violates social justice, a social virtue that the liberal must defend at all costs. Some of our best-selling fiction of recent years exemplifies this attitude. The hero blazes with indignation over people who are anti-Semitic, anti-Negro, or antilabor, but the hero himself (and the author) has no moral qualms about extramarital relations, abortions, blasphemy, and lying. In fact, these latter patterns of behavior are sometimes espoused as expressions of the free spirit and defended by the argument that they "do not hurt anybody."

With this peculiar definition of social justice as the only and ultimate criterion of social behavior, this type of liberal has been confronted with many problems in recent American history. He was anti-Hitler, but pro-Stalin. He was almost completely deceived by the Marxist line of pacifism in the early thirties and by the popular front before the second World War. He thought of the Chinese Communists as agrarian reformers. In spite of shattered illusions he is still in a dilemma concerning loyalty hearings, free speech in universities, and censorship of all kinds.

c) It is scientifically questionable if any society has ever had, or ever can have, a system of social behavior based on either absolute freedom or on a freedom limited only by the prohibition not to harm anyone. The liberalism proposed by the laissez faire philosophy of the last century has everywhere been found ineffectual. The logical basis of the liberal ideology is neither absolute freedom nor social justice but the "freedom to do what is right." But here we are still faced with the question of criteria and judgments of what is right and wrong. Freedom is a right highly valued in most major cultures, but it is a right which springs from, and is made possible by, the acceptance of a set of basic moral principles.

d) These basic principles have long been a part of the American core values. Neglect of them is the extent to which the extreme liberal fails to share in the American value system. American liberalism, as interpreted by the ordinary citizen, is not an ideology of extremes. It is ultimately based on innate human dignity, on those principles we have called the intrinsic criteria of values, on the conception of the social person as a morally accountable and inviolable human being. The qualities of accountability and inviolability are inherent in people and are not the result of investiture by an enlightened and benign society.

There can be no quesiton that America is a liberal and progressive society that highly values individual freedom and promotes the innate dignity of man. The generally accepted American concept of freedom is quite different from that of extreme and naïve liberalism. Americans object strenuously to the formal controls of a police state, to any form of totalitarianism, and to any concept of absolute authority invested in a person, a class, or a party. But Americans are also faced with the social facts of power and authority, of functioning officialdom, of social stratification, and of social order. Without being servile or docile, the normal American adult submits to the necessary restraints and limitations these social facts impose.

The realistic social scientist finds everywhere that freedom is limited, relative, and conditioned. The human being is not the economic man, working individually and rationalistically for his own profit, that the liberals of the last century considered him to be. He is a total personality with rights and obligations; he is immersed in and responsible for his society. His social conscience cannot replace his personal conscience any more than social morality can take the place of personal morality. Limitations on freedom come from within through self-control as well as from without through social control. Both the rights and the obligations of a liberal society have their roots ultimately in the value of the human being.

5. Social Problems

It appears to be the nature of the American society that it constantly creates social problems. This statement may discourage the beginning student who feels that social science should be a tool for the alleviation of social problems. But, given the characteristics of American values, it is logical to assume that our social problems will never completely disappear. In a sense, it is also the lesson of human history that social problems are inevitable concomitants of society.

This is, of course, a matter of degree. A relatively static culture may strive for and achieve a kind of permanent good order in which there are few major disturbances. Primitives tend to "accept" the facts of social life in a way that is impossible for contemporary Americans. One of the dominant notes of our culture is a belief in perfectibility and in the necessity for attempting to work it out. A dynamic society in which the sights are always being raised must inevitably continue to have social problems.

a) The rising level of education in the United States has contributed to the recognition of social problems. This recognition is a specific part of the curriculum in the expanding area of social science. In this kind of culture the inquiring mind projects into the future. Data are available in more abundant detail, and no area of dislocation and disorganization has been left unexplored. Americans now know more about social facts than ever before. While it is true that social science adheres to the discovery, analysis, and discussion of social facts, the student of social science, as an interested citizen, also dwells almost necessarily upon the social possibilities for the future.

Increasing education helps to make Americans dissatisfied with present conditions. It not only recognizes social problems but in this sense it tends to "create" them. Large numbers of educated persons seek for themselves a greater participation in American values, but they also promote those values for the whole society. It is no accident that the American "intellectual" has larger dreams of a better society than the proletarian social reformer could ever envision.

b) Technological progress has been another large factor in the area of social problems. This refers principally to scientific inventions, the creation of material things, and the constant drive to make better things in better ways. But technology also affects and is applicable to social organization. The need to readjust one's self, not once but often, to the changing demands of invention and production prevents the achievement of a permanently stabilized social order. It holds out a challenge to our society to re-establish the proportion between our technical possibilities and our real patterns of behavior.

c) Rising material standards of living have also held out to the American people new notions of what "ought to be" and what "can be." This is part of the characteristic American mastery of physical nature and the basic fact that our country is endowed with tremendous natural resources. Many factors besides nature and technology have contributed to the constant rise in living standards, however. The channels of communication have made known the possibilities, and an excellent transportation system has brought them to remote places.

In combination, these three factors, education, technology, and material standards, have been aimed at the satisfaction of the social and cultural needs of the American people. In the very act of improving social conditions there has been a refinement and elevation of the criteria by which social conditions are measured. These criteria are values. The gap between social values and social conditions, which gives meaning to the concept of social problem, has not been closed. Both levels have been raised, and social problems remain.

The discrepancy between social values and social conditions is the difference between what "ought to be" and "what is." The sociologist studies both as social facts, and he notes that their relationship constantly moves to a higher level. As things improve we aspire for more. Standards of living our grandfathers tried to attain have been reached and surpassed. Their values have been transmitted to us, but we have raised them to higher levels. Our dynamic social philosophy apparently demands that the distance between values and conditions can never be bridged.

DISCUSSION QUESTIONS

1. What elements must be reconciled in the definition of social value?
2. What are the characteristics of social value?
3. Explain the difference between extrinsic and intrinsic sources of valuation.
4. Show the connection between values and mores.
5. Why do the social roles of the same person differ in value?
6. How do social values act as norms of behavior patterns?
7. Discuss: "Social processes depend upon the recognition of a body of values."
8. Explain briefly the bases for classification of values.
9. Explain the classification of values according to institutional functions.
10. Outline briefly the social functions values have.
11. In what sense do social values "cause" social problems?
12. Give some examples of the clash of values in American society.
13. If values are flexible and variable, how can the sociologist speak of a body of ultimate values?
14. Discuss: "American use of quantitative norms to measure success indicates that the American culture is pervadingly materialistic."
15. Give examples of the increasing concern of Americans for humanitarian values.
16. Describe the typical opposition to increasing humanitarianism.
17. List and explain the principal values upon which most Americans agree.
18. What is the relationship between liberalism and the criteria of morality?
19. Discuss: "For the ordinary citizen, American liberalism is not an ideology of extremes."
20. In what sense are education, technology, and higher living standards factors for the recognition of social problems?

SUGGESTED READINGS

HILLER, E. T. *Social Relations and Structures*. New York: Harper & Bros., 1947, chaps. xiii, xiv.

LUNDBERG, G. A. *Can Science Save Us?* New York: Longsmans, Green & Co., Inc., 1947.

LYND, ROBERT S. *Knowledge for What?* Princeton, N.J.: Princeton University Press, 1939.

MYRDAL, GUNNAR. *An American Dilemma*. New York: Harper & Bros., 1944, chap. i.

QUEEN, STUART; CHAMBERS, WILLIAM; and WINSTON, CHARLES. *The American Social System*. Boston: Houghton Mifflin Co., 1956, chap. xix.

WILLIAMS, ROBIN M. *American Society: A Sociological Interpretation*. New York: Alfred A. Knopf, Inc., 1952, chap. xi.

CHAPTER FOURTEEN

Mobility

Mobility is a social phenomenon gaining more and more attention from both scientific and lay observers in the modern world. In its most general interpretation, "mobility" refers to any movement or migration of people in time, in physical space, or in a social framework. The term is not used, however, by social scientists to refer to a social movement, which is defined as a concerted, continuous, organized agitation by a group with a program directed toward social goals. A mass movement, or a movement for social reform, is not included under the head of either physical or social mobility.

Obviously, all mobility must occur in time and place, but there is a difference between physical and social mobility. The latter refers to a change of social status by a person or group. We have already discussed status and stratification, and we are aware that positions in the social structure are higher or lower in relation to one another. Movement upward or downward among these social positions is called *social mobility*.

Physical mobility is usually called migration. It is the movement of people from one geographical spot to another, and it is a phenomenon of increasing frequency in modern society. It includes forced relocation of large groups of people, eviction and dispossession of unwanted people, voluntary permanent migration from one country to another or from one region to another within the same country, as well as local residential change. Physical mobility includes also the so-called fluidity exemplified by people commuting from home to office or factory, making business trips, and taking vacations.

Types of Geographical Migration

History is filled with accounts of the migrations of peoples. These have been of two general kinds, *voluntary* and *forced*. The voluntary movement of people from one geographical area to another is determined by numerous factors, but since it is a free movement, its effects upon the persons involved are quite different from those of forced migration. This latter type of movement takes several forms: the expulsion of unwanted people, the herding of people into reservations and concentration camps, the transportation of enslaved individuals and groups.

Geographical mobility always implies movement over a physical distance and is often from one country to another. *Internal mobility*, that is, movement within the territorial boundaries of a nation, is also of great sociological significance. There are few nomadic peoples, herdsmen and hunters, in the modern world, but most large countries include groups of migratory workers, journeymen, peddlers, gypsies, circus people, farm harvesters, and so forth. These are permanent itinerants who have no fixed domicile and who move mainly for economic reasons.

In large industrial societies there is almost a continuous movement of people out of the rural areas into towns and cities. This voluntary one-directional mobility is selective. Women tend to move to commercial cities and men to centers of heavy industry, and most of both sexes are young adults. International migrants have most often been individuals while internal migrants tend to move as whole families. There are, however, many exceptions to both these statements. There appears to be no convincing evidence that the energtic (or conversely, the shiftless and unsuccessful) migrate more than other people.

Reasons for Voluntary Migration

The reasons why people move from one country or region to another are numerous and complex. Traditionally, the *economic* factor is a major influence, whether one speaks of nomads seeking better food supplies, workers looking for better jobs, or families trying to improve their material standards of living. The decreasing need for agricultural workers tends to *push* people out of rural areas, while the increasing industrialization *pulls* them toward opportunities in large population centers.

But many non-economic factors also motivate mobility. People have migrated to escape *political* oppression and *racial* discrimination; they have migrated in search of a place where they could enjoy *religious* liberty. Families sometimes change their residence to take advantage of better *educational* facilities for their children, or to be closer to congenial friends and relatives. Migrants often follow a pattern in moving to those places where their previous neighbors and acquaintances now live.

Effects of Migration

The migration of people from one place to another has various effects upon both the migrants themselves and the groups and structures into which they move. Historically, the most significant result of migration has been the *diffusion of culture*. It has meant contact and communication between peoples who had been culturally and geographically isolated. Patterns of behavior have been exchanged, new ideas have been combined, and culture has been enriched and expanded. This does not mean that the mingling of people has always been a peaceful process or that it produced immediate social progress.

Cultural diffusion and convergence occur when people migrate, intermarry, and interbreed. Racial stock that has been preserved through centuries of isolation is mingled with other racial strains as a result of geographic mobility. The notion of a "pure race" in the large contemporary societies has been discarded by social scientists. *Biological mixtures* have always occurred through migration, whether this was invasion and conquest, peaceful wandering, or deliberate colonization. In the most mobile, large societies, ethnic strains become so entangled that they cannot be traced back more than a few generations.

The effect of internal migration in large modern societies has been an *urbanization of the culture*. Urban ways of thinking and acting, urban social relations and structures, and increasing secondary associations reach more and more of the population as people crowd into the cities. City families are smaller and the urban birth rate is lower than that of the rural areas. The sex ratio tends to decrease, that is, there are fewer males than females, as the population becomes more urbanized. Medical, educational, and recreational facilities become more available for the people.

The effect of migration on the individual varies according to social situations. The migrant does not always find himself a "complete stranger" in his new environment. He usually moves into localities in which his "own kind" are already living. For this reason, urban neighborhoods can often be identified by the ethnic, religious, or other similarities of the people in them. Even in the most open society two or more generations are required before the migrants are assimilated into the general population. In the early stages of this assimilative process the migrant is often a marginal person but not a total stranger to either his previous or his present environment.

Types of Social Mobility

Geographical mobility is movement in physical space, while social mobility is movement of a person, group, or category from one social position or stratum to another. We have previously seen that every group or society has a social structure in which persons and positions are at different levels of stratification. Conceptually the parts of the structure are both co-ordinated and distant from one another, and social mobility may be defined as any shifting of position within the structure.

From the point of view of "direction" of change in position, social mobility is classified as horizontal or vertical. *Horizontal mobility* means movement back and forth on the same social level from one similar social group or situation to another. Theoretically, people of the same social class have access to one another because they share roughly in the same degree the same criteria of status. Concretely, however, especially in large population concentrations, various "social sets" on the same plane do not always have social relations with one another. The permanent movement of an individual from one set to another is horizontal social mobility.

This horizontal mobility is significant to the persons immediately involved in the movement because they have changed the set of people with whom they associate. The need of the social personality to adapt itself to "new" people is not demanding if the persons involved are really in the same social class. One sees this smooth transition frequently in the marriage of people whose families, though strangers to each other, are in the same social class. Since there are often fine shadings of distinction among subclasses in the same general stratum, this change involves a certain amount of vertical mobility also.

Vertical mobility is a more widely discussed and more significant type of movement than horizontal mobility. It is defined as the movement of people from one social status to another, from one class to another. The factors and conditions for vertical mobility are more numerous and complex than those involved in the relatively simple movement along the same social plane. Obviously, vertical social mobility can be either upward or downward. The person may shift to a higher status, or he may slip to a lower status, and the difference between the two is deeply significant to the individual.

Role Mobility

The social personality is defined as the sum of all the social roles an individual enacts. Since the individual is the social person in action, and since people usually perform only one function at a time, there is necessarily a shifting from role to role. This is what we mean by role mobility. If we observe the individual in action, we find that this type of mobility may be analyzed on three levels.

a) Every person enacts multiple roles, even while he remains a total, integrated personality. Each different group in which he participates calls for the enactment of a different role. In the course of a day, the husband and father shifts from these familial roles to his economic and recreational roles, perhaps also to his political and religious roles, and then back again to his familial roles. Through constant repetition, as well as through knowledge and interest in the various functions and goals of the different groups, the individual usually makes these transitions smoothly and consistently. This kind of role mobility is so commonplace that it is not noticed until an individual breaks down, or becomes frustrated by contrasting demands of the different roles.

b) A second observable type of role mobility is the normal successive assumption of new roles. During the course of lifelong socialization the individual person develops gradually from role to role. In early childhood he first learns familial and recreational roles, then the formal patterns of the educational and religious roles, and somewhat later undertakes the obligations of the economic and political roles. He assumes new roles again when he marries and becomes a parent. Obviously, this assumption of new roles does not mean the abandonment of previously learned roles. The social personality, as we have seen, contains many roles, and the point we make here is that the principal social roles are assumed successively and not simultaneously.

c) A third kind of shifting of roles is that of occupational mobility, characteristic of some large, urban, industrial societies. This role mobility takes two main forms: Upward mobility by promotion from job to job, as well as downward mobility by demotion, within an economic structure is a type that has been much commented on by sociologists. Since the economic role is frequently the key role for the individual and the role upon which his family's social status often depends, it is given attention as an instrument of general upward social mobility. The person who starts as an office boy and works his way to the presidency of a bank exemplifies this type of occupational mobility.

Occupational mobility is also horizontal, the shifting from one kind of job to another. The high-school teacher gets a job as real estate salesman. The factory laborer becomes a taxicab-driver. The medical technician gives up her job and becomes a private secretary. When we say that an industrial society develops and requires a mobile labor force, we are speaking not only of the ability to migrate from one place to another but also of this willingness to shift to different types of employment. Perhaps no society has exemplified this kind of role mobility as much as the American society has in its economic system.

Circulation of the Elite

Since mobility goes in two directions, people from the upper classes descend socially while people from the lower classes move upward. This is an oversimplification if it is applied to the social mobility of an individual person within his own lifetime. The mere fact that family background is one of the criteria of social status seems to demand more than one generation as a time span in which an extreme change can occur. This is true even in an open-class society and is logically more the case in traditional, rigidly stratified societies.

It is sometimes asserted that an open-class society with much upward mobility disintegrates relatively quickly. According to this hypothesis, the "best people" fail to reproduce themselves, lose their social vigor, and become degenerate and disorganized, so that they and their progeny "disappear" or slip from their high status. Into their places move people from the lower classes, people who are not endowed with noble character, social awareness, and leadership qualities. Behind the hypothesis are certain biological assumptions about the inheritance of innate abilities, as well as psychological implications concerning the lower mentality of the masses.

This theory is not only unpopular in modern democratic societies, but it appears to have been disproved by the experiences of countries like Canada and the United States. The children and grandchildren of uneducated, lower-class, white immigrants have moved into the middle and upper classes without any apparent detriment or "degeneration" of the society. Biological and psychological testings have dispelled the old-fashioned notion that class or race accounts for innate tendencies toward intelligence or morality. Social scientists generally agree that the concept of the "elite" is a culture-bound concept, varying in meaning from one people to another.

It must be pointed out that social mobility is not a continuous uninterrupted movement but one that proceeds by stages. It is somewhat analogous to the physical movement of people from farm to small town, to large city, to suburbs. It requires time, even in a relatively dynamic society; and upward mobility tends to be that of families rather than of individuals. Furthermore, the great majority of persons remain in relatively the same social status all their lives, moving neither upward nor downward. The exceptions are those who have been able to take advantage of opportunities for personal achievement.

Channels of Mobility

As we have seen, social status is measured by a combination of criteria so that the person has a position in the total community and society. Social status, however, is not a mere abstraction. It is exemplified in and through people who are in association with others. Thus the channels of mobility are the actual groupings in which the individual participates. A person moves upward or downward only in relation to other persons with whom he is in some way associated and who can observe and judge the extent to which he possesses the highly valued cultural criteria.

In the major groups of every society there is successful and unsuccessful social striving. It is here that the individual enacts his social roles, and since his roles require the total personality, they provide an opportunity for the scrutiny and judgment of social status of the whole person. The individual becomes the head of a family, the president of a college, the governor of the state, or the bishop of a church. Whatever function he performs within these groupings, he is seen to advance or regress in relation to other functioning individuals.

It must be further noted that these groups, like the individual himself, exist in concrete societies. We have seen that social mobility is relatively slow in the communal type of society and relatively rapid in the associational type of society. This means that mobility does not go on at the same rate, and it does not affect the same proportion of people in all parts of any large society. The differences of rate and proportion do not rest in the individual so much as in the type of social and cultural environment around him.

Usually the stable, rural, and village community does not have great class differences or a wide range of status to and from which persons can move. In the large industrial and commercial cities the number of positions and the opportunities for change are usually very great. In an associational society, dominated by the economic institutions, occupational mobility is an important criterion of shifting class position. This mobility is not always upward, especially where the institutionalization of occupational roles requires large assemblages of clerks, typists, stenographers, machine-tenders, and other semiskilled workers. People often get stranded permanently in one of these occupational categories.

Briefly stated, the urban milieu is more favorable for upward social mobility than the rural. The stratification system is greater in the sense that there are more layers or strata and a larger differential from the top to the bottom. City people usually emphasize achievement of status more than ascription of status. This, together with the fact that the rewards are more numerous, motivates urban people to strive for higher status. Finally, the more numerous secondary associations and groupings open up more channels of upward mobility in the city.

Factors of Upward Mobility

We have seen that the various criteria of social status are intimately bound up with the social values existing in a culture. The possession of these valued criteria is the measurable determinant of the particular social status of the individual. It is obvious that the person who is striving for upward mobility must have access to the objects that give high status. Thus, the conditions that help or hinder this access may be called the factors of mobility.

For any particular individual who has the personal abilities as well as the desire for upward mobility, the following conditioning factors must be taken into consideration. They exist, of course, in combination, but any one of them may be more important than the others at a given time and place.

a) The policy and practice of immigration into a total society and into a local community will greatly affect the possibilities of upward mobility. If the immigrants are numerous and if they are mainly working people from abroad or from rural areas, they usually come in at the "bottom" of the social structure. This almost automatically pushes up some of the local natives and long-term residents so that they rise in social status.

b) Differential fertility of the social classes is also an important conditioning factor of mobility. It is sometimes said that there is "always room at the top," and this is probably true of occupational status in an expanding economy. In the general social structure, however, the upper class is always small. If these people have large families, the upward mobility of the lower classes is slowed down; if they do not reproduce themselves, it is accelerated.

c) The presence or absence of individual competition as a value in the culture significantly affects mobility. If competition is valued, there must be goals for which the successful competitor can strive. There must be opportunities for status advancement and social prestige for the "self-made" man. A competitive society actually encourages upward mobility but it also permits downward mobility of unsuccessful persons.

d) The availability of opportunities to prepare one's self for the competitive process is a secondary factor. If education is universally obtainable, it may act as a short cut to upward mobility in the sense that the individual can prepare himself for the business and professional roles that carry high prestige. It is necessary, of course, that the occupational positions be open to those who best qualify for them.

e) The patterns of equality and inequality in a society have much to do with the chances of social mobility. If there is a categorical attitude of discrimination against a racial, religious, or ethnic plurality, upward mobility will be slow, if not impossible, for people in these categories. Inequality of treatment on the basis of age and sex is also a hindrance, as, for example, when young persons and women are held back from opportunities of advancement in role and status.

It must be remembered that these factors must be studied in combination as they function in real social situations. Briefly stated, it may be said that the possibilities for upward mobility for the individual are greatest in a society in which the lower classes are increasing either by immigration or birth and the upper classes are not reproducing themselves, and in which competition is encouraged and the opportunities for self-improvement are available to all without discrimination. Conversely, the degree to which these factors are absent from a society will indicate the lack of upward mobility.

Mobility and Social Personality

To the extent that higher social status is the result of personal achievement there are as many channels of mobility as there are social roles the person enacts. The competence of the individual must be tested in the social groupings in which he participates. Since each person has a key role, this is usually the one in which he does the most to achieve status, but all the groups and roles are possible avenues of mobility. A woman may move upward by marriage into a higher class or by competence in a profession. A man may achieve status through his political or educational activities.

Striving for higher status is often accompanied by certain strains and frustrations for the individual person. For example, it is not enough for him to have abilities, he must also show results that can be measured in terms of the cultural values. Results are particularly pertinent in the occupational role but are also necessary in political, religious, and other social roles. Furthermore, it is not always true that ability and efficiency are rewarded with higher prestige. There are frustrating situations for an individual in which another person is rewarded on the basis of unearned privileges that have little relation to his competence.

Another source of frustration occurs when the individual simply does not have the competence to achieve higher status even though he may have a desire and drive for it and the social pressure for upward mobility may be very strong. The demands and the expectations of group life are often "too much" for this type of individual. The competitive process in which social mobility is worked out is also a strain for him. Competition implies some rough equality among the competitors, and the less competent person finds himself pushed beyond his limitations. He desires higher status and the rewards that accompany it, and he is frustrated in his failure to achieve it.

The attempt to achieve higher status in competitive groups sometimes results in an unbalanced social personality. This occurs usually when the key role, the main instrument of higher prestige in any individual, is emphasized at the expense of the other social roles. A balanced social personality does not imply that the individual's time, interest, and effort must be distributed equally among all the social roles. This is sociologically unnecessary and psychologically impossible. The imbalance occurs when the individual neglects the demands of lesser social roles in order to concentrate on those functions and activities through which he can more successfully achieve upward mobility.

It must be obvious that downward social mobility also carries its own social and personal costs. People who are "left behind" in the competitive struggle for social status, or who slip to a lower class, suffer strains, frustrations, and disappointments. If this happens in later adulthood, the person finds adaptation and readjustment to his new position very difficult. The "genteel poor" and the disillusioned clingers to the upper class suffer from this phenomenon.

Compensation for Downward Mobility

We must remember that social mobility is characteristic of the open associational type of society and that social stability characterizes the closed communal type. Since neither upward nor downward movement occurs to any extent in the latter kind of social structure, the strains, frustrations, rewards, and compensations are not present in it. On the other hand, "standing still" socially, or merely holding one's own, can be a frustrating experience in an associational society; and downward mobility is usually a disturbing experience.

Certain compensations, however, appear to be built into the cultural values of a society in which upward mobility is expected but in which the expectations cannot be universally realized. For example, the presence of large ethnic and racial minorities in the society assures the individual that he still has an appreciable degree of social status. Furthermore, the individual subjectively may still identify himself with a higher social status even though he has actually lost the objective criteria by which that status is measured.

a) The disappointments and frustrations of downward mobility are cushioned somewhat by the traditional conservatism of the middle class. This is especially true in societies where the middle class is large and important, and where many members of the middle class have satisfying recent memories of having risen out of the lower classes. The inclination toward conformity and the satisfactions that come from it help to compensate for some loss of social status by those who were formerly of a higher class. There are both strength and consolation in numbers of others who share one's own social experiences.

b) Resentment over loss of status may never completely disappear from the individual but it is modified by the fact that he need have little contact with his former associates of higher status. Constant association with people on the same social level can be satisfying for the normal personality. The demands of society are that everyone adjust himself to reality, and this adjustment is made largely subconsciously through social relations in real situations. The human environment, the presence of people who have similar aspirations and problems, tremendously influences a person to accept reality.

c) There is often also a rationalization of downward social mobility that helps to sooth the ego. A person in this situation may feel that there have been "miscarriages" of social assignment, that some people who have achieved higher status have not done so through honest effort and competence, and that some of those who have slipped from higher status have done so through no fault of their own. A curious twist on this rationalization is the opinion that the maintenance of social status is not worth all the trouble and worry it requires.

d) It is a compensation also for the person who has suffered downward mobility in a large industrialized society that there is no significant status visibility. The quality of his clothing may be different from that of higher-status persons but the style of clothing is not a mark of status. Unlike a rigid closed social structure, there are no caste marks on either the person or his possessions in an open associational type of society. Many of the public activities and most of the public facilities are available to the persons of all social classes.

e) Finally, consolation derives from the belief that one's children may regain the social status that one has himself lost. A decrease in social prestige may be more or less permanent for the older person who has suffered it, but in an open-class society there is a strong drive to give children the advantages parents did not have or have lost. To the extent that parents "live again" in their children they often spend less effort in improving or maintaining their own social status than they do in providing opportunities and advantages for their offspring's social progress. In this there is satisfaction for the person who has suffered downward social mobility.

AMERICAN MOBILITY

1. Mobility within the Church

We have seen that the major social groups are the principal channels in which and through which upward social mobility takes place. One of the chief criteria of social status is functional utility, and since the American culture is dominated by economic institutions, most people think of their gainful occupation as the main index of social status. Because of this emphasis, there has been a neglect, and perhaps a misunderstanding, of other important groups in which upward mobility is possible.

The religious groups of the American society present a varied and complex area of research in this regard. A religious body obviously has a social structure and the church members have possibilities for vertical social mobility within the structure. There are different strata within the official and formal organization of the church, and there are also certain informal criteria according to which social status is measured.

A significant difference exists between the Catholic and the Protestant social structure, and some differences exist among the varieties of Protestant organizations.

In the social structure of the Catholic church there is a clear-cut distinction between the laity and the professional functionaries. The priesthood, brotherhood, and sisterhood are traditional arrangements through which the individual "leaves the world" and is "set apart" from the laity. The persons who function professionally in these systems have a relatively high social status among their fellow Catholics. They have a distinctive garb, are bound by certain obligations, follow a certain rule of life, and receive deference, respect, and financial support from the laity.

There is less distinction between laity and ministry in Protestant and Jewish religious bodies, although the person who dedicates himself to God in these religions has higher status. There is a great variation depending upon other criteria of status: type and amount of education, attitudes toward wealth and family background, the kind of stratification within the religious body, and the social status the particular religion itself enjoys in the society.

The diocesan priesthood in the Catholic church is a striking example of opportunities for upward mobility within a religious structure. Theoretically, any competent boy from the lowest social class can be accepted into the seminary, receive holy orders, and climb to the highest position in the ecclesiastical structure. This is a peculiar characteristic of a church in which the son of an illiterate peasant can become a pontiff. This potential mobility demands, of course, that the individual possess certain moral and intellectual qualities, specific kinds of knowledge and virtue, and an adaptive personality.

The concept of a "hereditary" ministry and of the influence of family on the admission and rise of the religious functionary also shows variations. It is not uncommon to find that a rabbi is a descendant of a long line of rabbinical ancestors. It is possible also for the son of a Protestant minister to follow in his father's footsteps. In the Catholic church the celibacy of priests, brothers, and sisters prevents the establishment of hereditary privileges or of a self-perpetuating caste. In the United States the recruitment of candidates to the Catholic religious status is from all strata of society and not limited to any particular social class.

The Negro Protestant churches are a dramatic example of the extent to which social status can be achieved, not only within the religious structure as such, but also in the large community. The Negro preacher has long been an important figure as a leader among the people. The ministry itself has been an avenue to higher status for some who have become educators, labor leaders, civic leaders, and political officials. Many factors have made the religious group more important for Negroes than for whites, and this importance of the church has often attracted the socially aspiring and the more competent persons.

Since the laity form the largest portion of any religious body, the question of religious mobility must include them. An interested, able, and active Protestant lay person has many avenues in which to raise his social status within the church. While there are many professional functionaries—bishops, superintendents, and ministers—there is also a wide opportunity for lay persons to participate directly in the activities of the church. Lay boards of administration with full power to fix policies, make rules, manage finances, and even with some power to influence dogmatic and moral teachings, are common among Protestant groups.

These opportunities for the upward mobility of lay persons appear to be more available in the congregational type of structure than in the presbyterian, and also in the sect or cult rather than in the denomination. Generally speaking, we may say that the religious body in which the status differential between the laity and the religious functionary is smallest is also the one in which the laity is allowed the greatest amount of direct participation in church affairs, but it is also one in which there is the least potential range in religious status.

There appears to be no comparable ladder of social mobility for the laity of the Catholic church. From a functional point of view there are few status-giving actions that the laity can perform. The lay person is not permitted within the sanctuary where the sacred rites are performed; he cannot ascend the pulpit to preach the Word of God; he has no voice in ecclesiastical government, and in the United States he has no direct participation in the administration of church properties.

To the extent that status is achieved through functions, the Catholic laity is at best an adjunct and auxiliary to the clergy. The able lawyer, physician, educator, and businessman, however, can make important auxiliary contributions to the non-sacred functions of the church. Since the ultimate responsibilities and decisions are in the hands of the clergy, these contributions can be advisory or they can be services under direction. Upward mobility, therefore, appears to be possible only for the laity who competently perform permitted actions in co-operation with the clergy.

This brief survey of the variant structure of American churches indicates how a prearranged stratified system affects the possibilities for upward mobility within a given religious body. The contrast is greatest within the Catholic church, where there exists no higher role and status for the layman but where any diocesan clergyman must start from the lowest ecclesiastical status and may reach the highest possible position. The Protestant churches in general have much more direct lay participation in church affairs and provide both roles and status of high order for laymen. The Negro Protestant churches have an even greater advantage for both lay and clergy because they often provide a starting point for higher social status in the non-religious groupings.

2. Declassed People

The concept of an organized social structure of status and class has no room for persons who have no social prestige and who are, as it were, "outside the pale" of society. The practice of ostracism is an ancient one, but the people so affected have usually been able to carry on their social relations in other groups within the larger society. In the United States there are at least three categories of people who are declassed, although they are commonly assigned by many observers to the lowest class. They are the habitual criminals, the hoboes, and the city bums.

a) The habitual criminals have been the subject of some intense sociological research in recent years. They constitute a large category of declassed people and suffer the accompanying disesteem especially when they are in prison. Often enough, however, they do have connections "on the outside" even while they are serving their prison terms. With co-operation, effort, and a certain amount of good fortune, they may be able to regain their lost social status with their family and associates in the approved social structure.

Criminal society operates in ways similar to that of the normal social structure. It contains people of higher and lower social status, and some of the criteria employed in non-criminal society to determine social status are also used in it. Since, however, these people have much contact, communication, and social relations with non-criminals, and since much of their behavior is normal social behavior, it is difficult in every instance to term them outcasts, or declassed people. It appears that this term would be appropriate only when the individual has been removed from the larger society and is confined in prison.

There are two other categories of people in the American population who may be considered either temporarily or permanently declassed. They are the hoboes and the urban bums, and these terms are by no means synonymous.

b) Hoboes are vagrants who move about the country with no steady means of support. They drift from one place to another and perhaps take an odd job occasionally, but they are not like the migrant workers we have discussed above because they work as seldom as possible. They hitch rides on trucks and freight trains and are forced to take makeshift sleeping and eating arrangements wherever they are.

Most hoboes are only temporary tramps. They are usually unmarried males from twenty to thirty-five years old. During the economic depression of the thirties there were vagrants who were older than this, and there were also a considerable number of female hoboes. Generally speaking, the hardships of this kind of life are such that only younger men are able and willing to endure them.

The hobo is only temporarily declassed. Since he possesses so few of the criteria of social status, he is looked down upon by the more stable members of society. He does not associate with "respectable" persons in normal social relations. He is unwanted by people in any social class and he is harassed by railroad detectives, state police, and town officials. Nevertheless, the hobo almost always has some place to which he can return, some connections with family or friends through whom he can again establish his social status and social relations.

It is to be expected that a restless, energetic population like that of the United States would produce a certain number of hoboes even in times of economic prosperity. These people have certainly experienced downward social mobility and in many cases appear voluntarily and temporarily to accept this situation. In most instances the hobo eventually comes in off the road and settles down to normal living. Whether his spirit of adventure has been satisfied, or whether the hardships are too great, or whatever the reason is, he abandons the life of vagrancy.

c) The city bum is quite a different phenomenon. He is usually a homeless male over fifty years of age. Since he has no post office address, no fixed domicile, no gainful employment, and no membership in formal social organizations, it is difficult to estimate the number of such men. City police estimate that there are thousands in every large American city. The city bum has experienced downward social mobility to its lowest terminal. He has skidded to the bottom of the social structure and is in some ways even outside the lowest social class.

Every large city in the United States has a Skid Row, a locality into which have drifted the social "has-beens." It is a terminal place. No one starts there; no one is born on Skid Row. It is the place where dirty and unkempt men, most of them suffering from malnutrition and alcoholism and dependent on the charity of others for food and shelter, live out their declining years in misery. Rescue missions have done much to alleviate their sufferings and are occasionally successful in reclaiming an individual to normal social living.

Skid Row is not the urban slum, which as we have seen has a certain degree of social organization, although it may be in the same physical place. Skid Row is an aggregate of people who have been heartlessly called the "offscouring" of society. Their personal histories show that each of them has descended from a previously higher social status. Some have even been successful business and professional men; all have been at least accepted and acceptable members of society. They constitute the extreme American example of downward social mobility.

We have discussed these three categories of declassed people mainly from the point of view of social class, status, and mobility. They are social deviants also in some of the external manifestations of behavior. These people have gone through the socialization process in the American society, however, and they can never completely release themselves from the influences of the American culture. Even though they violate many of the mores and folkways and are visited with the negative social sanctions that these violations entail, their basic behavior patterns are at least residually American. In this sense they still share in the American culture.

3. Education and Social Mobility

The amount and kind of education a person has constitute one of the most important criteria of social status, and this is basically in agreement with the facts of social mobility. Educational requirements are rising in all the major social groupings, and most of the social roles in the American industrial society demand technical knowledge and competence. From the point of view of social mobility, however, there is a difference of educational effect upon those who receive education and those who dispense education.

a) Those who receive education may use it as a stepping stone to higher social status. The elementary-school system, both public and private, has been a means of rapid socialization for immigrant children. Similarly the city schools are now extremely helpful to the children of migrants from rural areas. In this way the school is a kind of short-cut agency for upward mobility, more effective than the family, neighborhood, or church. It provides the basic knowledge and training without which one could hardly hold his own, much less move upward.

Several other educational factors must be taken into consideration. One is the *amount* of education the individual has—a college degree has become almost an imperative in current American society. The Master's and Doctor's degrees add significant prestige only in specialized and professional areas. Another factor is the *content* of the education, and it is probably true that a person who majors in science or business, rather than in philosophy or humanities, has a better instrument for future mobility. Similarly the *choice of a college or university* is important since some have in themselves higher prestige than others.

b) Those who teach are affected differently, for they actually achieve their social status within the educational groupings. Several serious changes have recently occurred in teaching. The social prestige of the teacher and educator is no longer as high, in comparison with other occupational statuses, as it once was. It appears that as the general level of education rises the American people no longer look upon the teacher with the same awe and respect.

Partly as a consequence of this lowered respect there are not so many young people who aspire to be teachers. This is due to other factors as well: the increasing school population, the relatively low salaries of teachers, the apparently increasing unruliness of pupils, especially on the public high-school level, and the attractive employment opportunities in non-educational areas. All these elements are lowering the high position the teacher once held in our American society and are decreasing the attraction of the teaching role as an aspiration for young persons.

The social status of the college and university faculty is somewhat higher than that of the elementary- or high-school teacher. But there are distinctions among the faculty. The general public often regards the college professor as a kind of impractical and fuzzy-minded person who lives in a world of ideals and who probably could not make a living in the world of reality. People in the business world frequently take this same attitude, especially if the professor is an "intellectual," like a philosopher, humanist, or social scientist. The social appraisal of physical scientists, laboratory experts, and accounting teachers is more approving.

Within the framework of the educational groupings, the individual educator may aspire to higher academic rank, to positions as chairman, dean, and president, and to reputation and office in learned societies. These are all means of upward social mobility, and they add appreciably to the social status of the individual who achieves them. The necessity for the expansion of educational facilities, which first affected the elementary and high schools, also affects the college level. Competent professors and administrators are at a premium, and lucrative offers are constantly being made to them from industry, business, and the professions.

Since faith in education is a deeply ingrained value in the American culture, it is probable that education will continue to be a means of upward social mobility for both the students and the educators. No society in the history of the world has ever made the investment in education—in terms of personnel, energy, time, money, and effort—that the United States has. The fact that most important universities and colleges and many of the secondary and elementary schools were founded and maintained by private initiative indicates that the social value of education is not merely the result of formal and official policy. It is deeply imbedded in the culture, and, as a widely accepted criterion of social status, it logically remains an important channel of upward social mobility.

4. Migration and Social Mobility

The American people are said to be the most migratory in a physical sense, and the most mobile in a social sense, of all people on earth. Both these phenomena are related; but their mutual influence is seldom noticed. The reason people migrate is frequently that they are seeking higher social status and sometimes that they have actually achieved higher status.

Throughout most of its history the United States has encouraged the immigration of foreigners into this country. Millions of Europeans came to America to find a better way of life and to make opportunities for their children's upward mobility. Although certain regulations were set for immigrants in the latter part of the last century, real restrictions and quotas were not put upon them until after the first World War. After the second World War these were somewhat relaxed to admit displaced persons and refugees.

The connection between migration and mobility is seen most clearly in the arguments American nativists have employed against the admission of foreigners. They argued that the flood of immigrants was a threat to American standards of living, to high wages and job opportunities, to standards of education, and to the general cultural welfare of the people. It is immediately apparent that these are all criteria of social status; they represent the valued items people seek to possess as they attempt upward social mobility. The anti-immigrationists argued that the foreigners would "take these away," and the implication was that the native-born would suffer in their aspirations to higher status.

American history shows that the opposite has been the case. A foreign immigrant can seldom move into the same social stratum in the new society that he occupied in his native society. Individual scientists and professional people are sometimes exceptions. Immigrants to the United States have always as a body moved in at the level of the lower classes and have therefore "pushed up" the native-born. At the present time, the migration of Puerto Ricans, Mexicans, and Negroes into the large American cities is countered with the same kind of argument. But because of their relatively low class status, their presence has not impeded the social mobility of the native-born.

Another aspect of the relation between migration and mobility is the phenomenal migrations of American urban people. The percentage of city dwellers who change their residence every year is larger than that of farm dwellers. So much emphasis has been placed upon the migration of people from farm to town and city that the internal urban change of residence is often overlooked. This change is most often a factor of upward social mobility.

Every large city and its suburbs demonstrate the relation between residential mobility and social mobility. Traceable patterns of movement from poor to better residential areas can be made on any urban map. Sections that were once the areas of the best families have gradually deteriorated physically. As lower- or middle-class families move in, upper-class families move out. Then as these families move upward in the class structure, they in turn seek more favorable sections into which they move. The tremendous migration of families to the suburbs has been largely by persons who can better express their improved social status in more acceptable physical surroundings.

With the growth and spread of large manufacturing and business concerns there has been a need for occupational mobility. The term "mobile labor force" refers generally to workers who are willing to move their place of residence as well as workers who are able to shift to other types of jobs in industry. In the ranks of sales and management the term "occupational mobility" refers usually to the opportunities for advancement within a company. These people must be ready to move their residence when an opportunity for advancement is offered in another city. Unwillingness to migrate physically may cancel out the chance to rise in social and occupational status.

There is, of course, a selectivity in both physical migration and social mobility, but the interrelated factors of this selectivity have not been thoroughly studied by social scientists. For example, more Negro women than men have migrated from the rural South to neighboring cities, and this disproportion lowers their chances for marriage. On the other hand, the Negroes who migrate to northern cities have been mostly men. Young adults of both races migrate more than older persons, but there is no conclusive evidence that the farms retain the less intelligent and less adventurous while the cities claim the more competent.

We return then to our original observation: some people change their place of residence because they have already achieved higher social status and others do so because they are seeking higher status. A young man may "seek his fortune" in the city or in a foreign country. A rising junior executive may move his family to a better residential area as a manifestation of his higher status. These examples demonstrate that physical migration may be both a cause and an effect of social mobility.

5. Success and Social Mobility

The American ethos contains a number of highly valued concepts that are directly related to the actual practice of social mobility. The high value placed by Americans upon activity, success, and quantity acts as both a cause and an effect of upward mobility. If the possibility of upward mobility in the open class society were not offered to people, these values probably would not exist. On the other hand, if we were not a "doing" society, constantly measuring our achievement by quantitative standards, we would not have people moving upward in the social structure.

a) The emphasis upon activity is seen in all the major groups of our society. It is strikingly apparent in the educational system, especially in the high schools and colleges, where there is a tremendous amount of extracurricular activity. One has to strain logic to find the educational significance of fraternities and sororities, of proms and homecomings, or of highly competitive football and basketball programs.

Another example is that of the religious groupings. The active church is one in which something is "always going on." This activity is to some extent directly spiritual, but the area in which the activity is most emphasized is usually only on the periphery of the spiritual. In either case, the value of activism prevails, and the members of the congregation are constantly being urged to work for the church.

b) The value of performance does not stand alone but must be somehow related to success. The American people have long been avid readers of an endless series of books on how to be successful. The books that tell us how to do things stress the importance of doing the thing successfully. The significant notion is that the best way to do it is to do it successfully. The millions of relatively unsuccessful people in our society tend to be considered below par, perhaps even mentally subnormal.

The success ideal glows like a steady flame in the sky of the American culture. Educated, urban people indoctrinated with this ideal have a special dread of failure. Success is expected and demanded in the raising of children, in the functioning of the household, in winning friends and influencing people, in salesmanship, in sports and recreation, and in all the institutionalized forms of social behavior.

c) A third value, about which we have already spoken, is that of quantity. The active, successful group is one in which large numbers frequently perform in a successful way. We look with respect at the biggest factory with the largest volume of products. We respect also the biggest university, political machine, hospital, church, and store. There is even a certain pride in being an inhabitant of a big city.

From the point of view of social mobility these values of activity, success, and quantity are extremely influential. Upward mobility means for any individual that he enjoys higher status than he previously had, and this change is in itself valued as an achievement. We have seen that the criteria of ascribed social status are numerous and that the functional role is only one of these. In American society, however, the status-giving property of the social role is greater than elsewhere, partly because the rewards in social prestige for the successfully functioning role are greater than elsewhere.

An analysis of this kind would lead us astray if we did not view it in the total ethical framework of the American culture. We must not have the impression that the striving for higher social status is the all-absorbing purpose of American living. It is probable that the great majority of Americans are not consciously striving for, or deliberately aware of, the relationship between upward social mobility and the factors of achievement, success, and bigness. It would be a scientific error to assume that the people are grossly acquisitive or heartlessly materialistic in a naïve pursuit of higher social status.

The success ideal places the emphasis on the rewards of achievement, and in the American context these are personal rewards for personal activities. But this competition is not merely a ruthless struggle which results in the survival of the fittest. The factors that help people to status and power and thus promote upward social mobility are not in practice divorced from the ultimate values of charity, brotherhood, democracy, personal and social rights, and human dignity.

A subtle distinction here seems to escape many negative critics of the American culture. The American people do not interpret achievement, success, and quantity merely as practical means to higher social status. On the other hand, they do not interpret them as absolute ends in themselves. They assume the moral goodness and social propriety of achievement, success, and quantity. They believe it is both personally and socially beneficial to work hard, to succeed in work, and to have big measurable results to show for successful achievement. Upward social mobility is then assumed to be a logical corollary of these factors.

DISCUSSION QUESTIONS

1. What is the difference between physical and social mobility?
2. Explain and give examples of the main types of geographical mobility.
3. List the principal factors and effects of migration.
4. What is the difference between horizontal and vertical social mobility?
5. What is meant by "role mobility"? Give examples.
6. Explain the theory of "circulation of the elite."
7. Compare the rate of mobility in the communal and associational types of society.
8. List and explain the factors that facilitate upward mobility.
9. To what strains is the individual subject in the struggle for upward mobility?
10. What compensations exist for downward mobility?
11. How do clergy and laity of the Catholic church differ in their prospects of upward mobility within the church?
12. How can the laity achieve status within the Protestant churches?

13. How can people be "declassed" and still share in the American culture?
14. Define and compare the main types of declassed persons.
15. Explain how the recipients of education benefit in terms of mobility.
16. What factors lower the social prestige of teachers?
17. Show the relation between migration and mobility from the arguments of American nativists.
18. How is urban, residential change related to social mobility?
19. Explain how activity, success, and quantity contribute to social status.
20. Is the American success ideal merely another term for the struggle for survival? Explain.

SUGGESTED READINGS

BROOM, LEONARD, and SELZNICK, PHILIP. *Sociology: A Text with Adapted Readings.* Evanston, Ill.: Row, Peterson & Co., 1955, chaps. vi, ix, xi.

GREEN, ARNOLD. *Sociology: An Analysis of Life in Modern Society.* New York: McGraw-Hill Book Co., 1952, chaps. xi, xv.

HERTZLER, J. O. *Society in Action.* New York: Dryden Press, 1954, chap. xv.

MACIVER, ROBERT, and PAGE, C. H. *Society: An Introductory Analysis.* New York: Rinehart & Co., Inc., 1949, chaps. xiii, xiv, xxviii.

MARTINDALE, DON, and MONACHESI, E. D. *Elements of Sociology.* New York: Harper & Bros., 1951, chaps. xix–xxii.

YOUNG, KIMBALL. *Sociology: A Study of Society and Culture.* New York: American Book Co., 1949, chaps. xiii, xvi, xxii, xxviii.

CHAPTER FIFTEEN

Change

Every society and every culture, no matter how traditional and conservative, is constantly undergoing change. This means that the subject matter of our study—social and cultural phenomena—can never be completely static. Change is inherent in its very nature. The central unit of society, the social person, is subject to the universal facts of birth, maturation, aging, and death; and eventually the total personnel of a society disappears and is replaced by another. The minimum unit of culture, the behavior pattern, while more durable than the persons who perform it, is also subject to many factors of change.

Change is defined briefly as a variation from a previous state or mode of existence. There is always something that undergoes the variation, and this changed object represents a reformation and combination of previously existing modes. The social scientist here faces the old philosophical problem of permanence and fluidity, of unity in variety. We have seen that the basic sociocultural phenomena must be permanently present, even though they keep changing. The basic groups and institutions—familial, educational, economic, political, religious, and recreational—may change in form and content, but they are necessarily present wherever there is organized social life.

Recurrent and Novel Change

All the phenomena we have studied in this book—patterns and roles, status and values, processes and institutions, and others—are universally existent and comparable. If this were not true there could be no reliable body of knowledge called social science. Furthermore, these phenomena are always subject to change, and change itself is a permanent phenomenon subject to sociological analysis and study.

For purposes of clarity and utility we must distinguish between recurrent permanent change and change that represents a shared modification of behavior. The changes of behavior patterns a child experiences as he grows up, or the change any adult undergoes when he meets a novel situation, are nothing "new" to the society. Temporary fads and fashions, like those in speech, dress, songs, and games, are simply recurrent variants of the same phenomenon. Similarly, seasonal cycles in business, in clothing, in foods, drinks, and household arrangements are merely expected fluctuations of behavior. In the technical sense, it is only when some cultural element is accepted as a new arrangement and shared by many people that we can say a genuine cultural change has occurred.

This distinction between recurrent and novel change makes it possible for us to discuss separately social mobility in one chapter and deviation in another. Social mobility, as well as geographical migration, occurs to some degree wherever group life exists. Like social and cultural deviation, which is found to some extent wherever people live together, it is a relatively permanent phenomenon. Mobility and deviation are obviously kinds of change, and it is merely for purposes of analysis and clarity that we discuss them as constantly recurring changes, distinguishable from novel changes.

Aspects of Change

For a fruitful interpretation of sociocultural change it is necessary to understand certain general aspects from which change can be viewed. It is obvious that all change is *temporal*. The passage of time is an important condition under which change takes place, but time alone does not cause change. Sociocultural change is not analogous to the biological aging process in human beings; society or culture does not become tired and worn out. Time is required for both the renovation and the discarding of behavior patterns.

Change is also *environmental;* it has to take place in concrete surroundings that are both physical and cultural. The geographical environment is constantly undergoing changes, some of them induced by man's control over nature and others through the uncontrolled powers of nature itself. We have seen that the cultural environment greatly influences the behavior of people and that it in turn is changed by them.

In so far as it has sociological significance, all change has also a *human* aspect. The fact that people effect change and are themselves affected by it makes change extremely important. Furthermore, every society's personnel, viewed both as individuals and as pluralities, is constantly shifting. People move in and out of groups so that the size and type of group membership vary. Over a period of time the total personnel of any society is completely replaced by another.

In combination all three of these aspects of change are the necessary conditions under which change occurs. This is another way of saying that change must occur at some time, in some place, and with some people. At this point we discuss these aspects of change as conditions, not as causes. If we clearly conceptualize all three aspects as combined and necessary conditions we shall find the study of change itself more meaningful.

Sequence of Change

Change involves a question of the sequence of the changing phenomena—what follows what—which in turn involves the question of the rate and direction of change. One may see that a total society is roughly in the transitional period between an agricultural and an industrial stage, or that a democratic culture is changing into a totalitarian culture, or that a kinship system is shifting from the consanguine to the conjugal type.

Most sociologists have abandoned the notion that there is an inevitable single direction of sociological change or that there are any universal laws of acceleration or deceleration of the rate of change. Earlier speculations concerning the evolution of society and culture through neatly arranged stages from lower to higher forms have lost their meaning. We need not be concerned with the vague historical assumptions, for example, that sexual promiscuity among primitives changed to group marriages, then to polygamy, and finally to monogamy, or that religion developed from magic to polytheism and then to monotheism. The empirical study of contemporary primitives has dispelled theories of this kind.

The *comparative analysis* of cultures has shown that the rate of change varies enormously. In fact, the rate of change has been one of the useful criteria sociologists employ in classifying societies. The difference between slow and rapid change constitutes a highly relevant index to the difference between a communal and an associational type of society, open and closed societies, rural and urban subcultures, and others.

The *internal analysis* of a society shows that change occurs at different rates of speed from one grouping to another. Even when we remark that an industrial, urban culture changes very rapidly we must realize that some of its institutions remain relatively traditional and conservative. We have seen that the theory of the cultural lag is based upon this observation. In a technologically successful society the economic institutions and groups change more rapidly than the religious and familial institutions and groupings.

Planned and Unplanned Change

Both the rate and direction of change depend largely upon whether the change is deliberate or non-deliberate. By induced, *deliberate change* we mean that which is effected by social control, engineering and planning, by leaders, inventors, reformers, and pressure groups. People, from a variety of motives, foresee the direction in which they would like society and culture to move, and they make efforts to bring about the desired change. A manufacturer builds a factory to produce a new invention, for example. There are sometimes unanticipated consequences of these efforts, like slums in a rapidly expanding industrial city, but the general direction is intended to be one of forward progress.

The "great-man theory" of history is not an exclusive and universal explanation of social and cultural change; every great reformer must work under favorable conditions. Nevertheless, there cannot be any doubt that individual men (saints, heroes, dictators, and others) have been instrumental in effecting important changes. They have employed, in crude or refined forms, the various techniques of propaganda and pressure. Mass movements, inspired by these individuals, have swept across whole countries.

Non-deliberate change is generally unforeseen. It occurs often as the result of natural catastrophes, like floods, droughts, and earthquakes, and the significance of its effects depends upon its severity and the ability of the society to absorb it or react to it. These catastrophes are in themselves sudden changes, and they usually require people to make rapid readjustments in their behavior. There are also certain non-deliberate biological factors of change, like new diseases and even genetic mutations, that cannot be traced to human agencies.

Any theory of determinism that attributes all social and cultural change to these non-deliberate occurrences must be scientifically suspect. Human and non-human agencies of change act and react upon each other. Blind, inevitable determinism, as the sole or even the principal factor of change, is no longer a scientifically respectable theory. As man, through his technical knowledge and administrative competence, gains more and more control over his physical environment, the importance of unplanned change and of "blind" forces of nature decreases.

Factors of Change

Social scientists have discarded the early evolutionary notion of change through inevitable, progressive stages of development. Similarly, they have abandoned the easy explanation of single causality for changes in culture and society. Factors of change cannot be isolated and treated as though they were single, sufficient causes. There is a basic fallacy in selecting geographical environment, biological heredity, supernatural providence, or personal genius as the single complete cause of change. It is also contrary to the historical facts to emphasize a general principal cause of change as do the proponents of economic determinism, idealistic emanationism, psychic emergence, and others.

We have seen that change can be either planned and deliberate or fortuitous and non-deliberate. Single factors of change can be recognized and introduced, and certainly minor changes in society and culture can be traced to these single factors. We know in general that changes in the law and its enforcement can have a wide influence upon the mores and folkways. We know that a change in the credit system or in mechanical production may start a whole chain of actions and reactions, some of them unforeseen. We also know with complete certitude that no one of these factors is an all-embracing cause that brings about all changes in society and culture.

Despite the available scientific and empirical knowledge in regard to multiple causality, there is still frequent and slipshod use of the single-factor theory. People still attribute the "present state of affairs," that is, the whole social and cultural system, to racial heredity, or geographical environment, or supernatural intervention, or to any number of mysterious factors like blind destiny, automatic evolution, and dire fate. It is true, of course, that *physical* factors like climatic shifts, droughts, and soil erosion, and *biological* factors like pestilence, lowered fertility, and increased senility may change the normal and expected course of a society. But the extent to which these factors can be and have been controlled lessens the force of their causal influence.

Change and Progress

The analysis of the direction of change immediately involves assessing whether any given change is an example of advancement and progress or of degeneration and regress. Induced change is generally intended to be beneficial and progressive, while non-deliberate and unanticipated changes may be either harmful or beneficial. The assessment of change appears to depend in most instances on what the people in a society consider desirable and undesirable. In most general terms, therefore, progress is a conscious movement in an approved and desirable direction.

It is scientifically questionable, however, to employ exclusively a criterion of this kind. It means basing an estimate of progress upon *values,* either those held privately and subjectively or those existing objectively in the culture. If a person measures social progress according to his own value criteria, he is in danger of private, relatively non-scientific, interpretation. If he employs the common values of the culture, he is in danger of succumbing to the "fallacy of numbers," that is, of concluding that what many people desire is intrinsically progressive. He simply multiplies private interpretation into mass interpretation.

The way out of this dilemma appears to be the use of the goal-means relationship as a criterion of progress. For example, every major institution has as its goal the satisfaction of certain social and cultural needs of the people. The means used within each institution can be carefully analyzed, and a rough generalization can be made of the extent to which these institutional goals are being achieved in the total culture. Since no society stands still, the extent to which changes increase or decrease these cultural satisfactions is the extent to which society is progressive or regressive.

It must be noted, however, that not all goals can be clearly defined or objectively appraised. There are some institutional areas in which goals and means are not clearly understood, partly because there are large gaps in our scientific knowledge of society and culture and partly because people lack the willingness and ability to use rational means to intended goals. For example, at certain levels of the educational and political institutions, there is not only a conflict of values but a diffusion of purpose so that we cannot say with accuracy that one line of achievement is more progressive than another.

Certain basic levels, however, of all of the major institutions can be appraised by the goal-means relationship. If we recognize that the production of more goods at cheaper prices is an objective goal of the economic institution, we can readily see that mechanized mass production is superior to, and more progressive than, a system of hand labor. If we recognize that the assurance of justice and the protection of the law to the largest number of citizens are objective goals of the political institution, we can compare the degree to which different societies have achieved these goals.

It must be emphasized that rapid change is not synonymous with progress. In some instances the most rapidly changing cultures of the modern world are those that have made great advances in the technological, industrial, and material aspects of the society. The attempts to induce change through five-year plans in industry have resulted sometimes in the dislocation of the non-economic institutions. This sort of experience indicates that the student of society must scrutinize the rate and direction of all of the institutions within a society and then judge each on the basis of the goal-means relationship.

It appears also that an intelligent and fruitful comparison of cultures requires the study and appraisal of parallel institutions. Progress in the educational system of one society cannot be compared with the progress of the political institution of another, or the economic institution of a third. This is precisely the area in which ethnocentrism and misinterpretation operate. The ethnocentric person uses the progress of a particular institution in his own culture as the measuring rod of the total culture of another society. It is a basic rule of logic that only comparable objects can be compared.

Functional and Structural Change

We have seen that there are wide differences in the patterns of behavior from one culture to another. The various ways in which different people pursue their social goals indicate that social and cultural functions are subject to change. Here again the rate and kind of change differ from one society to another. Communication at a distance may still be performed in some societies by means of smoke signals and drum beats, while in other societies it has changed over the course of a century from surface mail to air mail and to telephone, radio, and television communication.

The study of *functional change* within a culture is important to the sociologist. What people do and how they do it indicate the recurrent uniformities of social behavior that can be compared from one culture to another. Since culture is a dynamic reality, its principal changes and evolutions can be accurately traced by an observation of the functions of the people in group life, that is, of people in their various social roles in the major groupings of the society. Tracing the development of the paternal role, the worker role, the citizen's role, and others, over a period of time provides a fruitful insight into functional change.

The concept of social structure is not that of a rigidly static arrangement of parts. While every society has an orderly system of personal and group statuses and of interrelated social positions and strata, this whole structural system is a "going concern." In it are two kinds of simultaneous change: the movement of the total structure through time, and the movement of the parts in relation to one another within the total structure. These two aspects of change are so closely intertwined that they can be separated only conceptually and analytically.

Structural change is involved in phenomena like the following: the development of bureaucracy, the contraction of the unskilled worker class, the expansion of the middle class, the multiplication of role specialists, and the shifting of social power from economic to political groupings. These are all examples of the way in which the relative position of persons, classes, and groups undergoes change. A change in any one of these involves changes in other related segments of the society and a gradual re-alignment of the total structure.

This distinction between functional and structural change is sometimes roughly equated with the distinction between cultural and social change. The notion is that the cultural system is dynamic and the social system static; and this distinction may be useful in some aspects of sociological research. The fact is, however, that the components of a culture are structured in relation to one another and that the components of a society are functioning objects. It seems more logical to define cultural change as that which occurs among the units of the culture and social change as that which occurs among the units of the society. Since culture and society in the concrete situation are closely allied, even this distinction has to be employed with caution.

Conditions of Change

There is sometimes an erroneous overlapping of meaning between the concepts of condition and factor. By the *conditions* of change we mean simply those circumstances in which change is likely to occur, and by the *factors* of change we mean those causes that can produce change. The passage of time is obviously a condition, and not a cause, of change. The physical environment is from one point of view a condition of change, since all change must occur somewhere, but it may at times also be a factor of change.

Assuming the presence of physical and biological environment as the circumstances in which change occurs, the social scientist focuses more directly upon social and cultural conditions. There are several general conditions under which sociocultural change is likely to occur:

a) The recognized needs of the people in any society are usually cared for by the traditional institutionalized ways of behavior. But when "new" needs appear—created, imaginary, or actual—they provide a situation in which change is often attempted, and perhaps effected. For example, the automobile complex has created a whole chain of needs which have been satisfied by superhighways, motels, drive-in theaters, auto clubs, collision insurance, and many other innovations. The creation of needs is especially characteristic of a mass-producing, industrial, and commercial society.

b) Need is closely aligned to readiness for change, the attitudes of expectation and anticipation people have in a society. Those who are more or less satisfied with the status quo and are suspicious of innovations do not provide fruitful conditions for change. Where people are eager for new and "better" ways to train children, to distribute income, to streamline government, or to promote religious values, they provide a condition favorable to change.

c) The accumulated store of knowledge is an important condition for change because new modes of doing things always build on already existing forms. The condition depends on both the amount and the kind of knowledge at hand. The extent to which this knowledge is rich, varied, organized, and transmissible will help to determine the basic starting point from which further knowledge is available. A culture in which the store of knowledge is rigid, conservative, and dogmatic does not provide a condition of easy change. Conversely, the greater the usability of the knowledge, the more accelerated the changes will be.

d) The type of dominant values that exist in a culture and the general attitude or orientation of the people toward them are significant as a circumstance of change. If the scientific spirit of inquiry is coupled with a pragmatic belief in social perfectibility, deliberately induced changes are almost inevitable. An emphasis on traditional, quietistic values provides a condition in which change occurs only slowly.

e) The degree of complexity of the social and cultural structure is also a condition for change. A society in which there is a great differentiation and multiplication of status and class, a specialization and division of functions, and a facile system of communication and transportation is one in which change is likely to occur.

It must be noted that all these conditions favorable to change are present simultaneously in a society where frequent change occurs; they complement one another. It is difficult to determine which is most important because any one of them, when taken separately, would probably not provide a sufficiently favorable condition for change. Furthermore, all these are in the realm of the "non-material" culture, and they presuppose the favorable physical and biological environment of which we have spoken. In general, non-material conditions are much more important and revealing than material conditions in the study of sociocultural change.

Invention and Diffusion

Although we have discussed both the factors and conditions of change, it is necessary to ask still a third question concerning the *source of change*. Since we are concentrating on the social and cultural, that is, the human, element in change, we are asking who originates change. The answer is that a new modification of behavior patterns is either invented or borrowed. It is only through invention within the culture, or through diffusion from another culture, that social and cultural changes occur.

Invention may be defined as a creative variation that puts into a new combination two or more elements already existing within the culture. *Diffusion* is the introduction of a behavior modification from another culture. These two sources of change are often studied as though they were different, but they have many common features. Contact and communication are essential to both, and the society that enjoys a great deal of intercultural contact is likely to be the one in which changes are more numerous and rapid.

The crucial common factor in both invention and diffusion is, however, the way in which a society accepts an innovation. The comparative study of cultures shows that there is a *selectivity* of change, that societies do not accept all innovations whether their origin is from within or from without the culture. There is no single criterion by which we can judge this cultural selectivity. Utility of the change is a partial index, but there are occasions when a society rejects an obviously useful change. The appropriateness, or fitness, of the change is also a partial indicator, but it is merely another word for the combination of conditions we have described above.

Internal invention and external diffusion are originating sources that have a cumulative, mutual influence on change. The society that shows a willingness to accept imported ideas, behavior patterns, and cultural traits from other societies is usually ready also to make its own innovations. An internally inventive society also seeks knowledge through contact with other societies. In a sense, every social change is strange and foreign, whether it originates at home or abroad. In spite of this strangeness, the exigencies of time and locality make the rapid acceptance of the domestic rather than the imported innovation more likely.

Resistance to Change

While it is true that change is a universal phenomenon we must remember that societies and cultures are relatively permanent and durable. They differ widely in rate and direction of change, in the degree to which conditions are favorable to change, and in the way in which the factors of change are allowed to operate. The social and cultural functions and structures do not change "overnight" even in the most dynamic populations. Certain resisters of change have become institutionalized.

The clearest intracultural demonstration of this resistance to change is the comparison between mores and usages. We have seen that mores endure because they are characterized by the widest conformity, the highest values, and the strongest social pressure. Those behavior patterns the society considers really worthwhile are the ones to which the people must and do conform. Consequently they offer the greatest resistance to innovation. Usages carry neither the same compulsion nor the same resistance, and they change more readily.

Similarly, from an institutional point of view, those major institutions in which the mores are deeply imbedded are the most resistant to change. This helps to explain why the religious and familial institutions change more slowly than the other major institutions and why they have a greater strength than others through revolutions and natural catastrophes. It is the very nature of institutionalized mores that they are traditional, that through repetition and habituation they have endured the longest time.

SOME AMERICAN ASPECTS OF CHANGE

1. Superstitious Explanations of Change

The difference between scientific prediction and general forecasting is well known to students of society. The first is based upon an accurate knowledge of the facts, while the other is at best guesswork of probabilities. Nevertheless, both are similar in that they are concerned with the factors, conditions, and explanations of change. One might expect the American people to be intelligent enough to prefer scientific prediction to the various sources of forecasting that are frequently used.

Superstition is defined as the attribution of supernatural or preternatural power to an object that does not have such power. In modern America there is a widespread and irrational belief that some objects or actions can, of their own power, influence the future course of action. This belief is different from that professed by crystal-gazers, tea-leaf readers, card manipulators, fortunetellers, and other charlatans who simply claim that they can read the future without being able to influence it. They employ various objects as indicators but not as causes of future occurrences.

Following are some of the more widespread superstitious practices current among Americans:

a) Certain forecasters pretend to find a causal link between the object they are "reading" and some future event. In this sense they are handling factors of change. Examples are palmists and phrenologists who forecast that because of certain physical characteristics the subject will act in certain ways in the future. The lines on the palm of the hand are supposed to be causes of future acts, and the variations in cranial structure are supposed to be explanations of behavior.

b) Diviners and spiritualists who act as a medium between the spirit world and their customers are for the most part tricksters. They fraudulently claim to have the power to bring messages from the outer world, but they do not personally believe in these superstitious practices. They do, however, constitute a culturally significant focus for the many Americans who employ their services and attend their seances. The customers are the superstitious people who are not merely curious about extraordinary spiritual appearances but also seek guidance for the future. They believe they can learn what is going to happen and can take steps to change their behavior.

c) On a different superstitious level are the large numbers of people who carry good-luck charms—a rabbit's foot, a horseshoe, a four-leaf clover, and many other lucky symbols. There are others who associate bad fortune with spilled salt, black cats, open umbrellas, stepladders, or who think that thirteen is an unlucky number and that three people should never light their cigarettes from the same match. Businessmen who wear a certain suit when closing an important deal, women who insist upon a certain chair when they play cards, athletes who lace their shoes in a special way, are all examples of otherwise intelligent Americans who superstitiously believe they can influence the future.

d) The most curious of the superstitious practices is the modern revival of astrology. The influence of the stars and planets upon human behavior was once considered a reasonable scientific pursuit, but serious scientists have long since abandoned it as a field of study. Nevertheless, there are millions of literate and perhaps educated Americans who consult horoscopes, buy books and magazines on astrology, and study almanacs to make sure that the "signs are right" before undertaking anything important. Many newspapers carry a horoscope column, and the astrology business enjoys an annual income of millions of dollars.

It is a curious phenomenon that many Americans actually try to effect social change through superstitious practices. Americans have not learned all the secrets of nature; we have not reached the limit of inventions and discoveries; but our store of knowledge is sufficient to provide for us a reasonable methodology and an intelligent guide to social change. We maintain a tremendous, complex, and expensive educational system mainly for the purpose of teaching people how to live rationally. Our technological equipment and our scientific experience can be compared favorably with those of any other modern society.

This contradiction between scientific and superstitious behavior is modified by the fact that the superstitious practices of most Americans are limited only to some areas of behavior. If the person has an intense desire for something—happiness in marriage, a raise in salary, or victory in a game—he may follow all the intelligent steps to the objective, but add the strength of a four-leaf clover "just for luck." Especially if there is a strong element of chance, so that predictability is difficult, the individual may rely on charms. Finally, if there is a certain confusion or lack of knowledge in the area where the change is desired, he resorts to superstition. When these conditions are combined, they indicate that although superstitious practices persist among Americans, they are often merely supplementary behavior.

The incongruous presence of these irrational patterns of behavior side by side with the most advanced scientific systems in the world is a dramatic demonstration of the tenacious persistence of folklore. Even persons who do these things jokingly and without belief serve as carriers of traditional and outmoded practices. They are also sometimes the most critical of the magical rites of primitives, of oriental beliefs, of peasant practices, and even of valid religious symbolism in their own society.

2. Social Trends and Change

We have seen that one of the important differences between a science like sociology and a science like physics is the predictive behavior of the objects studied in each field. The physicist knows with some accuracy the necessary conditions under which certain changes will occur and he is more or less able to control those conditions; predictability in his field is much higher than in sociology. As the storehouse of social science grows larger, however, the sociologist can outline trends of human behavior and can make some limited suggestions for the direction of these trends.

This empirical approach is typical of the American social scientist. The broad theories of social and mental evolution no longer hold more than historical interest here. The greatest American sociologists have been hard at work gathering factual data, studying social factors and conditions, and plotting statistical curves over long periods of time. Out of this research has come reliable knowledge of social and cultural trends, some of which we indicate here:

a) The long-term trend in American race relations, when statistically charted, traces a zigzag line, but it runs in the general direction of racial integration. The Negro's struggle for full acceptance into the American society shows a history of gains and losses in different regions of the country and different segments of the society; but over the long term the setbacks become less frequent and serious while the gains become more numerous and important.

b) A similar trend is seen in the interrelations of American religious bodies over the course of the past century. Occasional acrimony flares up; there are still charges and countercharges and evidences of bigotry and prejudice. The general direction of change in this instance has not been the unification and integration of the churches but a mutual understanding and toleration of theological differences.

c) Over the last century there has also been a trend toward low birth rates. The line of decline has not been straight, even when the rate in the total population is traced. It shows peaks and depressions and regional and class differences. The general direction of the birth rate has been downward, but the likelihood of further decline seems to be limited to certain classes or categories of the people.

d) The trend in working conditions has also been in one general direction, toward higher pay, shorter hours, more security, safe work places, and especially toward more co-operative efforts between the representatives of management and of organized labor. In spite of periodic depressions, fluctuations in the business cycle, and transitional unemployment, the direction of these changes is clear.

e) A major and somewhat abstract trend has been toward the cultural homogeneity of the American people. There is ample evidence that the processes of assimilation and accommodation have accelerated in recent decades, and there is little doubt that this trend will continue in the same direction.

Many other American sociocultural trends can be recognized from the examples interspersed throughout this book: the development of the educational system and its extension to more people; the increase of leisure time and its utilization in recreation and arts; the application of medical discoveries to the major diseases; the higher material standard of living with its emphasis on expanding varieties of consumption; and the increasing responsibilities of governmental agencies in aid of voluntary, subsidiary groups. These trends in sociocultural changes can be observed, measured, and plotted by the social scientist.

We have given the more obvious examples of the numerous social and cultural trends that can be plotted for the United States. Others are of shorter duration; some are of less social significance. The development of automation—the productive techniques in which some machines are used to operate other machines—is a trend so well known that it hardly requires description. Its broader consequences are studied with considerable interest by social scientists.

There are two cautionary remarks to make about analyzing these trends. The first is that we cannot use the term inevitable in its strictest meaning with regard to them. For example, the inevitable consequence of the downward trend in the birth rate would be the disappearance of the American population. The second is that the scientific prediction of any trend must be based upon given conditions, and in the analysis of human affairs no one can completely and accurately know in advance these conditions.

These two cautions are, of course, mutually dependent. In physical science the expert can usually control and manipulate the conditions under which any experiment, or any series of experiments, is conducted. He can make sure that the given conditions are observed, and by this very fact he can insure the "inevitability" of the scientific trend. The scientist has not gained full mastery over nature, and there are many instances not subject to experimentation in which trends can be interrupted and reversed. The sociologist's material is even less controllable.

American sociologists are fully aware of these cautions in the study of social and cultural trends. Nevertheless, they continue to accumulate pertinent knowledge, to analyze the relationships among cultural items, and to interpret the direction toward which social change is moving. This scientific study and analysis is the central difference between the younger and the older sociologists, and between the American sociologists and those of more traditional and less dynamic societies.

3. Limits of Change

The adventurous and progressive "spirit" of the American culture, and the dramatic material success of the American people, have led some foreigners to observe that the United States is a country of "unlimited possibilities." Some Americans share this naïve faith in progress and the future. The notion is particularly prevalent in the field of material and technical changes that can be measured by miles of concrete highways, underground telephone cables, and air-flight routes, and by numbers of automobiles, television sets, and refrigerators.

The fact that this multiplication has been so phenomenal, has brought benefits to so many persons, and has been so rapid leads to the conclusion that it has no foreseeable end. We have become habituated to rapid progress, and we define progress in measurable terms. Some Americans have come to the conclusion that physical science has merely "scratched the surface" of the potentialities of nature and that mechanical wonders will never cease.

a) While it is not the sociologist's task to judge the limits and potentialities of the physical sciences, a realistic scientific appraisal of social trends and changes indicates some areas in which trends must end and changes are limited. For example, if there is a long-term trend toward a lower average age of marriage, there is also a point where this trend must stop. There are not only biological barriers but also cultural taboos against child marriage. The percentage of married persons in our population has been increasing for a long time.

but this, too, must reach a saturation point. There is a limited number of possible sex pairs in any society.

b) Social change is limited by the readiness of the people and the institutions to accept change. In many instances this may be called a limit to the "suddenness" or rapidity of change. It is commonly asserted that engineers have already designed radically novel automobiles, airplanes, and trains but that the public will not accept them now. The limit of suddenness is seen in the twenty years that elapsed between industry-wide collective bargaining and the guaranteed annual wage; there were also about two decades between the admission of a Negro to a southern white university and the universal prohibition of public school segregation.

c) Any trend that involves numbers of people and physical actions must necessarily have a limit. In the area of cultural developments of a non-material nature the limitations are not always present. If the increase in education is measured by the number of years and of people involved, it is certainly limited; if it is measured by the progress of knowledge, there appears to be the possibility of continuing perfectibility. Similarly, if the improvement in group relations is analyzed in terms of the social virtues of justice and love, there appears to be no point at which it must be limited.

d) Social and cultural change is limited by the number of forms the principal phenomena can assume. The number and kind of social roles an individual can enact and a society contain are finite. The form the political institution can take has certain outside limits; and the possible major variations in the institutionalized economic system are also relatively few. In other words, there are boundaries beyond which change cannot go; and if it were otherwise there could be no reliable core of sociological science.

Generally speaking, however, the American people are not interested in the so-called lateral variations of sociocultural phenomena. The basic forms of our major institutions and groupings have become well established; certain internal variations are permitted and even encouraged. The main interest is in the lineal, "forward and upward" direction of trends and changes. The expectation is not that capitalism, democracy, or Christianity will change to some other essentially different economic, political, or religious system but that these institutions will continue to "get better." The common notion seems to be that if there are any limits to the benefits derived from these institutions, we have not even remotely approached them.

In summary, we may make the following observations about the limits of change in the American society and culture. (*a*) Some trends have an obvious saturation point, as those with biological bases in sex and age. In other trends, involving the multiplication of material products, the level of saturation is not so clearly seen. (*b*) Trends in the development of non-material culture, such as education, knowledge, and social virtues, appear to contain the possibility of continual perfectibility. (*c*) There seem to be built-in limitations to the suddenness of change that result from both the exigencies of time and the readiness of people to accept change. (*d*) There is also a limitation to the number of major institutional forms available to any culture. The American people seem intent on improving those that are established rather than exchanging them for others.

4. Change Begets Change

A belief in single causality of social change is one of the most widespread errors in social thinking among the American people, and perhaps among most other people. One sees this error in everyday social situations. Many people appear to have a favorite single solution for one problem or for all problems. We hear that "The only way to prevent gambling is to pass a law" or "The only way to solve the race question is through education." Or people may say that the eradication of Communists, or of Catholics, or of Jews would be the solution of all of America's problems.

This scientific error is prevalent among persons who want quick, pragmatic answers and are ignorant of the deeper complexities of society and culture. This simplicist approach ignores the demonstrable fact that every social change involves a series of other changes, that the web of action and reaction spreads more widely in the more complex societies, and that absolute stability and balance are impossible in the sociocultural phenomena. These three facts indicate why social change cannot be attributed to single causality and cannot eventuate in total solutions.

a) Every change involves many other changes. Let us take an actual American case. A Catholic bishop decrees that henceforth there is to be no more segregation between white and colored children in the parochial schools. This does not mean simply that the children of both races sit together in the same classrooms; they also play together in the schoolyard, eat together in the cafeteria, participate in dramatics, debates, picnics, teams, bands, and other organized programs and groupings. Anything sponsored by the school—athletic contests, parties, and dances—will include children of both races.

But the causal chain does not stop with the children. The parents' club of the school now contains both Negroes and whites who co-operate in the meetings, discussions, and fund-raising programs. There can no longer be discrimination in hiring employees in either a particular parochial school or in the school superintendent's system. Most of the teachers are members of religious orders, and these must now include members of both races. Since heretofore Negro schools existed in Negro parishes and white schools in white parishes, the whole system of segregated parishes is removed.

b) The complex American society allows the causal web to spread widely. In the same case, the bishop's decision to desegregate was an action interrelated with many others. Desegregation had occurred, or was occurring, in most of the non-religious institutions. White colleges, universities, and high schools had admitted Negroes. The armed services had long since abandoned the policy and practice of racial separation. Employment policies had been liberalized; labor organizations promoted integration. The major recreational agencies had created opportunities for Negroes.

What we have said earlier concerning the mutual dependence and interlocking of the society is demonstrated in the causal influence of social change. Differentiation of roles and functions always implies complexity, and this in turn requires relative uniformities in the total system. In spite of lags from one institution to another, the total culture tends to change as a whole. What happens in one major segment of the society affects what happens in others.

c) The third fact, concerning the impossibility of an absolute equilibrium, requires an understanding of the dynamics of sociocultural phenomena. Strictly speaking, balance can never be restored because there never was and never can be balance. Balance is a static concept not applicable in social science. We say that the children, parents, teachers, and employees had to "adjust" to the bishop's decision to integrate the parochial schools. What we really mean is that they had to change their patterns of behavior; they had to learn new ways of meeting new people and new situations.

The American's sense of orderliness and efficiency is offended because causality does not work in the area of sociocultural phenomena as it does in that of material things. If he puts so many pieces of matter together according to a certain pattern, he has a house. But if he brings so many persons together to form a group for a certain purpose, he has to be ready for any number of variable factors. If he has learned something about the causes, direction, rate, and extent of change, he is not likely to be disappointed or to expect neat, balanced, and permanent solutions.

This elementary analysis of the manner in which change affects a total society is of great significance to both the ordinary citizen and the active social reformer. Confusion and frustration on the part of individuals seem to be traceable to an ignorance of the facts themselves. People living in the midst of an ever changing culture are often oblivious to the meaning of the behavior patterns in which they themselves participate. The reformer with more zeal than knowledge is almost certain to be subjected to disappointment and chagrin. Many of these difficulties can be obviated by a closer study of the changing American sociocultural system.

5. Trends in Knowledge

Most Americans recognize that the day of the "universal scholar" is over. One may well be skeptical that the so-called intellectual giants of the past would attempt to embrace all knowledge if they lived in our day. The mental capacities of man have not degenerated, for there appears to have been neither mental evolution nor devolution in the whole history of the human species, but the store of human knowledge has increased tremendously. No modern genius can encompass more than a small proportion of it.

This change in the amount of knowledge has demanded a change in the approach to scholarship and education. The age of the specialist has behind it a whole series of interlocking causes. It is not merely the aftermath of human decisions to concentrate on segmental areas of knowledge; nor is it merely a simple imitation of the successful rationalization of industrial production. The spirit of inquiry and the capacity for scientific thought have existed throughout recorded history, but it is only in recent centuries that the store of knowledge has become unmanageable except through an increase of scholars and other specialists.

In the United States it is possible to trace in rough outline the change of emphasis and direction in three major areas of teachable knowledge. The educationists recognize three broad divisions: the humanities, the natural sciences, and the social sciences. Without attempting to force all college courses and all research projects into some one of these major categories, we are able to make some generalizations about the kinds of change and the reasons for change. If we recognize that the American cultural values of pragmatism and progressivism are influential in institutionalized education, we may evaluate these changes according to the norms of *utility* and *applicability*.

a) As taught in our colleges and universities, the humanities include the "great literature" of the past, the important "ideas" that have gone into the development of civilization. While the proponents of the humanities often stress knowledge for its own sake and insist upon philosophical thinking as a means for developing the intellect, their most effective argument appears to be that knowledge of the past helps us to understand the present and the future.

This is an important insight. The American culture is not geared to a "return to the past." The humanists and philosophers cannot seriously propose to Americans the restoration of historical grandeurs; nor do they attempt this. We have only to ask what happened to the Latin and Greek literature our grandfathers studied so laboriously in the original texts, to the systematic courses in philosophy and theology once considered essential for the educated man. These fields are no longer judged directly useful in our kind of society and culture.

b) The tremendous progress of the natural sciences has done much to change the concept of the educated man. These sciences have obtained results. They have taught man to master nature; they have given students the attitudes and skills that find outlet in the American industrial society; they satisfy and promote the cultural values we profess. It is no mere historical accident that they have in many colleges replaced the humanities as the focus of higher education.

The statement that the natural sciences are useful and practical does not mean that the resulting human product is merely a glorified mechanic. They require a high level of abstract thinking probably comparable in depth and breadth to that of any humanist or philosopher. But it is the empirical approach and the empirical result that has "paid off" and has brought the natural sciences into the leading position in the American educational scene. They appear to fit most aptly in our kind of culture.

c) The rise of the social sciences as a significant area of knowledge in higher education has been relatively recent. Several factors have been important in this change. One was the change of focus from historical speculation and social philosophy to an impirical and scientific approach. The further the social scientists got away from the speculative generalizations of the humanities and the closer they got to the methodology of natural sciences, the more successful they have been. The general and vague concern of Americans about the effects of technological advance on society and culture has also brought increased interest in the social sciences.

Social science has advanced further in the United States than elsewhere in the world. As researchers and writers, and particularly as teachers, our social scientists are answering a need in higher education. They have vastly increased the storehouse of sociocultural knowledge, have attracted an increasing audience of students and scholars, and have spread the conviction that this kind of knowledge is useful and practical for Americans.

In summary, it may be said that a society develops the kinds of knowledge it requires and deserves, and that its changes and trends in the areas of knowledge can be measured against its principal values. In this rough tracing of the American educational trends, we have mentioned only two value norms, pragmatism and progressivism. A mere reference to the total core of American values (including rationality, success, activism, freedom, tolerance, and others) would show that our cultural ethos is compatible with the changing status of three major areas of knowledge—the dominance of the natural sciences, the increasing importance of the social sciences, and the relatively diminishing position of the humanities.

DISCUSSION QUESTIONS

1. Why is it impossible for any sociocultural system to remain static?
2. What is the difference between recurrent and novel change?
3. Explain the inherent aspects of change.
4. Is there a universal and specific sequence of change? Explain.
5. List and explain some of the non-deliberate factors of change.
6. Can change be explained by single causality? Explain.
7. What is the difference between change and progress?
8. How can progress be scientifically measured?
9. How does the study of social roles help in the understanding of functional change?
10. Give some examples of structural change.
11. List and explain the conditions under which change is likely to be accelerated.
12. What is the crucial common factor in both invention and diffusion? Explain.

13. Discuss: "Certain resisters to change have become institutionalized."
14. List some of the superstitious explanations of change.
15. Explain the contradiction between scientific and superstitious behavior.
16. Give examples of some of the main social trends in America.
17. What are the cautions to be observed in the analysis of social trends?
18. What are the principal areas of limitations to change?
19. Demonstrate with an example that "change begets change."
20. Why is "equilibrium" a term not applicable to society?
21. Show how certain major areas of teachable knowledge have been influenced by the norms of utility and applicability.

SUGGESTED READINGS

BARNETT, H. G. *Innovation.* New York: McGraw-Hill Book Co., 1953, chaps. ii, iii.

DAVIS, KINGSLEY. *Human Society.* New York: Macmillan Co., 1949, chap. xxii.

GILLIN, J. L., and GILLIN, J. P. *Cultural Sociology.* New York: Macmillan Co., 1948, chap. xx.

MERRILL, F. E., and ELDREDGE, H. W. *Culture and Society.* Englewood Cliffs, N.J.: Prentice-Hall, Inc., 1955, chap. xxvi.

OGBURN, WILLIAM F. *Social Change.* New York: Huebsch, 1922.

TOZZER, ALFRED. *Social Origins and Cultural Continuities.* New York: Macmillan Co., 1925, last chap.

YOUNG, KIMBALL. *Sociology: A Study of Society and Culture.* New York: American Book Co., 1949, chap. vi.

CHAPTER SIXTEEN

Social Control

Social control is an extension of the socialization process. We have seen that socialization, whether of the newborn child in his society or of the migrant into a new society, means ultimately that the social person learns and enacts the expected patterns of approved behavior. Persons and patterns are brought together so that a systematic way of life can be pursued. Social control is the mechanism that perpetuates this process by inducing and maintaining conformity of the people to the patterns.

It may be helpful to recall here what we have said about social pressure. The range of behavior patterns from strict mores to mere usages is measured by the three criteria of values, conformity, and pressure. When we analyze social control we are studying the ways in which social pressure is exerted. Social control puts pressure on people so that they will conform to the kind of patterns, roles, relations, and institutions that are highly valued in the culture.

A preliminary caution in the study of social control is to avoid the restriction of this concept only to the area of governmental and political control. In contemporary society the dominant power of the state over individuals has been recognized and feared. As a matter of fact, however, the demands of the political institution are in most societies quite indirect and impersonal. The influence of other groupings is much more powerful, and it is axiomatic that small primary groups have greater and more immediate control over individual behavior than have large secondary associations.

Levels of Control

Social control exists on different levels of society and operates in different kinds of human relations. On the level of the social person, we tend to think of the control by the society or group over the individual. The total society influences all its members; but social control is exerted also by primary and secondary associations over their members. Since the social roles are the functional connecting link between the person and the groups in which he participates, the actual conformity of the person is recognized in the way in which he enacts these roles. Hence the role is the channel through which control is exerted upon the person from his familial, economic, religious, and other groups.

Social control is not, however, directed only from the plurality to the individual. There is also a reverse control through which an individual, usually designated a leader, influences a group to conform to the patterns and values he promotes and approves. We shall discuss in some detail this function of leadership in society.

Besides the influence of the plurality upon the individual and of the individual upon the plurality, there is also social control exerted by the relatively small group over the total society. This control has been historically demonstrated by the dominance of a military group, a small upper class, or a rich and powerful political minority. Social control on this level operates more subtly, but often just as effectively, by special interest groups and pressure groups. This latter type of group has perfected scientific and refined techniques for getting the larger society to conform to the patterns they promote.

Kinds of Control

The classification of social control can be made from various points of view, depending upon the interest and purpose of the student of society. We discuss here briefly the three general classifications of *positive and negative* control, *formal and informal* control, and *group and institutional* control.

a) Certain positive mechanisms, like persuasion, suggestion, education, and rewards, are useful in influencing people to practice the behavior and to hold the attitudes that are socially approved. Other forms of control may be termed negative, like threats, orders, commands, compulsions, and penalties. They are employed to prevent people from antisocial behavior and attitudes.

Societies and groups try to get people to do certain things and to avoid other things, but this contrast between positive and negative controls can be made only in the abstract order. Both appear to operate together in the concrete order toward the goal of social conformity. Human motivation is complex, and the individual may act in socially approved ways either because he seeks rewards or because he avoids penalties, or because of both kinds of sanctions simultaneously.

b) A further classification is that of formal and informal controls. Every society and group institutes certain measures that are formally devised to bring about social conformity. These are the public enactments, ordinances, and laws established by political authority; they are the constitutions and by-laws of a country club, the regulations and commandments of a church, the official rules of a school or college. They are called formal because they are carefully planned, fully promulgated and obligatory on all persons who submit to the authority of the law-makers. There is also usually some sort of enforcement procedure of an official kind in formal controls.

Informal social controls are more subtle but equally effective. They are employed to enforce the kind of behavior "everybody knows" should be performed and to prohibit patterns that are obviously socially disapproved. The informal controls operate positively through applause and other expressions of commendation and through gestures like a nod of approval or a pat on the back. Negatively they operate through sneering, hissing, and ridicule.

c) A third classification is that of group and institutional controls that we shall analyze in more detail below. Briefly, group control achieves conformity through conscious, voluntary, and deliberate action on the part of both controller and controlled. The control may be positive or negative, formal or informal, but the distinguishing note is that it is deliberate and recognized. Institutional control is the subconscious, often non-rational response of the individual to the cultural environment. The person carries out unthinkingly patterns of behavior to which he has become accustomed through long experience in his particular culture.

The Person and Social Control

The person controlled is not an automaton. It is important to recall that persons are not inert creatures of their culture or mechanical puppets of their society. Socialization is often stressed as a process that happens *to* the human person, and immediate situational interaction is often thought of as an influence *upon* a person, but we must remember that the person is an *actor* in both the process and the situation. He both acts in, and reacts to, socialization and cultural situations.

We have seen that a human being is a person because he is a thinking and deciding animal; he can store up abstract knowledge and has the power to use it in planning and in self-direction. Thus, it is scientifically absurd to suggest that he is nothing more than an unwitting victim to cultural forces. Nevertheless, it is obvious that man is a crea-ture of social custom, that he does not stop to reflect and plan every thought and action, that he finds life much simpler when he accom-modates himself to routines of behavior.

This patterning and routinization is quite different from the process of stimulus and response through which brute animals learn. In human beings, the fact is that self-control is an essential ingredient of social control. It is only in rare and extreme cases, where an individual has become "dehumanized" or "brain-washed" or rendered irresponsible through mental or physical torture, that one can speak of social control without self-control. For these individuals, and for mentally subnormal persons, the term "social control" is logically inapplicable.

Why do normal people consciously submit to social control? To say that man is a habit-forming animal is simply to go back to the social-ization process through which his habits were formed. To say that he is by nature a conforming animal is simply to say redundantly that he submits to social pressure. The suggestion that man is a status-seeking animal is a retreat to another general catch-all explanation of human behavior, like utilitarianism or self-interest.

The social fact of conformity to cultural norms and pressures is so obvious that it requires no demonstration, but the conscious and intrin-sic motivation behind it poses a problem of some complexity. There can be no doubt that human beings seek their own good, in so far as they consciously conform to norms and standards of approved conduct. They seek the recognition and approval of their fellow men because these are the evidences of status, and because it is to the interest of the individual to preserve social status.

Together with all these motives, and deeper than any of them, is the fact that every normal social person has a developed *sense of right and wrong*. Most of the expressions of this sense emerge during the process of socialization, but the source of the expressions is the human con-science. The social person learns how to use his conscience by living in society and by learning the cultural expectations. Like the basic abilities to know and to judge, the basic feeling for right and wrong is a human quality. It is a characteristic only of human beings, and therefore only of social persons; and it is the ultimate—though not the only—personal explanation why people submit to social control.

Group Control

It is essential to the maintenance of every group that some degree of conformity be achieved and that some type of social control be exercised. The primary groupings need conformity more than the secondary associations, and there is also a difference between them in the types of control they employ. The members of the primary group tend to display a voluntary, spontaneous and informal submission to social control. In the secondary groups controls are more impersonal and formal.

A further distinction in control and conformity is found in an analysis of the major groups universal to every society. Each of these, together with their numerous subgroups, is interested in having persons conform to its norms of behavior and belief. It is possible to rank these major groups according to the closeness and amount of control exercised in each, a ranking that depends to some extent upon the importance of the behavior patterns performed in each major group.

The mores valued by any group are more strictly enforced than the usages. This means, of course, that the group is not equally concerned with imposing conformity to all the behavior patterns. We have said that social pressure varies, and that it is greatest in those areas of conduct where high values are involved and wide conformity is attained. This is simply another way of saying that social pressure and social control have much in common. In highly ritualized behavior, as in secret lodges and fraternities and in some religious groups, exact conformity is often required even in minute and apparently non-essential details of behavior.

a) The closest control over group members is exercised in familial and educational groups. In these groups the socialization of persons is of greatest importance: social relations are most intimate; values engendered are high; and conformity to norms is a deliberate purpose of the group. In these groups there is relatively little variety and freedom of choice. The persons of authority are easily identified, and the members know that observing the rules is basic to the maintenance of the group and to the pursuit of their own welfare.

b) The economic and political groups rank next in the strength of their social controls. The conditions of gainful employment vary greatly, but for the great majority of human beings they include obedience and conformity. The expectations concerning function, time, and procedure in economic activities are often rigid and formal, so that the individual has no choice except to conform or to resign. Politically, at those points where the citizen comes into contact with civic and public regulations, he is compelled to relatively close conformity. The controls are as strong in political as in economic groupings, but they are not applied so frequently.

c) The recreational and religious groups have the least amount of control over their members. These groups are, in general, more loosely knit than the others; there is much more freedom of movement and of choice by individuals; there is neither the need, nor often the possibility, of enforcing rigid conformity. The purposes of these groups are achieved more through voluntary co-operation of members than through strict social controls. This does not mean that there exist no strictly disciplined and authoritarian religious groups, and even recreational groups. Here again social control and conformity are a matter of degree.

It must be noted that this ranking of groups from the point of view of social control may vary from society to society and from time to time. A totalitarian system would differ from a democratic one; it would tighten all controls and would shift the emphasis onto obedience to the political center. A culture in which religious values are high would probably de-emphasize economic conformity and insist upon closer adherence to sacred norms. In spite of these variations, however, there is always discernible a ranking of group control.

Institutional Control

Institutional control is the effective influence of the patterned cultural environment as exhibited by the subconscious response of the people of the group or society. In the conceptual framework of our study of sociology we have seen that persons use patterns, groups use institutions, and the society uses culture. The cultural patterns and institutions show us not only what people do, but what they are expected to do. These expectations and demands of patterned behavior indicate that culture is in some sense self-enforcing. This is what we mean by institutional control over people. Institutionalized behavior is the "thing to do" and this fact by itself exerts social pressure.

The analysis of social control requires an understanding of both group pressure and institutional pressure. The latter is largely impersonal and subconscious. It is a general, environmental influence upon behavior rather than a specific, personal ordering of an individual to this or that particular pattern of behavior. The two kinds of control go hand in hand. The group verbally demands conformity of the individual, but the group also gives an example of conformity because the institutionalized patterns are followed by everyone. The constant repetition of the same behavior patterns in relatively the same way develops social acceptance in people, and this is why we can say that custom both enforces and reinforces itself.

The ranking order of the degree and amount of social pressure exerted by the major groups of a society becomes clearer when we analyze it from the point of view of the institutions these groups employ. Shared patterns of behavior and close agreement on norms have to exist in the primary group more than in the secondary association. Similarly, mores identified with familial and educational institutions become more strongly patterned—and consequently exert greater pressure over a longer period of time—than those in the recreational and political institutions.

The institutional environment exerts control over the behavior of the person. From another point of view, however, institutions exert varying degrees of social pressure on one another and on the total society and culture. We have said that every culture contains a recognizable *pivotal institution* that demands more conformity and has more influence than any of the other institutions. Examples can be drawn from various cultures to show that in one the economic institution is dominant and that in another the political, or familial, or religious institution has the greatest influence. The environmental control exerted by the pivotal institution affects the institutionalized behavior throughout the culture. Since the major institutions must necessarily exist in every culture, this control of the pivotal institution can never destroy or replace the other institutions.

Institutional control varies in its effectiveness from one society to another; it varies within the same society, and from one period of time to another. So-called tradition-bound people accept institutionalized restraints of long-established behavior patterns much more readily than the people of a restless, dynamic, individualistic society. Older people conform more steadily than younger people to institutional patterns. The dominance of a major institution may vary according to the exigencies of the time and the needs of the society, as, for example, in large-scale warfare when the political institution requires great conformity and co-operation.

Leadership and Social Control

From our observations about group control and institutional control we must not come to the conclusion that the deliberate influence of leaders is of little importance. The presence and the action of dominant personalities are significant means for bringing about the conformity of people to the social norms and standards. Leaders can be classified in many ways, from the point of view of effectiveness, of techniques used, of types of groups served, and others. From the point of view of social control they are characterized as follows:

a) Positional leadership refers simply to the status dominance a person has in a group or society. This leadership is ascribed, since the person who is born into a royal or other prominent family, or who fills a position in a bureaucracy or hierarchy, has influence attributed to him by virtue of this fact alone. People who are asked to "lend their names" to programs and causes have this kind of leadership; it is abstracted from any particular skill or competence they may personally possess.

b) Personal leadership, on the other hand, is for the most part achieved. Its exercise as a means of social control depends upon the qualities of leadership the individual possesses. The person pursues a functioning social role, and because of his success in this role, he can, directly or indirectly, influence the behavior of others. Three recognized general categories of personal leadership are as follows:

Expert leadership in a specific area of technical competence is enjoyed by specialists. The best brain surgeon, the best atomic physicist, and the best lawyer are persons who are leaders in their fields even though they may not be consciously striving to exert control over others. In most instances, the wider importance of this indirect influence is through the transfer of leadership; for example, the expert mathematician exerts leadership by expressing his opinions in politics, religion, art, and other fields in which he is not an expert. His opinions are listened to in these other areas, even when they are erroneous, because people tend to accept the statements of an "important" person.

Charismatic leadership evolves out of certain emotional qualities an individual possesses and exhibits. He is able to convince his followers that he is preordained, inspired, and enlightened in special ways. The charismatic leader inspires personal devotion to himself in others and depends upon it in the use of his influence. People intensely believe in him. The historic heroes, the Fathers of a country, the crusaders in a great cause, the successful generals, the prophets and preachers, have been men in whom this special charism is recognized.

The most general type of leadership is managerial, which usually includes executive expertness and a touch of charism. The managerial leader has deep insight into complicated problems, a large comprehension of all the facets involved in them, an ability to make decisions and to follow them through to a conclusion. He knows how to delegate functions and authority to others and his executive ability is not confined to one profession or industry. He is the superorganizer, the "trouble-shooter," who can function expertly in government, industry, or any other organized system.

Communication and Social Control

The expectations of behavior must somehow be communicated to the people who are to conform to them. All the various mechanisms of socialization—written and spoken words, symbols, and examples—are used to convey the prohibition or approbation of behavior to people. If the group or the leader cannot get essential norms across to the members, there is no possibility of conformity and control.

In any system of conscious, deliberate social control the *edict* is the most common form of communication. It is expressed by "do" and "don't." It may be a new law or a revision of an old law, a command, a regulation, or a decision by persons in authority. In most instances, especially in primary relations and informal groupings, the edict is accompanied by reasons, explanations, and persuasions.

Advertising is one of the most carefully planned forms of communication in obtaining social conformity because the advertiser explains in precise detail what he wants people to do. He is attempting not only to build up a favorable attitude toward his product; he also wants people to purchase and consume his product. *Propaganda* is another deliberate medium for obtaining conformity to certain values and conceptual patterns. By its very nature and purpose it cannot be as detailed as the advertising medium, but it is nonetheless a powerful instrument of social control.

The *educational process* is the channel through which the society transmits its culture to succeeding generations. The social purpose of education is to train persons to accept and conform to the highest behavior norms of the culture. It works through both formal systems and informal procedures, but its end product is a person who knows the difference between approved and disapproved behavior, and who can take his place as a conforming member of the society.

Social Engineering and Control

Just as man occasionally thinks about his environment, himself, and his future, so also every social group does a certain amount of planning. Group members and especially leaders are conscious of the functions and goals of the group and of the fact that these are subject to design and direction. Even the informal primary group, which appears to be quite casual and spontaneous, requires the forethought and decision that are the basis of planning. Secondary associations construct budgets, hold meetings, arrange for elections and terms of office, issue statements of purposes and programs, and make analyses of their success and failure. All this is a simple demonstration that planning is essential to organized groups and societies.

Social engineering means more than planning; it means also social action, the carrying through of plans. Engineering implies a detailed analysis of parts, a specific and technical design for making them workable, and a scheduled program for manipulating them toward predetermined ends. This definition is, of course, a mechanical analogy, and it can be interpreted only with the proper understanding of the strictly sociological phenomena involved. The basic units analyzed and manipulated are behavior patterns and social persons and their various combinations, and we have seen the conditions and limitations under which these function toward given ends.

From the point of view of social control, social engineering presents one of the central problems of group life. We have seen that socialization is the process through which the person is inducted into society and learns the patterns of culture. This results in general conformity to the accepted norms and standards. Social engineering goes beyond this and demands a more specific conformity to rationally planned behavior. The problem lies in the working relationship between the individual and the group. Engineering that minimizes the initiative and voluntary co-operation of the individual defeats its own purposes. Engineering that does not exert sufficient control over individuals to arrive at its end is meaningless.

It is possible to have social control for its own sake without engineering; but it is impossible to have effective social engineering without some control and conformity. An effective type of social engineering requires that the people have some participation in both the planning and the execution of the social design. The type of social goals set, the speed at which the plan is executed, and the kind of pressures and sanctions applied all require a general knowledge of social change and a specific knowledge of pertinent trends. In addition to this knowledge, effective social engineering requires great understanding of the social personalities involved in the proposed change.

SOCIAL CONTROLS IN AMERICA

1. Resistance to Social Control

It is important to remember that even in a progressive and pragmatic culture like that of the United States there are many traditionalists among the people and many who resist social control. Every attempt at *social reform*, or induced social change requiring social control, engineering, and planning, has been met by opposition. We must not think of the American society as a sort of pliant, fluid, passive system which is easily controlled and in which change takes place almost automatically.

Every major social reform, which has required planning and control, has had to overcome the opposition of those who said the change would do "more harm than good." A list of reforms taken at random demonstrates this point: the shortened workweek, political suffrage for women, safety rules in mines and factories, infant and maternal care, public health benefits, public housing, old age pensions, child labor laws, extension of education, public parks and playgrounds, released time from school for religious instruction, fair employment practices, and many others.

All these have required a change in both conceptual and external behavior patterns, a conformity on the part of Americans to new social situations, and consequently a submission to social control. We cannot here make an exhaustive analysis of the reasons why objections are raised to social reform, but we present the following as a partial explanation of resistance to social control.

a) The virtue of prudence is often invoked to bless and justify opposition to social reform. Correctly used, "prudence" is an essential virtue of every scientist who makes sure of his facts before drawing a conclusion. Incorrectly defined, the self-styled prudent man leaves the facts and the conclusions where they are and does nothing about them.

An ill-defined concept of prudence is used as a rationalization against reform.

b) It is more comfortable to continue doing things in the same old way. Older people especially seem to magnify the costs of reform in terms of their own comfort and convenience. The creature of long habit is disturbed at the prospect of changing his attitudes even in cases where no change in his external patterns is required. This inertia is characteristic of many people.

c) A more positive aspect of this characteristic is self-interest. The fear of losing status or some of the criteria of status motivates people to a staunch defense of the present order of things. This fear is part of the constant though often imaginary conflict between self-interest and public interest, between personal gain and social gain. It cannot always be demonstrated that what will benefit the total society will also benefit the individual, and the strong individualist is unwilling to experiment in order to discover whether this is so.

d) Ignorance of social trends is one of the strongest obstacles to social reform. Fear of the unknown, past and present, reinforces fear of the future. It is a curious fact that those who know least about the technical areas of society and culture are frequently the most dogmatic in prophesying exactly and in detail the harm that will ensue from any given proposal for social reform. Fortunately, the diffusion of social science among Americans is decreasing this obstacle.

e) Pressure groups are often positive means of social control, but they act in many instances as preventives of social change. The pressure group functions to protect the interests of some organized segment of the population and may exert an influence far out of proportion to its importance or its numbers. The notion that a proposed reform will "do more harm than good" implies usually that the group fears danger to itself rather than to the total society.

The traditionalists who are prophets of doom in the face of every proposed social reform display a curious set of reactions after the reform has been in effect for a considerable period. First, they learn to live with it, to conform to the change, and even to approve it. Second, they forget the fact that their worst fears were unfounded and that their dire predictions did not come true. Third—and this is most frustrating to the social reformer—they use precisely the same arguments ("it will do more harm than good") when a program of further social reform is proposed.

It is probably true that certain types of social personality—authoritarian, ethnocentric, paranoid—are more likely than others to oppose social reform. At the present time we have no reliable studies to indicate whether these people are increasing in the American population. The hope and expectation of the student of society is that they are not increasing but that the spread of knowledge about society and culture is increasing the number of Americans who welcome and approve social progress.

2. Variations of Institutional Control

Institutional pressure varies throughout the culture. Although all the major institutions affect in some way the behavior of all the people, they do not have an even and equal influence on all. The total American culture is influenced more by the economic institution than by any other. This presents, however, only the general picture. There are many variations of pressure within the sociocultural system, and it may be useful to make a rough analysis of these variations:

a) From the point of view of people in any group, the force of the institutionalized patterns differs according to the function and role of the individual. The inner and higher functionaries are forced by their position to adhere closely to the strongest mores of the group. Those who are relatively passive members and hangers-on have less pressure upon them, while outsiders are only lightly influenced. These generalizations are valid for all major groupings.

b) There are also local variations in pressure. For example, American farmers are more likely to be influenced by familial and religious mores, while urban people are under greater pressure from the economic and recreational patterns. To the extent that local subcultures exist there are also regional differences in institutional control.

c) There appears to be also a class differential in the strength of, and the response to, institutional pressure. One can recognize "middle-class morality" in the United States; behavior conformity is greater among those who are class-conscious and especially among those who are straining for higher status. Often enough, at least in certain areas of conduct, socially secure, upper-class people take institutional pressure lightly. There are examples also of lower-class persons who disregard the educational and religious mores of the culture even though they yield to strong pressure from the economic and political institutions.

d) There is an uneven age variable in both the kind and the degree of institutional control. It may be said that controls are personally applied by the group more to young persons than to adults; but the impersonal institutional pressure is greater on adults than on youth. Older people are conformists by habit and by inclination; it is more convenient to conform than to resist. It is obvious also that the institutional environment of younger people is mainly that of the familial, educational, and recreational systems.

e) The time variable is noted by a glance at recent American history. During the second World War there was an emphasis on patriotic mores, on military conduct, and on nationalistic behavior. The total American political institution demanded conformity in ways that subsided later during peacetime. In periods of national catastrophe and depression it is said also that the influence of the religious institution increases.

f) The social pressure from institutions varies also according to the values held in a culture, and there can be no doubt that the institutionalized economic values have taken precedence in contemporary United States. Directly and immediately for the adult working population, and indirectly and mediately for the rest, there is a subconscious feeling for the appropriateness of the economic mores. The number of people, the amount of time, the degree of interest, and the extent of subservience that surround the demands of the economic system indicate where the highest values of the American culture lie.

This list of the fundamental variations of institutional control gives a hint of the complex network of social pressure. It makes us realize that institutional conformity is no automatic, evenly distributed result of a mechanically operating force. Not all Americans are affected in the same way by the same institutional pressures. There are times and situations when these pressures work in opposite directions, as when a conflict arises between familial and economic patterns, or between political and religious norms. The tremendous increase in leisure-time activities in our society has raised the recreational institution to a force of ever widening influence and has placed the values of work and play in contrast.

In spite of these variations and complexities it is possible for the careful student to obtain a general appreciation of institutional control in a given culture at a given time. Consideration of this control is necessary in any attempt to characterize the American people or any other society. Certain signposts point the way to generalizations without which the valid construction of a social science would be impossible.

As we obtain more knowledge through sociological research of the American culture we obtain also a clearer understanding of the workings of institutional controls.

3. Impersonal Conformity of American Workers

The increasing trend toward secondary relations and associations has interfered with personal and mutual loyalties in America. This decrease in personal involvement and in face-to-face relationships is apparent in all large-scale organizations, in educational, religious, and political associations; but nowhere is it more striking than in the economic system. Mass production of goods in our industrial economy has required a disciplined conformity to the demands of the machine, demands different from those in any other work situation.

The fact that American workers do conform to this kind of system and produce successfully and abundantly is witness to the resilience of the social personality. From the point of view of social control this conformity is remarkable because it is largely the result of technological planning and it occurs largely without benefit of personal and mutual loyalty between employer and employee. Social reformers who decry the "inhumanity of the machine" and who rue the passing of both economic individualism and paternalism do not seem to realize that personal fealty to the employer is a practical impossibility in the present work situation.

Following are a few social facts that help to explain why American workers conform to the plans of employers without having deep personal relations with employers.

a) The high cultural value of independence has characterized the American worker throughout our history and has been coupled with an aversion to paternalistic authority. The worker rejects anything that resembles servitude, bondage, or peonage, and the society itself puts legal prohibitions on this kind of work arrangement. The absence of a docile and humble servant class in America is symptomatic of the general unwillingness of workers to become personally dependent upon employers.

b) As labor unions have become larger and stronger they have acted as an agent for the worker. They make collective agreements for him, arranging the details of hours, wages, seniority rights, and other conditions. They step between the employer and the employee and in this sense discourage the need for personalized relationships between the two.

c) To some extent the government has also helped to depersonalize this relationship. The successful functioning of our gigantic industrial economy is a national and federal concern. A certain amount of regulation and control is essential. Labor laws have been made and remade by the Congress and they deal in considerable detail with the content—the rights and privileges—of the labor-management relation.

d) The basic corporate structure of big industrial enterprises is necessarily a formal, legalistic, and impersonal arrangement. The thousands of owners of a large corporation are themselves represented by management in the control of the business. Hired executives and specialized functionaries are themselves employees even though they are on the "side" of management in the direction of operations. Nevertheless, they often develop a "loyalty to the firm" difficult for the ordinary worker to achieve.

e) The mobility of the work force, or at least of a significant portion of it, appears to be a permanent concomitant of our kind of industrial economy. A local solidarity and a set of close personal relations between worker and employer would interfere with this mobility. The fluid labor force responds to the changes and pressures always at work in our economy.

f) The tendency to conceptualize labor as simply another cost item in the production of goods also has a depersonalizing effect. This is in line with the general commercialization of materials, goods, and services, and it must be remembered that the constant effort to cut down the cost of production has been a large factor in the increase of purchasing power of the consumer. A rigid and stable relationship between employer and employees, especially one of loyalty and personal solidarity, would have an effect upon this concept.

g) Finally, the specialization of functions compartmentalizes labor and separates the worker from the employers. The sheer quantity of technical knowledge required, especially on the higher levels of the industrial function, makes it impossible for a worker to be proficient in more than a few jobs within an industry. This means that his day-to-day social experience is narrowed to a relatively small circle of fellow workers.

This list must not be construed as a total explanation of the work situation in American industry. Sufficient research has been done in factories and plants to show that the impersonal conformity of workers to the demands of the job does not imply automatic or mechanical social relations. Peer groups of people with mutual respect and loyalty exist everywhere. Techniques have been devised for maintaining human relations within the factory, and many programs have been established as substitutes for personal employer-employee relationships.

As the present system of relations becomes more and more institutionalized, the workers become accustomed to it, take it for granted, and submit to it with only a vague realization of the "rules of the game." Most workers are conditioned to the kind of conformity their jobs demand, and, as long as there are no patent injustices, they probably prefer to have it this way.

4. Political Control of Industry

We have seen that the major institutions of the American culture are necessarily interlocking systems, mutually influential and interdependent. Persons who naïvely speak of complete separation of the political and religious institutions are usually those who also complain about the intrusion of the "welfare state" into the economic order. There are many points at which the government and the economy meet; and it is difficult to see how this merger could be avoided, or to imagine that this avoidance could be sociologically helpful.

The notion that the government could be a mere arbiter among economic pressure groups, or that it could be an aloof umpire over the general economy, is as outmoded as the individualistic philosophers who proposed it. The American government from its beginning has exerted control over the economy; and as the economic system grew larger and more complex this political control also had to increase. We may sketch very briefly the two directions of this relationship between the political and the economic institutions: the one is *implementation* and the other *regulation*.

a) Probably the more important aspect of political influence is found in the tremendous service the government has rendered to American business. Our economy would be unworkable if the government did not control currency and counterfeiting, support the banking system, operate a patent office, set norms for the stock exchange, and provide a legal framework for everything from the establishment of corporations to the procedures for bankruptcy and reorganization. The enforcement of property laws and contract terms, the provision of direct subsidies, and the establishment of tariffs are all mechanisms the government provides in order to facilitate the operation of the economy.

For the benefit of the whole economy the government maintains research departments and information bureaus for almost every economic function. Mining, forestry, agriculture, heavy and light industry, and producers and distributors of all types are helped by these services. The physician who condemns farm subsidies gets assistance from the Public Health Service; the farmer who fears socialized medicine gets help from federal and state agricultural stations. The Securities and Exchange Commission aids investors; the Bureau of Labor Statistics gives information on employment trends; the Bureau of Standards does research for consumers.

b) Besides these and many other supportive mechanisms the government also regulates economic activities, primarily in order to restrain monopoly and promote competition. Government regulations have been made to prohibit deceptive business practices, misleading advertising, the bootlegging of trade marks, and so forth. These have been helpful regulations for which the great majority of honest and efficient businessmen have been grateful. Nevertheless, the cry of "interference" is almost always heard whenever the Justice Department suggests an investigation of monopolistic practices.

In recent years the government has been called upon by both sides to "balance" the power between giant corporations and giant unions. The attempts by Congress and the administration to promote industrial harmony have become major issues in each political campaign, enmeshing the political institutions even more deeply with the economic institution. Because we have never developed a large American labor party, both of the major political parties contend for the labor vote.

These two aspects of political control, *supportive* and *regulative*, are not always initiated by the government. Farmers, workers, businessmen, and professional people are forced to comply with many governmental regulations and they readily accept governmental support. But much of this political "interference" has come at the request of pressure groups, lobbies, and interest groups, and some is a result of the inability of the various economic agencies to maintain an orderly system.

Although for purposes of analysis we distinguish between political and economic functions, the concrete situation shows a close intermeshing of the two. It is safe to predict that the economy would collapse if there were any serious attempt to withdraw the political from the economic institution, or even to return to the governmental policies of fifty years ago.

From the point of view of our institutionalized value system, economic values have penetrated government more than political values have influenced the economy. Americans depend upon the government to promote prosperity and to take preventive measures against economic depression. Economic problems, like inflation and the high cost of living, have become a central concern of the government, and the American people apparently believe that only the government is "big enough" to do something about them.

5. Social Planning and Morale

America is one of the few large societies of the world without mass movements. The political apathy of Americans is particularly noticeable, and even much of the success of organized economic movements has come through the work of relatively small interest and pressure groups. Besides this lack of mass action there has also been a lack of confidence in any obviously dictatorial individual who has tried to assume control.

It may be said in general that in the United States, deliberate social engineering succeeds best when it is promoted by small groups with high morale. This may appear to be an anomaly in a country where large-scale projects are carried out by big organizations requiring the co-operation of large numbers of people. The appearance is deceptive because we tend to look at the results of planning, that is, thousands of people in co-ordinated action, rather than the planning process that brings about the action. To discover the planning process we have to watch the committees, boards, bureaus, and small groups of people who are dedicated to change, reform, and control.

The quality characteristic of all of these groups is high morale, which in turn is the result of a combination of factors. We have seen that teamwork is effective when three conditions are fulfilled: first, if the action to be performed is concrete; second, if the responsibility for performance can be placed; and third, if the action to be performed is considered worthwhile by the participants. Morale among the members of the group is an added element, and even groups with excellent leadership and emotions of righteousness do not succeed without it.

Empirical research has shown that morale is present in a group when there is (a) a clearly defined goal of real value to all the members; (b) a deep conviction that the goal can be reached, or at least that a worthwhile portion of the end can be achieved; (c) some empirical evidence that they are making progress toward the goal; (d) a feeling of solidarity among the members of the group; and (e) finally, an awareness of danger or threats from outside the group. External threats tend to unite and "uplift" the members.

These conditions of high morale can be recognized in all groups that successfully plan and execute social reform. This is exemplified in many instances in the American society: in the small group that engineered the prohibition amendment, in the group that fought for and won suffrage for women, and in any number of citizens' committees that have cleaned up vice, gambling, and political corruption in various cities in the United States.

One of the most dramatic examples of the effects of high morale is that of the small committee on industrial organization that formed within the American Federation of Labor in the 1930's. They had the whole tradition of the trade-union movement as well as the most powerful labor organization in the country against them. They were a close-knit group, convinced that their goal was both worthwhile and attainable, and they had almost immediate success in organizing the industrial workers. It is true that there were some defections, but these occurred only after the group had become the powerful Congress of Industrial Organizations.

The importance of high morale is demonstrated also by its absence in large numbers of unsuccessful social planners. The history of the country is dotted with abortive movements of social reform, and especially of groups that resisted strong social trends. The morale of many socialist and Marxist groups has been broken because one or more of these conditions was not present. New groups have formed for the same purpose and have also been unsuccessful over the long term.

It appears that negative and destructive goals, like those of the Ku Klux Klan, are not sufficient to sustain the enthusiasm of members. When external dangers turn out to be ephemeral, and when it appears that the goal is hopelessly in the future, the group members lose interest. A group of this kind that suffers defeat after defeat cannot expect to keep up its morale. Solidarity is lost and the people turn to other social relations and functions.

High morale ultimately makes the difference between mere social planning and genuine social engineering. One of the qualities of the leader is that he follows through in social action the ideas he proposes. Similarly, the test of the planning group is the endurance of its morale through the transitional period into the actual program of social reform. The members of the small planning group do not perform all the functions required in the total program. The program necessarily requires some co-operation from many persons. But progressive ideas remain only in the planning stage unless morale remains in the group into the engineering stage.

DISCUSSION QUESTIONS

1. Discuss: "Social control is an extension of the socialization process."
2. Explain with examples the different levels of social control.
3. Outline the various classifications of social control.
4. In what sense is self-control an essential ingredient of social control?
5. Rank the major groups according to the strength of their controls.
6. What is meant by saying the "culture is self-enforcing"?
7. Why are there variations in institutional control?
8. What is the difference between positional and personal leadership?
9. Explain with examples: expert, charismatic, and managerial types of leadership.
10. Explain the main forms of communication through which control is exerted.
11. What is meant by social engineering?
12. What are the main reasons why social control meets resistance?
13. Describe the traditionalist's reactions to social reform.
14. List the main variables in the pressure of institutions.
15. What is the difference in the age variable and the time variable in institutional control?
16. List the main reasons why personal loyalty to employers is decreasing in the American industrial system.
17. Explain the supportive control of business by government.
18. How does the government exert regulatory control over the economy?
19. Under what conditions does a group have high morale?
20. In what sense do negative goals impede successful social planning?

SUGGESTED READINGS

BERNARD, L. L. *Social Control*. New York: Macmillan Co., 1934, chaps. i–iii.

LANDIS, PAUL H. *Social Control*. Chicago: J. B. Lippincott Co., 1939, chap. xviii.

LAPIERE, RICHARD T. *A Theory of Social Control*. New York: McGraw-Hill Book Co., 1954, chaps. ii–ix.

MERRILL, F. E., and ELDREDGE, H. W. *Culture and Society*. Englewood Cliffs, N.J.: Prentice-Hall, Inc., 1955, chap. xxvii.

MURRAY, RAYMOND W. *Sociology for a Democratic Society*. New York: Appleton-Century-Crofts, Inc., 1950, chap. xviii.

WILSON, LOGAN, and KOLB, WILLIAM. *Sociological Analysis*. New York: Harcourt, Brace & Co., 1949, chaps. xi, xxiii.

CHAPTER SEVENTEEN

Deviation

In previous chapters we have noted that social change is any variation from a former mode of existence and that social control is the process through which change to, or maintenance in, social conformity is effected. Both change and control are concerned with regularities and norms. Both are regularized, recurrent sociocultural phenomena, for change is inherent in social life and control is a necessary condition of society and culture. Induced social change is always directed to the values and norms current in the culture, and control is directed to the conformity of people to those norms.

The Deviant and the Abnormal

Social and cultural deviation refers to abnormalities and irregularities. The social scientist uses the term "normal" to refer to anything regularized, standardized, patterned, recurrent, and characteristic. This means, of course, that these regularities of behavior and structure are themselves used as norms by which to discover and evaluate that which is "abnormal." It is assumed that normal behavior receives the approval of the society and abnormal behavior its disapproval and that the study of deviation involves to some degree the values of the culture. In strictly scientific terms, however, deviation does not imply the subjective approval or disapproval of the observer.

If social control is a mechanism for making people conform to the normal patterns of the culture, then deviation is a process in which people "get out of control." Persons who do not perform in normal ways, that is, do not conform to the normal, recurrent regularities of behavior, are called abnormal or deviant. They are not "normless" or anomic. Subjectively, every rational person entertains a set of behavior norms, but in so far as these subjective norms differ, conceptually and externally, from those commonly accepted in the culture, he is a deviant. From the sociological point of view, the normal persons in any society are those who share the commonly held patterns of belief and conduct. Those who depart from these patterns are deviant.

Positive and Negative Deviation

Every culture contains both ideal and real patterns of behavior. The ideal patterns are interpretive of the highest values; they are expressed in the basic principles to which the society subscribes, but they are never fully attained. It is not these but the real patterns of behavior that we employ as a norm of conformity or deviation. Thus, the mores and the folkways are the normal regularities and uniformities against which the social scientist must measure deviation.

a) Positive deviation is that which moves in the direction of the ideal patterns of behavior. It is attempted and approximate conformity to those ideal norms the society itself considers superior and to those forms of behavior people term "more virtuous." The positively oriented and upwardly deviant person or group "rises above" the commonplace, oft-repeated, real patterns of thought and action. The deviants involved in this are the extraordinary persons, the saints, models, and exemplars of behavior. It is often easier to discern this type of person in the literature of a people than it is to recognize him in concrete social situations.

There are many historical examples of persons who were termed radicals and fanatics during their lifetime but who were later recognized as positive deviants. Political and religious revolutionaries were sometimes persecuted. Inventors and discoverers were often ridiculed by their contemporaries. Similar treatment was accorded to prophetic social reformers and to innovators in the fields of painting, sculpture, and architecture. These examples indicate that time perspective is important in the recognition of positive deviants and that both tolerance and objectivity are required of the scientific social observer.

b) Negative deviation is a movement in the direction of disapproved, inferior, and inadequate behavior. It means conformity to modes of conduct that are substandard in the culture, that is, "below" the real patterns. This substandard behavior is the most commonly used meaning of the term "deviation" in sociological literature. Books on social problems deal with negatively deviant behavior because it is a downward departure from the level of normal behavior acceptable in a society. The persons and groups involved in negative deviation usually have low social status and are looked down upon by the society in general.

It will be recalled that three indexes are employed by social scientists to distinguish among the mores, folkways, and usages in a culture.

These are the real patterns of behavior, and they are measured by the amount of social pressure exerted upon their observance, the extent of conformity among the people, and the degree of value in which they are held. Similarly, the analysis of deviation becomes meaningful in a scientific way only when we have a knowledge of these three indexes and can measure the deviant behavior against them.

The difficulty of analysis arises, however, in the fact that these indexes must be used in combination. Generally speaking, deviant behavior of a negative nature is that which is accompanied by low social values; relatively few people enact it or urge that it be enacted. Recognized criminal and other antisocial behavior readily fit this description. Positive deviation toward superior and more virtuous behavior fits the highest values in the culture but does not fulfil the two other qualifications. There are relatively few persons in the society who perform it, and there is little effective pressure to force compliance. Thus, positive deviation, although in accord with the highest cultural values, must still be termed deviation.

Types of Negative Deviants

The people who are deviants are different and abnormal compared to the average person and the average kind of behavior. But there are kinds of differences and degrees of abnormality in every society. People may be extreme non-conformists or only moderate non-conformists; they may be abnormal from the physical, mental, moral, or cultural point of view. This approach classifies rather than explains, but at least a partial explanation of deviation may be surmised from the type of classification made:

a) The mentally defective and the psychologically unfit constitute a category of negative deviants. Their behavior is erratic in various degrees because they are unable to adjust themselves to the normally accepted ways of society. Included among these are morons, idiots, and simple-minded persons as well as those who suffer from severe psychotic and neurotic disturbances. Their antisocial behavior may range from that of the violent, destructive person to that of the harmless, helpless person.

Negative deviants of this kind are said to be "out of touch with reality," and they require the care of society for their own protection and for the sake of others. Their behavior is random and eccentric since they cannot recognize and duplicate the real patterns considered normal in society. Calling them "deviants" does not imply a moral or ethical judgment since they are not responsible or accountable for their conduct.

b) The physically or organically handicapped are another category of negative deviants to the degree that they cannot pursue the normal patterns of life in society. These people are quite different from both the psychologically and the morally abnormal deviants. Deaf-mutes, the crippled and paralyzed, and the chronically ill constitute a problem for themselves and for society. Through training and personal abilities, they may learn to participate to some degree in the culture and society, but they can never quite reach the level of behavior considered normal and acceptable.

c) Those who may be called dependent deviants are in a third category. In a sense they are declassed people who have little or no social status within the normal structure and are dependent upon the society. These are the homeless, the drifters, the socially disorganized "bums" and paupers. This category includes dependent orphans and illegitimate children, although it is possible that they will take their place as normal social persons in adulthood.

d) Criminal or delinquent deviants are subject to a different standard of judgment by society than are the mental, physical, and dependent deviants. The former are non-conformists who deliberately violate the value norms of the culture. It is only because they are accountable for their conduct that they are visited with penalties imposed by the society itself. Their deviant behavior ranges from serious to light offenses, and their irregularities from relatively habitual to merely occasional actions.

Deviation and Social Roles

Uniformities of behavior can be meaningfully analyzed from the point of view of social roles. When a person deviates markedly from the normal expectations of his social roles, we observe a lack of uniformity and regularity. Since the role satisfies a specific need and functions toward a recognized goal, it provides for us a clue to the cultural significance of conformity and non-conformity. The effective and integrated social personality is one in whom all the social roles are functioning in normal and expected ways.

This approach through the social roles helps to avoid the oversimplification that a person is all good, or all bad, or that deviation is a total condition of the social personality. An adequate analysis of the roles indicates that most non-conformists are only partial deviants and that most conformists occasionally act abnormally. An absolute conformist appears to be a sociological impossibility since both conformity and deviance are relative to the person, the role, and the culture.

From the point of view of role content society readily permits a degree of variation and deviation in the performance of usages. This permissive attitude is less in regard to folkways and turns into a prohibition in regard to mores. Thus, in the parental role the individual is permitted no choice on the level of compulsory duties toward children. Deviation here from the strict mores is not tolerated by society. But on the level of usages the parent has a certain freedom of choice, limited only by extreme eccentricities. The father may not starve his children, but he may restrict their eating of certain foods.

We have seen that the norms for social roles are developed, not in the society as a whole, but in the various social groupings in which the role is enacted. Thus, in the socialization process, the individual does not learn merely a general total social role, but the several specific social roles in the major groups in which he participates. Logically, therefore, the normal uniformities of behavior are pertinent to the functions and goals of each group and differ from group to group. A man does not act in the same way in a golf foursome as he does in a church choir or at a sales meeting. The same set of behavior patterns that is perfectly normal in one situation would be deviant or abnormal in another situation.

Role Deviation and the Social Personality

The acceptable social personality avoids deviation by learning not to "mix" his roles. The society judges him on his ability to adapt his behavior to given times, situations, and groups and to follow the behavior expectations of each role as it is enacted. Usually, however, deviation of the social personality does not occur merely by substituting one role for another, as by playing the choir member's role in an economic group. This would be total non-conformity and would be considered outright abnormality by the other participants.

Role deviation is seen more frequently in the uneven enactment of the various social roles. A man may fulfil adequately his roles as husband and father and his recreational and political roles but depart from the norms of behavior expected in his business practices. The adolescent daughter may conform normally in all her social roles with the exception of her student role. Conversely, the model student may be an incorrigible family member, conforming to the demands of school behavior but failing in the expectations of the familial role.

It is probable that in the internal comparison of social roles enacted by the individual person, all human beings are to some degree social deviants. Here again it is necessary to make the distinction among mores, folkways, and usages and to realize that deviation in most instances is a temporary aberration. Even the normal social personality is sometimes a deviant in some aspects of his social roles. A certain amount of elasticity is overlooked, and even expected, by society. A "slip" here and there is hardly noticed and sometimes even approved because it makes the person "more interesting." However, a person who is consistently a non-conformist in one social role, although he may fully conform in his other roles, certainly fits the definition of the social deviant.

Institutionalized Deviation

Since patterns of behavior become institutionalized it is obvious that the normal person is one who conforms to the general demands of the institutions. The uneven enactment of social roles by individuals is often paralleled and sometimes caused by a certain amount of inconsistency among the various institutions of a culture. The highest values of the religious institution may be at odds with those of the economic or political institution. This institutional inconsistency or impersonal deviation probably exists in every culture; and since we define deviation as a lack of conformity it is probably best evaluated against the norms of the pivotal institution.

Aside from the abstract level of the basic cultural ethos that seems to penetrate all institutions, the people tend to measure all institutional norms against those of the pivotal institution. If the culture is dominated by the values of family and kinship there is a tendency to bring all other institutional arrangements in conformity with them and to judge as a deviation those patterns that do not conform. In this sense, deviation becomes a more or less static concept of inconsistency.

One of the knottiest problems of sociological analysis lies in the fact that every culture contains patterned, and apparently approved, deviations of conduct. Anthropologists report that primitive tribes countenance occasional orgies and that in simple societies these act as a psychological release of tension. Whatever the explanation, the fact is that even highly developed and complex societies permit similar deviations.

These institutionalized deviations are sometimes called "patterned evasions." They are more or less regularized ways of contravening the approved and established norms of conduct. They are deceptive and paradoxical and may be called "normal abnormalities." Surreptitious punishment and deprivation of racial and minority groups, the passive co-operation of the police in these practices, and the tacit approval given to them by upper-class people combine in an established pattern of deviation. Various forms of prostitution and illegal gambling, ticket-fixing, graft, fee-splitting, and similar practices are recognized as "undesirable" behavior. They satisfy real or imagined needs of people, and even though they contradict the expressed values of the culture, they develop into systematized and institutionalized deviations.

Deviant Situations

Besides the more or less established forms of institutional deviation, the social scientist also recognizes the infrequent abnormal situation. This is a temporary phenomenon in which people tend to "forget themselves" and act almost completely out of their accustomed roles. For example, a panic or crises occurs and normal social persons act in strange and unanticipated ways. A riot or street fight may bring together people who have never met before and involve them in unaccustomed and unco-ordinated behavior. The definition of a mob implies a plurality of persons in an abnormal situation.

Not every deviant situation of this kind is sudden and unexpected. Periods of increasing social friction and of tense human relations often precede the panic, riot, or mob action. A labor strike may be well organized, and the intentions of the pickets may be quite peaceful, but the situation often lends itself to a social eruption. Similarly, a rebellion may be secretively planned over a considerable period of time, but when it does occur it creates an abnormal situation. The rebels themselves are non-conformists, and the action they pursue is abnormal.

If we view sociocultural deviation as a situation in which socially disapproved behavior is performed by a plurality of people, we can distinguish three situational levels. The first is the more or less established routine of deviation, like the "fixing" of tickets for traffic violations, that is merely tolerated by the people. The second is the temporary and unexpected behavioral aberration that occurs in crises or panics. The third is the temporary, but often anticipated, social eruption, like that of violence and conflict. Numerous and varying influences are at work in each deviant situation in this trilevel analysis.

Deviant Groups

The analysis of every society shows the presence of the major basic groups: the familial, educational, economic, political, religious, and recreational. It is rarely, however, that there is complete co-ordination and conformity of all the segments within each major group. The sub-groups may range from those that comply with the highest values and norms to those that are almost extreme non-conformists. The latter we call deviant groups.

In the large, complex, and dynamic society numerous examples of deviant groups can be classified under these major headings. Cults and sects break off from the large religious bodies, and radical movements emerge and make demands for reform within the parent body. Political parties have their groups of internal dissenters who sometimes form splinter parties. In the business world there are positive deviants who venture into new systems of production and distribution and negative deviants who operate shady enterprises. Similar forms of organized deviations are found historically in the recreational, educational, and familial groupings.

We have seen that social persons may be classified as deviants psychologically, physically, economically, or ethically. From the point of view of group classification, the ethically deviant groups are the ones that attract the most attention and present the largest problem to organized society. These groups are made up of lawbreakers, whether they are temporary aggregates forming riot and lynch mobs or relatively permanent associations of various kinds of criminals. Illegal and morally deviant groups, gangs, and even crime "syndicates" are present to some degree in every large society.

The student of society must understand that these criminal groups and associations are only partially deviant. An analysis of their functions and structures indicates that they exist and operate according to all the sociological generalizations we have made about non-deviant groupings. The individuals perform patterns of behavior, enact roles, and have status within the structure. They require the various processes and relations, as well as control and administration. These groups are stratified with leaders and followers; their shared behavior is institutionalized. They are sociologically different from non-deviant groups, however, because *some* of their values and actions differ from those approved and accepted in the larger society.

The goals of negatively deviant groups vary somewhat, but they point in the general direction of exploitation of the total society. It is probable that the main motivation of some of the youthful gangs is the desire for thrills and recreation, while that of the corrupt political machine may be a desire for power. Generally, however, the ethically deviant group exploits the society for material gain. In this sense, they are economic groupings, seeking financial "profit" through illegal channels and in ways disapproved in the culture.

The distinction between the law-abiding and the law-breaking groups in a society is not so clear-cut as this description may indicate. If sufficient data were available about individuals, we would be enabled to construct a continuum of persons, ranging from the full-time professional criminal to the honest upright citizen. But somewhere along the continuum are numerous persons who are esteemed as honest citizens but who participate regularly in illegal activities. We have seen that every culture contains patterned evasions, or institutionalized deviation. For example, the whole area of "white-collar" crime contains deviant groups of people who enact these patterns.

Marginal Groups

In terms of the accepted norms of the culture, we have seen that persons and groups may be either positively or negatively deviant, the first superior to the patterned behavioral norm, the latter inferior to it. Some persons, groups, and types of behavior are at the "margin" of the accepted limits of the sociocultural system. They are not completely within it, nor are they completely outside it.

The concept of cultural marginality does not necessarily connote an ethical or moral judgment. The marginal man is one who has not been fully assimilated or accommodated to the social and cultural norms of the society in which he lives. The marginal person is different, and in this sense he is a deviant, even though he may be striving earnestly to follow the mores and to be accepted by the majority.

Marginal groups are obviously *minority groups,* and from the broad view of the total society they are more technically termed "social categories." They are made up largely of immigrants and newcomers, who still exhibit the characteristics of their socialization in a different culture. Marginal categories may also be racial or religious minorities that, except for this specific characteristic, fully share the culture of the majority population.

Marginality is measured on the *general criteria of social status,* and in a large modern society it is necessarily a dynamic concept. The marginal person does not have in sufficiently high degree some of the valued items that increase status in the society, whether they are wealth, skin color, type of education, religion, or others. Most of these items change gradually in the persons who possess them, and their evaluation may change also over a period of time in the minds of the majority members. The marginal group is peripheral to the total culture and must be conceptualized as moving toward it, unless there are accepted castelike arrangements in the social structure.

The *degree of deviation* of the marginal group depends ultimately on what is considered normal in the total sociocultural system. The deviant group can gain acceptance only to the extent that it can "achieve" normality. The concept of achievement emphasizes the social role, while the concept of acceptance emphasizes the social status. The former is much more effective for the person or group already contained within the major society, while the latter is more important for the marginal person or group. Marginality is consequently a special aspect of deviation since the marginal deviants frequently cannot do anything about removing the source of their deviation.

Social Problems and Progress

Social deviation is a peculiar phenomenon in that it creates both social problems and the conditions for social progress. If society were a nicely balanced mechanism functioning in an exactly repetitive way, it would be subject to neither abnormalities nor improvements from within. Every sociocultural system is subject to internal change and to deviation from previously accepted regularities and normalities.

Sociologists who employ the "value approach" define a *social problem* as a discrepancy between the value norms and the actual social behavior in a society and imply also that there are always conflicts between different sets of values. Whether or not this approach is used, the social problem appears always to be related to a deviation from the accepted standards of behavior. The list of social problems ordinarily analyzed by the sociologist—poverty, crime and delinquency, substandard housing, ill-health, and many others—suggests that a considerable number of people do not, or cannot, participate normally in the valued items of the culture.

It is obvious that the term "social problem" has to do with negative deviation. Whether it is defined as social pathology or as social disorganization, it is behavior that swerves "downward" from approved and desired social standards. The collective attempt at solution or amelioration of social problems must include the attempt to narrow the gap between the behavioral norms and the concrete situation. The attempt to eliminate this deviation is an attempt to "restore" the society to its level of normality.

Social progress is not simply the removal of social problems or a decrease in the amount of negative deviation in a society. Nor can one imagine even a relatively stagnant society in which permanent normalities exist. Social progress, no matter how one defines it, moves in the direction of positive deviation and has its source in positively deviant persons and groups. If cultural uniformities were rigid, if people repeated the same behavior patterns in exactly the same way, if human beings could not foresee, plan, and execute new programs of action, there could be neither positive deviation nor social progress. The accumulated experiences of people form the normal and expected patterns of the current culture, but they are also the bases from which new sociocultural patterns are projected.

Temporary novelties, like fads and fashions, are not significant deviations, although they indicate that a certain culture may be highly volatile. Important progress evolves from long-term, large-scale positive deviations that raise the level of normality. The extension of the protection of human rights to more and more people in the society is this kind of progressive deviation. The introduction of new institutional forms through which group conflict can be lessened, the expansion of opportunities for social and cultural participation, the elevation of standards of family living—all these are examples of deviation in the direction of more acceptable and valued norms.

DEVIATIONS IN AMERICA

1. Leisure as Deviation

One of the most remarkable changes occurring in the American society is the development of a leisure culture. The traditional emphasis on hard work as a means of both material prosperity and eternal salvation has not been lost among Americans, but the continual advance of machine power has lifted much of the drudgery from manual labor. The Puritan notion that "idleness is the Devil's workshop" is still to some degree extant, and even our leisure time has been filled with feverish activity. Roughly speaking, we may say that the previous emphasis on production has shifted to an emphasis on consumption.

This transition of emphasis from a work culture to a leisure culture is not, of course, a complete reversal. The work continues, but the patterns of work have greatly changed; there has always been leisure, but new patterns of leisure are emerging. This emergence of institutionalized leisure may be called a form of social and cultural deviation. It is a departure from the standardized attitudes and behaviors that had previously existed in the recreational institution. It is a new direction forming new normalities and regularities, and it is having a tremendous effect upon the total culture.

The analysis of this recreational deviation shows several broad lines of conduct. These patterns are not rigidly set and probably cannot be as long as our culture continues its rapid change, but they are sufficiently established to be recognized as quite different from previous patterns.

a) In the general field of entertainment there has been a marked relaxation from the so-called Victorian and Puritan standards. Movies featuring love scenes that would have been embarrassing to an all-male audience fifty years ago are now played in every neighborhood theater. Pulp magazines have changed from stories in which the healthy hero always wins over the forces of evil to stories in which weird heroes from outer space perform fantastic stunts. Suggestive songs that would have shocked Americans of two generations ago are hummed by almost every adolescent.

b) In the general field of what the moralists call "self-indulgence" there have also been remarkable changes. We spend more money per capita for tobacco than for public education. The prevalence of smoking among women is a complete reversal of previous patterns. The consumption of alcoholic beverages, especially of mixed drinks, has not only increased tremendously but has also directly affected the pattern of entertaining guests. Various changes in attitudes and conditions have permitted a sexual freedom never before possible in the American society.

c) One of the broadest generalizations that exemplify the new American leisure and wealth can be studied under the category of conspicuous consumption. Pretentious standards of living have been used as symbols of status in many societies, but among Americans many items that were once luxuries are now considered necessities. Beyond this, however, we find people who never read books buying and displaying shelves of serious volumes; people who do not swim building a swimming pool in the backyard; people who need only one automobile building and maintaining a three-car garage; and women wearing mink stoles when the temperature requires a light cloth coat.

There are degrees of conformity to these newer norms of conduct, and there are differences among the deviant personalities who induce or accept the change. A strip-teaser is still considered a deviant personality by most people, as is the adolescent who commits a murder modeled upon one of the crime-magazine stories he has read. The upper-class drunkard is called an alcoholic and is treated with a certain amount of sympathy. The person who has a TV antenna on his roof but no television set inside the house or the man who drives an expensive car he cannot afford may be ridiculed by his neighbors, but he is a person who knows and strives for the newer patterns of conduct.

Whatever one's moral judgment concerning the goodness or badness of these changes, the causes of the deviation are not simply good or bad people. Changed attitudes toward sin and virtue unquestionably have an effect upon external patterns of recreation, but the deviation in question is more than a personal matter. In a sense, the American people have had leisure "thrust upon them" and perhaps have not yet learned to live with it. There are signs of popular interest in music and painting, of developing patterns of self-help in handiwork in the home, of an appreciation of natural scenic beauty through touring and sight-seeing.

These three broad lines of development—entertainment, self-indulgence, and conspicuous consumption—must be kept in the perspective of our question of recreational deviation. It would be an error to exaggerate them as external patterns of behavior currently pursued by the majority of Americans. It is probably true that most Americans are in some way affected by them; they are therefore sociologically significant. From a negative point of view, they are deviations no longer protested by most people; and from a positive point of view, they are deviations admired and desired by many people.

2. Deviations of Religion

The American culture contains an extremely large number of internal religious deviations. Almost every known form of worship ritual can be found in practice somewhere among the religious bodies of our country. Most of the religious oddities and abnormalities, however, are practiced by relatively few people. Most churchgoers adhere to a few basic well-known patterns of worship.

Besides these internal deviations, which have been widely studied and commented upon, there is also the important aspect of religious deviation as an influence upon non-religious institutions. Here we consider the ways in which behavior patterns accepted and practiced in a religious group are extended beyond the group as an attempt to reform non-religious patterns. From the point of view of social deviation, this means that behavior considered normal within the religious group but abnormal by the great majority of Americans was introduced as a general pattern for the total society. Sometimes the new pattern was successfully established, and at other times it was not.

a) The best-known experiment along these lines was the Eighteenth Amendment to the Constitution, known as the prohibition law. Certain fundamentalist religions that taught that the use of intoxicating beverages is sinful were able to get sufficient political support to outlaw the sale of liquor. The real pattern of liquor consumption among the people was not changed into one of abstinence, and the national law was ultimately repealed. The drive against gambling, also promoted by these religious groups, has been successful in some places.

b) The question of the teaching of religion in the public school system has had some curious variations. All churches hold that children should be taught religion, but there are so many churches in the United States that there could be no agreement on what to teach. Even the Protestant version of the Bible is no longer taught in most public schools, and the system of "released time" from school for religious instruction at church has been set up in many places. The pattern of religious instruction has been established, and the percentage of children receiving it has increased, but the people teaching it are not public school employees.

c) To some degree the churches have been successful in extending the concept of racial brotherhood into wider areas of American life. In many instances, churches had first to abandon their own internal patterns of racial segregation and to develop a doctrine of Christian solidarity before promoting it in the non-religious structure. While the religious groups have not been the only agency of racial integration in the American society, the influence of religious leaders has been very great in establishing the new patterns. What were once considered peculiar local and group deviations in this regard are now gradually becoming accepted as standardized practice throughout the society.

d) On the level of conceptual patterns of economic justice, the principles of the papal encyclicals and of various other pronouncements by religious leaders have had wide acceptance. These have been realized through direct action of religious representatives, such as chaplains in industry and ministers acting as strike arbitrators, and through the religious services of Labor Day, the publication of labor papers, and the establishment of labor-management institutes. The notion that the religious institution has "something to offer" to the economic institution is no longer strange to most Americans.

The examples given here are a few indications of the ways in which induced change has been deliberately attempted in order to carry over religious patterns into other areas of life. The opposite trend, the so-called "secularization" of our culture, has often been pointed out. Other examples can be given of the religious patterns that have persisted as long-established customs—the celebration of Christmas, Easter, Thanksgiving, and Memorial Day and the religious ceremonies observed for birth, marriage, and death. These patterns can hardly be termed deviations since they have long been accepted as normal behavior.

To some extent the acceptance of religious deviations into non-religious institutions involves the various phenomena of social change, control, and integration. It is probable that as the American culture grows older, its major institutions will acquire closer co-ordination and more interchange of patterns. This requires that some deviations be tolerated in the various institutions and that the people who have deep convictions about these deviations be permitted to propagate them. The American society has provided a fertile field for experimentation in religious beliefs and practices, and while most of the deviations remain weak or disappear, some of them become accepted normalities in the total culture.

3. Law Deters Deviation

The American legal system acts as both a positive and a negative control over social deviation, because it promotes conformity to norms and employs formalized techniques for punishing non-conformists. The home, the church, and the school are important instruments for encouraging conformity, for instilling an appreciation of the highest social values, and for standardizing the conduct of people. These and other institutionalized groups succeed in promoting a respect for the law, but they do not have the clear-cut definitions of behavior norms nor the apparatus of enforcement and punishment the law possesses.

In spite of their tradition of individualism and their rapidly changing culture, the American people are by and large law-abiding. Sensational reports about non-conformity, from the minor delinquencies of juvenile gangs to the planned murders by organized criminals, overlook the fact that the large majority of Americans are never involved in law violations. Whether our rate of crime is higher or lower than that of other countries is beside the point here. We are interested in the fact that the law acts among us an an impediment to serious social deviation.

a) To the extent that the norms of other groupings are ineffective, the law acts as the ultimate means of control. Punishment by a parent, expulsion from a school, excommunication by a church, or ostracism imposed by any other group or association may in particular cases suffice as a control mechanism. The individual may "return to the fold," or he may accept the uniformities of behavior prevalent in other groups; but if he persists in serious deviation, he must ultimately reckon with the law.

b) American law is more precise and detailed in the behavior norms it sets up than are any of the other institutionalized systems of control. Every formal association has rules and regulations, but these are limited only to the immediate membership, are often vaguely and inefficiently worded, and are taken seriously only in crisis situations. The canon law of the Catholic church is the only conspicuous exception to this, but it is in itself a legal system.

c) The laws that define prohibited and deviant behavior have been written and interpreted by technical experts and discussed and enacted by municipal, state, and federal assemblies deliberately constituted for this purpose. In no other area of human activity is it the precise purpose of a large body of persons to establish the norms of behavioral conformity and the criteria by which deviation can be judged. Nowhere else in the society is such rational effort devoted to the elaboration of standards which tell us what is beneficial and what is harmful to the society.

d) The law is a relative and changing system, but the legal norms at any given time tend to be absolutistic. While legislative and juridical lags may exist, there is still a demand for conformity to the legal norms. Since law can be changed and improved, it can cope with any new and large-scale deviations that may threaten the American culture. The unchanging principles of the natural moral law are recognized as the basis of all American law, but the application of the law fits the needs and interests of the total society.

e) Strictly interpreted, the objectivity of the law requires that the criminal deviant be punished, not because he is antisocial or immoral, but because he has violated the specific legal norms of behavior. In effect, however, the whole system of law and law-enforcement, with its police and courts and prisons, provides pressure to conformity to minimum standards of behavior. It is essential to the welfare of society that this minimum conformity be maintained.

These statements concerning the utility of law as a deterrent to social and cultural deviation do not mean that all criminals are caught and punished or that all aspects of the legal system operate efficiently. The fact that a law is "on the books" does not mean that it is rigidly enforced or even that a majority of the people accept it. The body of laws in any society is not a reliable indicator of the actual behavior of the people. A severe code of laws may be only laxly enforced in one society, while a less severe code may be rigidly enforced in another society.

The American legal system therefore can be sociologically analyzed only in relation to the actual behavior patterns of the American people. There exists a certain amount of public corruption; there are occasional miscarriages of justice; there are fee-splitters and ambulance-chasers among the lawyers and incompetent personnel within the total system. In spite of these deficiencies, the law continues to act as a preventer and punisher, and sometimes as a reformer, of criminal deviants.

It is probably true that a sociocultural system gets the kind of law it deserves. The pluralistic American society is in many ways tolerant of deviation; it has grown from groups that have had many variations in culture patterns; it has absorbed both ideas and persons from many different societies. Tolerance of differences has certain outside limits, and it is principally the legal system that sets those limits when people and patterns appear to be getting out of hand.

4. The Pattern of Divorce

The nineteenth-century traditions of the United States showed a remarkable record of marital durability. In the middle of the century the general and ideal pattern of marriage was one of permanence and indissolubility. There were, of course, also cases of unhappy marriages, infidelity, and even desertions. The churches were unwilling to remarry divorced persons; the law in general made it difficult to obtain a divorce; and cultural pressure was strong upon married people to remain together. By 1890 there was one divorce in about seventeen marriages; the current annual divorce rate in urban places is about one in four.

The contemporary pattern of divorce in America deviates from the normalities of the last century. The divorce laws in some states are extremely lax; many courts apparently allow collusion; the alleged causes for divorce are often trivial; some churches place little negative sanction upon their divorced members; and social disapproval is not always visited upon the divorced person.

The changed conception concerning divorce requires a changed conception concerning marriage. Thus there is really a twofold deviation involving the essential quality of the indissolubility of the marital contract. This solemn agreement appears in some cases to be less binding than a mortgage contract or an agreement to pay for goods delivered. It is probable that most persons who enter marriage intend at the time to remain married permanently to each other. The intended conditions of the contract appear to change under the pressure of experience, and because of these changed conditions the spouses often feel justified in voiding the contract.

Following are some aspects of deviation which are a general result of the spread of divorce:

a) Not all divorced persons are parents, and childlessness may sometimes be a contributing factor to divorce. Nevertheless, the children of divorced persons are required to make numerous adjustments. Living with one parent and paying a weekly visit to the other, or getting used to a "new" father or mother at home with still another to greet him on his weekly visit, can be a most confusing experience. Whether the child lives at home, or is boarded with foster parents, or lives in a children's institution, he is still the product of a broken home, and his socialization process is deeply affected by this experience.

b) The divorced persons themselves must necessarily make adjustments to the new situation. The patterns of behavior of people who have lived together become quite different, once they have parted from each other. The woman especially is placed in a new category that appears to provide good opportunities for remarriage and consequently provides difficulties for the divorcée who does not believe in remarriage. The man is also faced with new problems as he attempts to live as a bachelor again.

c) In spite of the relative independence of the conjugal unit in the American society, marriage does develop a loose system of contact and communication among the blood relatives of both spouses. The longer the marriage lasts, the more likely are the in-laws on both sides to become acquainted with one another. Divorce often causes an awkward rearrangement of these social relations. If small children are involved, some of the relatives become sponsors for their baptism or confirmation, and the grandparents also maintain interest in, and contact with, the children. Few social arrangements are more peculiar than the wedding of children of divorced parents. No satisfactory protocol for this situation has yet been established.

d) Similarly, but to a less embarrassing degree, divorce requires a realignment of the friendship circles of both spouses. Invitations to parties, to dinners, and other congenial gatherings now require selective care. Married couples develop and maintain at least a small circle of friends with whom they "do things" together. If the divorced persons remain in the same community and continue to belong to the same church clubs, country clubs, and other primary groupings, the contacts with their mutual friends may often be awkward.

The deviations in both marriage and divorce patterns may be rooted in the personal, rather than the social, aspect of the marital relation. An analysis of divorced persons and their children, relatives, neighbors, and friends, however, indicates that neither marriage nor divorce can be a purely personal affair. Even in the American system of the conjugal family that emphasizes the spouses rather than the total group of the consanguine family, there is need to recognize the broader sociocultural effects of marriage. Deviations in so basic a relationship as that of marriage are certain to effect deviations in the wider circle of people.

The emphasis on the self, on one's personal desires and privileges, which characterizes the divorce pattern contravenes an important American social trend toward collective morality. In almost all other areas of social problems there is progress toward better co-operation, more cohesive group relations, social justice, and guaranteed social rights to more categories of citizens. The increase of social welfare and collective action in the American society appears to correlate with the wider acceptance of social values and the wider conformity to the virtues of love and justice.

The divorce pattern is a deviation in this respect, too. It not only causes new patterns of behavior in the divorced persons and in others; it also deviates from the general American trend toward social integration and cohesion.

5. Mental Abnormalities

We have indicated that most social deviants are only partial deviants, that is, that they occasionally depart from the expected mores or that they deviate in only one of their social roles. Mentally abnormal persons are also abnormal in their social behavior. They range from the total deviant to the person who is only moderately disturbed. The social scientist is not directly concerned with organic psychotics whose mental disease is traceable to some defect in the structure or physiology of the organism. These present primarily medical problems and only secondarily social problems.

The so-called functional psychotics constitute the largest percentage of Americans who suffer from mental abnormalities, and their psychoses have been traced to no known physical or organic cause. They are of interest to students of society not only because they involve all kinds of behavior aberrations but also because some of them appear to suffer the effects of the social and cultural environment. Functional psychoses are increasing in the United States, and more than half the hospital beds at any given time are occupied by these patients.

The statistics concerning mental diseases in our country have caused considerable controversy. Large numbers of young men were rejected by the armed services for various forms of personality disorders, and the numbers of Americans being treated for these disturbances are increasing faster than the population growth. Whether this increase is due to the fact that more precise diagnoses are now being made and more attention is being paid to these mentally disturbed people, or whether there is an actual increase in the incidence of the disease, has not yet been made clear.

Schizophrenics and manic-depressives constitute well over half of all Americans who suffer mental disorders, and these functional disturbances are said to be increasing. They are sometimes roughly called "split personalities," although only the latter type exemplifies extreme shifts of the personality back and forth from excitement to depression. Both these types not only occur more frequently but also remain under treatment longer than others.

Almost a half-million Americans are resident patients in all types of mental hospitals. Some of them are curable; others are hopelessly and permanently out of touch with the realities and normalities of behavior. All of them constitute a large category of Americans who are behavioral deviants. Their responsibility is decreased, and they cannot be classified as moral deviants. Some of the possible sociocultural sources of these mental diseases are the following:

a) The rapidity of change in the American society is often alleged to be a causal factor of mental abnormalities. The need to adjust one's self to new situations, patterns, and values is said to cause mental confusion. The less endowed individual cannot keep up the pace; the frequent demands are too much for him, and he has a "nervous breakdown."

b) The United States has the most competitive culture the world has ever seen. Competition is itself a highly valued social process, and people are trained from childhood to be successful competitors. But competition implies that some persons must fail to achieve the desired prize or goal. The losers are expected to accept defeat graciously but especially to try again; and in some cases frequent failure leads to discouragement and mental unbalance.

c) The complexity of the American society is an overwhelming problem to some people. There are so many factors that are too big and complicated for the individual to understand or control. The general areas of war and peace, economic prosperity and depression, and political and religious mores do not lend themselves to easy analysis. The individual feels helpless before these gigantic problems, and this frustration may lead to mental disturbances.

d) The inconsistencies of the culture, either real or imagined, are also a disturbing element for many people. We have spoken of the patterned evasions and incongruities in many areas of American life. To many people these do not "make sense." They portray a kind of disorder that annoys and confuses the person who wants everything reasonably and neatly arranged. People of simple intelligence, particularly, are often very literal and precise in their expectations of others and are therefore frequently disappointed and frustrated. They do not understand why the real patterns do not always coincide with the ideal patterns of our culture.

e) Much has been made also of the secularization of the American culture as a factor in mental abnormalities. Man apparently requires many moral supports for a stable personality, and if confidence is lowered in the supernatural, one of these traditional supports is removed. Emphasis on the effectiveness of this-worldly factors often implies a de-emphasis on prayer and divine grace. Curiously enough, the opposite can lead to frustration; that is, the neglect of the secondary causes of the material world leads people to an unreasonable presumption upon the supernatural First Cause. They expect miracles, and when they are disappointed, they conjure up their own miracles.

These are the social scientist's tentative explanations for the apparent increase of functional psychoses in the American society. Psychiatrists are paying more attention than ever before to the cultural envirunment as a factor in mental abnormalities. Since conceptual patterns are an integral part of the culture, there can be no doubt that at least in many instances a correlation exists between the personal internal aspects and the impersonal external aspects of the culture.

DISCUSSION QUESTIONS

1. Distinguish between normal and abnormal social behavior.
2. Does the sociologist use "ideal" patterns as a norm for measuring deviant behavior? Explain.
3. How does negative deviation differ from positive deviation?
4. Explain with examples the main categories of negative deviants.
5. In what sense does society permit deviation in role performance?
6. Discuss: "The acceptable social personality does not mix his roles."
7. What is meant by "normal abnormalities"? Give examples.
8. Explain with examples the different levels of deviant situations.
9. Give examples of deviant pluralities under each of the major groupings.
10. Is cultural marginality an ethical deviation? Explain.
11. What is the connection between social progress and deviation?
12. What are the broad lines of development in recreational deviation?
13. Explain the change of emphasis from a work culture to a leisure culture in contemporary America.
14. In what ways has religion effected deviations in non-religious institutions?
15. Show how the legal system acts as an impediment to negative deviation.
16. Discuss: "The enacted laws are not a reliable index of behavior."
17. In what sense is the contemporary pattern of divorce a form of deviation?
18. What are some of the deviant consequences of the divorce pattern?
19. Discuss: "Mental abnormality is accompanied by social deviation."
20. List and explain the sociocultural conditions that are alleged factors in the development of mental diseases.

SUGGESTED READINGS

BARNES, H. E. *Society in Transition*. New York: Prentice-Hall, Inc., 1939, chap. xviii.

CUBER, JOHN. *Sociology: A Synopsis of Principles*. New York: Appleton-Century-Crofts, Inc., 1955, chap. xiv.

DAVIS, KINGSLEY. *Human Society*. New York: Macmillan Co., 1949, chap. x.

MARTINDALE, DON, and MONACHESI, E. D. *Elements of Sociology*. New York: Harper & Bros., 1951, chaps. xiii, xiv.

MURRAY, RAYMOND. *Sociology for a Democratic Society*. New York: Appleton-Century-Crofts, Inc., 1950, chaps. xi, xxi.

YOUNG, KIMBALL. *Sociology: A Study of Society and Culture*. New York: American Book Co., 1949, chap. xxvii.

CHAPTER EIGHTEEN

Sociocultural Integration

Up to now in this book we have analyzed the various segments that constitute society and culture. Together with this analytical "fragmentation" we have also frequently pointed out that society and culture are so closely intertwined that they must ultimately be viewed as a total, single, sociocultural system. This totality—how it can be recognized and how it is achieved—is the object of the present chapter.

Static and Active Integration

The term "integration" is often used synonymously with terms like "cohesion," "solidarity," "unity," "balance," "adjustment," and "harmony." All these terms have meaning to the social scientist only if they include the kinetic as well as the static aspects of sociocultural phenomena. In other words, integration implies not only order and structure but also action and function. In this final chapter we study integration of both structure and function in both society and culture.

Sociocultural integration does not mean strict homogeneity throughout the whole society and culture. We have seen that differentiation is an essential quality of social relations and that it is a prelude to integration. One cannot speak of integration unless there are different segments to be integrated. Integration does not refer to a highly formalized society of rigidly obedient people. An authoritarian society may be only externally regimented without inner, meaningful solidarity. People and patterns that are identical with others are not necessarily united to them.

The term "integration" often signifies social processes like assimilation, amalgamation, socialization, and acculturation. For example, the migrant from the farm to the city, or from one country to another, goes through a process of sociocultural integration as he gradually takes on the behavior patterns of the new environment and develops social relations with people who were formerly strangers to him. This example and others like it simply indicate that integration can be viewed as both a process and a product and that the former is always going on because the latter can never be complete.

Because of the relativity and mutability of the sociocultural system, several precautionary statements must be made concerning the concept of integration. (*a*) We cannot always say that a "well-integrated" society functions better toward its goal than a loosely integrated society. The best we can say is that a certain degree of integration is a necessary condition for social and cultural functioning. (*b*) The assessment of the degree of integration existing anywhere is not an intuition or a concealed value judgment. It requires a knowledge of the recognizable conditions under which integration occurs. (*c*) This assessment cannot be made from a mere list of all cultural items that happen to coexist within the same territorial boundaries. We shall see that certain cultural objects have a greater integrative significance than others.

Basic Requisites

It must be clear from what we have said in this book that every sociocultural system requires for its very existence two fundamental elements: (*a*) the maintenance of co-operation and (*b*) the satisfaction of needs. These are the minimum sociological requirements. They presuppose the presence of all the biological and physical elements, the presence of resources and people, and the geographical and material conditions in which social and cultural life occur. Thus, integration must be studied in sociological terms and not reduced to biological or physical factors.

a) The maintenance of co-operation means that persons are able to function with one another at least at that minimum level at which the system can be called a going concern. This minimum requirement refers to those social processes or basic forms of human relations we have called positive or conjunctive. Roles, statuses, groups, and strata are fairly well co-ordinated through the associative processes without disabling interference from negative and dissociative processes.

b) The satisfaction of sociocultural needs means that the people have found systematic and acceptable ways to achieve the purposes of the major institutions and groups. We have seen that these needs cannot be satisfied individually or in isolation and that they are found universally wherever people live together. A sociocultural system cannot exist—it cannot be imagined—unless it contains institutions and groups that fulfil the familial, educational, economic, political, religious, and recreational needs of the people.

These are basic requirements, and it is possible to measure roughly the extent to which the requirements are met. A society in which these sociocultural needs are poorly supplied is obviously one in which the people are not efficiently co-operative. The cause of this failure at any given time may lie outside the sociocultural system, in a lack of resources, in overpopulation, in changes of climate and other physical catastrophes. Aside from all these external factors, it is possible to measure the manner in which the people are trying to achieve the goals and the extent to which they succeed.

These basic prerequisites for integration operate through and with people. They exist in the real order of sociocultural phenomena, but they can be analyzed meaningfully only when they are abstracted from the concrete social situations in which they exist. Hence, we must study separately the integration of the culture and the integration of the society. It is in this way that we can bring together the segments of a vast and complicated system in which people behave toward one another in patterned ways.

Cultural Integration

We have seen that the total culture is made up of the major and subsidiary institutions and that each institution can be analyzed into its co-ordinated patterns of behavior. From this point of view the cultural system can be studied on three levels: (a) that of behavioral patterns, (b) that of the institutions, and (c) that of the total culture. This appears to be a horizontal approach, but it must be understood that these levels are vertically co-ordinated. The institutions contain the patterns, and the culture contains the institutions.

a) The integration of behavior patterns means that the generalized uniformities of conduct are co-ordinated in each social personality and between one person and another. This is what is meant by structured, arranged, or ordered behavior. The segments of behavior are consistent with one another. They make sense to both the actor and the observer. This notion is best demonstrated by its opposite—random, erratic, and unco-ordinated behavior is immediately detectable, and the individual who pursues it is often alluded to as a disintegrated or disordered personality.

Since the social person is not an isolated individual and since social science deals only with shared and generalized patterns of behavior, we must note also the integration of relational patterns. A man regularly and in the same way fulfils the paternal roles in the family. The other members of the family know what to expect from him; they recognize the consistent and recurring uniformities, and they respond with their own behavior patterns. Thus, integrated patterns include consistent reciprocity. Integration is observable when the reciprocal behavior patterns of two or more persons meaningfully "fit together."

b) On the level of the institution itself we find integration when the segmental patterns and roles are consistently co-ordinated. Any one of the major institutions in a culture can be analyzed from the point of view of its numerous subsidiary institutions, which in turn must be interrelated if the larger institution is integrated. For example, the regularized behavior in courtship and dating, in the training and raising of children within the home, in the relations of husband and wife, must somehow "fit together" if the familial institution is to be integrated.

Institutional integration is seen in the interdependence of the various subfunctions. A capitalist economy must have institutionalized ways of planning production, of assuring credit, of gathering stockpiles of raw material, of cost accounting, and so forth. These and many other subsidiary institutions function together, and if any one of them suffers a serious breakdown, the whole system tends to disintegrate. These are all differentiated functions, but they point toward the total institution. It would be physically impossible in an industrialized system for the same person to extract the raw material, finance production, build and assemble the commodity, and advertise and distribute it to the consumer. When all these functions are performed by different people, and when their functions are co-ordinated, the institution is integrated.

c) The integration of the total culture means that the various major institutions are mutually consistent and co-ordinated. A lack of integration on this level is one of the most serious problems a society can face. The functions and goals of one major institution differ from those of another, but in an integrated system they must ultimately serve the society. For example, the maintenance of public order through the political institution is not the same as the production of goods through the economic institution, but the fact that they pursue different immediate and mediate goals does not mean that they can be completely disconnected.

What we are saying in effect is that the integrated culture functions as a total system of distinct contributing patterns, roles, and institutions. Since the culture itself is a constantly changing system, there are always minor inconsistencies and lags. The parts of the culture do not change with the same rapidity or even move in the same direction. One institution may develop more rapidly than the others; the mores change more slowly than less important usages; certain roles become more demanding than others; some values are emphasized more than others.

Social Integration

In the conceptual framework of this book we have seen that people enact behavior patterns, that groups use institutions, and that the whole society has a culture. The major segments of the society are its numerous groups, and each group is composed of social persons. Social integration, therefore, can be analyzed on the three levels of: (a) the social personality, (b) the major groupings, and (c) the entire society. Here again, as in the conceptualization of culture, integration occurs both horizontally and vertically.

a) From the sociological point of view, the integration of the social personality refers to the fact that the individual enacts his various social roles in a co-ordinated and consistent way. This approach presupposes the psychological definition of the normal, integrated personality, an area of study outside the field of social science. The integrated social personality exhibits no apparent conflict of behavior patterns as he moves from one group to another and as he carries out the functions of his different roles. His behavior in a recreational group is different from, but not contradictory to, his conduct in his family, his business, and his other groups.

b) Group integration means that the members of the group enact their reciprocal roles interdependently toward the goals of the group. An integrated group is one which achieves its purposes with a minimum of conflict. It is not only well structured, but the social relations of its members proceed in a productive and peaceful way. They emphasize the social processes of co-operation, accommodation, and assimilation.

The test of group integration is not external order and observable co-operative functioning toward common goals. External orderliness may result from the coercive power of a dominant minority, as in the case of a prison or a concentration camp. Thus, the absence of a disabling amount of overt conflict is not a sufficient proof of solidarity. There must also be, on the conceptual level, a consensual sharing of institutionalized culture patterns. This point we shall discuss later.

c) The integration of an entire society refers to the fact that not only the major groups but also the multitude of subgroupings are able to co-operate successfully. In the integrated society, the school, home, and playground do not pull the child in opposite directions. Business office, church, and political party are not at odds with one another in competing for the interest and loyalty of the adult. Within each of these larger areas, the smaller subgroups are necessarily co-ordinated if the society is integrated.

Social integration is not the result of the complete similarity of all the people in the society. Integration is a matter of structure and function rather than of identity or similarity. It cannot be emphasized too often that within any large society people differ and groups vary; statuses and roles are multiple. Thus, unity is a logical concept, and it means in society that the people and the groups are brought together in a meaningful way and that their social needs are satisfied in an orderly way. Social integration does not dispel differences; it co-ordinates and directs them.

Integration of Culture and Society

It must be remembered that the separate discussion of culture and society is possible only on an abstract level. Each can be studied in its various parts, as we have studied them throughout this book, but neither can exist in the real order without the other. The persons who are organized into groups in society are the people by, through, and for whom the cultural patterns and institutions are developed. Culture and society are inseparable entities, and this very fact indicates that there is at least a minimum degree of integration between the two.

That culture and society must somehow be integrated requires little factual demonstration. We need only compare two widely different sociocultural systems and attempt to interchange their cultures. For example, China has a culture and a society, and so has Italy. It would be impossible for the Chinese society to combine with the Italian culture and still remain the Chinese society. The ways in which the Italian people conduct their behavior patterns, social relations, statuses, groups, and institutions are very different from the Chinese ways.

Although culture and society are inseparable in existence, they do not have an equal mutual influence for integration. We have seen that it is possible to arrange, discipline, and direct a social aggregate into a form of external social cohesion. This aggregate of semiautonomous persons, as in a police state, may give the appearance of an integrated social order, but it does not have genuine sociocultural solidarity. In other words, the meaningful integration of the society depends more upon the integration of the culture than vice versa. From the point of view of total integration, therefore, the culture is a more influential factor than the society.

We may say that it is the culture that puts the society into action or that the action, both conceptual and external, of the people in society is the culture. *Lack of cultural integration throws the whole society into confusion,* depending upon the degree to which it is lacking. Without cultural integration the social persons cannot adequately enact patterns and roles, the groups cannot properly employ institutionalized forms, and the total society becomes disjointed into unco-ordinated and even conflicting factions. We have seen that inconsistent behavior patterns result in split social personalities, and inconsistent institutions result in contravening roles and groups.

Sociocultural integration is not a rigid absolute. Although a degree of integration of the culture and the society must essentially and always exist, we must warn again that sociocultural integration is a relative phenomenon. Human nature, as well as the very nature of social relations among men, prevents a rigid, permanent integration between society and culture. If integration were complete, there would be neither change nor progress; and while sociocultural progress is not inevitable, sociocultural change is a constantly present phenomenon.

Essential Factors of Integration

We have described in general the meaning of sociocultural integration and how the various social and cultural segments are interdependent on one another. It remains now to answer the important question how this integration is effected and maintained. What factors account for this integration? Here again we cannot say that all the factors are of equal importance, since conditions and situations change. Nevertheless, we can attempt to arrange them in a rough order of importance.

a) Social scientists in general agree that value consensus heads the list of factors for meaningful sociocultural integration. The continuing operation and the essential solidarity of any society require a minimal sharing among the people of an ultimate body of values and norms. The majority of the people conform voluntarily to a common set of significant values. Value consensus excludes the simple hypotheses of either an instinctual gregariousness innate in all persons or a rationalistic and formal social contract emerging out of the dim recesses of history.

Consensus on common values does not imply total agreement upon all the detailed norms regulating specific social relations and patterns. We have seen that there is great diversity of conduct among the people of a large society but that there is also basic and common adherence to ideal patterns of behavior. Many of these values are, and perhaps must be, vaguely formulated in terms like "loyalty," "democracy," "brother-hood," "progress," "opportunity," "equality," and "liberty." These values cannot be easily spelled out in concrete action, but they supply the generalized meanings to which the people give consensus, and they appear to be the principal factor of sociocultural integration.

b) The sharing of common functions is another important factor of integration. People who together do things they believe are worth doing are drawn closer together. This simple conclusion is drawn from empirical observation by many social scientists. The reasons why people co-operate may lie deeply hidden in their motivation and probably involve the appreciation of values and goals as well as appreciation of the people with whom they share the function. Here again the degree of voluntariness is significant, since we are not talking about external cohesion resulting from either force or automatic routinization.

c) The third factor of sociocultural integration is the multiple participation of persons in different groups with varying cultural patterns. This integrating factor is more conspicuous than commonly shared values, and it is empirically observable when persons share common functions. The same person usually enacts his different social roles in groups made up of sets of different people. Lawyers are most often active in political and economic groups; clergymen are active in both educational and religious groups; the mother of a family may play active roles in recreational, religious, and other groups. The integrative element is therefore the social personality as it is expressed through the multiple roles in relation to other social personalities.

We are analyzing three factors that are inseparable in the concrete sociocultural situation. If the total combination is viewed from any of its three parts, it demonstrates mutual and reciprocal influence, as in the following three statements: (1) persons are integrated with one another because they share common functions and values, or (2) common values bring people together in the same functions, or (3) common functioning increases the participants' appreciation of each other and of the commonly shared values. Each of these three statements is empirically verifiable, and all three together indicate the most important integrating combination in the whole sociocultural system.

Auxiliary Factors of Integration

Besides these essential factors of integration there are several others that are auxiliary rather than essential factors.

a) One of them is the external pressures, threats and dangers, to which the members of a society respond. These threats are most obvious when they come from an enemy in wartime. If the danger is not overwhelming and if there is hope of successful resistance, the reaction is an increase in co-operation. In wartime the society is unwilling to tolerate deviants, shirkers, and traitors. The common sacrifice in a common cause of averting danger, even unpleasant and distasteful in detail, condenses the culture and integrates the society.

b) There are also numerous more or less deliberate mechanisms and techniques employed by society to insure sociocultural integration. We have spoken of these in the chapter on social and cultural control. Conformity to behavior patterns is reinforced through techniques of authority and obedience. Social status and personal sanctions help to keep the primary groups integrated, and systems of collective representation are an integrative factor in large secondary associations. This network of overlapping techniques operates throughout the total society; and its largest and most obvious exemplification is that of a national system of formal laws.

c) A general recognition in a society of the interdependence of interests is still another factor for sociocultural integration. Individuals and groups continue to interact and to avoid conflict on the basis of gains each anticipates from the maintenance of the social framework essential to interaction. This is the empirical antidote to the hypothesis that social progress and the general commonweal emerge from the pursuit of self-interest. The interests and motives of many groups are different and separable, but in the total society many of them are interdependent. Even religious bodies with conflicting dogmas have some interests in common. There may be certain conflicting interests between an economic group and a political group, but they have also some congruent interests.

These three latter factors—external pressure, deliberate techniques, and interdependent interests—are ancillary, rather than master, factors of sociocultural integration. An understanding of them requires a certain amount of insight into the structure and function of the total sociocultural system. Their operation requires a certain degree of rational planning toward integration. This analysis goes beyond the crude and outmoded notions about the automatic balance of power, or the inevitable readjustment of forces, or the blind play of symbiotic interdependence. In other words, the sociological explanation of integration does not lie in physical or biological factors; it is found in the persons and groups who constitute the society and who employ the culture.

Communal and Associational Integration

Although sociocultural solidarity is possible—and necessary—in every type of society, it differs in kind and degree from one society to another. We have seen that a culture is usually dominated by one of its major institutions and that a society gives greatest importance to one of its major groupings. In this case the *pivotal institution and grouping* are a focus of solidarity for the total system. We may say, for example, that the Chinese society was integrated around its family system and that the people of medieval Europe were mainly united through their religious system. Similarly, a large society may find its principal focus of solidarity in its political or its economic system.

We have discussed also the further general classification of societies into the communal and the associational types. Either one of these may be dominated by any of the major institutionalized groupings. The *small, simple, communal society* is frequently a strongly familistic society in the sense that the kinship system is a weighty factor for sociocultural integration. This type of society also adheres to traditional values and is largely controlled by the mores; it is usually preindustrial and slow to change; it has a narrow range of stratification and little contact with out-groups. Together these elements form a subconscious, informal, and almost automatic sociocultural solidarity.

The *large, complex, associational type of society* is characterized by certain elements opposite from those of the communal society. Human relations are contractual rather than familistic. Values are relatively volatile; social control is exerted through formal legal systems; there are numerous classes and categories; and change is rapid. Solidarity must exist in the associational society if it is to maintain itself as a distinct and functioning sociocultural unit. But in this kind of society integration depends upon different factors and requires rational effort and planning.

The complex, large-scale society, with its numerous conflicting pressure groups, varying institutional values and diverse goals, cannot depend upon the automatic and spontaneous operation of solidaristic processes. The greater the differentiation of roles and statuses, functions and goals, interests and values, the more deliberate must be the techniques of co-operation. This does not mean the communal society is "natural" and the associational "artificial," but it does mean that certain inherent advantages for solidarity present in the former are absent from the latter. They have to be supplied by conscious, scientific, and technical effort. The people must discover, devise, and employ mechanisms that maintain sociocultural integration.

INTEGRATION IN AMERICA

1. Loyalties and Integration

The United States has, of course, a pluralistic and heterogeneous sociocultural system. We have observed that all our people are of immigrant lines from various ethnic and racial sources and that much of our culture was originally imported from foreign places. For several centuries the processes of cultural assimilation and biological integration have been going on, and there has been an accelerated trend toward a monistic and homogeneous sociocultural system.

Meanwhile there is still more heterogeneity here than there is in any other large country. We can identify in general two large—Protestant and Catholic—and one smaller—Jewish—religious orientations; and even among these there are many variations. There are in addition many minor groups. The disparities of national and ethnic backgrounds are gradually decreasing, but there are still recognizable categories of Spanish-speaking immigrants and of peoples from eastern and southern Europe. The differences in class and caste status are also diminishing with the rise of organized labor and the integration of Negroes.

The general goal of this trend toward integration seems to be that each person should become a "true American." The belief of some observers, especially foreign visitors, has been that this goal is impossible because various and conflicting loyalties interfere with a centralized loyalty to the country itself. Americans, however, maintain their allegiance to all kinds of groups: family, political, religious, economic, and others. In this kind of society, in which authority is polyphasic and values are multiple, Americans find multiple allegiance not only possible but desirable.

Some of the factors that make this paradoxical situation workable are the following. They help to explain how Americans foster allegiance to many apparently contradictory groups and values and still maintain loyalty to the central cultural ethos.

a) A toleration of differences is apparently built into the American value system. The defense of individualism and independence has gradually brought about the realization that others must also be allowed their individualism and independence. Tolerance is the result of practical necessity. No single group, whether religious, economic, or political, has been large or strong enough to impose its own way of life upon all the other groups. Toleration has been the necessary and positive compromise.

b) In concrete group relations there is rough procedural agreement on the "rules of the game." The competing groups are expected to grant one another a fair chance; those that gain an advantage expect to be challenged again; and those that lose out are expected to accept the situation gracefully. This is, of course, a general attitude. There are instances of "poor sports" and "bad losers." In spite of bitter labor disputes, vicious political campaigns, and occasional recriminations among religious groupings, the general attitude of sportsmanship that prevails in the recreational institution helps people to recognize and follow the rules of fair play in other institutions.

c) Multiple participation in groups is an extremely important and little-recognized factor of integration. Especially in the urban milieu, it is impossible for a Catholic to associate only with Catholics in his neighborhood, business, civic, recreational, and other activities. Americans do and must associate with other Americans who differ from them even in their deepest convictions. Given the general attitudes of toleration and procedural agreement mentioned above, this common functioning and face-to-face relationship constitutes a practical form of integration. The individual participates in each group with other individuals who share the values and functions of that particular group, even though they may refuse to share the values and functions of other groups.

d) The American people try to avoid overt disagreements by de-emphasizing contradictory values. They seem to skirt controversial issues wherever possible. A conscious effort is often made to find areas of agreement, as when people of differing religious faiths agree that "after all, we all believe in the same God; and we are all going to the same heaven." What may be merely superficial conformity and integration appears to be necessary in the pluralistic culture. Furthermore, external patterns of conformity tend to break down prejudices against other groups even when deep-seated value differences remain.

These four factors are at work particularly among urban, middle-class Americans. They bring about a kind of practical integration that works as a temporary mechanism of co-operation even while individuals continue to maintain loyalties to numerous differing groups. If present trends of assimilation continue, this temporary and external mechanism may someday be abandoned. Certain lines of internal cultural integration have been developing for many decades, as we have seen in discussing the ultimate American core of values, but it is improbable that total integration will eventuate, or even be desirable, in our kind of sociocultural system.

2. War and Solidarity

It is sometimes observed that war is a universal culture pattern and that the results of war are always destructive and disintegrative. In the conceptual framework of this book we classify the preparation for and the conduct of war as a *subsidiary institution* under the major political institution of the culture. Except for the Civil War, the American participation in armed conflict has had in general an integrative influence upon our sociocultural system.

a) The two world wars of 1917–18 and 1941–45 did more than any other events in our history to achieve co-operation among the American people. In both instances, there were conscientious objectors throughout the struggle; there were many who opposed our entrance into war; and there were some traitors and shirkers. But by and large, the war effort, with everything it entailed in training and fighting by the armed forces and in production and sacrifices by the civilian population, brought the American people together at a relatively high level of sociocultural integration.

b) It is an axiom of social science that the threat of external danger tends to unify a society internally. For purposes of co-operative functioning it was necessary, of course, that the people be aware of this danger. Hence, the importance of propaganda to the home country; a constant stream of slogans reiterated the necessity of "saving the world for democracy" and of "keeping the world free of tyranny." Except for the persons in uniform, the immediate danger from the outside was not always apparent. A consciousness of the threat had to be aroused and maintained.

c) The first World War was the major test of the possibility of integrating the many ethnic and national strains of the American population. The unwillingness of Irish-Americans to fight on the side of England, of German-Americans to break their ancestral ties, and of other

Americans to participate in a "foreign entanglement" they considered none of their business was a source of considerable anxiety to the national leaders before the first World War. No large society had ever before faced this kind of sociocultural problem. The United States emerged from the first World War not only as a major international power but also as a society of united people.

d) The spirit of patriotic unity engendered by the war effort is necessarily a short-lived phenomenon. The concentration of co-operation is pointed to a precise goal—victory over the enemy—and the psychological intensity of the effort cannot be maintained at the same high level during peacetime. The notion of "getting the job done" is not expected to carry over after the job is actually done. We must note, however, that although the spirit of unity subsides somewhat after each world war, the level of sociocultural integration is higher after than it has been before the war.

e) These two major wars had an immediate effect in bringing together Americans from widely separated sections of the country and of various sociocultural backgrounds. The war factories drew workers from the rural, agricultural areas to the urban, industrial areas, while the induction centers and training camps brought in persons from all over the country. Many had never before experienced this physical mingling. Contact and communication, however, merely provided the necessary conditions under which the process of assimilation could occur. The essential factor was that these persons in factories and in the armed services shared common functions in the pursuit of common and valued goals.

f) One of the most far-reaching integrative effects of the second World War was the deliberate plan to remove racial and religious discrimination within the armed services. The plan is an example of the manner in which intelligent leadership, through the use of approved legislative and administrative functions, is able to influence the real patterns of behavior. The executive order to remove segregation and discrimination came from the Commander-in-Chief, President Truman, after the war. It was carried out in all branches of the service—in the academies that educate and train officers as well as in all American military installations throughout the world. It was shown to work successfully during the Korean conflict.

The armed forces were not the only agency for this type of sociocultural integration. When we analyze a society and culture, we necessarily concentrate upon one segment of an institution or group at a time. Other changes were going on concurrently in educational, economic, religious, and other areas at the time when integration was being planned and promoted in the armed forces. The fact that millions of young men of draft age had this practical experience of integration was most significant in its broad influence. It provided a sociological demonstration that persons of varying ethnic, religious, and racial backgrounds could function together in relative harmony. It affected these young men in their postservice experiences in schools, churches, factories, and communities.

The general and positive integrative consequences of war upon the American sociocultural system do not, of course, prove a universal means-end relationship. Given the circumstances and the trends in our country, as well as the fact that we have been fairly successful in waging war, the logical result has been a higher level of sociocultural integration. In other societies, where the circumstances are different and the trends are in other directions, the effects of war are often likely to be destructive and disintegrative.

3. International Competition

Every society suffers a certain degree of internal inconsistency because of the discrepancy between its ideal and real patterns of behavior. The United States is no exception to this generalization. Our Constitution, Bill of Rights, and general social philosophy uphold ideals of conduct based upon the natural moral law. There have been, however, numerous patterned evasions of these ideals. The contemporary American trend seems to be in the direction of higher ideals, and one of the most compelling factors in this trend is our present status in world affairs.

a) At the risk of oversimplification, we may say that the international factor of domestic solidarity emerges from the competitive roles of the American and the Communist systems. Americans have been loud in their denunciation of authoritarian governments, critical of the denial of human rights in other parts of the world, and boastful of the freedom and prosperity that accompany the democratic system. People of other countries, with equal ethnocentrism, have been critical of America for preaching a sociocultural idealism it does not practice. The result is a sharp re-evaluation by Americans of the inconsistencies between ideal and real levels of behavior.

b) American leadership has been forced to take cognizance of this international challenge. The Communists boast throughout the world that their system can bring economic security to all working people; various former colonies and protectorates are suspicious of Caucasian pretensions to racial superiority; smaller countries, at a lower level of technological advancement, demand respect, recognition, and independence from the two power centers, Russia and the United States. This situation has forced America to accelerate the trend toward the fulfilment of democracy at home and thus toward sociocultural solidarity.

c) America has been "put on the spot"; Americans are asked to demonstrate to the world that our sociocultural system contains the promises we claim for it. In concrete measurable terms, this demonstration includes numerous programs: practical plans to improve both housing and health; extension and improvement of the educational system; enforcement of democratic principles of racial equality; the protection of workers' rights; the increase of purchasing power to more and more Americans; various programs for the economic relief of agriculture; and many other similar indications of sociocultural progress.

d) It must be noted that there is an intimate connection between these programs of progress and the American system of sociocultural solidarity. The ideals of freedom and justice are neither novel nor exclusively American principles, but in the American ethos they are closely allied to the notions of equality of opportunity, brotherhood, mutual responsibility, and other solidaristic principles. Similarly, the striving for national prosperity and for the material progress of the common people is not an exclusively American invention, but in the American society these are considered the right of the people to be obtained through democratic co-operation and participation.

e) If all these cultural threads are pulled together, we perceive a network of interacting principles and ideals supporting internal American solidarity. If brotherhood and equality are translated into concrete social situations, they imply both mutual responsibility of people and a common sharing of social and cultural benefits. Democracy is not a mechanical institution that automatically produces prosperity, nor does the material prosperity of the people inherently guarantee the processes of democracy. The political slogan that "it is people who make democracy work" means that there must be common effort to elevate the real patterns of conduct closer to the ideal patterns.

In effect, this elevation has taken place during the so-called "cold war" period following the second World War. America has been competing for the good will of other nations not merely through economic, political, and military support to them but also by developing an internal example of democratic solidarity. Obviously, international competition is not the only factor at work in this process, but the challenge of other societies does find a response in the ethical sensitivity of the American people.

4. Secondary Groups

We have seen in other parts of this book that the American society is characterized by a trend away from primary relations and groups toward secondary relations and associations. We have seen also that the individual person learns the mores, appreciates social values, and develops solidarity in small face-to-face primary groupings. The family and neighborhood, the work and play groups, are essential to the ongoing society, and they are essential also to the socialization of the individual. The sociologist sees an American dilemma: If the decline of primary groups is making the individual less solidaristic, how can the increasing number of large secondary associations develop a satisfactory solidarity for the total society?

a) Secondary groupings are numerically large; social relations are formal and impersonal; the social structure is loosely organized; social control operates through rules and regulations. These characteristics are seen in urban America with its gigantic labor unions, business corporations, political parties, large-scale recreational centers, and even religious associations. On the upper layers of these organizations individual persons and subgroupings are represented rather than participants in common functions.

b) From this perspective of large-scale organizations the importance of the millions of interacting basic primary groups can be appreciated. Psychological security for the individual is anchored in these smaller units—families, work groups, friendly meetings and activities. Through them the individual escapes the anonymity that appears to be a concomitant of secondary associations, and in them he participates in sociocultural integration with other individuals. The basic layers of primary groups are in many ways related to the larger and broader layers of secondary groupings. The same persons are present in both primary and secondary groups, but the manner of their social relations is notably different at each level. The total aggregate of people cannot participate directly in the higher centers of administration and communication.

c) The type of sociocultural integration differs at these two levels. In the primary groups, solidarity is taken for granted; it may be called spontaneous, natural, and subconscious; the individuals do not deliberately work at its achievement. In the secondary associations, solidarity is deliberately contrived; it is often arbitrary, planned, and devised. The recognition of this difference is an important insight into the nature of the sociocultural integration characterizing the United States. The observation of solidarity on the level of secondary groupings reveals two facts: first, that there are professional people whose function it is to plan and execute integration and, second, that the major decisions of these top people must take cognizance of the interests of other large organizations and of the total society.

d) The fact that professional co-ordinators are becoming increasingly important in the American society means that integration is in part a strictly technical problem. We have seen that occupational roles are becoming more and more institutionalized and that bureaucracies are necessary in these large associations. There can no longer be a reliance on "nice" personalities, on hit-or-miss techniques, or on old-fashioned paternalistic relations, to integrate the persons and roles in large organizations. Skilful practitioners with a knowledge of social science, like labor specialists, psychologists, sociologists, statisticians, and social workers, are employed for the purpose of applying the techniques of solidarity.

e) Paradoxically, the most successful of these experts in human relations are those who have studied the workings of primary groups within the large secondary organizations. For example, a detailed knowledge of the mores and folkways, the status aspirations, and the prejudices and preferences of the members of small factory groups has been of great value in understanding and implementing the total structure of solidarity. This kind of painstaking research has produced more integrative results than the philosophical maxims, moral exhortations, and peremptory edicts of employers. Similar comparisons can be made of the scientific analysis of social relations in churches, schools, hospitals, and other large organizations.

These experts are employed mainly by large corporations and industries and to some extent in educational, political, and religious associations and even in athletic organizations. They are not numerous at this time, and the body of reliable knowledge with which they can work is only beginning to emerge from the various research projects constantly being conducted by social scientists. Nevertheless, they are

contributing invaluable service in dealing with the problems of conflict and tension that occur within large secondary associations and
with the larger problems of public relations and communication on
the national level.

f) It is true that within the total sociocultural system these large
secondary associations pursue different goals—the objectives of a medical association differ from those of a lumbermen's organization, and
these again differ from the objectives of a political party, a ministerial
alliance, or an automobile workers' union. It is true also that large associations within the same major institutional framework—like rival
auto-makers, religious bodies, and educational groups—are imbued with
competitive and often conflicting values. At the top level, however,
they are gradually developing techniques of negotiation, arbitration,
and compromise. They often achieve voluntary co-ordination among
themselves and sometimes have it forced upon them by public opinion
or even by the intervention of political and legal authority.

This brief analysis of the relationship between social solidarity and
secondary associations introduces an area in which much research is
being conducted. We must realize that primary groups are necessarily
functioning within the large secondary associations. Both the kind of
goals pursued and the type of integration achieved are on a different
level from those of primary groups. Nevertheless, the work of the scientific researchers and of professional co-ordinators indicates that a
relatively successful form of integration can be achieved.

The degree of sociocultural integration attained among Americans
appears to depend ultimately upon the integrative success of the large
secondary organizations. It is fatalistic to suggest that these large
groupings must necessarily "gobble up" the smaller groupings, or that
they will inevitably crumble from their own gigantic size, or that they
can achieve solidarity only by developing into an authoritarian and
totalitarian political system. These negative and hypothetical approaches are belied by the obvious fact that their dire prophecies have
not been fulfilled during the past half-century.

5. Symbolic Integration

The American likes to think of himself as a hardheaded, reasonable,
practical kind of person who knows what he is doing and where he is
going. Social scientists, however, have presented enough evidence to
indicate that this self-evaluation is somewhat inaccurate. Perhaps we
Americans are not so suggestible to the influence of slogans and sym-

bols as people of some other societies; it is certainly true that we are influenced by different types of slogans and symbols. We feel there is something odd about the political banners and heroic posters in Communist countries, but we blithely accept advertising jingles and commercial slogans.

On a more serious level Americans are drawn together by certain symbols of national unity without precisely defining their ideological content. As a matter of fact, the integrative effect of the sharing of common symbols requires only a vague reference to their specific meaning. In our kind of pluralistic culture, we would probably find many grounds for disagreement if we attempted to define, for example, what the national anthem really means to the different people in an audience while it is being played.

a) The "Star-spangled Banner" had great symbolic value when it was so frequently played during wartime. The custom of using it as a kind of invocation before public gatherings has carried over into peacetime. A reverent hush falls over the crowd; everyone faces the flag; men remove their hats. The pledge of allegiance to the flag itself, as well as the songs written in honor of it, provide a kind of psychological security. It is as though people were saying, "Here, at least, we have something upon which we can depend and about which we do not disagree."

b) The Constitution acts as another common symbol that has important integrative effects. The symbol is not the Constitution in detail with all the interpretations and definitions worked out by scholars, legal experts, and judges during our national history. The integrating symbol is the general notion of the Constitution as a kind of sacred focus of reverence that somehow or other protects us all and remains a dependable bastion in a hectic and changing world. Even those who disagree violently with the findings of the Supreme Court cling tenaciously to the Constitution and sometimes challenge these judicial interpretations as an "assault" upon the Constitution.

c) Historical heroes, and to some extent political figures, act as a common symbol of integration for Americans. Washington and Jefferson, John Paul Jones and John Pershing, exemplify the supposed national virtues. The highest political officials—the President, governors, and senators—make a deliberate effort to represent all their constituents, or at least they create the impression that they are doing so. In this case the common symbol of unity is more frequently the public office itself rather than the incumbent of the office. The fact that high governmental office is closely associated with other symbols like the flag and the Constitution reinforces it as a factor of generalized solidarity.

There are other types of heroes who, because they represent successful achievement of common aspirations, act as a symbolic focus of integration. Successful businessmen, well-known scientists, eminent literary and artistic figures, and even athletic heroes and entertainment stars are in this category.

d) Certain physical, inanimate objects in our country are also endowed with meaning and value. National parks, monuments, and buildings, as well as "natural wonders" like Niagara Falls, the Grand Canyon, and the Mississippi River, have the trade mark "America" stamped on them. These act in subtle and subconscious ways as symbolic integrators of the American people.

e) In spite of differences in creed and of numerous people who are not directly church-affiliated, the common fatherhood of God acts as a symbol of unity to many. The meaning of the Lord's Prayer is sufficiently generalized to be acceptable to people of any religious persuasion, and there is a vague notion even among non-churchgoers that it is a "good idea" to have a Father in heaven. Innumerable public and official meetings are opened with prayer for divine guidance, and this action is, if nothing else, a satisfying formula for a generalized unity.

The immediate connection between sociocultural integration and these various kinds of common symbols has not been studied with scientific precision. To understand the validity of this connection, however, it is necessary to distinguish the specific and interpretable content from the generalized and vague symbolism of these phenomena. Group cleavages are numerous on the level of specific interests and values within our society, but there does exist in America an observable type of sociocultural unity, and one of the factors that influences it is found in the common symbols.

DISCUSSION QUESTIONS

1. Discuss: "Sociocultural integration does not mean social homogeneity."
2. What precautionary statements must be made concerning integration?
3. What are the basic prerequisites for an integrated system?
4. Explain the levels on which cultural integration must be studied.
5. Why are there always lags and inconsistencies in a culture?
6. Show how social integration occurs both horizontally and vertically.
7. Discuss: "Culture and society can never exist separately."
8. What is meant by saying that "culture puts the society into action"?
9. Explain with examples the essential factors of integration.

10. Why are other integrative factors called "auxiliary"?
11. In what way is the pivotal institution a focus of solidarity?
12. Compare the degree of integration in the communal and the associational types of society.
13. List the evidences of heterogeneity in contemporary America.
14. Discuss: "In spite of multiple and contradictory allegiances, Americans have a central loyalty to the country."
15. In what sense can it be said that American participation in armed conflict has integrated our people?
16. How has the "challenge of Communism" acted as a factor for internal American solidarity?
17. What is meant by the "network of interacting principles and ideals" that support internal solidarity?
18. How does the type of integration differ in primary and secondary groupings?
19. Why are professional co-ordinators becoming increasingly important in the American society?
20. List some of the common American "cultural symbols" and show how they contribute to national solidarity.

SUGGESTED READINGS

ANGELL, ROBERT C. *The Integration of American Society*. New York: McGraw-Hill Book Co., Inc., 1941, chap. ii.

BARKER, ERNEST. *National Character and the Factors in Its Formation*. New York: Harper & Bros., 1927, chap. v.

BENNETT, J. W., and TUMIN, M. M. *Social Life, Structure and Function*. New York: Alfred A. Knopf, Inc., 1948, chaps. xxx, xxxi.

HILLER, E. T. *Social Relations and Structures*. New York: Harper & Bros., 1947, chaps. xxxix, xl.

OGBURN, W. F., and NIMKOFF, M. F. *Sociology*. New York: Houghton Mifflin Co., 1946, chaps. xxiii, xxvi.

WILLIAMS, ROBIN. *American Society: A Sociological Interpretation*. New York: Alfred A. Knopf, Inc., 1952, chaps. xiii, xiv.

Indexes

Index to Bibliographies

Subject Index